MANAGING RISK IN PHYSICAL THERAPY

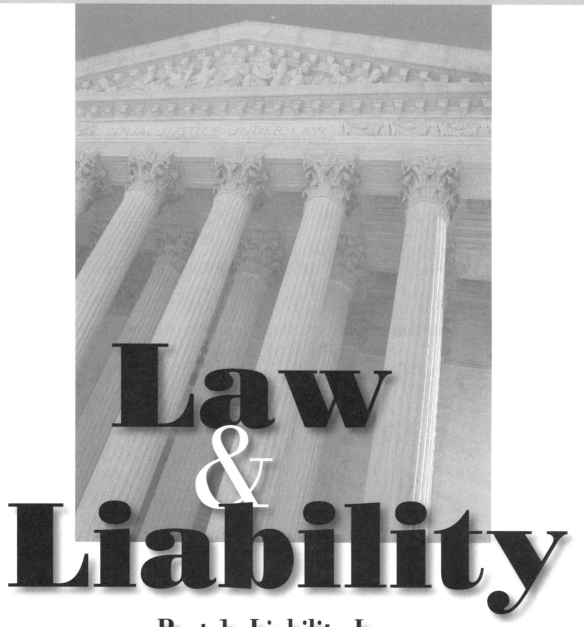

Law & Liability

Part 1: Liability Issues

AMERICAN PHYSICAL THERAPY ASSOCIATION

Table of Contents

Acknowledgements

We gratefully acknowledge Ronald W Scott, JD, PT, OCS, who has contributed in so many ways to *PT Magazine*'s coverage of law and liability issues—from full-length articles, to companion pieces, to columns, to general review and consultation.

We also are grateful to the following individuals who reviewed the contents of the original edition as well as suggested additions for this second edition to ensure that the articles continue to be relevant, useful, and accurate. Thanks to Kathy Lewis, PT, MAPT, JD, Laura Lee (Dolly) Swisher, PT, PhD, Cathy Thut, PT, MBA, and Mary Ann Wharton, PT, MS.

And to the many authors of the articles that are included in this volume—thank you.

Introduction

A physical therapist shall comply with laws and regulations governing physical therapy and shall strive to effect changes that benefit patients/clients. (APTA Code of Ethics, PRINCIPLE 3 [HOD 06-00-12-23])

APTA recognizes the unique challenges physical therapists (PTs) confront every day to understand and apply all the laws that relate to physical therapist practice. The APTA *Standards of Practice, Code of Ethics* and *Guide for Professional Conduct* direct PTs to comply with all applicable laws that govern the jurisdiction in which they practice. All physical therapists, from new practitioners to experienced clinicians, face legal considerations in all aspects of practice.

It is essential for PTs to understand and apply their knowledge of law and liability to their everyday practice, whether to employee relations or patient care.

However, law is not static—new legislation is passed, and current regulations are amended. In order to uphold their legal and ethical obligations, physical therapists must keep up with developments in laws to protect patients from harm, laws to uphold PTs' rights in dealing with payers, laws to protect the physical therapy profession from encroachment, and many more. The sheer amount of information can be overwhelming to the busy professional.

Recognizing this, APTA publications, including its professional issues magazine, *PT—Magazine of Physical Therapy*, frequently have covered both specific legislation affecting physical therapist practice and general trends in liability. Articles and columns have explained particular laws, examined risk management strategies, discussed repercussions of breach of confidentiality, and analyzed issues related to physical therapist practice beyond the scope of licensure. APTA's official peer-reviewed journal, *Physical Therapy*, has published manuscripts that have dealt with any number of legal considerations. In 1996, APTA's commitment to keeping readers up-to-date on these topics was supported by the launching of a *PT Magazine* column, "Liability Awareness," that continues today and from which many of the articles in this book were drawn.

This second edition of the two-volume *Law and Liability* is now part of APTA's Risk Management in Physical Therapy series, which also includes the two-volume *Ethics in Physical Therapy* and *Risk Management in Physical Therapy: A Quick Reference*. The second edition includes relevant articles published between 2000 and 2005, as well as the still-applicable articles from the first edition.

Both volumes in *Law & Liability—Part 1: Liability Issues*, and *Part 2: Professional Issues*—will be relevant to all PTs across all practice settings, including articles in Part 1 on licensure, documentation, liability insurance, malpractice, and patient relations, and articles in Part 2 on pro bono services, contracting, and principles of risk management.

In addition to articles with broad appeal, Part 2 also includes items on disability legislation, advertising, delegation and supervision, making referrals, and the hiring process. There is even a section in Part 2 specifically geared toward practitioners in specific settings, such as home health, continuing education, and aquatics.

Both volumes include several of APTA's core documents, policies, guidelines, standards, and procedural documents that represent the Association's stance on the basics of safe, ethical physical therapy practice that meets the appropriate standard of care. A list of suggested readings complements these, directing the reader to specific resources for in-depth information. Together with the articles, these guidelines and references provide physical therapists with a set of tools to help them understand their legal obligations, know their rights, minimize risk, and provide physical therapy services in accordance with the high standards of their profession.

* Readers should note that articles related to specific laws or citations of specific APTA documents provided current information at the time of original publication and may be outdated due to changes in the legal code or revisions in APTA official documents. None of the articles in this publication is intended to provide specific legal advice for any particular individual. Personal advice can be given only by personal legal counsel, based on current and applicable state and federal law.

APTA documents are current as of September 2005. They may change based on annual APTA House of Delegates actions. Visit APTA's Web site, www.apta.org, for the most current versions of all documents.

APTA Disciplinary Action (Judicial Process)

American Physical Therapy Association

Guide for Professional Conduct

APTA
American Physical Therapy Association
The Science of Healing. The Art of Caring.

Purpose

This *Guide for Professional Conduct* (Guide) is intended to serve physical therapists in interpreting the *Code of Ethics* (Code) of the American Physical Therapy Association (Association), in matters of professional conduct. The Guide provides guidelines by which physical therapists may determine the propriety of their conduct. It is also intended to guide the professional development of physical therapist students. The Code and the Guide apply to all physical therapists. These guidelines are subject to change as the dynamics of the profession change and as new patterns of health care delivery are developed and accepted by the professional community and the public. This Guide is subject to monitoring and timely revision by the Ethics and Judicial Committee of the Association.

Interpreting Ethical Principles

The interpretations expressed in this Guide reflect the opinions, decisions, and advice of the Ethics and Judicial Committee. These interpretations are intended to assist a physical therapist in applying general ethical principles to specific situations. They should not be considered inclusive of all situations that could evolve.

Code of Ethics

Preamble

This *Code of Ethics* of the American Physical Therapy Association sets forth principles for the ethical practice of physical therapy. All physical therapists are responsible for maintaining and promoting ethical practice. To this end, the physical therapist shall act in the best interest of the patient/client. This Code of Ethics shall be binding on all physical therapists.

Principle 1

A physical therapist shall respect the rights and dignity of all individuals and shall provide compassionate care.

Principle 2

A physical therapist shall act in a trustworthy manner toward patients/clients and in all other aspects of physical therapy practice.

Principle 3

A physical therapist shall comply with laws and regulations governing physical therapy and shall strive to effect changes that benefit patients/clients.

Principle 4

A physical therapist shall exercise sound professional judgment.

Principle 5

A physical therapist shall achieve and maintain professional competence.

Principle 6

A physical therapist shall maintain and promote high standards for physical therapy practice, education, and research.

Principle 7

A physical therapist shall seek only such remuneration as is deserved and reasonable for physical therapy services.

Principle 8

A physical therapist shall provide and make available accurate and relevant information to patients/clients about their care and to the public about physical therapy services.

Principle 9

A physical therapist shall protect the public and the profession from unethical, incompetent, and illegal acts.

Principle 10

A physical therapist shall endeavor to address the health needs of society.

Principle 11

A physical therapist shall respect the rights, knowledge, and skills of colleagues and other health care professionals.

Adopted by the House of Delegates
June 1981
Last amended June 2000

PRINCIPLE 1

A physical therapist shall respect the rights and dignity of all individuals and shall provide compassionate care.

1.1 Attitudes of a Physical Therapist

A. A physical therapist shall recognize, respect, and respond to individual and cultural differences with compassion and sensitivity.

B. A physical therapist shall be guided at all times by concern for the physical, psychological, and socioeconomic welfare of patients/clients.

C. A physical therapist shall not harass, abuse, or discriminate against others.

PRINCIPLE 2

A physical therapist shall act in a trustworthy manner toward patients/clients, and in all other aspects of physical therapy practice.

2.1 Patient/Physical Therapist Relationship

A. A physical therapist shall place the patient's/client's interest(s) above those of the physical therapist. Working in the patient/client's best interest requires knowledge of the patient's/client's needs from the patient's/client's perspective. Patients/clients often come to the physical therapist in a vulnerable state and normally will rely on the physical therapist's advice, which they perceive to be based on superior knowledge, skill, and experience. The trustworthy physical therapist acts to ameliorate the patient's/client's vulnerability, not to exploit it.

B. A physical therapist shall not exploit any aspect of the physical therapist/patient relationship.

C. A physical therapist shall not engage in any sexual relationship or activity, whether consensual or noncsonsensual, with any patient while a physical therapist/patient relationship exists. Termination of the physical therapist/patient relationship does not eliminate the possibility that a sexual or intimate relationship may exploit the vulnerability of the former patient/client.

D. A physical therapist shall encourage an open and collaborative dialogue with the patient/client.

E. In the event the physical therapist or patient terminates the physical therapist/patient relationship while the patient continues to need physical therapy services, the physical therapist should take steps to transfer the care of the patient to another provider.

2.2 Truthfulness

A physical therapist has an obligation to provide accurate and truthful information. A physical therapist shall not make statements that he/she knows or should know are false, deceptive, fraudulent, or misleading. See Section 8.2.C and D.

2.3 Confidential Information

A. Information relating to the physical therapist/patient relationship is confidential and may not be communicated to a third party not involved in that patient's care without the prior consent of the patient, subject to applicable law.

B. Information derived from peer review shall be held confidential by the reviewer unless the physical therapist who was reviewed consents to the release of the information.

C. A physical therapist may disclose information to appropriate authorities when it is necessary to protect the welfare of an individual or the community or when required by law. Such disclosure shall be in accordance with applicable law.

2.4 Patient Autonomy and Consent

A. A physical therapist shall respect the patient's/client's right to make decisions regarding the recommended plan of care, including consent, modification, or refusal.

B. A physical therapist shall communicate to the patient/client the findings of his/her examination, evaluation, diagnosis, and prognosis.

C. A physical therapist shall collaborate with the patient/client to establish the goals of treatment and the plan of care.

D. A physical therapist shall use sound professional judgment in informing the patient/client of any substantial risks of the recommended examination and intervention.

E. A physical therapist shall not restrict patients' freedom to select their provider of physical therapy.

PRINCIPLE 3

A physical therapist shall comply with laws and regulations governing physical therapy and shall strive to effect changes that benefit patients/clients.

3.1 Professional Practice

A physical therapist shall comply with laws governing the qualifications, functions, and duties of a physical therapist.

3.2 Just Laws and Regulations

A physical therapist shall advocate the adoption of laws, regulations, and policies by providers, employers, third-party payers, legislatures, and regulatory agencies to provide and improve access to necessary health care services for all individuals.

3.3 Unjust Laws and Regulations

A physical therapist shall endeavor to change unjust laws, regulations, and policies that govern the practice of physical therapy. See Section 10.2.

PRINCIPLE 4

A physical therapist shall exercise sound professional judgment.

4.1 Professional Responsibility

A. A physical therapist shall make professional judgments that are in the patient's/client's best interests.

B. Regardless of practice setting, a physical therapist has primary responsibility for the physical therapy care of a patient and shall make independent judgments regarding that care consistent with accepted professional standards. See Sections 2.4 and 6.1.

C. A physical therapist shall not provide physical therapy services to a patient/client while his/her ability to do so safely is impaired.

D. A physical therapist shall exercise sound professional judgment based upon his/her knowledge, skill, education, training, and experience.

E. Upon accepting a patient/client for physical therapy services, a physical therapist shall be responsible for: the examination, evaluation, and diagnosis of that individual; the prognosis and intervention; re-examination and modification of the plan of care; and the maintenance of adequate records, including progress reports. A physical therapist shall establish the plan of care and shall provide and/or supervise and direct the appropriate interventions. See Section 2.4.

F. If the diagnostic process reveals findings that are outside the scope of the physical therapist's knowledge, experience, or expertise, the physical therapist shall so inform the patient/client and refer to an appropriate practitioner..

G. When the patient has been referred from another practitioner, the physical therapist shall communicate pertinent findings and/or information to the referring practitioner.

H. A physical therapist shall determine when a patient/client will no longer benefit from physical therapy services. See Section 7.1.D.

4.2 Direction and Supervision

A. The supervising physical therapist has primary responsibility for the physical therapy care rendered to a patient/client.

B. A physical therapist shall not delegate to a less qualified person any activity that requires the professional skill, knowledge, and judgment of the physical therapist.

4.3 Practice Arrangements

A. Participation in a business, partnership, corporation, or other entity does not exempt physical therapists, whether employers, partners, or stockholders, either individually or collectively, from the obligation to promote, maintain, and comply with the ethical principles of the Association.

B. A physical therapist shall advise his/her employer(s) of any employer practice that causes a physical therapist to be in conflict with the ethical principles of the Association. A physical therapist shall seek to eliminate aspects of his/her employment that are in conflict with the ethical principles of the Association.

4.4 Gifts and Other Consideration(s)

A. A physical therapist shall not invite, accept, or offer gifts, monetary incentives, or other considerations that affect or give an appearance of affecting his/her professional judgment.

B. A physical therapist shall not offer or accept kickbacks in exchange for patient referrals. See Sections 7.1.F and G and 9.1.D.

PRINCIPLE 5

A physical therapist shall achieve and maintain professional competence.

5.1 Scope of Competence

A physical therapist shall practice within the scope of his/her competence and commensurate with his/her level of education, training, and experience.

5.2 Self-Assessment

A physical therapist has a lifelong professional responsibility for maintaining competence through on-going self-assessment, education, and enhancement of knowledge and skills.

5.3 Professional Development

A physical therapist shall participate in educational activities that enhance his/her basic knowledge and skills. See Section 6.1.

PRINCIPLE 6

A physical therapist shall maintain and promote high standards for physical therapy practice, education and research.

6.1 Professional Standards

A physical therapist's practice shall be consistent with accepted professional standards. A physical therapist shall continuously engage in assessment activities to determine compliance with these standards.

6.2 Practice

A. A physical therapist shall achieve and maintain professional competence. See Section 5.

B. A physical therapist shall demonstrate his/her commitment to quality improvement by engaging in peer and utilization review and other self-assessment activities.

6.3 Professional Education

A. A physical therapist shall support high-quality education in academic and clinical settings.

B. A physical therapist participating in the educational process is responsible to the students, the academic institutions, and the clinical settings for promoting ethical conduct. A physical therapist shall model ethical behavior and provide the student with information about the *Code of Ethics*, opportunities to discuss ethical conflicts, and procedures for reporting unresolved ethical conflicts. See Section 9.

6.4 Continuing Education

A. A physical therapist providing continuing education must be competent in the content area.

B. When a physical therapist provides continuing education, he/she shall ensure that course content, objectives, faculty credentials, and responsibilities of the instructional staff are accurately stated in the promotional and instructional course materials.

C. A physical therapist shall evaluate the efficacy and effectiveness of information and techniques presented in continuing education programs before integrating them into his/her practice.

6.5 Research

A. A physical therapist participating in research shall abide by ethical standards governing protection of human subjects and dissemination of results.

B. A physical therapist shall support research activities that contribute knowledge for improved patient care.

C. A physical therapist shall report to appropriate authorities any acts in the conduct or presentation of research that appear unethical or illegal. See Section 9.

PRINCIPLE 7

A physical therapist shall seek only such remuneration as is deserved and reasonable for physical therapy services.

7.1 Business and Employment Practices

A. A physical therapist's business/employment practices shall be consistent with the ethical principles of the Association.

B. A physical therapist shall never place her/his own financial interest above the welfare of individuals under his/her care.

C. A physical therapist shall recognize that third-party payer contracts may limit, in one form or another, the provision of physical therapy services. Third-party limitations do not absolve the physical therapist from making sound professional judgments that are in the patient's best interest. A physical therapist shall avoid underutilization of physical therapy services.

D. When a physical therapist's judgment is that a patient will receive negligible benefit from physical therapy services, the physical therapist shall not provide or continue to provide such services if the primary reason for doing so is to further the financial self-interest of the physical therapist or his/her employer. A physical therapist shall avoid overutilization of physical therapy services. See Section 4.1.H.

E. Fees for physical therapy services should be reasonable for the service performed, considering the setting in which it is provided, practice costs in the geographic area, judgment of other organizations, and other relevant factors.

F. A physical therapist shall not directly or indirectly request, receive, or participate in the dividing, transferring, assigning, or rebating of an unearned fee. See Sections 4.4.A and B.

G. A physical therapist shall not profit by means of a credit or other valuable consideration, such as an unearned commission, discount, or gratuity, in connection with the furnishing of physical therapy services. See Sections 4.4.A and B.

H. Unless laws impose restrictions to the contrary, physical therapists who provide physical therapy services within a business entity may pool fees and monies received. Physical therapists may divide or apportion these fees and monies in accordance with the business agreement.

I. A physical therapist may enter into agreements with organizations to provide physical therapy services if such agreements do not violate the ethical principles of the Association or applicable laws.

7.2 Endorsement of Products or Services

A. A physical therapist shall not exert influence on individuals under his/her care or their families to use products or services based on the direct or indirect financial interest of the physical therapist in such products or services. Realizing that these individuals will normally rely on the physical therapist's advice, their best interest must always be maintained, as must their right of free choice relating to the use of any product or service. Although it cannot be considered unethical for physical therapists to own or have a financial interest in the production, sale, or distribution of products or services, they must act in accordance with law and make full disclosure of their interest whenever individuals under their care use such products or services.

B. A physical therapist may receive remuneration for endorsement or advertisement of products or services to the public, physical therapists, or other health professionals provided he/she discloses any financial interest in the production, sale, or distribution of said products or services.

C. When endorsing or advertising products or services, a physical therapist shall use sound professional judgment and shall not give the appearance of Association endorsement unless the Association has formally endorsed the products or services.

7.3 Disclosure

A physical therapist shall disclose to the patient if the referring practitioner derives compensation from the provision of physical therapy.

PRINCIPLE 8

A physical therapist shall provide and make available accurate and relevant information to patients/clients about their care and to the public about physical therapy services.

8.1 Accurate and Relevant Information to the Patient

A. A physical therapist shall provide the patient/client accurate and relevant information about his/her condition and plan of care. See Section 2.4.

B. Upon the request of the patient, the physical therapist shall provide, or make available, the medical record to the patient or a patient-designated third party.

C. A physical therapist shall inform patients of any known financial limitations that may affect their care.

D. A physical therapist shall inform the patient when, in his/her judgment, the patient will receive negligible benefit from further care. See Section 7.1.C.

8.2 Accurate and Relevant Information to the Public

A. A physical therapist shall inform the public about the societal benefits of the profession and who is qualified to provide physical therapy services.

B. Information given to the public shall emphasize that individual problems cannot be treated without individualized examination and plans/programs of care.

C. A physical therapist may advertise his/her services to the public. See Section 2.2.

D. A physical therapist shall not use, or participate in the use of, any form of communication containing a false, plagiarized, fraudulent, deceptive, unfair, or sensational statement or claim. See Section 2.2.

E. A physical therapist who places a paid advertisement shall identify it as such unless it is apparent from the context that it is a paid advertisement.

PRINCIPLE 9

A physical therapist shall protect the public and the profession from unethical, incompetent, and illegal acts.

9.1 Consumer Protection

A. A physical therapist shall provide care that is within the scope of practice as defined by the state practice act.

B. A physical therapist shall not engage in any conduct that is unethical, incompetent, or illegal.

C. A physical therapist shall report any conduct that appears to be unethical, incompetent, or illegal.

D. A physical therapist may not participate in any arrangements in which patients are exploited due to the referring sources' enhancing their personal incomes as a result of referring for, prescribing, or recommending physical therapy. See Sections 2.1.B, 4, and 7.

PRINCIPLE 10

A physical therapist shall endeavor to address the health needs of society.

10.1 Pro Bono Service

A physical therapist shall render pro bono publico (reduced or no fee) services to patients lacking the ability to pay for services, as each physical therapist's practice permits.

10.2 Individual and Community Health

A. A physical therapist shall be aware of the patient's health-related needs and act in a manner that facilitates meeting those needs.

B. A physical therapist shall endeavor to support activities that benefit the health status of the community. See Section 3.

PRINCIPLE 11

A physical therapist shall respect the rights, knowledge, and skills of colleagues and other health care professionals.

11.1 Consultation

A physical therapist shall seek consultation whenever the welfare of the patient will be safeguarded or advanced by consulting those who have special skills, knowledge, and experience.

11.2 Patient/Provider Relationships

A physical therapist shall not undermine the relationship(s) between his/her patient and other health care professionals.

11.3 Disparagement

Physical therapists shall not disparage colleagues and other health care professionals. See Section 9 and Section 2.4.A.

Issued by the Ethics and Judicial Committee
American Physical Therapy Association
October 1981, Last amended 2004   P-6

American Physical Therapy Association

Guide for Conduct of the Physical Therapist Assistant

Purpose

This *Guide for Conduct of the Physical Therapist Assistant* (Guide) is intended to serve physical therapist assistants in interpreting the *Standards of Ethical Conduct for the Physical Therapist Assistant* (Standards) of the American Physical Therapy Association (APTA). The Guide provides guidelines by which physical therapist assistants may determine the propriety of their conduct. It is also intended to guide the development of physical therapist assistant students. The Standards and Guide apply to all physical therapist assistants. These guidelines are subject to change as the dynamics of the profession change and as new patterns of health care delivery are developed and accepted by the professional community and the public. This Guide is subject to monitoring and timely revision by the Ethics and Judicial Committee of the Association.

Interpreting Standards

The interpretations expressed in this Guide reflect the opinions, decisions, and advice of the Ethics and Judicial Committee. These interpretations are intended to guide a physical therapist assistant in applying general ethical principles to specific situations. They

should not be considered inclusive of all situations that a physical therapist assistant may encounter.

STANDARD 1

A physical therapist assistant shall respect the rights and dignity of all individuals and shall provide compassionate care.

1.1 Attitude of a Physical Therapist Assistant

A. A physical therapist assistant shall recognize, respect, and respond to individual and cultural differences with compassion and sensitivity.

B. A physical therapist assistant shall be guided at all times by concern for the physical and psychological welfare of patients/clients.

C. A physical therapist assistant shall not harass, abuse, or discriminate against others.

STANDARD 2

A physical therapist assistant shall act in a trustworthy manner towards patients/clients.

2.1 Trustworthiness

A. The physical therapist assistant shall place the patient's/client's interest(s) above those of the physical therapist assistant. Working in the patient's/client's best interest requires sensitivity to the patient's/client's vulnerability and an effective working relationship between the physical therapist and the physical therapist assistant.

B. A physical therapist assistant shall not exploit any aspect of the physical therapist assistant– patient/client relationship.

C. A physical therapist assistant shall clearly identify him/herself as a physical therapist assistant to patients/clients.

D. A physical therapist assistant shall conduct him/herself in a manner that supports the physical therapist–patient/client relationship.

E. A physical therapist assistant shall not engage in any sexual relationship or activity, whether consensual or nonconsensual, with any patient entrusted to his/her care. Termination of patient/client care does not eliminate the possibility that a sexual or intimate relationship may exploit the vulnerability of the former patient/client.

F. A physical therapist assistant shall not invite, accept, or offer gifts, monetary incentives or other considerations that affect or give an appearance of affecting his/her provision of physical therapy interventions. See Section 6.3.

2.2 Exploitation of Patients

A physical therapist assistant shall not participate in any arrangements in which patients/clients are exploited. Such arrangements include situations where referring sources enhance their personal income by referring to or recommend-ding physical therapy services.

2.3 Truthfulness

A. A physical therapist assistant shall not make statements that he/she knows or should know are false, deceptive, fraudulent, or misleading.

B. Although it cannot be considered unethical for a physical therapist assistant to own or have a finan-cial interest in the production, sale, or distribution of products/ services, he/she must act in accordance with law and make full disclosure of his/her interest to patients/clients.

2.4 Confidential Information

A. Information relating to the patient/client is confidential and shall not be communicated to a third party not involved in that patient's care without the prior

---

Standards of Ethical Conduct for the Physical Therapist Assistant

Adopted by the House of Delegates June 1981, Last amended June 2000

Preamble

This document of the American Physical Therapy Association sets forth standards for the ethical conduct of the physical therapist assistant. All physical therapist assistants are responsible for maintaining high standards of conduct while assisting physical therapists. The physical therapist assistant shall act in the best interest of the patient/client. These standards of conduct shall be binding on all physical therapist assistants.

consent of the patient, subject to applicable law.

B. A physical therapist assistant shall refer all requests for release of confidential information to the supervising physical therapist.

STANDARD 3

A physical therapist assistant shall provide selected physical therapy interventions only under the supervision and direction of a physical therapist.

3.1 Supervisory Relationship

A. A physical therapist assistant shall provide interventions only under the supervision and direction of a physical therapist.

B. A physical therapist assistant shall provide only those interventions that have been selected by the physical therapist.

C. A physical therapist assistant shall not provide any interventions that are outside his/her education, training, experience, or skill, and shall notify the responsible physical therapist of his/her inability to carry out the intervention. See Sections 5.1 and 6.1(B).

D. A physical therapist assistant may modify specific interventions within the plan of care established by the physical therapist in response to changes in the patient's/client's status.

E. A physical therapist assistant shall not perform examinations and evaluations, determine diagnoses and prognoses, or establish or change a plan of care.

F. Consistent with the physical therapist assistant's education, training, knowledge, and experience, he/she may respond to the patient's/client's inquiries regarding interventions that are within the established plan of care.

G. A physical therapist assistant shall have regular and ongoing communication with the physical therapist regarding the patient's/client's status.

STANDARD 4

A physical therapist assistant shall comply with laws and regulations governing physical therapy.

4.1 Supervision

A physical therapist assistant shall know and comply with applicable law. Regardless of the content of any law, a physical therapist assistant shall provide services only under the supervision and direction of a physical therapist.

4.2 Representation

A physical therapist assistant shall not hold him/herself out as a physical therapist.

STANDARD 5

A physical therapist assistant shall achieve and maintain competence in the provision of selected physical therapy interventions.

5.1 Competence

A physical therapist assistant shall provide interventions consistent with his/her level of education, training, experience, and skill. See Sections 3.1(C) and 6.1(B).

5.2 Self-assessment

A physical therapist assistant shall engage in self-assessment in order to maintain competence.

5.3 Development

A physical therapist assistant shall participate in educational activities that enhance his/her knowledge and skills.

STANDARD 6

A physical therapist assistant shall make judgments that are commensurate with his/her educational and legal qualifications as a physical therapist assistant.

6.1 Patient Safety

A. A physical therapist assistant shall discontinue immediately any intervention(s) that, in his/her judgment, may be harmful to the patient/client and shall discuss his/her concerns with the physical therapist.

B. A physical therapist assistant shall not provide any intervention(s) that are outside his/her education, training, experience, or skill, and shall notify the responsible physical therapist of his/her inability to carry out the intervention. See Section 3.1(C) and 5.1.

C. A physical therapist assistant shall not perform interventions while his/her ability to do so safely is impaired.

6.2 Judgments About Patient Status

If in the judgment of the physical therapist assistant there is a change in the patient/client status, he/she shall report this to the responsible physical therapist. See Section 3.1.

6.3 Gifts and Other Considerations

A physical therapist assistant shall not invite, accept, or offer gifts, monetary incentives or other considerations that affect or give an appearance of affecting his/her provision of physical therapy interventions. See Section 2.1(F).

STANDARD 7

A physical therapist assistant shall protect the public and the profession from unethical, incompetent, and illegal acts.

7.1 Consumer Protection

A physical therapist assistant shall report any conduct that appears to be unethical or illegal.

7.2 Organizational Employment

A. A physical therapist assistant shall inform his/her employer(s) and/or appropriate physical therapist of any employer practice that causes him or her to be in conflict with the *Standards of Ethical Conduct for the Physical Therapist Assistant.*

B. A physical therapist assistant shall not engage in any activity that puts him or her in conflict with the *Standards of Ethical Conduct for the Physical Therapist Assistant,* regardless of directives from a physical therapist or employer.

Issued by the Ethics and Judicial Committee
American Physical Therapy Association
October 1981, Last amended 2004   P-135

American Physical Therapy Association
Disciplinary Action Procedural Document

The American Physical Therapy Association (Association or APTA) has developed this *Procedural Document on Disciplinary Action* (Procedural Document) to establish a procedure to process claims that a member of the Association has violated the Association's *Code of Ethics* (Code) or *Standards of Ethical Conduct for the Physical Therapist Assistant* (Standards). This document encompasses the procedures for the investigation and hearing of such claims.

This Procedural Document will be followed when a Chapter President receives a signed complaint relating to a member of the Association or otherwise becomes aware of information indicating that a member has violated the Code or the Standards. The Appendix accompanying this Procedural Document is for informational purposes only. All time periods provided herein may be varied only for good cause consistent with fundamental fairness. Wherever this Procedural Document calls for the use of certified mail, return request requested, an alternative form of delivery may be used, provided that it generates a reliable record of receipt.

The Ethics and Judicial Committee of the American Physical Therapy Association will review all complaints, records, and recommendations that are initiated or generated at the Chapter level. At any time in the course of the disciplinary process the Ethics and Judicial Committee has the authority to assume responsibility for management of the ethics proceeding at the Chapter level. Questions of a legal nature may be addressed to Association headquarters.

1. INITIATION OF ETHICS PROCEEDING BY CHAPTER PRESIDENT

A Chapter President may initiate an ethics proceeding in response to a complaint or on the basis of reliable information that comes to his/her attention.

(a) **Complaint.**

(1) **Receipt, Forwarding, and Acknowledgment.** Any person who believes that a member has acted in violation of the ethical principles or standards of the Association may submit a signed written complaint to the President of the Chapter to which the member is assigned. The President may proceed on the basis of a signed complaint submitted by fax but not on the basis of any email complaint. A complaint must describe the conduct which the complainant believes constitutes an ethical violation, but it need not cite specific sections of the Code or Standards. Within three (3) days of receiving a complaint, the President must forward a copy to the attention of the Ethics and Judicial Committee at Association headquarters (1111 North Fairfax Street, Alexandria, Virginia 22314). Upon receipt of a copy of a complaint Association staff shall assign a case number for use on all documents in the proceeding and shall communicate the case number to the Chapter President. The Chapter President and the Chapter Ethics

Committee (CEC) must use this case number on all documents he/she or it issues in the proceeding. The Chapter President and the CEC may not send any communication to a complainant or respondent unless its heading includes the case number assigned by Association staff. Within fifteen (15) days after being advised of the case number, the President shall give the complainant written acknowledgment of receipt of the complaint, which acknowledgment shall enclose a copy of the Procedural Document and shall advise the complainant of the respondent's right to learn the identity of the complainant.

(2) **Alternative Recipient of Complaint.** In any case in which a person has a complaint against a Chapter President, a member closely associated with the Chapter President, or an elected or appointed leader of the Association or of any APTA chapter or section (or in which other circumstances exist which give rise to the appearance that the Chapter President may be unable to act impartially), the complainant may address the complaint to the Association's Ethics and Judicial Committee at the Association's headquarters. The Ethics and Judicial Committee, upon determining that the complaint falls within the foregoing sentence, shall proceed to carry out the functions hereunder of the Chapter President with respect to the complaint; in such a case, references in this Procedural Document to the Chapter President shall be deemed to be to the alternative recipient. The Ethics and Judicial Committee, upon determining that this paragraph does not apply, shall so notify the complainant (who will remain free to resubmit the complaint to the Chapter President).

(b) **Chapter President's Action With Respect to a Complaint.** The responsibility of a Chapter President with respect to a signed complaint is to decide whether to initiate an APTA ethics proceeding by issuing a notice of charges as described in subsection (b)(2)(C) below. The Chapter President shall consult with the Chair of the CEC in making this decision.

The Chapter President first shall determine whether the complaint, fairly construed, alleges conduct by the Association member that would constitute a violation of the Code or Standards. For purposes of this analysis, the President shall assume that the specific facts alleged are true, unless the allegations are plainly baseless.

(1) **No Allegation of Ethical Violation.** If the Chapter President determines that the conduct alleged would not constitute an ethical violation, he/she must send the Ethics and Judicial Committee written notice advising that he/she is declining to issue a notice of charges and briefly explaining his/her rationale. The Chapter President shall send the complainant a copy of such notice of decision not to initiate an ethics proceeding.

(2) Allegation of Ethical Violation. If the Chapter President determines that the conduct alleged would constitute an ethical violation, he/she still must exercise his/her best judgment as to whether to refer the case to the CEC, taking into account the nature of the alleged conduct, the ability of the CEC to investigate and dispose of the case, and other relevant considerations. The Chapter President may decline to issue a notice of charges on the ground that:

(i) the conduct alleged would constitute only a de minimis violation such that referral to the CEC is not warranted;

(ii) the conduct alleged occurred sufficiently long ago that referral to the CEC is not warranted; or

(iii) the ultimate determination whether the conduct violates the Code or Standards would require resolution of legal or other issues beyond the competence of the CEC and/or the Ethics and Judicial Committee, so that referral to the CEC is not warranted.

(A) Decision Not To Initiate an Ethics Proceeding. If the Chapter President makes a discretionary decision not to refer the case to the CEC, he/she must send the Ethics and Judicial Committee written notice advising that he/she is declining to issue a notice of charges and briefly explaining his/her rationale. At the same time the Chapter President shall forward the complete file to the Ethics and Judicial Committee and shall send the complainant a copy of the notice of decision not to initiate an ethics proceeding.

(B) Decision To Initiate an Ethics Proceeding; Notice of Charges. If the Chapter President decides that a complaint's allegations of ethical misconduct should be referred to the CEC, he/she shall initiate an ethics proceeding against the member (respondent) by promptly sending a notice of charges to the respondent, with copies to the Ethics and Judicial Committee and the CEC. The President shall send the notice of charges to the respondent by certified mail, return receipt requested.

(C) Notice of Charges. The notice of charges shall describe, in the President's words, the conduct which, if proven, would constitute a violation of the Code or the Standards. The notice must describe the conduct in sufficient detail to apprise a reader unfamiliar with the case of the behavior in which the respondent allegedly engaged. The notice must specify which provision(s) of the Code or Standards the conduct, if proven, would violate. The notice of charges may, but need not, specify any provision(s) of the *Guide for Professional Conduct* or the *Guide for Conduct of the Physical Therapist Assistant* which the Chapter President believes is (are) relevant to the conduct in question. The notice of charges shall state that the President is referring the matter to the CEC and shall identify the Chair of the CEC (name, address, and telephone number). The President shall enclose a copy of the complaint with the notice of charges, and the notice shall advise the respondent that a copy of the complaint is enclosed. The President shall refer the matter to the CEC by sending it a copy of the notice of charges and shall transmit also the underlying complaint, and any other documents in the President's possession that may be relevant to the proceeding.

(c) Chapter President's Action Based on Reliable Information. A Chapter President may initiate an ethics proceeding without having received a signed complaint, but only in accordance with this subsection. A proceeding may be initiated on the basis of written information that is available publicly, obtained from authorized agencies, or otherwise properly obtained, if such information reliably indicates that an APTA member engaged in conduct that would constitute a violation of the Code or Standards. Such information may include evidence that a member has violated a state or federal criminal law or that a state licensing agency has taken disciplinary action against a member.

(1) Receipt of Information. Association staff may forward to a Chapter President reliable information that might be the basis for initiation of an ethics proceeding, in which case staff shall assign a case number to the matter and communicate that case number to the Chapter President.

A Chapter President who obtains reliable information that might be the basis for initiation of an ethics proceeding from a source other than Association staff must forward a copy of the information to the attention of the Ethics and Judicial Committee at Association headquarters within three (3) days of obtaining such information. Upon receipt of a copy of such information, Association staff shall assign a case number for use on all documents in the proceeding and shall communicate the case number to the Chapter President. The Chapter President and the Chapter Ethics Committee (CEC) must use the case number assigned by Association staff on all documents he/she or it issues in the proceeding. The Chapter President and the CEC may not send any communication to a respondent unless its heading includes the case number assigned by Association staff.

(2) Chapter President's Action With Respect to Information Reliably Indicating Misconduct. The responsibility of a Chapter President with respect to information reliably indicating that a member engaged in unethical conduct is to decide whether to initiate an APTA ethics proceeding issuing a notice of charges as described in subsection (b)(2)(C) above. The Chapter President shall consult with the Chair of the CEC in making this decision.

The Chapter President first shall determine the facts that have been reliably established (e.g., by a guilty plea or verdict in a criminal proceeding or by a consent decree in a licensing action). Because such determinations often involve the interpretation of legal documents, the Chapter President shall consult with the Association's legal counsel as needed.

(A) No Evidence of Ethical Violation. If the Chapter President determines that the conduct reliably established would not constitute an ethical violation, he/she must send the Ethics and Judicial Committee written notice advising that he/she is declining to issue a notice of charges and briefly explaining his/her rationale.

(B) Evidence of Ethical Violation. If the Chapter President determines that the conduct reliably established would constitute an ethical violation, he/she still must exercise his/her best judgment as to whether to refer the case to the CEC, taking into account the nature of the conduct, the ability of the CEC to investigate and dispose of the case, and other relevant considerations. The Chapter President may decline to issue a notice of charges on any ground specified in subsection (b)(2) above.

(i) Decision Not To Initiate an Ethics Proceeding. If the Chapter President makes a discretionary decision not to refer the case to the CEC, he/she must send the Ethics and Judicial Committee written notice advising that he/she is declining to issue a notice of charges and briefly explaining his/her rationale.

(ii) Decision To Initiate an Ethics Proceeding. If the Chapter President decides that an ethics proceeding based on reliable information should be initiated, he/she shall do so by promptly sending a notice of charges to the member (respondent), with copies to the Ethics and Judicial Committee and the CEC, in accordance with the requirements specified in subsection (b)(2)(C) above.

2. PROCEEDING BASED ON SERIOUS CRIME OR REVOCATION OF LICENSURE

(a) Serious Crimes. A member's commission of a crime which (i) is substantially related to the qualifications, functions, or duties of a physical therapist or physical therapist assistant and (ii) is classified as a felony by the applicable federal, state, or territorial law, or is punishable by imprisonment for six months or more, is *prima facie* evidence of a violation of the ethical principles or standards of the Association. The procedures in this section shall apply in the event of (a) a member's plea of guilty or nolo contendere to a charge involving such a serious crime, (b) a finding of guilt after trial, or (c) a member's conviction of such a serious crime. Such a plea (if not withdrawn), finding, or conviction shall be deemed presumptive evidence that the member has engaged in the activity alleged in the criminal charges to which he/she pleaded, as to which there was a finding of guilt, or of which he/she was convicted.

(b) Revocation of Licensure. A member's engaging in conduct which would justify revocation of professional licensure is *prima facie* evidence of a violation of the ethical principles or standards of the Association. The procedures in this section shall apply in the event a state licensing agency revokes a member's license (except that this section shall not apply if the revocation of the member's license is stayed). Such a revocation shall be deemed presumptive evidence that the member has engaged in the conduct on which the revocation was based.

(c) Chapter Responsibilities. If a Chapter President, through receipt of a complaint or other information, becomes aware that a member has committed a crime such as described in subsection (a) above or has had his/her license revoked as described in subsection (b) above, the President shall forward the complaint or other information to the Ethics and Judicial Committee. If a CEC becomes aware of information such as described in subsection (a) or (b) above concerning a member who is a respondent in a case before the CEC that relates to the crime or the basis for the license revocation, the CEC shall forward the information and the complete record of the case to the Ethics and Judicial Committee.

(d) Ethics and Judicial Committee Responsibilities. If the Ethics and Judicial Committee receives reliable information (from a Chapter President or any other source) indicating that a member has made a plea (which has not been withdrawn), been found guilty, or been the subject of a criminal conviction such as described in subsection (a) or that a state licensing agency has taken action such as described in subsection (b), the Ethics and Judicial Committee shall initiate (or continue) an ethics proceeding by preparing and sending a notice of suspension and charges to the member (respondent) by certified mail, return receipt requested.

(e) Notice of Suspension and Charges. The notice of suspension and charges shall advise the respondent that the Ethics and Judicial Committee has preliminarily suspended the respondent (ie, temporarily removed his/her membership rights as provided in Section 4), effective thirty (30) days after the date of the notice and continuing until the Ethics and Judicial Committee's decision. The notice shall describe the conduct which appears to constitute a violation of the Code or the Standards and shall specify which provision(s) of the Code or Standards the conduct appears to have violated. The notice of charges may, but need not, specify any provision(s) of the *Guide for Professional Conduct* or the *Guide for Conduct of the Affiliate Member* which the Ethics and Judicial Committee believes is (are) relevant to the conduct in question. The notice shall advise the respondent that the Ethics and Judicial Committee will consider the case at its next regularly scheduled meeting (or, if the date of the notice is sixty (60) or fewer days before the start of that meeting, at the first regularly scheduled meeting thereafter) and that the respondent may choose to appear before the Committee or to submit a written statement.

(f) Ethics and Judicial Committee Action. At the appropriate regularly scheduled meeting the Ethics and Judicial Committee shall consider the respondent's case. If the respondent exercises his/her right to appear before the Ethics and Judicial Committee, the hearing shall be limited to one hour.

(1) **Serious Crime.** With respect to any proceeding based on commission of a serious crime, the Ethics and Judicial Committee shall consider: whether the respondent in fact entered a plea of guilty or nolo contendere, was found guilty, or was convicted; the nature of the conduct underlying the criminal charges to which the respondent pleaded or was found guilty or convicted; the relationship of the criminal conduct to the qualifications, functions, or duties of a physical therapist or physical therapist assistant; the relationship of the criminal conduct to the provision(s) of the Code or Standards specified in the notice of suspension and charges; and any other matters which the Committee in its discretion deems relevant.

(2) **Licensure Revocation.** With respect to any proceeding based on revocation of licensure, the Ethics and Judicial Committee shall consider: whether the respondent in fact was the subject of administrative action resulting in revocation of licensure; the nature of the conduct upon which the licensing authority based its adverse action; the relationship of such conduct to the qualifications, functions, or duties of a physical therapist or physical therapist assistant; the relationship of such conduct to the provision(s) of the Code or Standards specified in the notice of suspension and charges; and any other matters which the Committee in its discretion deems relevant.

(3) **Ethics and Judicial Committee Decision.** The Ethics and Judicial Committee shall make a decision, based on the information available to it, to dismiss the charges or to impose any form of disciplinary action described in Section 4. The Ethics and Judicial Committee shall mail notice of its decision to the respondent, by certified mail, return receipt requested, within fifteen (15) days following the decision. If the Ethics and Judicial Committee decides to continue the suspension the notice of decision shall specify the length of the continuation (which shall be deemed the specified time of initial suspension for purposes of any future termination of suspension).

3. CHAPTER ETHICS COMMITTEE PROCEEDINGS

The CEC shall be responsible for processing any proceeding the Chapter President refers to it under Section 1. All CEC decisions shall be determined by a majority vote of members present and voting. The Chapter President, after referring a matter to the CEC, shall not participate any further in the proceeding.

(a) **Appointment of Investigator.** Within 30 days after receipt of the notice of charges, the CEC by letter (with a copy to the Ethics and Judicial Committee) shall appoint an investigator (who may be a member of the CEC and who need not be an Association member) to conduct and investigation of the charges set forth in the President's notice of charges. The CEC shall provide the investigator with the complaint (if any), the documentation underlying any proceeding initiated by the President under Section 1(e), the President's notice of charges, and any other documents or information the CEC determines to be relevant to the investigation.

(b) **Investigation.** The investigation shall be an appropriately comprehensive and unbiased review of the circumstances of the alleged unethical activity. As a part of the investigation, the complainant and the respondent will be offered an opportunity to submit a statement of position or other evidence with respect to the allegations against the respondent. The investigator shall advise the respondent of all adverse evidence developed in the course of the investigation and shall give the respondent the opportunity to respond to all adverse evidence.

(c) **Investigative File; Date of Receipt.** The investigator shall prepare an investigative file which includes the complaint (if any), any documentation on which the President relied in initiating a proceeding under Section 1(e), the President's notice of charges, and other information and documents acquired or created during the investigation. The investigative file shall not include a recommendation concerning the CEC's action on the case. The investigator, within ninety (90) days of his/her appointment, shall submit to the CEC a cover letter enclosing the investigative file. The investigator shall be available to be called at the hearing (if any) to clarify the contents of the investigative file. The CEC shall make a record of the date of its receipt of the investigative file (e.g., by memorandum to file).

(d) **Confidentiality.** In order to protect the legitimate interests of the respondent, complainant, witnesses, and others, the confidential nature of a proceeding under this Procedural Document shall be preserved (except as explicitly provided herein). The Chapter President, the members of the CEC, and the investigator shall take due precautions to assure the confidential nature of the proceeding; they shall endeavor to restrict knowledge of the existence and substance of any proceeding to those individuals having a need to know (e.g., witnesses, legal counsel, expert advisors or witnesses, stenographers, Chapter or Association staff with support responsibilities, etc.). The Chapter President, the CEC, and the investigator may seek information and documentation from state licensing agencies (and courts) relating to disciplinary (or criminal) proceedings involving the respondent, but they shall not reveal to state licensing agencies (or other parties) information or documentation developed in the course of the proceeding under this Procedural Document. Upon the respondent's request, the investigator shall disclose to the respondent any publicly available documents or information upon which the Chapter President relied in initiating a proceeding under Section 1(e). Except when the CEC dismisses the charges summarily without a hearing, the respondent shall have the right to obtain a copy of the complete investigative file, which shall contain a copy of the underlying complaint (if any). The Association's Chief Executive Officer or President may take appropriate steps (including cessation of the processing of ethics complaints and charges in a state) to protect the interests of individual participants in the ethics process (including respondents and witnesses), the Chapter, and the Association itself upon determining (i) that the law or practice of any state requires (or could require) the disclosure of the existence of a complaint or proceeding under this Procedural Document or the reporting or disclosure of information or documentation developed hereunder and (ii) that such requirement would be unfair to affected parties or could expose any participant, the Chapter, or the Association itself to an undue risk of civil or criminal liability.

(e) Summary Dismissal Without a Hearing. If the CEC determines, based upon its preliminary review of the investigative file, that the evidence does not substantiate the violation(s) specified in the notice of charges, the CEC may dismiss the charges summarily. In such a case the CEC shall prepare a notice of summary dismissal, which shall state the CEC's rationale. The CEC shall send the notice of summary dismissal to the respondent by certified mail, return receipt requested, with copies to the Ethics and Judicial Committee, the Chapter President, and the complainant (if any).

(f) Notice of Right to Copy of Investigative File and Hearing. If the CEC does not dismiss the charges against the respondent summarily under subsection (e) above, the respondent shall have the right (i) to obtain a copy of the investigative file, and (ii) if the respondent still is an APTA member, to have a hearing before the CEC.

In such a case, the CEC, after receiving the investigative file, shall send the respondent a notice of his/her rights, in substantially the following form:

> This Committee has conducted a preliminary review of the investigative file and determined that it contains evidence that could substantiate the charges against you specified in the [date] notice of charges that the Chapter President sent to you. Under the APTA's *Procedural Document on Disciplinary Action*, you have the right (i) to obtain a copy of the investigative file, and (ii) if you still are an APTA member, to have a hearing before the CEC. If you wish to exercise any such right, you must submit a written request for a copy of the investigative file or for a hearing within fifteen (15) days of your receipt of this notice.

The CEC shall send this notice by certified mail, return receipt requested, with a copy to the Ethics and Judicial Committee. The respondent shall have fifteen (15) days from receipt of the notice in which to request in writing a copy of the investigative file and/or a hearing.

(1) Respondent's Election of Hearing. If the respondent makes a timely election to have a hearing, then the CEC shall notify the respondent in writing of the date, time, and place of hearing at least thirty (30) days in advance. The hearing shall be scheduled within sixty (60) days of the CEC's receipt of the investigative file.

(2) CEC's Calling of Hearing. If the respondent declines the opportunity to have a hearing or fails to make a timely response, the CEC has the prerogative to call and convene a hearing (eg, if the CEC wishes to hear the

respondent testify) to be held no later than sixty (60) days after the CEC's receipt of the investigative file. In such an event the CEC shall notify the respondent in writing of the date, time, and place of hearing at least thirty (30) days in advance.

(3) No Hearing. If no hearing is held the CEC shall proceed as described in Section 4 of this Procedural Document.

(g) Hearing. The CEC shall conduct the hearing to review the pertinent facts, including the calling of witnesses and the production of pertinent documents. Except for the purpose of offering testimony, attendance at the hearing is limited to members of the CEC, the respondent, the respondent's legal counsel (if any), the Chapter's legal counsel (if any), and a transcriber (if any). Additional persons may be allowed to attend with the mutual agreement of the CEC and the respondent. The respondent may call a witness(es) to the hearing. Witnesses, including the complainant, shall not be allowed to attend any part of the hearing in which they are not directly involved. The respondent shall have the right to appear at the hearing in person to present and question witnesses and examine evidence. If legal counsel for the respondent or the CEC is present at the hearing (or at any stage of the ethics proceeding including proceedings before the Ethics and Judicial Committee or Board of Directors of the Association) the scope of involvement of such counsel shall be to provide consultation and advice to the respective parties. Rules of evidence shall not be applied strictly, but the CEC shall exclude irrelevant or unduly repetitious evidence. An oral affirmation of truthfulness will be requested from each witness. All documents accepted by the CEC, including the investigative file, shall be made a part of the record of the hearing.

(h) Failure of Complainant To Participate. If a proceeding was based on a complaint and the situation arises where the complainant no longer participates, the CEC may continue the ethics proceeding.

(i) Termination of Respondent's Membership During Proceeding. If during an ethics proceeding the CEC learns that a respondent's membership in the Association has ended, the CEC shall still complete the collection of all available information to facilitate a later reopening of the case if the respondent at any time rejoins the Association. In such a case the CEC shall review the investigative file. The CEC may dismiss the charges summarily on the basis of the investigative file, in which case it shall send notice of such summary dismissal in accordance with subsection (e). Otherwise, the CEC shall notify the respondent in accordance with subsection (f) and shall conduct a hearing (if any) in accordance with subsection (g). If a hearing is held the CEC may dismiss the charges, in which case it shall so notify the respondent by certified mail, return receipt requested, with a copy of the notice to the Ethics and Judicial Committee. If the CEC does not determine to dismiss the charges against the respondent, the CEC shall forward the complete record of the case (including the investigative file and the record of any hearing) to the Ethics and Judicial Committee. In any such case the CEC may (but need not) make a recommendation to the Ethics and Judicial Committee concerning the disciplinary action that it deems would have been appropriate if the respondent had been a member throughout the time the proceeding was before the CEC. In any such case the Ethics and Judicial Committee shall proceed pursuant to Section 5(e).

(j) **Stay of Proceeding.** The CEC may (but need not) vote to stay any proceeding before it if the conduct in question is the subject of investigation or action by federal, state, or local governmental authorities. If the CEC stays any such proceeding it shall review its decision to stay at intervals of no more than six (6) months.

(k) **Communications With Ethics and Judicial Committee.** The Ethics and Judicial Committee may prescribe a form of Disciplinary Action Worksheet to be used to track the progress of any proceeding. The Chair of the CEC shall advise the Ethics and Judicial Committee periodically (and upon request) of the status of any matter pending before the CEC.

4. CHAPTER ETHICS COMMITTEE CONCLUSIONS AND RECOMMENDATIONS

(a) **Dismissal or Recommendations of Disciplinary Action.** The CEC shall take action based on the evidence contained in the investigative file and obtained at a hearing (if any). The CEC shall take one of the following actions:

(1) dismiss the charges; or

(2) recommend that the Ethics and Judicial Committee impose one of the following disciplinary actions:

(A) **Reprimand**—a statement of recognition that the respondent's behavior was contrary to the Code or Standards. A reprimand is issued with the understanding that the respondent will correct the violation immediately (if he/she has not done so already). Ongoing conditions may not be added to a reprimand.

(B) **Probation**—a stronger reprimand with conditions for corrective action that the respondent shall complete within a given time period, not less than six (6) months nor more than two (2) years. The CEC shall monitor compliance with the conditions of probation. Failure to comply with the conditions of probation shall result in review by the Ethics and Judicial Committee as described in Section 7(a).

(C) **Suspension**—a temporary removal for not less than one (1) year of the rights and privileges of membership as identified in Article IV, Section 2 of the Association's *Bylaws*, "Rights and Privileges of Members," with the exception of B.(11). The affected rights and privileges shall be restored after the termination of the specified time of initial suspension, in accordance with Section 7(b), provided that there has been compliance with Article IV, Section 5 of the *Bylaws*, "Good Standing," during the suspension;

(D) **Expulsion**—a removal of membership which is subject to reinstatement only as stipulated in Article IV, Section 7 of the Bylaws, "Reinstatement."

If the CEC recommends the imposition of disciplinary action, the recommendation must specify (i) the evidence that the CEC believes supports its recommendation and (ii) the Principle of the *Code of Ethics* or the Standard of the *Standards of Ethical Conduct for the Physical Therapist Assistant* that the CEC believes is implicated. The CEC shall not make any finding that the respondent has violated an ethical principle or any law or regulation.

(b) **Notice to Respondent.** The CEC shall mail a copy of its dismissal of the charges or its recommendation for disciplinary action to the respondent by certified mail, return receipt requested, within thirty (30) days of the hearing, or if no hearing is held, within seventy (70) days of the CEC's receipt of the investigative file. In either case the CEC shall send a copy to the Ethics and Judicial Committee. If the CEC recommends that the Ethics and Judicial Committee impose disciplinary action, the CEC must include notice of the respondent's right to have a hearing before the Ethics and Judicial Committee and to make a written submission. The notice shall be in terms substantially similar to the following:

Under the APTA's *Procedural Document on Disciplinary Action*, this Committee has authority to recommend but not to impose disciplinary action. The APTA's Ethics and Judicial Committee has authority to impose the disciplinary action recommended by this Committee, to impose less severe disciplinary action, or to dismiss the charges against you. You have thirty (30) days after your receipt of this letter in which (i) to request in writing a hearing before the Ethics and Judicial Committee and/or (ii) to make a written submission to the Ethics and Judicial Committee for its consideration.

(c) **Transmission of the Record.** The CEC, within the same time frame as above, shall mail to the Ethics and Judicial Committee the entire original of the record, including an updated Disciplinary Action Worksheet, the investigative file, the record of hearing (if any), and evidence of the receipt of all items required to be sent by certified mail, return receipt requested. The CEC shall retain a duplicate copy of the entire record until and unless directed by Association staff in writing to destroy such copy.

5. DECISION OF THE ETHICS AND JUDICIAL COMMITTEE

(a) **Time of Ethics and Judicial Committee Action.** The respondent, within thirty (30) days after receipt of the CEC's recommendation of disciplinary action, by written notice to the Ethics and Judicial Committee may request a hearing before the Ethics and Judicial Committee. Within the same period the respondent may make a written submission to the Ethics and Judicial Committee for its consideration. The Ethics and Judicial Committee shall consider the case at its first regularly scheduled meeting after the respondent's receipt of the CEC's recommendation of disciplinary action if: (i) the Ethics and Judicial Committee receives a timely written request for hearing, a timely written submission, or a written waiver of the unexercised right(s) forty (40) or more days before such meeting; or (ii) the period for the respondent to request a hearing and/or make a written submission expires forty (40) or more days before such meeting. Otherwise, the Ethics and Judicial Committee shall consider the case at the immediately succeeding regularly scheduled meeting.

(b) Notice of Hearing; Hearing. If the respondent elects to have a hearing then the Ethics and Judicial Committee shall mail the respondent notice of the date, time, and place of the hearing at least thirty (30) days before the hearing. If a hearing is held, the hearing shall be limited to one hour. The respondent's presentation shall be limited to matters relevant to the charges.

(c) Decision of Ethics and Judicial Committee. The decision of the Ethics and Judicial Committee shall be based on only the record of the CEC, any oral or written testimony presented by the respondent, and any other information that fairness requires to be heard. The Ethics and Judicial Committee shall not set aside the CEC's dismissal of charges unless it is not supported by substantial evidence, it resulted from a misinterpretation of procedures or of the Association's ethical principles or standards, or there is evidence of actual or apparent impropriety in the dismissal of the charges.

The decision of the Ethics and Judicial Committee with respect to a CEC's recommendation of disciplinary action shall be to:

- impose the disciplinary action recommended by the CEC and specify the effective dates thereof;

- impose less severe disciplinary action than recommended by the CEC or dismiss the charges; or

- remand to the CEC with appropriate directives.

If the Ethics and Judicial Committee decides to impose disciplinary action, its decision shall specify (i) its findings as to the conduct in which the respondent engaged and (ii) the Principle of the *Code of Ethics* or the Standard of the *Standards of Ethical Conduct for the Physical Therapist Assistant* that it believes was violated. Within thirty (30) days after the Ethics and Judicial Committee has considered the CEC's recommendations and any oral or written testimony, the Ethics and Judicial Committee shall prepare its decision and mail it to the respondent by certified mail, return receipt requested, with a copy to the CEC (and to the Chapter President who initiated the proceeding, if the decision is to approve a dismissal of charges). The Ethics and Judicial Committee shall include an explanation of the appeals procedure. All records of the proceeding shall be kept by the Ethics and Judicial Committee for at least the longer of three (3) years from the date of the decision or one (1) year after the termination of any probation or suspension, except that the records of any proceeding resulting in expulsion shall be kept for at least ten (10) years from the date of the decision.

(d) Publication of Disciplinary Action. If an Ethics and Judicial Committee decision that becomes final under Section 6 imposes suspension or expulsion, the Ethics and Judicial Committee shall publish the name of the respondent, the disciplinary action taken, and the effective date(s) of such action in *PT Magazine* and *Physical Therapy* and make appropriate communications regarding the matter wherever the public welfare requires.

(e) Non-Member Respondent. In a case where the respondent's membership has ended the Ethics and Judicial Committee may dismiss the charges if the evidence does not substantiate the violation(s) specified in the notice of charges, but it may not impose any disciplinary action upon a nonmember. If the Ethics and Judicial Committee does not dismiss the charges, it shall stay the proceeding until the respondent rejoins the Association. In such a case the Ethics and Judicial Committee shall maintain the record of the proceeding for at least ten (10) years from the date of the lapse and shall request the Association's staff to notify the Ethics and Judicial Committee upon the respondent's rejoining the Association so that the stay may be lifted and the proceeding brought to a conclusion.

6. APPEAL TO BOARD OF DIRECTORS

(a) Time for Taking Appeal; Notification of Finality If No Appeal. Within thirty (30) days after receiving the final decision of the Ethics and Judicial Committee, the respondent may appeal the decision by delivering a notice of appeal to (i) the Association's Board of Directors and (ii) the Ethics and Judicial Committee. If the Ethics and Judicial Committee does not receive a notice of appeal within thirty (30) days the decision shall become final and unappealable, and the Ethics and Judicial Committee shall forward a copy of its decision and a notice that the decision is final to the Chapter President, the CEC, the complainant (if any), and the Board of Directors.

(b) Time of Board Consideration. If the Ethics and Judicial Committee receives a timely notice of appeal, then the Committee shall assemble the record of the proceeding and forward it to the Association's Board of Directors. The Board of Directors shall hear the appeal at its next regularly scheduled meeting which is not scheduled concurrently with the Annual Conference, provided that meeting begins thirty-five (35) or more days after the date of delivery of the notice of appeal to the Board of Directors. Otherwise, the Board of Directors shall hear the appeal at the immediately succeeding regularly scheduled meeting which is not scheduled concurrently with the Annual Conference.

(c) Notice of Board Consideration. The Board of Directors, at least thirty (30) days prior to the date of its consideration of the appeal, shall mail the respondent a notice, by certified mail, return receipt requested, stating the date, time, and place of the consideration of the appeal. The Board's notice shall advise the respondent that he/she may elect to have a hearing before the Board of Directors and/or to make a written submission. The respondent must exercise any such election in such manner and within such time as the Board's notice prescribes. If the respondent timely elects to have a hearing he/she may appear and present testimony. The hearing shall be limited to one hour.

(d) Decision on Appeal. The Board shall base its decision on appeal upon the record before the Ethics and Judicial Committee and any newly available information which the Board may decide to consider. The Board of Directors shall restrict its consideration of the appeal to the question whether the decision of the Ethics and Judicial Committee is appropriate.

The decision of the Board of Directors on initial appeal shall be to:

- affirm the Ethics and Judicial Committee's decision;

- modify the decision by dismissing the charges or by imposing less severe disciplinary action than imposed by the Ethics and Judicial Committee; or

- remand to the Ethics and Judicial Committee with appropriate directives.

If the Board of Directors does not remand the case to the Ethics and Judicial Committee, then its decision to affirm or modify the Ethics and Judicial Committee's decision shall be final.

(e) Remand to Ethics and Judicial Committee. If the Board of Directors remands the case the Ethics and Judicial Committee shall follow the procedures (if any) prescribed by the Board in its remand. In the absence of any such prescription of procedures, the Ethics and Judicial Committee on remand shall afford the respondent the opportunity to elect to have a hearing before the Committee and/or to make a written submission. If the respondent elects to have a hearing, the hearing shall be limited to one hour. The Ethics and Judicial Committee shall make its decision on remand and give notice thereof to the respondent as in Section 5(c).

(f) Appeal From a Decision on Remand. The respondent shall have thirty (30) days after the receipt of the Ethics and Judicial Committee's decision on remand in which to appeal to the Board of Directors, in the same manner as in subsection (a).

(1) No Appeal From Decision on Remand. If the Ethics and Judicial Committee does not receive a copy of a notice of appeal within thirty (30) days, its decision on remand shall become final and unappealable, and it shall forward copies of its decision on remand to the Chapter President, the CEC, the complainant (if any), and the Board of Directors.

(2) Board Action on Appeal From Decision on Remand. If the Ethics and Judicial Committee receives a timely notice of appeal from its decision on remand it shall forward the record to the Board of Directors. On an appeal following a remand the Board of Directors shall either (i) affirm the Ethics and Judicial Committee's decision on remand or (ii) modify the decision on remand by dismissing the charges or by imposing less severe disciplinary action than imposed by the Ethics

and Judicial Committee. No further remand shall be ordered, and the Board of Directors' decision shall be final.

(g) Notice of Board's Final Decision. The Board of Directors shall notify the respondent of its decision, on initial appeal and upon appeal after remand, by certified mail, return receipt requested. The Board shall forward copies of a final decision (ie, one to affirm or modify the Ethics and Judicial Committee's initial decision or its decision on remand) to the Chapter President, the CEC, the complainant (if any), and the Ethics and Judicial Committee.

7. POST-DECISIONAL MATTERS

(a) Probation. In any case involving probation, responsibility for monitoring the respondent's compliance with the conditions of the probation shall lie with the CEC, which shall report to the Ethics and Judicial Committee as requested. If the Ethics and Judicial Committee determines that the period of probation has expired and that the respondent has complied with the conditions of probation, it shall send notice of the termination of the probation to the respondent by certified mail, return receipt requested, with a copy to the CEC (and appropriate notice to the staff of the Association responsible for maintaining membership records). If the CEC determines at any time that the respondent has violated the conditions of probation it shall promptly notify the Ethics and Judicial Committee in writing, with a copy to the respondent. Immediately upon receiving notification that a respondent has violated the terms of probation, the Ethics and Judicial Committee shall notify the respondent by certified mail, return receipt requested, that it will review the respondent's case.

(1) Notice of Review; Hearing or Written Submission; Time of Review. The notice of review shall advise the respondent that he/she may elect to appear before the Ethics and Judicial Committee (unless the Committee meets by conference call, in which case the respondent may participate in the call) and/or to make a written submission. The respondent must exercise any such election in such manner and within such time as the notice of review prescribes. If the respondent timely elects to appear before the Ethics and Judicial Committee (or participate in a conference call meeting), the hearing (or call) shall be limited to one hour. If the Ethics and Judicial Committee receives notification from the CEC forty (40) or more days before its next regularly scheduled meeting it shall review the case at that meeting. Otherwise, the Ethics and Judicial Committee shall review the case at the immediately succeeding regularly scheduled meeting or any special meeting. The Ethics and Judicial Committee shall notify the respondent of the date, time, and place of its review, by certified mail, return receipt requested.

(2) Ethics and Judicial Committee Action Upon Review. The Ethics and Judicial Committee, on the basis of the information available to it, shall have authority to impose more severe disciplinary action, including suspension or expulsion, as the circumstances warrant. The Ethics and Judicial Committee shall prepare its decision and mail it to the respondent by certified mail, return receipt requested, with a copy to the CEC, within fifteen (15) days after the decision. The respondent may appeal the Ethics and Judicial Committee's decision to the Board of Directors in accordance with Section 6, but only if the decision imposes more severe disciplinary action than the probation previously imposed.

(3) Transfer of Responsibility for Monitoring Compliance. If the respondent moves or changes his chapter assignment during the period of probation, the CEC or the respondent may seek to transfer the responsibility for monitoring compliance to another CEC by mailing a request to the Ethics and Judicial Committee with a copy to the other party. The Ethics and Judicial Committee in its discretion shall grant or deny the request.

(b) Termination of Suspension. A member suspended under Section 2(f) or Section 5 may seek restoration of the affected membership rights by submitting to the Ethics and Judicial Committee, at any time after the expiration of the specified time of initial suspension, a request for termination of the suspension. If the Ethics and Judicial Committee receives the request forty (40) or more days before the start of its next regularly scheduled meeting, then it shall consider the request at that meeting. Otherwise, it shall consider the request at the succeeding regularly scheduled meeting. The Ethics and Judicial Committee shall notify the respondent of the date, time, and place of its consideration of the request to terminate suspension.

(1) Membership in Good Standing Determination. The Ethics and Judicial Committee shall terminate the suspension of a member who complied with the conditions of Article IV, Section 5 of the *Bylaws*, "Good Standing," throughout the period of initial suspension. Accordingly, a request for termination shall include an answer to each of the following questions:

    (i) Did the respondent remain a member of the Association throughout the period of initial suspension?

    (ii) Did the respondent comply with the ethical principles or standards applicable to his/her membership class throughout the period of initial suspension?

    (iii) Did the respondent make timely payment of all Association and chapter dues throughout the period of initial suspension?

    (iv) Was the respondent under suspension or revocation of a license or certificate of registration to practice physical therapy or to act as a physical therapist assistant in any jurisdiction at any time during the period of initial suspension?

The request for termination may contain such other information as may be relevant to the Ethics and Judicial Committee's decision whether to extend the suspension in the event of a negative compliance determination. The Ethics and Judicial Committee, in determining whether the respondent was in compliance with the "Good Standing" conditions throughout the period of initial suspension, may rely upon the information contained in the request for termination of suspension and may make such further inquiry or investigation as it deems appropriate. If the Ethics and Judicial Committee proposes to make a negative determination based on information extrinsic to the request for termination, the Ethics and Judicial Committee first shall so notify the respondent and afford him/her reasonable opportunity to respond.

(2) Termination Upon Affirmative Compliance Determination. If the Ethics and Judicial Committee makes an affirmative compliance determination it shall terminate the suspension immediately, effective as of the expiration of the period of initial suspension. The Ethics and Judicial Committee shall send notice of the termination of suspension to the respondent by certified mail, return receipt requested, with a copy to the CEC (and appropriate notice to the staff of the Association responsible for maintaining membership records).

(3) Action Upon Negative Compliance Determination. If the Ethics and Judicial Committee makes a negative compliance determination it shall decide whether to terminate or extend the suspension. The Ethics and Judicial Committee in its discretion may terminate the suspension or extend it for any length of time (including an extension of less than one year). The Ethics and Judicial Committee shall mail its decision to terminate or extend the suspension to the respondent by certified mail, return receipt requested, with a copy to the CEC (and appropriate notice to the staff of the Association responsible for maintaining membership records).

(4) Extended Suspension. If the Ethics and Judicial Committee extends the suspension its decision shall specify the period of the extended suspension. Restoration of the affected membership rights shall be dependent upon compliance with the "Good Standing" conditions during the time of the extended suspension. A member under extended suspension may seek restoration of the affected membership rights by submitting to the Ethics and Judicial Committee, at any time after the expiration of the specified time of extended suspension, a request for termination of the suspension. Any such request shall be processed in the same manner as set forth above (substituting extended suspension for the initial suspension, as appropriate).

Appendix

Complainant's Responsibilities and Rights

1. Make written complaint to Chapter President (or Ethics and Judicial Committee) that a member has violated the ethical principles or standards of the Association. (Section 1(a))
2. Receive acknowledgment of receipt of complaint. (Sections 1(a))
3. Have the opportunity to submit to investigator a statement of position or other evidence with respect to the allegations. (Section 3(b))
4. May act as witness if hearing takes place. (Section 3(g))
5. Receive notice of final action of the Ethics and Judicial Committee or the Board of Directors. (Section 6(a) or 6(g))

Chapter President's Responsibilities

1. Obtain legal consultation from Association headquarters, as appropriate. (Introduction)
2. Receive written complaint. (Section 1(a))
3. Immediately forward copy of complaint to Ethics and Judicial Committee. (Section 1(a)(1))
4. Obtain a case number from APTA staff (Section 1(a)(1))
5. Send complainant acknowledgment of receipt of complaint. (Section 1(a)(1))
6. Decide whether to initiate an APTA ethics proceeding, in consultation with Chair of Chapter Ethics Committee (CEC). (Section 1(b))
7. Notify the Ethics and Judicial Committee if the President declines to issue a notice of charges based on complaint (Section 1(b)(1), Section 1(b)(2)(A))
8. Notify complainant of decision not to initiate an ethics proceeding. (Section 1(b)(1))
9. Forward to Ethics and Judicial Committee copy of any reliable information that might be the basis for an ethics proceeding (Section 1(c)(1))
10. Determine whether to initiate a proceeding based on reliable information indicating an ethical violation. (Section 1(c)(2))
11. Notify the Ethics and Judicial Committee if the President declines to issue a notice of charges based on reliable information (Section 1(c)(2)(a), Section 1(c)(2)(B)(i))
12. Prepare notice of charges describing conduct at issue, citing ethical Principle(s)/Standard(s), and referring case to CEC. (Section 1(b)(2)(C))
13. Send respondent notice of charges, with copy of complaint (if any), copy to CEC and Ethics and Judicial Committee. (Section 1(b)(2)(C))
14. Receive notice of final action of the Ethics and Judicial Committee or the Board of Directors. (Section 6(a) or 6(g))

Chair of Chapter Ethics Committee's Responsibilities

1. Consult with Chapter President as to whether to initiate an APTA ethics proceeding. (Section 1(b), Section 1(c)(2))

Chapter Ethics Committee's Responsibilities

1. Obtain legal consultation from Association headquarters, when appropriate. (Introduction)
2. Accept referral of case from Chapter President. (Section 1(b)(2)(C) or 1(c))
3. Appoint investigator. (Section 3(a))
4. Receive the investigative file and make record of date of receipt. (Section 3(c))
5. Determine whether investigative file has evidence tending to substantiate the charges in the President's notice. (Section 3(e))
6. Notify respondent, Ethics and Judicial Committee, Chapter President, and complainant (if any) of summary dismissal of charges. (Section 3(e))
7. Notify respondent of rights to obtain copy of investigative file and (if respondent is still a member) to have a hearing before the CEC. (Section 3(f))
8. Provide respondent copy of investigative file, if requested. (Section 3(f))
9. Notify respondent of date, time, and place of hearing (if any). (Section 3(f)(1))
10. Conduct hearing (if demanded by respondent or chosen by CEC). (Section 3(g))
11. If respondent ceases to be a member complete collection of available information to facilitate later reopening, and forward record to Ethics and Judicial Committee. (Section 3(i))
12. Report status of case to Ethics and Judicial Committee. (Section 3(k))
13. Issue a decision dismissing the charges or recommending disciplinary action. (Section 4(a))
14. Mail to respondent CEC's decision, including notice of right to request a hearing before Ethics and Judicial Committee and to make written submission, with copy to Ethics and Judicial Committee. (Section 4(b))
15. Mail entire original record to Ethics and Judicial Committee. (Section 4(c))
16. Retain duplicate copy of entire record until and unless directed by APTA staff in writing to destroy such copy. (Section 4(c))
17. Receive notice of Ethics and Judicial Committee's action with respect to CEC's recommendation of disciplinary action. (Section 5(c))
18. Receive notice of final action of the Ethics and Judicial Committee or the Board of Directors. (Section 6(a) or 6(g))
19. Monitor probation and report noncompliance to Ethics and Judicial Committee. (Sections 7(a))

Ethics and Judicial Committee's Responsibilities

1. Receive copy of complaint filed with Chapter President. (Section 1(a)(1))

2. Serve as alternative recipient of complaint -- for responsibilities, see Chapter President's responsibilities. (Section 1(a)(2))

3. Assign case number to proceeding. (Section 1(a)(1) and 1(c))

4. Receive copy of Chapter President's decision not to initiate an ethics proceeding. (Section 1(b)(1), 1(b)(2)(A))

5. Receive copy of notice of charges prepared by Chapter President. (Section 1(b)(2)(C) or 1(c)(2)(b)(ii))

6. Forward to Chapter President reliable information indicating an ethical violation. (Section 1(c))

7. Receive from Chapter President or CEC complaint (or other documentation) indicating commission of serious crime or revocation of licensure. (Section 2(c))

8. Prepare and send notice of suspension and charges in case of serious crime or revocation of licensure. (Section 2(d) and 2(e))

9. Dismiss charges based on serious crime or revocation of licensure or impose disciplinary action or impose disciplinary action. (Section 2(f)(3))

10. Receive copy of CEC notice of summary dismissal. (Section 3(e))

11. Receive copy of CEC notice of respondent's right to hearing and to obtain copy of investigative file. (Section 3(f))

12. Receive copy of CEC decision to dismiss or to recommend disciplinary action. (Section 4(b))

13. Receive entire original record together with CEC's dismissal of charges or recommendation for disciplinary action (if any). (Section 3(i) and 4(c))

14. Receive from respondent request for hearing or written submission. (Section 5(a))

15. Notify respondent notice of date, time, and place of hearing. (Section 5(b))

16. Make decision on CEC's recommendation and notify respondent and CEC. (Section 5(c))

17. Retain record of the proceeding for time required. (Section 5(c))

18. Publish fact of suspension or expulsion in PT Magazine and Physical Therapy after decision becomes final. (Section 5(d))

19. Alert staff as to respondent whose membership lapsed and maintain record of case for reactivation. (Section 5(e))

20. Forward copies of unappealed decision to Chapter President, CEC, complainant, and Board of Directors. (Section 6(a) and 6(f)(1))

21. Receive copy of notice of appeal and forward record to Board of Directors. (Section 6(b) and 6(f)(2))

22. Make decision on remand in accordance with directions from Board of Directors and Procedural Document. (Section 6(e))

23. Receive CEC notice of noncompliance with conditions of probation; send notice of review to respondent; review case; notify respondent and CEC of decision. (Section 7(a)(1) and 7 (a)(2))

24. Receive respondent's request for termination of suspension; determine compliance with "Good Standing" conditions of Bylaws; give respondent opportunity to respond to proposal to make negative compliance determination. (Section 7(b)(1))

25. Terminate suspension and notify respondent, CEC, and staff if compliance determination is affirmative. (Section 7(b)(2))

26. Decide whether to terminate or extend suspension if compliance determination is negative; notify respondent. (Section 7(b)(3))

Respondent's Responsibilities and Rights

1. Right to receive from Chapter President notice of charges describing conduct at issue and citing ethical Principle(s)/Standard(s) allegedly violated. (Section 1(b)(2)(C) or 1(c))

2. Receive notice of suspension and charges from Ethics and Judicial Committee in case involving commission of serious crime or revocation of licensure. (Section 2(d))

3. Right to have hearing before or make written submission to Ethics and Judicial Committee concerning serious crime or revocation of licensure. (Section 2(e))

4. Receive notice of Ethics and Judicial Committee's decision concerning serious crime or revocation of licensure. (Section 2(f)(3))

5. Right to submit statement of position or other evidence with respect to charges against respondent. (Section 3(b))

6. Right to be advised by investigator of adverse evidence and to respond. (Section 3(b))

7. Right to confidentiality as provided in Procedural Document. (Section 3(d))

8. Receive notice of CEC's summary dismissal of charges. (Section 3(e))

9. Receive notice of right to obtain copy of investigative file and (if still an APTA member) to have a hearing before CEC. (Section 3(f))

10. Receive CEC's notice of date, time, and place of hearing. (Section 3(f)(1) or 3(f)(2))

11. Attend the CEC hearing; right to examine and cross-examine witnesses, produce documents, consult with counsel. (Section 3(g))

12. Receive notice of recommended disciplinary action or dismissal of complaint. (Section 4(b))

13. Request hearing before Ethics and Judicial Committee or make written submission to Ethics and Judicial Committee. (Section 5(a))

14. Receive Ethics and Judicial Committee's notice of date, time, and place of hearing. (Section 5(b))

15. Attend the Ethics and Judicial Committee hearing. (Section 5(b))

16. Receive notice of the Ethics and Judicial Committee's decision and explanation of appeals procedure. (Section 5(c))

17. Appeal Ethics and Judicial Committee's decision to Board of Directors. (Section 6(a))

18. Receive Board's notice of date, time, and place of hearing; appear and present testimony or make written submission. (Section 6(c))

19. Receive notice of Board of Directors' decision on appeal. (Section 6(g))

20. Receive notice of Ethics and Judicial Committee's decision on remand (if any) with explanation of appeals procedure. (Section 6(e))

21. Receive copy of CEC notice of noncompliance with conditions of probation. (Section 7(a))

22. Receive notice of Ethics and Judicial Committee's review as to noncompliance with probation and right to appear and/or make written submission. (Section 7(a)(1))

23. Receive Ethics and Judicial Committee's decision as to noncompliance with probation; right to appeal to Board of Directors if result is stricter disciplinary action. (Section 7(a)(2))

24. Submit request for termination of suspension to Ethics and Judicial Committee. (Section 7(b))

25. Receive notice of proposed determination of noncompliance with "Good Standing" conditions if based on evidence extrinsic to request for termination. (Section 7(b)(1))

26. Receive Ethics and Judicial Committee decision to terminate or extend suspension. (Section 7(b)(3))

Investigator's Responsibilities

1. Conduct objective unbiased investigation. (Section 3(b))

2. Give respondent and complainant opportunity to submit a statement of position or other evidence bearing on the charges. (Section 3(b))

3. Give respondent opportunity to respond to adverse evidence developed. (Section 3(b))

4. Transmit investigative file, with no recommendation, to CEC. (Section 3(c))

5. Be available if hearing takes place to clarify the contents of investigative file. (Section 3(c))

Board of Directors' Responsibilities

1. If no appeal is taken, receive copy of final decision of Ethics and Judicial Committee. (Section 6(a))

2. Receive notice of appeal from respondent. (Section 6(b))

3. If appeal is taken, receive record of proceedings of Ethics and Judicial Committee. (Section 6(b))

4. Notify respondent of date, time, and place of consideration of appeal. (Section 6(c))

5. Hear and make decision on appeal. (Section 6(d))

6. Notify the respondent of its decision. (Section 6(g))

7. Forward a copy of a final decision to the Ethics and Judicial Committee, the Chapter President, the CEC and the complainant (if any). (Section 6(g))

APTA Ethics and Judicial Committee: Approved, Board of Directors: November 1999; Last Amended, Board of Directors: March 2004 [BOD R03-04-11-23]

LIABILITY AWARENESS
Staying Informed in Risk Management
by Jonathan M Cooperman, MS, PT, JD,
and Ronald W Scott, PT, JD, OCS

Disciplinary Action

When a member runs afoul of the APTA code of ethics,
there are consequences, both within
and external to the Association.

If asked, most physical therapists and physical therapist assistants probably would profess to practicing in a legal and ethical manner. However, it is an unfortunate reality for our profession that, occasionally, members are found to have violated APTA's *Code of Ethics*[1] or *Standards of Ethical Conduct for the Physical Therapist Assistant*.[2] Although all APTA members agree to abide by the Association's *Code of Ethics* as a condition of membership, few members may be familiar either with the sanctions that may be imposed if they do not abide by the *Code* or with the practical consequences of those sanctions.

A mark of our status as a profession is that we impose ethical standards upon our members and that we enforce them. APTA's Judicial Committee oversees both the interpretation of the *Code* and *Standards* (ie, by developing the *Guide for Professional Conduct*[3] and the *Guide for Conduct of the Affiliate Member*,[4] which are interpretations of the codes of ethics adopted by APTA's House of Delegates) and the disciplinary process.

Complaints of violations typically arise at the state level and initially are handled by the Chapter Ethics Committee (CEC). The *Procedural Document on Disciplinary Action*[5] ensures that all parties to the complaint receive due process. If a complaint arises, the CEC conducts an investigation, and the respondent (the person against whom the complaint is alleged) has a right to a hearing. Based on the information in the completed investigative file, the CEC will either dismiss the charges or recommend action to the Judicial Committee. If, after investigation, the CEC recommends that a specific sanction be levied, the Judicial Committee has several options: It may impose the disciplinary action recommended by the CEC, impose less severe disciplinary action, or dismiss the case. The Judicial Committee may *not* impose more severe sanctions than those recommended by the CEC.

Disciplinary Action

There are four specific disciplinary actions that the CEC may recommend to the Judicial Committee[5]:

Reprimand is a statement of recognition that the respondent's behavior was contrary to the *Code of Ethics* or the *Standards of Ethical Conduct for the Physical Therapist Assistant*. A reprimand is issued with the understanding that the respondent will correct the violation immediately (if he or she has not done so already). Ongoing conditions may not be attached to a reprimand, and this sanction is a private one; that is, it is not published.

Probation is a stronger sanction than a reprimand is, with conditions attached. The respondent must comply with the conditions within a specific time frame (which cannot be less than 6 months or more than 2 years). The CEC is charged with monitoring compliance with the conditions of probation. Failure to comply results in a review by the Judicial Committee, which may then impose more severe sanctions. For example, if a member is found to have violated the *Code* by failing to adequately document his or her involvement in patient care (Principles 2, 3.1), the CEC might require attendance at a continuing education course specifically related to documentation and/or might require the respondent to submit to random audits of his or her patient documentation. In cases in which the State Licensing Board has taken action, as in the case of substance abuse, the CEC will occasionally impose a probation that mirrors that required by the state. Probation, like a reprimand, is a private sanction and is not published.

Suspension is a temporary (not less than 1 year) removal of the rights and privileges of membership as outlined in the Association's Bylaws.[6] As a practical matter, the member must continue to pay dues and

~

Employers have a management prerogative to inquire of position applicants about relevant job-related matters, including any finding by APTA's Judicial Committee that an applicant violated the *Code of Ethics* or *Standards of Ethical Conduct for the Physical Therapist Assistant*.

~

will receive the Association's publications and nothing more. The suspended member loses all rights to vote, hold elected office, or serve on committees, at all levels of the Association. After the suspension has been served, and upon request, the respondent/member's rights and privileges will be restored, provided he or she has been in good standing during the suspension. The intent of suspension is to punish members for severe violations of the *Code* while allowing them to rehabilitate themselves and later enjoy all the rights and privileges of membership. The Association publishes the name of the respondent and the effective date(s) of all suspensions in both *PT* and *Physical Therapy*.

Expulsion is the removal of a member—the most severe sanction that an association can impose. There are no time frames or conditions accompanying this action, as an association has no power over a nonmember. Expulsions are published in the same way as suspensions are.

External Consequences

A finding of culpability for a breach of professional ethics may result in other adverse consequences external to APTA. Violations of health care professional ethics and violations of law have become blended, so that an allegation made to a professional association for ethical adjudication frequently is also reported by the complainant or another party to a state licensure entity, and perhaps to criminal legal authorities in the appropriate jurisdiction for possible prosecution. In some cases, an aggrieved party could file a civil lawsuit for physical therapy malpractice based on the same conduct that gave rise to the complaint of ethical violation.

As a matter of policy, APTA does not ordinarily communicate directly with the Federation of Boards of Physical Therapy or individual licensure entities concerning pending or adjudicated ethical cases. This policy reflects the fact that, unless it is protected by state statutes or case law in specific states, a private organization could face civil liability for such communications. The organization could be held liable for the intentional torts of invasion of privacy (specifically, "unlawful public disclosure of private facts") or defamation (if the assertions in the communication are untrue).[7]

This does not mean, however, that licensure entities cannot obtain information about ethical adjudication involving professional and affiliate APTA members; as stated above, such information is published in APTA periodicals.

Another potential adverse consequence of a finding of culpability for a breach of professional ethics involves prospective employment. Employers have a management prerogative to inquire of position applicants about relevant job-related matters, including any finding by APTA's Judicial Committee that an applicant violated the *Code of Ethics* or *Standards of Ethical Conduct for the Physical Therapist Assistant*. The fact that an applicant is not a member of APTA may itself give rise to inquiry by an employer as to why the applicant is not a member. This question requires a truthful answer, a declination to answer, or a deceitful answer. For a former member who has been expelled, these are all undesirable options.

A finding of an ethics violation subjects a member of APTA—or of any other health care profession's professional association—to potential serious adverse consequences far beyond membership status. Members facing such action should exercise all reasonable options to avoid or minimize the adverse consequences of a finding of culpability, including retaining legal counsel and carrying out an effective defense of a charge. *PT*

Jonathan M Cooperman, JD, MS, PT, is Director, Rehabilitation and Health Center Inc, Akron, Ohio. He is a member of APTA's Judicial Committee. He can reached via e-mail at jcooperman@aol.com. Ronald W Scott, JD, PT, OCS, is Associate Professor, Dept of Physical Therapy, School of Allied Health Science, University of Texas Health Sciences Center, San Antonio, Tex. He is past chair of the APTA Judicial Committee and is a member of PT 's Editorial Advisory Group. He can be reached via e-mail at scottr@uthscsa.edu.

References

1   *Code of Ethics.* Alexandria, Va: American Physical Therapy Association; 1998.
2   *Standards of Ethical Conduct for the Physical Therapist Assistant.* Alexandria, Va: American Physical Therapy Association; 1998.
3   *Guide for Professional Conduct.* Alexandria, Va: American Physical Therapy Association; 1998.
4   *Guide for Conduct of the Affiliate Member.* Alexandria, Va: American Physical Therapy Association; 1998.
5   *Procedural Document on Disciplinary Action.* Alexandria, Va: American Physical Therapy Association; 1998.
6   *Bylaws of the American Physical Therapy Association.* Alexandria, Va: American Physical Therapy Association; 1998: Article IV.
7   Scott RW, *Promoting Legal Awareness in Physical and Occupational Therapy.* St Louis, Mo: Mosby-Yearbook Inc; 1997.

Copies of APTA's *Code of Ethics* and *Guide for Professional Conduct* are available to members either through the APTA service center (800/999-2782, ext 3395) or via APTA's Web site at http://www.apta.org.

Licensure

Physical Therapist and Physical Therapist Assistant Licensure/Regulation
HOD P06-002133 [Initial HOD 06-91-25-33]

Physical therapists are licensed and physical therapist assistants should be licensed or otherwise regulated in all US jurisdictions. State regulation of physical therapists and physical therapist assistants should at a minimum: (1) require graduation from an accredited physical therapy education program (or in the case of an internationally-educated physical therapist, an equivalent education); (2) require passing an entry-level competency exam; (3) provide title protection; and (4) allow for disciplinary action. Additionally, physical therapists' licensure should include a defined scope of practice.

Consumer Protection in the Provision of Physical Therapy Services: Qualifications of Persons Providing Physical Therapy Services
HOD P06-01-20-20 [Initial HOD 06-72-10-13]

Protection of the consumer requires that physical therapy services be provided only by, or under the direction and supervision of, duly licensed physical therapists who have successfully completed physical therapist professional education. Physical therapist professional education includes graduates from 1926 to 1959 who have completed physical therapy curricula approved by the appropriate accreditation bodies. It also includes graduates from 1960 to the present who have successfully completed professional physical therapy education programs accredited by the Commission on Accreditation in Physical Therapy Education or determined to be equivalent.

Protection of the consumer further requires that the practice of physical therapists, which includes examination, evaluation, diagnosis, prognosis, and intervention, complies with well-defined regulations. In addition, physical therapist assistants, under the direction and supervision of the physical therapist, are the only individuals who assist in the provision of selected physical therapy interventions. The physical therapist assistant is a graduate of a physical therapist assistant program accredited by the Commission on Accreditation in Physical Therapy Education and is licensed or otherwise regulated.

Protection of Term, Title, and Designation
HOD P06-03-18-15 [Initial HOD 06-95-20-11]

The terms "physical therapy" and "physiotherapy" shall be used only in reference to services that are provided by or under the direction and supervision of a licensed physical therapist/physiotherapist and, when so used, the terms are synonymous. Only physical therapists may use or include the initials "PT" or "DPT" and only physical therapist assistants may use or include the initials "PTA" in their professional, technical, or regulatory designation. Additionally, the American Physical Therapy Association supports the inclusion of language to protect the exclusive use of these terms, titles, and designations in statute and regulations.

Protecting the Term 'Physical Therapy'

Protection of the term "physical therapy" is an issue gaining more and more visibility and attention across the country, and is unlikely to disappear from the profession's radar screen in the near future. Legislation is pending in several states, aimed at preventing the phrase from becoming a generic term rather than a term denoting a specific body of knowledge held by licensed individuals with distinct skills and education. Advocates of protecting the term contend that advertising or otherwise promoting physical therapy services by unlicensed individuals causes confusion among consumers about which health care professionals provide physical therapy services.

Here is a look at some recent actions:

- Legislation in Mississippi prohibits anyone from representing him- or herself, in any manner, as a physical therapist or someone who provides physical therapy services without a valid license as a physical therapist. The bill was signed into law by the governor in 1995.
- Robert Kroll, PT, of Milwaukee, who spoke at the Sixth Annual State Government Affairs Forum in October 1995, stated "Legislation addressing the term physical therapy is greatly influenced by chiropractors and their political action committee in Wisconsin. As PTs, we have our work cut out for us in Wisconsin."

Wisconsin's pending legislation would prohibit any person from claiming to render physical therapy or physiotherapy unless he or she is licensed as a physical therapist. The prohibition, according to an analysis by the state's Legislative Reference Bureau, would not apply to "a person who is lawfully practicing within the scope of a license, permit, registration, or certification granted by this state or the federal government, to certain persons who are assisting a physical therapist in practice while under the supervision of the physical therapist, to a student's education or training, or to a physical therapist who is licensed to practice physical therapy in another state or country and is providing a consultation or demonstration with a physical therapist who is licensed in this state." The proposed bill would not prohibit other licensed health care professionals from providing services within their own scopes of practice and which are granted by law.

- In Colorado, chapter members testified in 1995 before a state legislature committee regarding the use by chiropractors of the terms physical therapy, physiotherapy, physical therapist, physical therapy technician, and physiotherapist in advertising. Marcia Smith, MS, PT, of Denver, testified that physical therapy is an entire body of knowledge of a profession practiced by a licensed physical therapist. "Physical therapy is recognized as a unique, limited area of practice and as an established profession in all 50 states. The federal government recognizes physical therapy as an established, identifiable practice of the healing arts through Medicare laws and regulations," Smith told Colorado lawmakers.
- The Pennsylvania Physical Therapy Association (PPTA) is fighting a civil suit filed in federal court by the Pennsylvania Chiropractic Society (PCS) and one individual. The suit alleges that chiropractors' right of commercial speech is being abridged if they cannot use the term "physical therapy" in their advertising. Further, they want to be able to bill for physical therapy services. PCS wants to establish that the term is generic. The case now is in federal appeals court awaiting action. Ray Schaney, MS, PT, President of the Pennsylvania chapter, said in early December that no movement was expected until early in 1996.

How the Louisiana Chapter Protected the "Term"

The Louisiana Physical Therapy Association (LPTA) scored a major victory in 1993 when it succeeded in having state legislation passed to protect the term "physical therapy." Chiropractors had infringed on the term in advertising, and the Louisiana Board of Physical Therapy Examiners filed a request for an injunction against them. A state court judge threw out the request, saying that definitions in the two professions' practice acts were the same.

An agenda item at APTA's State Government Affairs Forum in October 1995 and a hot topic for the physical therapy profession in the '90s, protecting the term is a battle that's being fought in the legislative arena in a number of states. The LPTA's efforts in 1993 are a model for other state chapters looking to pass legislation protecting the term or fight potentially damaging efforts launched by chiropractors or others seeking to use the term in advertising.

Following the state court action, the Louisiana Chapter acted to revise the definition of physical therapy in the state practice act. Kevin Mayo, PT, legislative chair of the Chapter, stresses that the two key elements of the campaign were developing strong grass-roots efforts and analyzing the opposition's position. "We began by picking apart their argument, which revolved around how reimbursement occurs," Mayo says. "Chiropractors asserted that cornering the term 'physical therapy' would prevent them from billing for a physical therapy procedure, which was simply not true. The insurance code permits physical therapists and others, including chiropractors, to use the same Current Procedural Terminology (CPT) codes. Any licensed health care practitioner can bill utilizing CPT codes, and if chiropractors had problems, they were with insurers and were not linked to their ability to use CPT codes. Our opposition insinuated that 'physical therapy' was a generic term, and constituted nothing more than heat, light, water, sound, and electricity. We had to make the point that these are merely physical agents, not synonymous with physical therapy and cannot be called 'physical therapy' unless used by physical therapists. The use of physical agents is only

part of the body of knowledge practiced by the physical therapist."

Kyle Ardoin, LPTA's Director of Legislative Affairs, says the old adage about knowing your opponent better than yourself was crucial to the Chapter's success. LPTA thoroughly analyzed all of the chiropractors' arguments. "Then we educated legislators about what physical therapy is prior to the opening of the legislative session. This is critical because once the session starts there is little or no time to do the necessary educational work. We assigned LPTA members as 'buddies' for each senator and representative who met with lawmakers and kept them informed during the legislative process," Ardoin says. "We saw our success in hearings when senators and representatives repeated much of what we had provided to them in our background briefings."

Mayo, Ardoin, and other Chapter members wrote legislative language to modify the Physical Therapy Act. The proposed language modified the law by redefining the term "physical therapy" to include the "practice of physical therapy." It specified that it is a health care profession practiced by licensed physical therapists to evaluate and treat any physical or medical condition to restore normal function of the neuromuscular and skeletal system, relieve pain, or prevent disability. It modified the type and mechanical means used and included other treatment recognized by the Louisiana Board. The proposed law contained language stating that the law "shall not be construed to affect the scope of practice of chiropractors." Subsequent amendments to the proposed language also stated, "No provision in this Chapter [section of the bill] shall preclude other health care providers from billing for or being reimbursed for the physical medicine procedures which they are licensed to perform which fall within their respective scope of practice." Another amendment contained the statement that the law "precluded other health care providers from professing the practice of physical therapy and from the use of the term 'physical therapy' for

advertisement purposes unless licensed under this [section]."

The law at the time defined "physical therapy" as the art and science of physical treatment of any bodily condition to restore function, relieve pain, or prevent disability by the use of certain physical and mechanical means and included physical therapy evaluation, treatment planning, instruction, consultation service, and the supervision of

physical therapy supportive personnel.

"A first-term senator introduced the bill in the state legislature for us," Mayo continues. "A monumental lobbying battle with the chiropractors ensued. They were out in force. We rebutted every attempt by the chiropractors to cloud the issue."

LPTA flooded the fax lines at the Louisiana Capitol at the time the Chapter asked to have the bill moved from the Health and Welfare Committee, which was chaired by a chiropractor, to the Commerce Committee. The fax barrage continued for 3 days.

The bill was approved by the Senate committee and on the chamber's floor. Mayo says "The chiropractor's lobbying battle was intense at that point. We had set up a highly effective grass-roots phone and fax tree, and inundated the Capitol to the point that staff asked us to stop sending faxes. This helped establish us as a viable lobbying force and highlighted the widespread concern through the state over this issue..."

The drama intensified when the bill came up for a vote on the House floor. As the debate began, it was moving in favor of LPTA, but it turned nearly 180 degrees. It looked as though the LPTA might lose. In a procedural move, former Democratic Rep Tim Stine, who is paraplegic, did something unusual. In an unprecedented move,

he told the story of working with physical therapists following a diving accident when he was a youth. He had never told his story, but he said he wanted to "show the difference between physical therapists and chiropractors." He told fellow lawmakers that the reason he was able to talk, to sit in a wheelchair, to vote in the legislature, and do all the things that he was able to do, was because of physical therapists. When Stine finished, Democratic Rep John Travis, who was managing the bill, said he couldn't say much more and moved to pass the bill, according to Ardoin.

The bill passed by one vote. Gov Edwin Edwards signed the bill into law in June 1993. Mayo credits the victory to a strong grass-roots effort and the Chapter's ability to analyze the opposition well. "Legislators care less about what professional groups might say than what constituents in their home districts say. They respond to what they hear. We also didn't get emotional

about our arguments, and we got our rebuttals out in writing. Further, we rebutted the chiropractors' arguments as they occurred. It was an ongoing process. Everything seemed to fall into place. Our activity can be replicated by other chapters if they find themselves in a similar situation."

Ardoin recommends that chapters begin lobbying efforts on a physical therapy issue before a legislative session gets underway. "That is especially important in states that have short sessions. Activity becomes intense once a session begins, and legislators are getting material from many, many sources. They don't have time to absorb a lot of information. By working in advance, you lay a good foundation," Ardoin says.

"It is also critical that you dissect your opponents' arguments and have rebuttals ready. Being able to immediately rebut an assertion or argument is important. It helps keep the opposition off balance," Ardoin adds.   — **Paulette Dininny**

LIABILITY AWARENESS
by John J Bennett, Esq

Practicing Across State Lines –Part 1

In today's increasingly "global" practice environment, PTs may unknowingly expose themselves to criminal prosecution whenever their practice touches patients in other states. Be aware of the law!

Among the questions most frequently asked of APTA staff are inquiries about the legal implications of "practicing across state lines." As it relates to physical therapy, practice across state lines raises legal and/or liability issues in three areas: licensure, malpractice liability, and liability insurance. For a physical therapist whose practice somehow touches patients in states other than the therapist's home state, the basic practical questions are:

- Do I need to be licensed in the other state?
- Am I subject to a malpractice suit in the courts of the other state?
- Will my professional liability insurance cover me in a case involving a patient from the other state?

Part 1 of this column will address the first question; part 2, in next month's *PT*, will address the second and third questions.

Do I Need a License?

The discussion of licensure here is general in nature, and it therefore is subject to a crucial caveat. Licensure is a matter of state law, and the answer to any question always depends on the state practice act, as enacted by the state legislature and interpreted by the licensing agency (both in its published rules and in its unwritten enforcement practices) and the courts of the state.

Every state requires that a person be licensed in order to practice physical therapy. The consequences of noncompliance

with a state's licensure requirement typically are liability to criminal prosecution; for example, the New York Education Law makes unauthorized practice a crime.[1] In addition—and, perhaps, more importantly—noncompliance with one state's licensure laws can subject an individual to adverse licensing action in other states, including his or her home state.

The responsibility for enforcing licensure laws falls on public officials: the licensing agency and/or criminal prosecutors. Of course, the fact that a person has violated a state's prohibition against the unlicensed practice of physical therapy does not guarantee that enforcement action will occur. Some licensing agencies have little legal authority to proceed directly against unlicensed practitioners, and criminal prosecutors in general may be expected to place a relatively low priority on cases of unlicensed practice that do not involve harm to patients.

In some circumstances, the letter of the law requires licensure, but the likelihood of enforcement action actually may be very small. For example, in some states, a continuing education lecture with an element of "demonstration" that is delivered in a state in which the lecturer is unlicensed might be in clear-cut violation of the practice act, even though the chances of prosecution are slight. In light of the range of factors that influence enforcement decisions (including the details of the therapist's activity as well as governmental resources and pri-

orities), the primary focus of this article is on the meaning of state licensure laws rather than on the chances of apprehension or prosecution for violation of the law.

Some physical therapy practice acts provide that it is unlawful for a person to practice without a license "in this state," but even without such an explicit reference to location, a PT obviously must be licensed by the jurisdiction in which he or she is physically present while practicing. Strictly speaking, this rule applies even if the PT is present for only a limited time and even if the PT limits his or her activity to existing patients from his or her home state who are in the other state only temporarily. For this reason, the Georgia legislature passed a special law allowing out-of-state practitioners (including PTs) to treat athletes during the Olympics.[2] Without such special legislation, a PT licensed in another state would have been unable to treat an athlete in Atlanta, even if the athlete were a long-time patient.

A physical therapist whose office is in one state but who regularly travels to a neighboring state to evaluate or treat patients would be subject to the licensing requirement of that neighboring state. A state legislature *could* choose to exempt from the licensure requirement a practitioner who travels from a neighboring state in which he or she is licensed; for example, Missouri's medical practice act has an explicit provision that exempts from the licensure requirement a physician licensed in a border state who "attends the sick" in Missouri but who does not maintain an office there.[3] Currently, however, it does not appear that any physical therapy practice act has such an exemption for a licensee from a neighboring state.

Supervision

Clinical supervision of support personnel may be enough to subject a PT to state licensure requirements. A PT with supervisory responsibility over a physical therapist assistant who travels to a neighboring state to provide treatment (eg, home health care) very likely would be subject to the licensure requirement of that neighboring state, even if the PT never ventured across the state border. In states that license PTAs, the practice act typically provides that an assistant may practice only under the supervision of a PT licensed by that state (eg, see the California Business and Professions Code[4]).

If the supervising PT were not licensed in the state in which the PTA was treating patients, then both the PT and the PTA ordinarily would be in violation of the state's law. The PT might be deemed to be engaged in the unlicensed practice of physical therapy if the state's practice act included "supervision" as part of the definition of physical therapy.[5] In such a situation, the state might take action against the PTA for practicing without the requisite supervision, and it might take action against the PT not only for violating the supervision requirements applicable to therapists, but also for aiding and abetting the PTA's violation of the state's laws.

Not all supervisory relationships require licensure, however. Whether the PT's supervision of other personnel would trigger a licensure obligation might depend on whether the relationship involved business or clinical supervision (a distinction rarely—if ever—articulated in practice acts or regulations). That is, within any business setting, a person might stand over individuals engaged in the practice of physical therapy without thereby being subject to the licensure requirement. As an obvious example, the CEO of a hospital need not be licensed as a

PT merely because the hospital has a physical therapy department, because the CEO is not exercising clinical supervision over the PTs and the personnel supporting them.

In some cases, however, the distinction between business and clinical supervision can become blurred. For example, a PT in a managerial position in a multistate chain of facilities might provide guidance to subordinates (including other PTs, assistants, or aides) that has at least an element of clinical supervision. The closer the manager's behavior to clinical supervision, the more likely would it be to trigger a licensure requirement.

Activities That May Not Require Licensure

Certain kinds of activity typically do not constitute the practice of physical therapy for licensure purposes, and a PT ordinarily does not need to be licensed to engage in such

Whether the PT's supervision of other personnel would trigger a licensure obligation might depend on whether the relationship involved business or clinical supervision (a distinction rarely—if ever—articulated in practice acts or regulations).

activities in a state other than his or her home state. The rules can vary from state to state, however, and a PT who has a question *always* should seek guidance from the relevant state licensing agency.

Expert Witness Testimony. The widely established rule of evidence is that an expert need not be licensed in the state where the court is located in order to testify about a matter as to which he or she is qualified. Quite a bit of case law exists to support this rule.[6-16] In one case, a forensic pathologist licensed in Florida but not in Penn-

sylvania was permitted to testify as an expert.[17] In another case, the court's opinion was that "We do not believe that our Legislature intended that persons of great learning in the engineering field should be barred from testifying in our courts, and assisting the triers of fact, merely because they have not been licensed here in their respective fields of expertise."[18] As far as it appears, for PTs, the mere act of testifying as a witness does not constitute the practice of physical therapy for licensure purposes.

Utilization Review. Utilization review (UR) organizations provide insurers with retrospective review of the medical necessity or appropriateness of medical services rendered and/or prospective review of requests for admission to hospitals or the use of specialized services. For a PT who provides UR services relating to physical therapy treatment, the licensure question is whether that activity constitutes the practice of physical therapy under the practice act of the state where the patient resides or receives treatment.

Unfortunately, no state has yet answered this question with respect to physical therapy. However, in at least two states, the Attorneys General have taken the position that provision of UR services by a physician does not constitute the practice of medicine for purposes of the licensure law. In Kansas, the Attorney General ruled that the performance of UR (either retrospective or prospective) by physicians or nurses is not subject to the state's licensure requirements, on the theory that UR amounts only to consultation with an insurer about its contractual obligations.[19] In Mississippi, the state medical board sought an opinion from the Attorney General that out-of-state physicians performing review of services provided by a Mississippi practitioner must be licensed in Mississippi, but the Attorney General took the position that out-of-state physicians performing UR were not subject to licensure in Mississippi.[20]

The American Medical Association (AMA) has drafted model state legislation that calls for certain elements of UR to be included within the definition of the practice of medicine.[21] In addition, the AMA House of Delegates has a policy that says, in part, "Any physician who makes judgments or recommendations regarding the necessity or appropriateness of services or site of services should be licensed to practice medicine and actively practicing in the same jurisdiction as the practitioner who is proposing or providing the reviewed service and should be professionally and individually accountable for his or her decisions."[22] However, under current licensure laws in most states, because a reviewer typically does not have a professional relationship with the patient (especially in retrospective UR) or has an attenuated relationship (even in prospective UR), it seems likely that a PT providing UR services would not be deemed to be practicing physical therapy for purposes of the licensure requirement of the state(s) in which the patients reside or seek treatment.

Many states have passed laws specifically regulating UR activity (see Clifton's previous Utilization Review columns[23-24]), and some laws state that the organization providing the UR services must use physicians (or other practitioners) who are licensed. At least several such laws state that a practitioner is qualified to provide UR services if licensed in any state. In Arizona, for example, personnel conducting UR for an agent seeking certification must have "current licenses that are in good standing and without restrictions from

≈

The Attorneys General of two states have ruled that a PT may act upon a referral from a physician not licensed in that state if that physician is licensed in another jurisdiction

≈

a state health care professional licensing agency in the United States."[25]

Education. From a licensure perspective, teaching physical therapy, whether in a program offered by an educational institution or in a continuing education setting, is a somewhat gray area. APTA includes "engaging in ... education" as part of the model definition of physical therapy for state practice acts.[26] In a state where the practice act explicitly includes education or teaching within the definition of physical therapy, a teacher in an institutional or continuing education setting would be subject to the licensure requirement unless exempted. For example, the Illinois practice act includes the teaching of physical therapy but explicitly exempts from licensure requirement practice that is "part of an educational program by a physical therapist licensed in another state or country for a period not to exceed 6 months."[27] And in New York, a PT conducting a teaching clinical demonstration is exempt from the licensure requirement under certain circumstances.[28]

Referral. In states that do not authorize direct access to physical therapy, a PT may not evaluate and/or treat a patient without a referral from a physician (or other practitioner). Whether a PT may act upon a referral from an out-of-state physician is a matter of state law. The Attorneys General of two states have ruled that a PT may act upon a referral from a physician not licensed in that state if that physician is licensed in another jurisdiction.[29,30] A PT with a question about the permissibility of relying on an out-of-state referral would do well to consult with the physical therapy licensing board.

"Telemedicine." Modern telecommunications can enable a cardiologist to listen via satellite to the heartbeat of a patient located hundreds of miles away or permit a nephrologist to watch via interactive video the kidney dialysis of a distant patient. Such technological advances pose a challenge to traditional licensure regimes even greater than that posed by the ubiquitous telephone.

States have just recently begun to grapple with the applicability of licensure requirements to nonresident physicians whose practices make use of telecommunications. In 1995, the Attorney General of Mississippi ruled that a physician located out of state who interprets radiographs, CAT scans, MRIs, or other radiological workups communicated electronically (or via satellite) from Mississippi is not subject to Mississippi's licensure requirement.[31] Connecticut amended its medical practice act to make the licensure requirement applicable to nonresident physicians who, on an "ongoing, regular or contractual" basis, provide diagnostic or treatment services to persons located in Connecticut, including primary diagnosis of pathology specimens or written reports evaluating radiographs. The licensure requirement does not apply to a nonresident physician who, while outside Connecticut, "consults" on an "irregular basis" with a physician licensed in Connecticut.[32]

In April of 1996, the Federation of State Medical Boards (FSMB) endorsed a model practice act designed to regulate telemedicine. The FSMB's model act—which would apply to physicians interpreting specimens mailed interstate as well as to interactive

encounters via telecommunications—would require every physician who practices across state lines to hold a special purpose license in the state where the patient is located, but it would make obtaining such a license relatively simple, since the agency would have to license any person "holding a full and unrestricted license to practice medicine in any and all states ... in which such individual is licensed, provided there has not been previous disciplinary or other action against the applicant." The issuance of the special purpose license would subject the physician to the jurisdiction of the medical board, and the physician would have to agree to appear before the board in connection with any complaint.

Currently, no physical therapy practice act refers explicitly to practice across state lines by telecommunications, and it may be that the hands-on nature of physical therapy practice makes the issue less pressing than it is for some branches of medicine. The Federation of State Boards of Physical Therapy (FSBPT) is in the midst of a project to draft a model state practice act, which reportedly does not make any explicit reference to telemedicine. At this time, no clear guidance is available with respect to the application of state licensure requirements to physical therapy practice carried on by way of telecommunications.

This month's column addressed some issues of licensure and practice across state lines. Next month, part 2 of this column will explore some of those issues as they relate to malpractice liability and professional liability insurance.

John J Bennett, Esq, is APTA's General Counsel.

References

1 New York Education Law § 6512.
2 OC Ga Ann §43-1-26.
3 *Missouri Attorney General Opinion No. 19,* 1978 Missouri AG LEXIS 14, August 18, 1978.
4 California Business and Professions Code, §2655 (a-b).
5 225 Ill Comp Stat Ann 90/1.
6 *Hayes v United States,* 367 F2d 216, 222 (10th Cir 1966).
7 *Goodwin v Camp,* 852 SW2d 698 (Tex App 1993). 1993 Tex App LEXIS 1067.
8 *People v West,* 264 Ill App 3d 176, 636 NE2d 1239, 201 Ill Dec 807 (Ill App 1994). 1994 Ill App LEXIS 1080.
9 *Bordley v Gordon,* 609 A2d 668 (Del 1992). 1992 Del LEXIS 134.
10 *Costales v State,* 1991 Ark App LEXIS 718.
11 *State v Bricker,* 321 Md 86, 581 A2d 9 (Md App 1990). 1990 Md LEXIS 170.
12 *State v Jones,* 209 Kan 526, 498 P2d 65 (Kans 1972).Citing 32 C.J.S. Evidence 546 (92) pages 336-346.
13 *Dickey v Corr-A-Glass & Topping Bldg Serv,* 3 Kan App 2d 721, 601 P2d 691 (Kans App 1979).
14 *Kansas Attorney General Opinion No. 87-138,* 1987 Kansas AG LEXIS 56, Sept 18, 1987.
15 *Pearson v State,* 254 So2d 573 (Fla App 1971).
16 *Rose v State,* 506 So2d 467, 12 Fla Law W 1125 (Fla App 1987).
17 *Commonwealth v Brown,* 676 A2d 1178 (Pa 1996). 1996 Pa LEXIS 588.
18 *Owens v Payless Cashways, Inc,* 670 A2d 1240 (RI 1996). 1996 RI LEXIS 27.
19 *Kansas Attorney General Opinion No. 90-130,* 1990 Kan AG LEXIS 131, November 28, 1990.
20 *Mississippi Attorney General Opinion,* 1993 Miss AG LEXIS 280, May 18, 1993.
21 American Medical Association House of Delegates Policy H-285.995(7) Managed Care - Policy and Initiatives.
22 American Medical Association House of Delegates Policy H-285.998 Managed Care.
23 Clifton DW. Who's watching UROs? Part 1. *PT—Magazine of Physical Therapy.* 1996;4(10):25-27.
24 Clifton DW. Who's watching UROs? Part 2. *PT—Magazine of Physical Therapy.* 1996;4(11):26-28.
25 Ariz Rev Stat §20-2505(3).
26 *Model Definition of Physical Therapy for State Practice Acts,* BOD 03-95-24-64.
27 225 Ill Comp Stat Ann 90/1 and 90/2.
28 New York Education Law §6736(b)(3).
29 *Kansas Attorney General Opinion No. 93-61,* 1993 Kan AG LEXIS 54, May 5, 1993.
30 *South Carolina Attorney General Opinion,* 1986 SC AG LEXIS 66, October 3, 1986.
31 *Mississippi Attorney General,* 1995 Miss. AG LEXIS 867, December 8, 1995.
32 Conn Gen Stat §20.9(d), as amended by Public Act No. 96-148.

LIABILITY AWARENESS

by Rita Arriaga, MS, PT

Stories From the Front
Part 3: Practice Across State Lines

A scenario from real life illustrates some basic risk-management principles.

The final installment of *PT*'s three-part series of scenarios adapted from the claims files of APTA's endorsed professional liability insurance provider describes a complicated situation with a number of risky elements. As you read the scenario, consider the following questions:

1) What are the elements in this scenario that increase the PT's risk of professional liability?
2) What risk management techniques could have helped prevent that risk?

John had just moved to California after having lived and practiced in Arizona for a number of years. He held a physical therapist license in both states.

On the urging of a former client of his from Arizona, John agreed to assist a Florida-based neurosurgeon in a nationwide research project to determine whether a specific surgical procedure could improve the ambulatory capacity of patients with spinal cord injuries. The physician needed an Arizona-licensed PT who could perform preoperative physical therapy evaluations and design postoperative exercise programs for patients who lived in Arizona. A fitness clinic in Arizona was to be the site where the preoperative evaluations and postoperative intervention (exercises and ambulation) would occur.

John went to Florida, where he received training in the physical therapy protocol for pre- and postoperative evaluation and intervention. Thereafter, when an Arizona resident was scheduled for the surgery, John would do preoperative physical therapy evaluation and testing in Arizona, including a written report to the physician, and then fly to Florida with the patient to observe the surgery. John did not participate in the explanations to patients about the experimental nature of the surgery and expected outcomes. After surgery, John would consult with the hospital-based PTs on the patient's status and progress and perform a postoperative evaluation. He would also outline a plan for posthospital exercises, which would be supervised by the trainers at the fitness clinic upon the patient's return to Arizona.

The Arizona-based preoperative physical therapy assessments were billed using John's Arizona PT license. John subsequently found out that the exercise sessions carried out by the trainers at the fitness clinic in Arizona based on the postoperative plan he had developed were also billed as physical therapy, using his Arizona license number. In addition, patients were being billed for the postoperative in-hospital physical therapy evaluation performed by John in Florida as part of their hospital stay.

Patients unfortunately did not improve significantly as a result of the surgical procedures. They perceived John's physical therapy evaluations and interventions as contributory to the poor outcome, and they filed a claim of negligence against John, the Florida physician, and the Arizona clinic. John also was subsequently warned by his lawyer that he could be held liable for practicing without a license in Florida.

❖ ❖ ❖ ❖

Now, see the table opposite for a summary of risk elements and strategies and commentary on this scenario from a risk-management perspective.

LIABILITY AWARENESS

Risky Elements	Strategies for Risk Reduction
The PT was physically involved in physical therapy treatment in a state where he was not licensed.	If a PT is not licensed in the state where care is being provided, he or she should have a role as observer only and should not participate in any manner in provision of care.
The PT allowed use of his PT license number for billing for services that he did not directly provide or supervise.	The PT should always clarify and monitor use of his or her license number in any billing to ensure that it is consistent with his or her specific state practice act. A PT performing an evaluation should clearly state in the documentation whether he or she is taking responsibility for any postevaluation intervention.
The PT did not discuss the experimental nature of the treatment with the patient. In addition, the patient's perception was that the evaluating PT was in part responsible for the surgical outcome.	The PT should obtain clear and separate informed consent from the patient, explaining and documenting the exact nature, purpose, and goals of the physical therapy evaluation and intervention. A therapist should understand fully his or her role in any research project, including how (and which) services will or will not be charged and how they will be reimbursed. It is the therapist's responsibility to fully understand his or her scope of practice limits related to venue and location and to ensure that other members of the research team are so informed.

If a PT's practice involves such complex factors as practice across state lines, research involving human subjects, and development of a plan of care to be provided by someone who is not under the direct supervision of the PT, it is essential that the PT communicate clearly with all parties involved. Patients need to understand exactly where the PT's role begins and ends, especially if any care provided is of an experimental nature. In addition, because the PT is ultimately responsible for any services performed under the authority of his or her license, he or she should clearly establish in the documentation the portions of the care plan for which he or she takes responsibility. 𝒫𝒯

Rita Arriaga, MS, PT, is Assistant Clinical Professor in the Graduate Program in Physical Therapy, University of California at San Francisco, and is a member of APTA's Committee on Risk Management Services and Member Benefits.

The information presented here is not to be interpreted as specific legal advice for any particular provider. Personal advice can only be given by personal legal counsel, based on applicable state and federal law.

Documentation

Professional Fees for Physical Therapy Services
HOD P06-00-22-34

Physical therapists are professionally responsible for fees charged for their services. Physical therapists should charge fees for their services that are reasonable. In cases where the fee for service cannot be determined because of the payment methodology, the physical therapist should be aware of the payment methodology.

Physical therapists should:

- Be knowledgeable of practice or institutional fee schedules, contractual relationships and payment methodologies used in relation to physical therapy services.

- Participate, to the extent possible, in establishing practice or institutional fee schedules/contractual relationships and attempt to ensure that providers, agencies, or other employers adopt physical therapy fee schedules and contractual relationships that are reasonable and that encourage access to necessary services.

- Accurately document services provided including the selection of correct description and billing codes.

- Charge professional fees that are reasonable, never placing their own financial interest above the welfare of individuals under their care.

- Include, where feasible, their license number on all billing for their professional services.

- Seek guidance from the *Code of Ethics* and *Guide for Professional Conduct*, applicable state law, and other institutional or payer policies if any question or disagreement arises regarding professional fees.

Guidelines: Physical Therapy Documentation of Patient/Client Management
BOD G03-05-16-41 [Initial BOD 03-93-21-55]

Preamble

The American Physical Therapy Association (APTA) is committed to meeting the physical therapy needs of society, to meeting the needs and interests of its members, and to developing and improving the art and science of physical therapy, including practice, education and research. To help meet these responsibilities, the APTA Board of Directors has approved the following guidelines for physical therapy documentation. It is recognized that these guidelines do not reflect all of the unique documentation requirements associated with the many specialty areas within the physical therapy profession. Applicable for both hand written and electronic documentation systems, these guidelines are intended to be used as a foundation for the development of more specific documentation guidelines in clinical areas, while at the same time providing guidance for the physical therapy profession across all practice settings. Documentation may also need to address additional regulatory or payer requirements.

Finally, be aware that these guidelines are intended to address *documentation* of patient/client management, not to describe the provision of physical therapy services. Other APTA documents, including APTA Standards of Practice for Physical Therapy, Code of Ethics and Guide for Professional Conduct, and the Guide to Physical Therapist Practice, address provision of physical therapy services and patient/client management.

APTA Position on Documentation

Documentation Authority for Physical Therapy Services
HOD P06-00-20-05 [Initial HOD 06-97-15-23]

Physical therapy examination, evaluation, diagnosis, prognosis, and intervention shall be documented, dated, and authenticated by the physical therapist who performs the service. Intervention provided by the physical therapist or selected interventions provided by the physical therapist assistant is documented, dated, and authenticated by the physical therapist or, when permissible by law, the physical therapist assistant.

Other notations or flow charts are considered a component of the documented record but do not meet the requirements of documentation in or of themselves.

Students in physical therapist or physical therapist assistant programs may document when the record is additionally authenticated by the physical therapist or, when permissible by law, documentation by physical therapist assistant students may be authenticated by a physical therapist assistant.

Operational Definitions

Guidelines

APTA defines "guidelines" as a statement of advice.

Authentication

The process used to verify that an entry is complete, accurate and final. Indications of authentication can include original written signatures and computer "signatures" on secured electronic record systems only.

The following describes the main documentation elements of patient/client management: 1) initial examination/evaluation, 2) visit/encounter, 3) reexamination, and 4) discharge or discontinuation summary.

Initial Examination/Evaluation

Documentation of the initial encounter is typically called the "initial examination," "initial evaluation," or "initial examination/evaluation." Completion of the initial examination/evaluation is typically completed in one visit, but may occur over more than one visit. Documentation elements for the initial examination/evaluation include the following:

Examination: Includes data obtained from the history, systems review, and tests and measures.

Evaluation: Evaluation is a thought process that may not include formal documentation. It may include documentation of the assessment of the data collected in the examination and identification of problems pertinent to patient/client management.

Diagnosis: Indicates level of impairment and functional limitation determined by the physical therapist. May be indicated by selecting one or more preferred practice patterns from the Guide to Physical Therapist Practice.

Prognosis: Provides documentation of the predicted level of improvement that might be attained through intervention and the amount of time required to reach that level. Prognosis is typically not a separate documentation elements, but the components are included as part of the plan of care.

Plan of care: Typically stated in general terms, includes goals, interventions planned, proposed frequency and duration, and discharge plans.

Visit/Encounter

Documentation of a visit or encounter, often called a progress note or daily note, documents sequential implementation of the plan of care established by the physical therapist, including changes in patient/client status and variations and progressions of specific interventions used. Also may include specific plans for the next visit or visits.

Reexamination

Documentation of reexamination includes data from repeated or new examination elements and is provided to evaluate progress and to modify or redirect intervention.

Discharge or Discontinuation Summary

Documentation is required following conclusion of the current episode in the physical therapy intervention sequence, to summarize progression toward goals and discharge plans.

General Guidelines

- Documentation is required for every visit/encounter.

- All documentation must comply with the applicable jurisdictional/regulatory requirements.

- All handwritten entries shall be made in ink and will include original signatures. Electronic entries are made with appropriate security and confidentiality provisions.

- Charting errors should be corrected by drawing a single line through the error and initialing and dating the chart or through the appropriate mechanism for electronic documentation that clearly indicates that a change was made without deletion of the original record.

- All documentation must include adequate identification of the patient/client and the physical therapist or physical therapist assistant:

  o The patient's/client's full name and identification number, if applicable, must be included on all official documents.

  o All entries must be dated and authenticated with the provider's full name and appropriate designation:

    – Documentation of examination, evaluation, diagnosis, prognosis, plan of care, and discharge summary must be authenticated by the physical therapist who provided the service.

    – Documentation of intervention in visit/encounter notes must be authenticated by the physical therapist or physical therapist assistant who provided the service.

    – Documentation by physical therapist or physical therapist assistant graduates or others physical therapist and physical therapist assistants pending receipt of an unrestricted license shall be authenticated by a licensed physical therapist, or, when permissible by law, documentation by physical therapist assistant graduates may be authenticated by a physical therapist assistant.

    – Documentation by students (SPT/SPTA) in physical therapist or physical therapist assistant programs must be additionally authenticated by the physical therapist or, when permissible by law, documentation by physical therapist assistant students may be authenticated by a physical therapist assistant.

- Documentation should include the referral mechanism by which physical therapy services are initiated. Examples include:

  o Self-referral/direct access

  o Request for consultation from another practitioner

    – Documentation should include indication of no shows and cancellations.

Initial Examination/Evaluation

Examination (History, Systems Review, and Tests and Measures)

History:

Documentation of history may include the following:

- General demographics

- Social history

- Employment/work (Job/School/Play)

- Growth and development

- Living environment

- General health status (self-report, family report, caregiver report)

- Social/health habits (past and current)

- Family history

- Medical/surgical history

- Current condition(s)/Chief complaint(s)

- Functional status and activity level

- Medications

- Other clinical tests

Systems Review:

Documentation of systems review may include gathering data for the following systems:

- Cardiovascular/pulmonary
  - Blood Pressure
  - Edema
  - Heart Rate
  - Respiratory Rate
- Integumentary
  - Pliability (texture)
  - Presence of scar formation
  - Skin color
  - Skin integrity
- Musculoskeletal
  - Gross range of motion
  - Gross strength
  - Gross symmetry
  - Height
  - Weight
- Neuromuscular
  - Gross coordinated movement (eg, balance, locomotion, transfers, and transitions)
  - Motor function (motor control, motor learning)

Documentation of systems review may also address communication ability, affect, cognition, language, and learning style:

- Ability to make needs known
- Consciousness
- Expected emotional/behavioral responses
- Learning preferences (eg, *education needs, learning barriers*)
- Orientation (person, place, time)

Tests and Measures:

Documentation of tests and measures may include findings for the following categories:

- Aerobic Capacity/Endurance

Examples of examination findings include:

- Aerobic capacity during functional activities
- Aerobic capacity during standardized exercise test protocols
- Cardiovascular signs and symptoms in response to increased oxygen demand with exercise or activity
- Pulmonary signs and symptoms in response to increased oxygen demand with exercise or activity

- Anthropometric Characteristics

Examples of examination findings include:

- Body composition
- Body dimensions
- Edema

- Arousal, attention, and cognition

Examples of examination findings include:

- Arousal and attention
- Cognition
- Communication
- Consciousness
- Motivation
- Orientation to time, person, place, and situation
- Recall

- Assistive and adaptive devices

Examples of examination findings include:

- Assistive or adaptive devices and equipment use during functional activities
- Components, alignment, fit, and ability to care for the assistive or adaptive devices and equipment
- Remediation of impairments, functional limitations, or disabilities with use of assistive or adaptive devices and equipment
- Safety during use of assistive or adaptive devices and equipment

- Circulation (Arterial, Venous, Lymphatic)

  Examples of examination findings include:

  o Cardiovascular signs

  o Cardiovascular symptoms

  o Physiological responses to position change

- Cranial and Peripheral Nerve Integrity

  Examples of examination findings include:

  o Electrophysiological integrity

  o Motor distribution of the cranial nerves

  o Motor distribution of the peripheral nerves

  o Response to neural provocation

  o Response to stimuli, including auditory, gustatory, olfactory, pharyngeal, vestibular, and visual

  o Sensory distribution of the cranial nerves

  o Sensory distribution of the peripheral nerves

- Environmental, Home, and Work (Job/School/Play) Barriers

  Examples of examination findings include:

  o Current and potential barriers

  o Physical space and environment

- Ergonomics and Body mechanics

  Examples of examination findings for *ergonomics* include:

  o Dexterity and coordination during work

  o Functional capacity and performance during work actions, tasks, or activities

  o Safety in work environments

  o Specific work conditions or activities

  o Tools, devices, equipment, and work-stations related to work actions, tasks, or activities

Examples of examination findings for *body mechanics* include:

  o Body mechanics during self-care, home management, work, community, or leisure actions, tasks, or activities

- Gait, locomotion, and balance

  Examples of examination findings include:

  o Balance during functional activities with or without the use of assistive, adaptive, orthotic, protection, supportive, or prosthetic devices or equipment

  o Balance (dynamic and static) with or without the use of assistive, adaptive, orthotic, protective, supportive, or prosthetic devices or equipment

  o Gait and locomotion during functional activities with or without the use of assistive, adaptive, orthotic, protective, supportive, or prosthetic devices or equipment

  o Gait and locomotion with or without the use of assistive, adaptive, orthotic, protective, supportive, or prosthetic devices or equipment

  o Safety during gait, locomotion, and balance

- Integumentary Integrity

  Examples of examination findings include:

  Associated skin:

  o Activities, positioning, and postures that produce or relieve trauma to the skin

  o Assistive, adaptive, orthotic, protective, supportive, or prosthetic devices and equipment that may produce or relieve trauma to the skin

  o Skin characteristics

Wound:

- o Activities, positioning, and postures that aggravate the wound or scar or that produce or relieve trauma
- o Burn
- o Signs of infection
- o Wound characteristics
- o Wound scar tissue characteristics

- Joint Integrity and Mobility

  Examples of examination findings include:

  - o Joint integrity and mobility
  - o Joint play movements
  - o Specific body parts

- Motor Function

  Examples of examination findings include:

  - o Dexterity, coordination, and agility
  - o Electrophysiological integrity
  - o Hand function
  - o Initiation, modification, and control of movement patterns and voluntary postures

- Muscle Performance

  Examples of examination findings include:

  - o Electrophysiological integrity
  - o Muscle strength, power, and endurance
  - o Muscle strength, power, and endurance during functional activities
  - o Muscle tension

- Neuromotor development and sensory integration

  Examples of examination findings include:

  - o Acquisition and evolution of motor skills
  - o Oral motor function, phonation, and speech production
  - o Sensorimotor integration

- Orthotic, protective, and supportive devices

  Examples of examination findings include:

  - o Components, alignment, fit, and ability to care for the orthotic, protective, and supportive devices and equipment
  - o Orthotic, protective, and supportive devices and equipment use during functional activities
  - o Remediation of impairments, functional limitations, or disabilities with use of orthotic, protective, and supportive devices and equipment
  - o Safety during use of orthotic, protective, and supportive devices and equipment

- Pain

  Examples of examination findings include:

  - o Pain, soreness, and nocioception
  - o Pain in specific body parts

- Posture

  Examples of examination findings include:

  - o Postural alignment and position (dynamic)
  - o Postural alignment and position (static)
  - o Specific body parts

- Prosthetic requirements

  Examples of examination findings include:

  - o Components, alignment, fit, and ability to care for prosthetic device
  - o Prosthetic device use during functional activities
  - o Remediation of impairments, functional limitations, or disabilities with use of the prosthetic device
  - o Residual limb or adjacent segment
  - o Safety during use of the prosthetic device

- Range of motion (including muscle length)

  Examples of examination findings include:

  o Functional ROM

  o Joint active and passive movement

  o Muscle length, soft tissue extensibility, and flexibility

- Reflex integrity

  Examples of examination findings include:

  o Deep reflexes

  o Electrophysiological integrity

  o Postural reflexes and reactions, including righting, equilibrium, and protective reactions

  o Primitive reflexes and reactions

  o Resistance to passive stretch

  o Superficial reflexes and reactions

- Self-care and home management (including activities of daily living and instrumental activities of daily living)

  Examples of examination findings include:

  o Ability to gain access to home environments

  o Ability to perform self-care and home management activities with or without assistive, adaptive, orthotic, protective, supportive, or prosthetic devices and equipment

  o Safety in self-care and home management activities and environments

- Sensory integrity

  Examples of examination findings include:

  o Combined/cortical sensations

  o Deep sensations

  o Electrophysiological integrity

  - Ventilation and respiration

  Examples of examination findings include:

  o Pulmonary signs of respiration/gas exchange

  o Pulmonary signs of ventilatory function

  o Pulmonary symptoms

- Work (job/school/play), community, and leisure integration or reintegration (including instrumental activities of daily living)

  Examples of examination findings include:

  o Ability to assume or resume work (job/school/plan), community, and leisure activities with or without assistive, adaptive, orthotic, protective, supportive, or prosthetic devices and equipment

  o Ability to gain access to work (job/school/play), community, and leisure environments

  o Safety in work (job/school/play), community, and leisure activities and environments

Evaluation

Evaluation is a thought process that may not include formal documentation. However, the evaluation process may lead to documentation of impairments, functional limitations, and disabilities using formats such as:

- A problem list

- A statement of assessment of key factors (e.g., cognitive factors, co-morbidities, social support) influencing the patient/client status.

Diagnosis

Documentation of a diagnosis determined by the physical therapist may include impairment and functional limitations. Examples include:

- Impaired Joint Mobility, Motor Function, Muscle Performance, and Range of Motion Associated With Localized Inflammation (4E)

- Impaired Motor Function and Sensory Integrity Associated With Progressive Disorders of the Central Nervous System (5E)
- Impaired Aerobic Capacity/Endurance Associated With Cardiovascular Pump Dysfunction or Failure (6D)
- Impaired Integumentary Integrity Associated With Partial-Thickness Skin Involvement and Scar Formation (7C)

Prognosis

Documentation of the prognosis is typically included in the plan of care. See below.

Plan of Care

Documentation of the plan of care includes the following:

- Overall goals stated in measurable terms that indicate the predicted level of improvement in function
- A general statement of interventions to be used
- Proposed duration and frequency of service required to reach the goals
- Anticipated discharge plans

Visit/Encounter

Documentation of each visit/encounter shall include the following elements:

- Patient/client self-report (as appropriate).
- Identification of specific interventions provided, including frequency, intensity, and duration as appropriate. Examples include:
  - Knee extension, three sets, ten repetitions, 10# weight
  - Transfer training bed to chair with sliding board
  - Equipment provided
- Changes in patient/client impairment, functional limitation, and disability status as they relate to the plan of care.
- Response to interventions, including adverse reactions, if any.

- Factors that modify frequency or intensity of intervention and progression goals, including patient/client adherence to patient/client-related instructions.
- Communication/consultation with providers/patient/client/family/ significant other.
- Documentation to plan for ongoing provision of services for the next visit(s), which is suggested to include, but not be limited to:
  - The interventions with objectives
  - Progression parameters
  - Precautions, if indicated

Reexamination

Documentation of reexamination shall include the following elements:

- Documentation of selected components of examination to update patient's/client's impairment, function, and/or disability status.
- Interpretation of findings and, when indicated, revision of goals.
- When indicated, revision of plan of care, as directly correlated with goals as documented.

Discharge/Discontinuation Summary

Documentation of discharge or discontinuation shall include the following elements:

- Current physical/functional status.
- Degree of goals achieved and reasons for goals not being achieved.
- Discharge/discontinuation plan related to the patient/client's continuing care. Examples include:
  - Home program.
  - Referrals for additional services.
  - Recommendations for follow-up physical therapy care.
  - Family and caregiver training.
  - Equipment provided.

liabilityawareness

by Karen Stavenjord and Carol Schunk, PT, PsyD

Documentation to Reduce Regulatory Risk

Spelling out compliance policies and procedures is both good practice and good business.

Merriam-Webster Online Dictionary defines "liability" as "the quality or state of being liable," "something for which one is liable (especially pecuniary obligation)," and a "disadvantage" or "drawback."[1] There's a long list of things for which physical therapists (PTs) and physical therapist assistants (PTAs), as hands-on health care providers, face potential liability claims. That list includes but is not limited to patients' well-being and functional improvement, confidentiality of health information, recording of claims and supporting data, and development and use of policies and procedures designed to reduce risk in all areas of practice.

The best way for clinics to create a culture of compliance that reduces potential liability is to create policies and procedures manuals that encompass the subjects of regulatory compliance, internal monitoring, billing, and clinical documentation. That's a big job but one that's rendered much easier by the existence of a number of extremely helpful and easily accessible resources.

From the OIG. The US Department of Health and Human Services' Office of Inspector General's *OIG Compliance Program for Individual and Small Group Physician Practices*, a voluntary compliance plan issued in 2000, offers an excellent blueprint for creating clinical policies and procedures for claims submissions. (For the Internet addresses of this and other resources cited in this column, see the sidebar on page 30.) Don't be thrown by the term "physician practices" in the OIG document—this resource has high relevance for PTs and PTAs. The document's primary focus is claims submission to Medicare

and Medicaid, but the advice offered is equally applicable, with minor procedural modifications, to claims submitted to private payers.

The OIG resource outlines what the agency considers the seven essential components of a voluntary compliance plan:

❖ internal monitoring and auditing,
❖ written standards,
❖ a designated compliance officer to monitor all aspects,
❖ ongoing compliance training and education,
❖ appropriate response to and disclosure of any detected violations,
❖ strong lines of communication among staff regarding compliance, and
❖ publicizing and enforcement of disciplinary standards.

Implementing these seven components requires time and thought but is essential to limiting potential civil and monetary liability for improperly billed claims.

Provider bulletins. Another important way to limit potential liability is to read and share with employees—by means as simple as monthly in-services—the bulletins Medicare contractors send to alert health care providers to policy changes. Taking note of these bulletins is more that just good advice. Failure to read and heed them is considered "deliberate ignorance" under the False Claims Act (31 USC 3729-3733),[2] and fines under the act can be as steep as $5,500 to $11,000 per claim. Given the number of claims generated each day, suffice it to say it behooves practitioners to be well-informed and implement policy changes whenever they are required.

HIPAA resources. For compliance with the mandates of the Health

Insurance Portability and Accountability Act (HIPAA), *Standards for Privacy of Individually Identifiable Health Information* and *Security Standards for the Protection of Electronic Protected Health Information* are key documents. They require covered entities to develop policies and procedures to address each standard and implementation specification promulgated by HIPAA, and they mandate periodically reviewing and updating this documentation.

For the sake of both simplicity and cohesiveness, a policies and procedures manual for HIPAA can cover both privacy and security. Many of the concepts are similar. The manual should address, for instance, not only sanctions—up to and including termination—against employees for unauthorized disclosure of protected health information, but also proper documentation of those offenses and sanctions. Ensuring that compliance with HIPAA policies and procedures is well-documented, and that staff are kept up to speed on all policy and procedural changes, can go a long way toward quashing potential complaints.

Although HIPAA does not provide a private right of action, parties who feel their privacy has been violated by health care providers increasingly are testing the waters in civil lawsuits based on HIPAA provisions. Ed Shay, an attorney from the law firm Post Schell of Philadelphia who specializes in HIPAA, believes the power of mitigation in these situations tends to be underestimated. "Everyone knows that a covered entity under the HIPAA Privacy Rule is required to mitigate privacy violations as a component of its compliance obligations. There are good reasons to pursue mitigation vigorously," Shay says. "First, as the standards in

continued on page 30 ▶▶▶

liabilityawareness

continued from page 28

the Privacy Rule become increasingly recognized in privacy litigation as the standard of conduct, mitigation becomes directly linked to the financial outcome of that litigation. Most privacy lawsuits involve damages that are largely non-economic and recognize intangibles such as humiliation or injury to reputation."

Having a mitigation policy on the books not only is required for compliance with the HIPAA Privacy Rule, but also it makes good business sense. "Mitigation is a useful tool to minimize non-economic damages," Shay emphasizes. "It's required by the Privacy Rule, and failure to mitigate, when it's practicable to do so, is subject to civil monetary penalties. And mitigation works. Some well-timed efforts to lessen the harm caused by failure to comply with the

On the Web

- ❖ The Centers for Medicare and Medicaid Services continues to improve resources and guidance documents for covered entities. For answers to frequently asked questions on disclosure of protected health information in legal proceedings, go to www.hhs.gov and look for "Features" on the home page. Click on "Privacy of Health Information/ HIPAA," then "FAQs on Disclosing PHI in Litigation."
- ❖ The US Department of Health and Human Services Office of Inspector General's document on voluntary compliance can be found at www.oig.hhs.gov. Click on "Authorities & Federal Register Notices," "Federal Register Notices," then, under "2000," "Final Compliance Program Guidance for Individual and Small Group Physician Practices."
- ❖ Compliance resources for HIPAA transactions and code sets, privacy, and security can be found at www.cms.hhs.gov. Click on "HIPAA," then "HIPAA Administrative Simplification."
- ❖ Standards for Privacy of Individually Identifiable Health Information is available at www.hhs.gov. Look for "Features" on the home page and click on "Privacy of Health Information/HIPAA," then add "finalmaster.html" to the URL. Security Standards for the Protection of Electronic Protected Health Information is available at www.hipaadvisory. com. Click on "Regs," then "Security Standards."
- ❖ APTA has resources for HIPAA compliance at www.apta.org. Type "HIPAA" into the search box. Also, check out the APTA Consulting Service.

continued on page 33

liabilityawareness

continued from page 30

Privacy Rule go a long way to lessen the anger of injured individuals. No one ever should underestimate the power of a sincere apology." The power of well-documented policies and procedures for HIPAA compliance shouldn't be underestimated, either.

Most of the privacy complaints received by the US Department of Health and Human Services Office of Civil Rights (OCR), the enforcement agency for the HIPAA Privacy Rule, stem from provider-patient interactions. If the agency receives a complaint alleging a privacy violation, it first must first determine if it is a true violation. Many of the complaints received by the agency concern parties that are not considered "covered entities" under the regulations, or that have come about due simply to a misunderstanding of the regulations. According to a Government Accountability Office report released in September of 2004,[3] 5,648 complaints were filed between April 2003 and April 2004, but nearly two-thirds of the roughly 2,700 complaints the OCR closed during that time fell outside the scope of the Privacy Rule. Should your practice ever become the focus of a complaint, having documentation that clearly shows your implementation of HIPAA Privacy Rule and Security Rule provisions will go a long way toward resolving any questions.

Creating a culture of compliance within a physical therapy practice through the adoption of and adherence to policies and procedures is vital to protecting yourself and your practice.

Going back to the Webster's definition, such a culture addresses the "things for which one is liable—significantly reducing the potential "disadvantages" and "drawbacks" posed by liability claims. ℗

*Karen Stavenjord is assistant director of the Government Affairs Department at APTA. **Carol Schunk, PT, PsyD**, is a PT at Central Oregon Home Health and Hospice, a clinical consultant for TAOS (Therapeutic Associates Outcomes System), and editor of the APTA Geriatrics Section newsletter Gerinotes.*

References

1. *Merriam-Webster Online Dictionary.* Available at www.m-w.com. Accessed March 30, 2005.
2. False Claims Act (31 USC 3729-3733). Available at http://uscode.house.gov/search/criteria.php. Accessed March 30, 2005.
3. General Accounting Office. First-year experiences under the federal privacy rule. Available at www.gao.gov/highlights/d04965high.pdf. Accessed March 30, 2005.

liability awareness
by Rita Arriaga, PT, MS

Stories From the Front— Documentation and Clinical Decision Making

A real-life scenario illustrates some basic risk-management principles.

For the fourth straight year, **PT** is featuring a three-part Liability Awareness series presenting cases adapted from the APTA-endorsed professional liability insurance claims history. This year's series began in February with a scenario that illustrated the need for physical therapists (PTs) to manage risks up front in an effort to avoid burns, and to respond immediately and appropriately should burns occur in order to minimize health consequences

woman who injured her right knee when she fell off a hassock while dusting the top of a bookcase in her home. Within 24 hours she went to the emergency department of a local hospital, where she was examined and diagnosed with a tear of the anterior cruciate ligament (ACL). She was instructed to use crutches to keep all weight off the knee, to apply ice, and to see an orthopedist for follow-up care.

The following week she saw an ortho-

straight leg-raising exercise; then he used electrical stimulation to reduce pain and swelling. The patient was instructed to perform the straight leg-raising exercise at home and to visit the PT three times per week.

During the next two visits, the PT added bicycle and treadmill exercises. One week after the patient had begun physical therapy, the PT instructed her to begin using the leg press machine—which, in keeping with the protocol, was adjusted to limit range of motion (ROM) to 90 degrees of flexion with resistance no more than 50% of the patient's body weight. While she was using the leg press machine the patient reported to the PT that she experienced pain. The PT told the patient that it probably was related to scar tissue and instructed her to continue the leg presses. She performed three sets, with eight to 10 repetitions in each set.

> The PT told the insurance company that he didn't recall the incident, although he acknowledged that he did treat the patient on that date. However, there was no documentation for that visit in the physical therapy chart.

and professional liability. The March scenario spotlighted liability issues in two areas—communication with other health care practitioners and direction and supervision of personnel. This, the final scenario in the series, spotlights the importance of documentation and employing clinical decision-making skills rather than adhering strictly to a protocol.

As you read the scenario, consider these questions:

❖ What elements increase the PT's liability risk?

❖ What risk-management techniques could have been used to reduce that risk?

This case involved a 28-year-old

pedist who confirmed the diagnosis. Four days later, she had a successful surgical repair. During the patient's first post-op visit to the orthopedist, she was referred to physical therapy. Her first visit to the physical therapist (PT) was scheduled the next week, 2 weeks after surgery.

The referral from the orthopedist stated "ACL protocol." (The PT who accepted the patient for care had had prior experience with the referring orthopedist and was familiar with his preferred ACL protocol for post-op rehab.) The PT—a former clinical educator and a board-certified orthopedic specialist who also was certified in manual therapy—examined the patient, then began her on the protocol. The PT helped the patient perform a supine

The patient missed the following physical therapy appointment because of an unrelated illness, but returned for her next scheduled visit 2 days afterward. The patient told the insurance company that during that visit she heard and felt a "pop" in her right knee while using the leg press. She further stated that she related this information to the PT and did not resume using the leg press during that visit. The PT told the insurance company that he didn't recall the incident, although he acknowledged that he did treat the patient on that date. However, there was no documentation for that visit in the physical therapy chart.

On the next physical therapy visit following the incident, the patient presented with severe swelling in her right knee. The PT told her not to use the leg press machine that day, applied ice to the knee, performed ROM tests, and put the patient back on partial weight bearing. When the patient returned 2 days later with the same level of swelling, the PT called the orthopedist. X-rays taken by the orthopedist showed that the patient had fractured her right patella.

While a physician's statement 4 months later noted that the fracture had completely healed and the patient had regained almost full range of motion, the patient—who had switched to another PT after the fractured patella was diagnosed—maintained that she was continuing to experience severe pain in her knee, had difficulty climbing stairs, and was unable to resume running and playing recreation league basketball. She filed suit against her original PT, claiming that his actions—and lack of action—caused her to fracture her patella.

Now, turn the page for commentary on this scenario from a risk-management perspective, including a table summarizing factors that created risk and some of the APTA standards, policies, positions, and guidelines that specifically address them.

liability awareness

The PT could have exhibited better clinical decision-making skills—by conducting both a knee examination and a pain assessment after the patient first reported pain and also after she presented with severe swelling in her knee.

Violations of several APTA standards, policies, positions, and guidelines can be cited here. Among them: Principle 4 of the *Code of Ethics* (HOD 06-00-12-23) states that "A physical therapist shall exercise sound professional judgment." *Standards of Practice for Physical Therapy* (HOD-06-00-11-22) states that "the intervention is altered in accordance with changes in response or status." It also states, "The physical therapist reexamines the patient/client as necessary during an episode of care to evaluate progress or change in patient/client status and modifies the plan accordingly or discontinues physical therapy services."

The PT failed to document each physical therapy visit.

The message that PTs must fully document each episode of care is emphasized repeatedly in APTA documents. *Guidelines for Physical Therapy Documentation* (BOD 03-00-22-54) instructs PTs to examine and document their findings. *Documentation Authority for Physical Therapy Services* (HOD 06-00-20-05) states, "Physical therapy examination, evaluation, diagnosis, prognosis, and intervention shall be documented, dated, and authenticated by the physical therapist who performs the service." Criteria for Standards of Practice (BOD 03-00-22-53) states, "The physical therapist documents, on an ongoing basis, services provided, responses to services, and changes in the status of the patient/client relative to the plan of care."

The PT did not communicate appropriately with the orthopedist.

Standards of Practice for Physical Therapy states, "The physical therapy practice collaborates with all disciplines as appropriate." The standards further state that intervention "is interdisciplinary when necessary to meet the needs of the patient/client." *Professional Practice Relationships* (HOD 06-94-35-46) states, "APTA endorses a collaborative, collegial practice relationship between physical therapists and all other health care providers."

There are several instances in which the PT may have put the patient at risk and did put himself at unnecessary risk of liability.

The first time the patient reported pain—when she first began using the leg press machine—the PT should have assessed the patient's pain, reexamined the knee, and reassessed the intervention to determine whether it was contributory to or the actual source of the pain. While that would have been a prudent response under any circumstances, heightened public awareness of the importance of pain assessment and the development of standards by the Joint Commission on Accreditation of Healthcare Organizations have raised the profile of this specific component of patient assessment and treatment. Not only would conducting an assessment of the pain and its cause have better served the patient, but also it would have benefited the PT from a liability standpoint.

It is further worth noting that, while use of the leg press machine was in keeping with the protocol, the protocol is meant as a guide, not a definitive plan. Use of the leg press machine by this particular patient so soon after surgery may not have been prudent. In both instances—the PT's strict adherence to the protocol and his failure to reexamine the knee and reassess the intervention—the soundness of his clinical decision-making skills is open to question.

The lack of documentation of the visit during which, according to the patient, the patient's knee "popped" is even more problematic. Documentation would have shed light on some looming questions. Did the patient really mention a "pop" to the PT? The patient said she did, but the PT couldn't recall. Did the patient stop using the leg press machine prematurely that day? If so, why? Upon questioning, the patient said she made the decision to stop because of the pain she was experiencing. The PT said that, if the patient did indeed report the "pop," he must have told her to stop as a precaution. The lack of documentation turned what actually happened into a case of "he said, she said."

Finally, while the PT's response to the severe swelling in the patient's knee appears to have been clinically appropriate, the absence of a thorough reexamination/evaluation, including measurement of the swelling, increased the PT's risk exposure. Further, when the patient presented with acute signs of pain and swelling, the better decision would have been for the PT to have reported the situation imme-

> Not only would conducting an assessment of the pain and its cause have better served the patient, but also it would have benefited the PT from a liability standpoint.

diately to the orthopedist so that any further care or intervention would be clearly collaborative. **PT**

Rita Arriaga, PT, MS, is an Associate Clinical Professor in the Graduate Program in Physical Therapy and the Director of Rehabilitation Services at the University of California, San Francisco, and is a former chair of APTA's Committee on Risk Management Services and Member Benefits. She can be reached at 415/476-3453 or arriaga@itsa.ucsf.edu.

Suggested Readings

American Physical Therapy Association. Board of Directors policies. Available at www.apta.org/governance/governance_5/BODpolicies. Accessed February 11, 2002.

American Physical Therapy Association. Ethics and legal issues in physical therapy. Available at www.apta.org/PT_Practice/ethics_pt. Accessed February 11, 2002.

American Physical Therapy Association. House of Delegates policies. Available at www.apta.org/governance/HOD/governance_10. Accessed February 11, 2002.

A Normative Model of Physical Therapist Professional Education: Version 2000. Alexandria, Va: American Physical Therapy Association; 2000.

Guide to Physical Therapist Practice. 2nd ed. *Phys Ther.* 2001;81:9-744.

Risk Management for Physical Therapists: A Quick Reference. Alexandria, Va: American Physical Therapy Association; 2001.

Do you have risk-management questions or concerns? Insights into what PTs need or want to know will help APTA's efforts to educate members about the types of incidents occurring in the workplace and about appropriate risk-management techniques. Contact Jennifer Baker, Director of APTA Insurance and Member Benefit Services, at 800/999-2782, ext 3145, or jenniferbaker@apta.org.

liabilityawareness

by Kathy Lewis, PT, MAPT, JD

Do the Write Thing: Document Everything!

Meticulous record-keeping is a prime defense against a finding of liability, as well as a safeguard of high-quality patient/client care.

Mary, 53, injured her right elbow when she slipped on a wet floor while working at her job in a nursing home. After Mary underwent tendon repair surgery, her physician referred her to physical therapy three times a week for 1 month for moist heat, electrical stimula- tion, and passive range-of-motion (ROM) exercises.

After a month of physical therapy, Mary reported to her physical therapist (PT), John, that she injured her right shoulder and elbow in a motor vehicle accident that occurred during the previous weekend. Six months later, John was notified that Mary had filed a lawsuit alleging that John had "yanked" her right shoulder during physical therapy, causing a rotator cuff tear, and that he had performed physical therapy on the shoulder that was not included in the physician's order.

John successfully avoided liability because his documentation was thorough, timely, factual, and credible. Using John's documentation, his defense attorney was able to show that John had contacted Mary's referring physician, that Mary's credibility was questionable, that the physical therapy interventions John had performed met the professional standard of care, and that Mary's functional abilities began to decline after she learned that her workers' compensation benefits were terminated and that she could return to work.

What, specifically, did John do right? That's the focus of this column.

The potential for legal action is omnipresent in physical therapy—even when you, the PT, follow best-practice patterns, cultivate positive relationships with your patients/clients, and achieve successful patient/client outcomes. You can do all of that well, but where's the proof you'll need when a lawsuit is filed? A well-documented patient/client record is the hard evidence with which PTs can successfully defend themselves against legal action. In contrast, a poorly documented patient/client record can serve as powerful evidence in support of a suit, even when the accusations are frivolous. Here's a quick primer on how to manage your risk by doing what John did—by documenting everything.

Timeliness. Keep all patient/client records up-to-date to ensure the inclusion of all information that will provide evidence that appropriate care was provided. You may forget or inadvertently exclude important details of a patient/client visit if you let too much time lapse before documenting the visit. Documentation should be completed the day that services are rendered. Then, immediately after documenting the visit, look over the record to assess whether it is complete—as John did. You can make this determination by asking yourself what information you would need from the record if you were newly assuming management of the patient's/client's care. If everything you would need is in the record, your documentation is complete.

Decision-making rationale. Documentation of all of the elements of the patient/client management model—examination, evaluation, diagnosis, prognosis, and intervention—should harmonize. In Mary's case, when she reported injury to her right arm as a result of a motor vehicle accident, her patient/client record included this report. Documentation of Mary's responses to further probing questions (eg, "What problems are you having with your shoulder and elbow since this recent accident?") and the results of subsequent tests and measures (eg, flexibility and strength tests) logically built toward and supported John's subsequent decisions to call Mary's referring physician and to defer treatment of her right elbow until he received notice from the physician that X-rays of Mary's right shoulder and elbow were negative. John provided all the documentation necessary to "connect the dots" for any PT who might subsequently read Mary's record and provided ample evidence that the optimal standard of care was met at the time care was rendered.

Patient/client behavior. Document all missed and canceled appointments, instances of the patient's/client's failure or inability to follow instructions, patient/client reports regarding his or her condition, and patient/client violations of your department's conduct code. When the patient's/client's behavior is inconsistent with his or her chief report of pain/discomfort, or when the patient's/client's chief claims are inconsistent with tests and measures, his or her credibility becomes questionable. This cumulative record may suggest an unreliable client who may provide inconsistent testimony or have other character traits suggestive of questionable integrity. The credibility of parties to a lawsuit may be the most critical factor in the outcome of a case. Juries often sympathize with an injured plaintiff; documentation of a historical pattern that challenges the plaintiff's credibility can help counterbalance such sympathy.

In John's case, his careful documentation of Mary's statements and behavior proved a major asset in successfully countering Mary's charges. When Mary called to cancel appointments on a few occasions, stating in each case that she was too busy to come by the clinic, John documented each call and quoted Mary's stated reason for the cancellation. When Mary, on a few other occasions, simply failed to show up without having notified John's clinic, both the failure to attend and the failure to notify were recorded in Mary's chart. John also meticulously documented each instance in which Mary reported that she was performing functional activities at home (eg, lifting her grandchildren) that were inconsistent with her inability to perform less-demanding exercises during her physical therapy sessions. Mary's record clearly showed a substantial decline in her flexibility, strength, and functional ability during the visit after she was first advised that she had only 2 more weeks of reimbursed physical therapy, after which she could return to work.

Provider credibility. PTs who thoroughly and accurately document their compliance with professional standards of care in accordance with APTA's *Guidelines for Physical Therapy Documentation* (BOD-02-12-16-20) greatly strengthen their credibility. Conversely, documentation errors, omissions, or alterations of the record can form devastating evidence against that credibility. John took care to ensure that his documentation was complete and error-free.

Prior and concurrent treatment. The record should fully reflect prior and concurrent treatment of the patient/client by other health care providers and via alternative medicine and/or home remedies. Use quotation marks in the record to indicate the impressions of the patient/client or his or her family members regarding the effectiveness of other interventions. A patient may, for example, use a heating pad, liniments, or other substances on a wound or site of pain. Or a patient/client may currently be participating in more intense exercise (perhaps at a fitness center) than that called for in the physical therapy plan of care. By documenting all of this information, you are compiling a list of potential causes of alleged plaintiff injuries should legal action ensue.

liability awareness

In John's case, he documented that Mary reported having regularly visited a chiropractor during the past 2 years for relief of neck and shoulder pain.

Telephone conversations. Document every telephone conversation you have with patients/clients and health care providers. Include the name of the person with whom you spoke, the date and time, the specific points discussed, and the resolution of the call. Generally, it is advisable to follow up with a memo reiterating your understanding of the discussion and asking the other party to reply in writing if he or she has additions or corrections. If the party later claims disagreement or does not remember the conversation, you have a written record as evidence on your behalf.

Allegations of failure to follow up on patient/client care can be difficult to defend if you cannot prove that you made reasonable attempts to contact the patient/client who missed a scheduled appointment. Documenting telephone calls and the patient's/client's stated reason or reasons for missed appointments will provide you with a more defensible record against allegations of abandonment and may help suggest the questionable credibility of the plaintiff.

When Mary reported injury to John after her motor vehicle accident, John called Mary's physician to report Mary's information and to inquire about the necessity and urgency of Mary's being examined by the physician. John's docu-

mentation of that phone conversation was objective and complete, featuring the date, time, and relevant facts. John also explicitly documented a description of his subsequent communication with Mary (ie, the physician's recommendation that Mary come to his office that same day for possible X-rays and John's summary of the risks of harm if Mary elected to forgo this advice). John directed a member of his staff to draft a memo to Mary's physician advising the physician that John had relayed all of the physician's information to Mary. John further directed that a copy of the memo be placed in Mary's chart.

Informed consent and referral. Include documentation that you discussed with the patient your plan of care (including benefits, significant risks, alternative interventions, and the risks of forgoing intervention). Mary's record showed that John had explained to her all the details of her initial plan of care, and that John had referred Mary back to her physician after telephoning the physician about Mary's reported car accident. John's documentation also reflected compliance with requirements of the jurisdiction's workers' compensation board for preauthorization to continue or modify Mary's treatment plan.

Discharge instructions. Document all action-specific directives you give to patients/clients upon discharge. For example, "If you notice a decline in the movement of your elbow, contact me immediately." John's documentation showed that Mary was told to continue her exercises according to instructions until she was able to perform her daily functional activities without pain or discomfort.

Check-off forms. There is no question that check-off forms are time-saving devices for documentation of physical therapy visits, but using such forms can foster incomplete reporting. Assess your department's forms to ensure that their

Scenarios and Sources

The following are some selected scenarios in which inadequate documentation placed a PT or another health care professional at risk of liability. In each case, go to the link to read more.

1. Interventions were documented but the patient's reactions to those interventions were not. www.apta.org/Products_services/affinity_benefits/risk_management/articles/article4/series3part2 (You must be an APTA member to gain access to this information. Go to www.apta.org and click on "Products and Services," "APTA Affinity Benefits," "Risk Management," "Suggested Risk Management Readings"—at which point you will be asked your member number and last name—"Stories From the Front," then "Series Three, Part Two.")

2. The PT failed to report to the referring physician neurological changes of numbness and tingling. www.apta.org/Products_services/affinity_benefits/risk_management/articles/article4/series3part3 (You must be an APTA member to gain access to this information. Go to www.apta.org and click on "Products and Services," "APTA Affinity Benefits," "Risk Management," "Suggested Risk Management Readings"—at which point you will be asked your member number and last name—"Stories From the Front," then "Series Three, Part Three.")

3. The PT's use of a check-off form with wound care patients resulted in incomplete documentation. www.apta.org/pt_magazine/Oct97/liab.htm

Also, take a look at these resources that are available on the Web site of the Healthcare Providers Service Organization (HPSO): the "Case of the Month" and a directory of past cases (www.hpso.com/case/caseindex.php3); "Bringing Pain Management to the Forefront of Your Practice," an article by APTA member Rita Arriaga, PT, MS, that includes documentation tips (www.hpso.com/newsletters/3-2002/48850b.pdf); and a table of "Documentation Do's and Don'ts" (www.hpso.com/newsletters/1-2000/pt6.shtml).

usage will elicit all essential information. When using these forms, be sure to add narrative comments whenever necessary information might otherwise be excluded.

John used check-off forms to record the specific interventions he provided during each of Mary's physical therapy sessions. In addition, he recorded objective information about Mary's ROM, strength, endurance, and level of pain. John described the type of exercises Mary was doing, her apparent ability to perform them at home, and his observations about Mary's tolerance of each intervention.

Adverse incidents. Immediately complete incident report forms and delineate all the facts of the incident. Include the names of all witnesses, identify every piece of equipment involved, and describe everything you heard and saw. Avoid recording any judgments about causation, because causation generally is determined only after the facts have been investigated. Your organization's risk manager is familiar with relevant laws and should be consulted if you think the incident may lead to a malpractice claim. (Some organizations require employees to contact the risk manager whenever an adverse incident occurs.) Record only clinically pertinent incident-related information in the patient's/client's medical record. Do not record any information unrelated to patient care—eg, "incident report filed," "legal counsel notified." Incident reports may be protected from discovery (the pretrial disclosure of pertinent facts or documents) by a plaintiff's attorney if a lawsuit is later filed by the injured party. This protection may be lost if the patient's/client's medical record discloses any reference to incident reports. It is imperative that you strictly adhere to your organization's risk management guidelines about inclusions and exclusions in the patient's medical record when you encounter an adverse event.

There were no incidents to report during Mary's course of treatment. If Mary had cried out in pain during mobilization of her shoulder, however, completion of an incident report would have been appropriate.

What* not *to document. Do not use the medical record to air your grievances, concerns, and criticism of patients/clients, other health care providers, equipment malfunction, and health plan administrators. Rather, handle such matters through the appropriate chain of command within your organization. The Health Insurance Portability and Accountability Act of 1996 (HIPAA) and other recently enacted federal and state laws give patients/clients greater rights to see their medical records. Patients/clients and any other individuals who read the medical record may take even arguably derogatory or vaguely discriminatory-sounding remarks very seriously and use them as a stimulus to legal action. John's documentation contained nothing to which Mary could conceivably, reasonably take offense.

Although excellent documentation is no guarantee against legal action, it can deter those who threaten such action, function as a safety net when allegations are made, and decrease liability losses when suits are successful. Even more important, conscientious and thorough documentation promotes outstanding quality of care—our ultimate reason for being in the profession. **ⓅⓉ**

....

Kathy Lewis, PT, JD, is an Associate Professor in the Graduate Program in Physical Therapy at Wichita State University and is a member of APTA's Committee on Risk Management Services and Member Benefits. She can be reached at 316/978-6156 or dknlewis@worldnet.att.net.

Suggested Readings

American Physical Therapy Association. Board of Directors policies. Available at www.apta.org/governance/governance_5/BODpolicies. Accessed March 29, 2002.

American Physical Therapy Association. Ethics and legal issues in physical therapy. Available at www.apta.org/PT_Practice/ethics_pt. Accessed March 29, 2002.

American Physical Therapy Association. House of Delegates policies. Available at www.apta.org/governance/HOD/governance_10. Accessed March 29, 2002.

Guide to Physical Therapist Practice, 2nd Ed. *Phys Ther.* 2001;81:9-752.

Healthcare Providers Service Organization. HPSO risk advisor. Available at www.hpso.com/newsletters/newsindex.php3. Accessed March 29, 2002.

PL 104-191, Health Insurance Portability and Accountability Act of 1996. Available at http://frwebgate.access.gpo.gov/cgi-bin/getdoc.cgi?dbname=104_cong_bills&docid=f:h3103enr.txt.pdf. Accessed April 24,2002.

Risk Management for Physical Therapists: A Quick Reference. Alexandria, Va: American Physical Therapy Association; 2001.

liabilityawareness
by Rita Arriaga, PT, MS

Stories From the Front:
Documentation and Complex Medical History
A real-life scenario illustrates some basic risk-management principles.

PT's Stories From the Front series, featuring cases adapted from the claim files of the APTA-endorsed professional liability insurance plan, enters its fifth year this month with the first of three columns. The 2003 series will show that good risk management requires awareness of the implications of the patient's or client's health status and medical/surgical history on all aspects of his or her treatment—from evaluation through delivery and supervision of care.

The following scenario illustrates risk-management implications in the case of a patient with a complex medical history who is undergoing rehabilitation following rotator cuff surgery. As you read it, consider these questions:

❖ What elements increased the physical therapist's (PT's) liability risk?

❖ What risk-management techniques could have been used to reduce that risk?

This case involved a 70-year-old man with a history of left shoulder problems and rotator cuff injuries and tears. He had had polio as a child that left him with a non-functional right arm. Consequently, he was prone to overuse of his left arm. Despite his history of shoulder injuries, pain, and rotator cuff tears, surgery had not been performed because of his dependence on his left arm and his fear of being without its use for some time. He finally agreed to his orthopedist's recommendation for a complicated but neces-

sary surgical repair because of increasing pain and diminishing functional use.

The patient underwent rotator cuff surgery on his left arm in February. In March, after a few weeks of home care, he was referred to outpatient physical therapy for "gentle, passive range-of-motion only, left arm; advance to active assistive ROM after April 1." In mid-March, the patient presented for his initial visit to the physical therapy clinic with an immobilizer on his left arm. After taking a brief history and asking the patient questions about his pain, the PT removed the immobilizer in order to complete her initial evaluation. As part of her testing procedure, the PT asked the patient to raise his left arm as high as he could on his own, in order to establish a baseline measurement of his ability.

Following her initial evaluation, the PT embarked the patient on a program of ROM exercises. The patient visited the clinic four more times over the next 8 days, comprising two visits each with the initial PT and another PT. The physical therapy interventions documented in the clinic records by the two PTs over the course of the four visits included passive ROM exercises as well as notations that the patient performed wall ladder and pulley exercises in the clinic's gym.

On a return visit to his surgeon after the four visits, the man asked to be referred to a different PT clinic because he was having increased pain. Subsequently, the surgeon diagnosed a re-injury to the rotator cuff.

The patient's family filed a complaint claiming that the PT who initially evaluated the man tore the man's rotator cuff by applying excessive force and extending the patient's arm too far. They further alleged that this PT failed to properly monitor physical therapy interventions despite the physician's referral precautions and the patient's complaints of pain. The liability award in this case was high because the patient, who already was challenged by the impairment of his right arm due to polio, was left with very limited use of his left arm due to the reinjury to the rotator cuff. In addition, while there were notes documenting each visit, there was no indication that a plan of care had been designed emphasizing the need for only passive interventions prior to April 1.

Now, turn the page for a commentary on this scenario from a risk-management perspective and a listing of relevant APTA policies and guidelines.

Resources
APTA core documents, policies, and positions are available on the Association's Web site (www.apta.org). Click on "About APTA" for the links.

Also, consult these publications: *A Normative Model of Physical Therapist Professional Education: Version 2000, Guide to Physical Therapist Practice, 2nd ed,* and *Risk Management for Physical Therapists: A Quick Reference.* Descriptions and ordering information are available on APTA's Web site. Click on "Online Shopping," then "Order From Online Catalog."

liabilityawareness

Relevant APTA Policies and Guidelines

1. *Standards of Practice and the Criteria (HOD 06-00-11-22);*
   III. Provision of Services

❖ **B. Initial Examination/Evaluation/Diagnosis/Prognosis.** This section spells out the PT's responsibility to "incorporate appropriate tests and measures to facilitate outcome measurement." This implies not only performing appropriate tests, but also choosing the appropriate tests and knowing when conditions suggest that certain tests are contraindicated and therefore should not be conducted.

❖ **C. Plan of Care.** This section states that the PT establishes and describes (documents) a plan of care for the patient or client based on the results of his or her examination and evaluation and on the patient's or client's needs. It specifies that the documented plan of care should include interventions and treatment parameters. This implies that the plan of care is available and utilized by PTs not only as a record, but also as a form of communication.

❖ **D. Intervention.** This section states the PT's responsibility to alter the intervention in accordance with changes in the individual's "response or status"—which encompass such factors as pain and underlying medical conditions. This means PTs must monitor symptoms such as pain while managing the care of patients and clients.

2. *APTA Guide for Professional Conduct; Principle 4.1,*
   Professional Responsibility

❖ **Section E** states that upon accepting an individual for physical therapy services, the PT is responsible for evaluating, planning, implementing, and supervising the therapeutic program, and for maintaining sufficient records of the case.

❖ **Section G** states that when the patient or client has been referred from another health care practitioner, the PT "shall communicate the findings of the examination and evaluation, the diagnosis, the proposed intervention, and re-examination findings (as indicated) to the referring practitioner." Thus, when a referring practitioner prescribes a treatment program, any alteration of that program by the PT should be undertaken only in consultation with the referring practitioner.

3. *APTA Guide for Professional Conduct; Principle 5.3,*
   Professional Development

❖ This section states: "A physical therapist shall participate in educational activities that enhance his/her basic knowledge and skills." Thus, PTs always should be broadening their knowledge base. That includes currency in medical and surgical information that may have an impact on the management of physical therapy patients and clients.

4. *Guidelines for Physical Therapy Documentation (BOD 02-02-16-20)*

❖ **II. Initial Patient/Client Management, B1. Documentation of Appropriate History.** This section states that documentation of an "appropriate" history includes the history of the presenting problem and any appropriate precautions, pertinent diagnoses and the patient's or client's medical history, and co-morbidities that may affect goals or the plan of care.

❖ **III. Documentation of the Continuum of Care, 2. Documentation of Each Visit/Encounter.** This section states that documentation should include notation of "adverse reaction to interventions, if any" (eg, increasing pain).

A number of seemingly rudimentary elements of PT practice were violated in this scenario. It's important to note, however, that this summary is adapted from actual liability claims, and it's instructive to identify the risk-management strategies that should have been employed to ensure a better outcome.

In selecting and conducting tests and measurements during her initial examination of the patient, the PT overlooked several aspects of the patient's health status and medical history (not to mention the physician's written precautions), all of which added complexity to the patient's surgical repair process and rehabilitation. Even without the physician's written instructions that only passive movement exercises be used until April 1, the PT could and should have learned certain details while taking the patient's history that would have alerted her to be extremely careful in administering any movement tests and subsequent techniques.

The patient's history of overuse and repeated left shoulder injury, pain, and cuff tears were indicative of compromised tissue pre-operatively. The effects of age and surgical repair added further post-operative healing challenges to the tissue. Last, the patient's post-polio status should have been considered in planning, applying, and progressing interventions.

It is true that during the initial visit and prior to developing and initiating a plan of care, the PT should conduct tests to obtain baseline measures of a patient's or client's impairments and functional abilities. A sound risk management strategy, however, is for the PT to use knowledge obtained during this initial examination about a patient's or client's medical and surgical history to make decisions regarding the appropriate tests (and methods of measurement)

continued on page 28 ▶▶▶

liability awareness

continued from page 26

to employ. In this case, because the physician specifically noted that active movement was contraindicated until a later date, the PT should have deferred any active movement tests of the left shoulder. Even without direct written precautions from the physician, however, the patient's medical and surgical information should have led the PT to defer active tests until she had consulted with the physician to clarify the status of the surgical repair.

These same factors required further consideration by the initial PT as she designed a therapy plan and by both treating PTs when applying their physical therapy interventions. Good risk management demands that PTs be up-to-date on the implications of a variety of surgical procedures on the post-operative management of patients' and clients' physical therapy care.

Sound risk management also requires that PTs understand and appreciate the implications of age and medical conditions on post-surgical rehabilitation. In this case, the physician's written precautions should have guided the initial PT to design a plan of care using interventions that allowed only passive movement of the patient's left shoulder during the first few physical therapy visits.

The best form of collaborative communication would have been a well-documented treatment plan. Even without that, however, the second treating PT should have conducted a thorough review of the patient's records and recognized that the wall ladder exercises were *not*, in fact, passive exercise and, therefore, were contraindicated before

April 1. Both PTs shared responsibility for ensuring a very gradual progression of the parameters of any passive movement or exercise, and for closely monitoring the patient's pain throughout the treatment process.

Finally, good risk management in managing patient treatment requires timely and accurate documentation and the appropriate use of those records by each therapist involved in treating the patient. The plan of care, including appropriate interventions and their parameters based on the patient's or client's history and the PT's evaluative findings, always should be documented thoroughly and accurately.

This written plan of care then can serve as a guide to the PT, and any subsequent PTs who might also participate in the patient's treatment, regarding the therapeutic procedures, and any precautions, to be used with the particular patient or client. In this case, without a written plan of care on which to rely, it can be argued that both the initial PT and her peer lacked sufficient documented records to guide them in carrying out their interventions during subsequent sessions with the patient—and that this failure, in turn, resulted in the inappropriate application of active assistive techniques. **PT**

Rita Arriaga, PT, MS, is an Associate Clinical Professor in the Graduate Program in Physical Therapy and the Director of Rehabilitation Services at the University of California, San Francisco, and is a former chair of APTA's Committee on Risk Management and Member Benefits. She can be reached at 415/476-3453 or arriaga@itsa.ucsf.edu.

LIABILITY AWARENESS

by Ronald W Scott, JD, PT, OCS

Incident Reports: Protecting the Record

When is it necessary for you to report an adverse event? And how confidential will that report be kept?

*a*n incident report is a document created in the health care delivery setting to record information about an adverse event such as an injury to a patient, staff member, or visitor that occurs (or is reported to have occurred) on the premises. The incident report has two primary purposes. First, it serves to alert clinicians and management to safety concerns that may require further investigation and possible corrective action. In this regard, the incident report is a quality management (or quality improvement or assurance) tool. Second, the incident report serves as a powerful risk management tool to decrease the providers' and the facility's liability exposure to a tort (ie, "wrongdoing") claim by memorializing important facts about an adverse incident that can be relied upon in the event that litigation arising from the incident ensues.

When to Report

All health care organizations should have in place policies concerning the generation of incident reports, and all providers are responsible for being aware of what those policies are. No observed or reported incident involving injury should ever be considered too minor to report.

In addition to reports involving personal injury, incident reports may be created in response to a number of events, including:

- Expressions by patients of serious dissatisfaction with care or threats to pursue claims or litigation against the organization or its providers.
- Threats of violence or other harm by or against any person.
- Observations by staff, patients, or visitors of defective equipment or dangerous premises (such as an icy or unshovelled sidewalk).

The most prudent course of action that clinicians, support personnel, administrative staff, and managers—basically, any employee of the facility—can follow is to create an incident report *any time* that anything out of the ordinary occurs on the premises. There is never a problem with overreporting adverse incidents. The problem, from a risk management perspective, is that employees of health care organizations habitually underreport such matters. *When in doubt, generate an incident report!*

What to Report

The incident report has several parts. These include an administrative section in which patient or subject identifying information is recorded; a narrative section in which the reporting or percipient witness records factual information; and a section to record supervisory and administrative follow-up.

The narrative portion of an incident report should contain a concise—yet thorough—objective description of what a witness to

an adverse event perceived. The writer of the report must be careful to delineate statements attributable to other persons (ie, hearsay) with quotation marks. The report writer must also avoid speculating as to the possible cause of an adverse incident or attributing blame to any provider or other person.[1] Such matters will be addressed in a follow-up investigation.

When an adverse event involves a patient injury that is treated by the provider (eg, a patient twists her ankle and falls on a wet floor, and the PT puts ice on her ankle and refers her to a physician), a treatment record entry must be made in addition to the incident report. The focus of these two types of entries differs in that the treatment record entry addresses only (1) the fact or suspicion of injury, (2) any diagnosis reached about the patient's injury, and (3) the treatment measures, if any, carried out. *Never mention the existence of the incident report in the treatment entry.* Because the incident report is a business document wholly unrelated to patient evaluation or treatment, it does not belong in a patient's treatment record.

Will the Report Be Kept Confidential?

Incident reports normally are protected from release to persons or entities external to the organization. To enjoy this cloak of confidentiality, an incident report must always be identified either as a "quality assurance/improvement report" or as a risk management document "prepared at the direction of the facility attorney in anticipation of litigation." Because the privilege against disclosure varies from state to state, clinical managers must check with their legal advisors to determine the prerequisites for protection and the precise wording required to protect their particular incident reports.

There is a significant distinction between incident reports labeled as quality management documents and those labeled as risk management documents. In most cases, incident reports that are quality-focused enjoy broader immunity from release than do reports that are litigation focused. For example, the federal statute governing incident reports generated within the Department of Defense makes quality assurance documents absolutely nondiscoverable by patients and their attorneys and other persons outside the agency.[2] The rule is similar in most states. In a recently reported product liability lawsuit involving a patient allegedly injured by a neuromuscular stimulator,[3] a staff physical therapist made an incident report based on the patient's complaint of injury. The device manufacturer (the sole defendant in the case), in support of its contention that the hospital might bear legal responsibility for the patient's injuries, requested a copy of the incident report. The hospital refused to give the incident report to the device manufacturer, and the manufacturer sued to compel its release. The trial-level court initially ordered the hospital to release the incident report to the manufacturer; however, on appeal, the higher-level state court ruled that, as a quality assurance, peer-review document, the incident report enjoyed absolute immunity from involuntary release outside the hospital.

Incident reports that are risk-management-focused, rather than quality-focused, are considered to be "work products" of facility attorneys, and as such, these reports enjoy only limited protection from release to third parties. Because such reports contain ordinary facts about adverse incidents that occur within facilities, they may be ordered released if the party seeking them demonstrates substantial need for the information contained in them and an inability to obtain the substantial equivalent by other means.[4] However, to the extent that an attorney work product investigatory document contains "opinion work product," it enjoys greater immunity from discovery—similar to that enjoyed by quality-focused incident reports.[5]

In addition, the report from the follow-up investigation also may enjoy immunity from release as either a quality assurance or attorney work product document.

Regardless of whether an incident report is quality- or risk-management-focused, it may lose its protection from release by "waiver"— which includes disclosure to persons outside the organization—if a clinician, medical records clerk, or other facility employee inadvertently includes a copy of the incident report in a patient's treatment record.

The fact that an incident report is a privileged, confidential document does *not* imply that providers and managers are free to withhold all information about underlying adverse events from opposing counsel during pre-trial discovery processes (eg, depositions). The protection from release applies specifically to the report, not necessarily to all of the factual information contained in it. Even though a report is privileged, the person who prepared it may be compelled to testify about information contained therein.

Because incident reporting is so important to health care organizations and providers for quality and risk management, clinical managers should ask facility attorneys or other attorneys to present periodic in-service educational sessions (to include case examples and exercises) on the subject of generating incident reports.

Ronald W Scott, JD, PT, OCS, is Associate Professor, Department of Physical Therapy, School of Allied Health Sciences, The University of Texas Health Science Center, San Antonio, Tex. He is a member of PT 's Editorial Advisory Group.

References

1. Scott RW. *Legal Aspects of Documenting Patient Care*. Gaithersburg, Md: Aspen Publishers Inc; 1994:183-185.
2. Woodruff WA. The confidentiality of medical quality assurance records. *Army Lawyer*. 1987;May:5-12.
3. Community Hospitals of Indianapolis Inc v Medtronic Inc, Neuro Division. 594 NE 2d 448 (Ind App 1992).
4. Federal Rules of Civil Procedure, Rule 26(b)(3).
5. Boyle JJ. The Federal Work Product Doctrine: a "how to" for litigators. *Texas Bar Journal*. 1996;59(6):534-543.

Consider the following case:

C, a staff PT at a community hospital, enters the hospital room of Mr D, a 68-year old patient who recently had a cerebrovascular accident (CVA), to perform an evaluation for physical therapy. C immediately observes D on the floor next to his bed, right side-lying in the fetal position and moaning. D's wife is seated in a rocking chair next to D. When C asks D's wife what happened, she replies, "The nurses left the bed rails down. They always leave them down. D fell." C looks at the bed and notices that the rails are down. C quickly attends to D, and, finding no apparent injury, stabilizes him in his current position with pillows between his knees, under his head, and behind his back. C then calls for help.

How should an incident report be written for this? What should the treatment record in D's chart look like?

Incident Report, Narrative Section

On entering D's room, I immediately observed that D was on the floor, right side-lying in the fetal position, moaning. His wife was seated next to him, in a rocking chair. I observed D's bed rails to be down. In response to my question, "What happened?" D's wife stated, "The nurses left the bed rails down. They always leave them down. D fell." I quickly attended to D and found no apparent injury. I then placed a pillow between D's knees, one under his head, and one behind his back to stabilize him. I ran to the doorway and called for assistance. D's ward physician, Dr X, arrived within several seconds and assumed responsibility for D's further care. PT evaluation to be held until further orders. End of statement.

Treatment Record Entry

6/21/96/8:40 am: D discovered on floor next to his bed, right side-lying in the fetal position. On examination, no apparent injury. Stabilized in current position with three pillows. Called for assistance; Dr X assumed care. Hold initial PT evaluation until further orders.

Liability Insurance

Insurance Benefits for Physical Therapy Services
HOD P06-02-25-05 [Initial HOD 06-77-06-06]

The American Physical Therapy Association (APTA) shall pursue and promote the incorporation of physical therapy services in accordance with APTA policies, positions, guidelines, standards, and *Code of Ethics* as a benefit in all appropriate insurance policies. Such policies include those developed by any third-party payer, or state, federal, and other regulatory agency.

liability awareness
by Stuart H Platt, PT, MSPT

Taking It Personally

It's wise to consider individual professional liability insurance, even if you're covered by your employer's policy.

As physical therapists (PTs), we believe in autonomous practice and empowering our patients to ultimately self-manage their conditions. The question is, do we practice what we preach in our personal lives? Specifically, do we translate these concepts of autonomy and independence to ensuring that we have sufficient professional liability coverage?

Sadly, many of us do not even consider obtaining individual professional liability insurance for the protection of our current and future assets until it is too late. Also troubling is the fact that many of us rely on our employers' coverage without ever taking the time to assess whether or not it is adequate and appropriate to our needs.

Recent data from the APTA-endorsed Professional Liability Insurance Plan shows an increase in the frequency of claims—six claims per 1,000 physical therapy policyholders, versus 4.5 claims 5 years ago. The average payout has increased as well—to $49,000 from $29,000 5 years ago. These increases are the result of a confluence of factors, not the least of which is the litigious mentality that, unfortunately, has become part of our culture. They also reflect the pressures of a hectic clinical environment in which PTs, like other health care providers, must see greater numbers of patients in shorter amounts of time.

These trends point to the need for physical therapy practitioners to be proactive about risk management. That includes taking a closer look at individual professional liability insurance.

Now, I know you may be thinking you don't need such coverage because you don't have any assets to protect, and/or because your employer offers an excellent professional liability insurance policy. But let's explore both of these points.

Assets Aren't Static

It's important to realize that, depending on the statute of limitations for malpractice claims in your state, a claim may be filed against you months and sometimes years after the incident in question actually occurred. This means that while your "I've got no assets" rationale may be valid enough today, it may not be true when a future claim is made. Increased equity in your home, accumulation of retirement funds, inheritance, and other good fortune all can significantly change your asset mix over a period of just a few years. Do you want to run the risk of discovering that it's too late to protect yourself and your assets against an incident that occurred when you were unprotected?

It also is important to understand that personal assets jointly owned with a spouse, or held solely in a spouse or partner's name, are not necessarily immune from seizure as part of a malpractice settlement or judgment. The extent of protection is dependent on the laws of your state of residence and can be subject to change due either to changes in your state's law or to a change in your personal circumstances. For example, divorce or the death of you or your partner can affect the ownership of assets and create a situation in which the surviving partner is left

"holding the bag" for various debts and legal obligations.

The bottom line is that circumstances do change. Having an individual professional liability occurrence policy active at the time of an incident can provide the protection you need for assets that you own now and will own in the future, should a claim be filed against you years after the incident occurred.

Questions of Content

If you have exclusively relied on your employer's insurance benefits, do you know how well you are covered by that professional liability insurance policy? One way you can help protect yourself is by being well informed. Ask your employer for a copy of the professional liability insurance policy that applies to you. Once you have it, review it to determine whether you have adequate protection. Here's a checklist of key questions:

❖ What are the monetary limits of liability coverage for each incident?

❖ What are the aggregate annual limits of liability coverage for the company or hospital?

❖ How many other employees share in the limits of liability?

❖ What is not covered? Put another way, are any activities excluded from coverage under the policy? You'll want to ensure that all aspects of your physical therapy practice are covered. One major area that likely is not covered by an employer's policy is any physical therapy conducted outside the place of employment (eg, "moonlighting," volunteer work/screenings, "friendly" advice to family and friends, and so on).

❖ If you were named as a defendant in a lawsuit against your employer, would you be assigned your own attorney (to avoid conflict of interest issues)?

❖ What happens to your professional liability insurance coverage if your employer closes the practice or goes bankrupt?

❖ What happens to your professional liability insurance coverage if your employer fails to pay the insurance premium on the policy?

❖ If your employer merges with another employer, what assurances do you have that you'll be covered for incidents that occurred prior to the merger?

❖ If you terminate your employment (eg, move to another state or decide to leave work to raise a child), will liability coverage provided by your former employer's policy protect you from claims resulting from an incident that occurred when you were employed?

❖ What happens to your professional liability insurance coverage if your employer changes policies? Will there be any gaps in your coverage?

❖ Are you covered for legal representation if you're brought before your state licensure board for a disciplinary hearing as a result of a professional liability incident?

❖ Can your professional liability insurance coverage be cancelled? If so, for what reason or reasons?

If your employer is reluctant to share any of this information with you, or if your employer's answers give you some concern, the need for individual professional liability insurance policy should be even clearer. Also, remember that a patient or client has every right to sue you personally for alleged negligence—instead of or as well as your employer.

Investment in Your Future

Having your own professional liability policy ensures that, should a malpractice suit be brought against you, you will have your own attorney to defend you—and your interests alone. Also, when you buy your own insurance contract, you are in control of the policy. You have the right to request changes, to cancel the policy in favor of another, and to directly address all pertinent notifications from the insurance company. And maintaining your own policy means you always are assured of having the liability coverage you need.

While medical malpractice coverage for PTs remains available, premiums likely will continue to rise in the foreseeable future, according to APTA's Committee on Risk Management and Member Benefits, which tracks trends in the malpractice insurance market. In addition, the committee advises, individuals or firms with a claim history likely will continue to experience difficulty obtaining and keeping insurance in the mainstream market due to tightened underwriting guidelines.

The committee is aware that these difficult market conditions are negatively affecting some members, and encourages members with concerns to contact APTA staff for assistance. The committee welcomes member feedback regarding risk management needs and the Association's endorsed member benefit offerings. Questions may be directed to Jennifer Baker, director of APTA's Risk Management and Member Benefit Services Department, at jenniferbaker@apta.org.

Making informed decisions about professional liability insurance coverage is one way PTs can put the concepts of autonomy and independence we preach in the clinic into practice where we live. Personal professional liability insurance is an investment in your peace of mind and protection of your assets. **PT**

Stuart H Platt, PT, MSPT, a member of APTA's Committee on Risk Management and Member Benefits, is a principal with Appropriate Utilization Group, LLC. His practice focuses on chart audit, peer review, utilization review, and expert testimony in the rehabilitation arena. He can be reached at 404/728-1974 or splatt2208@yahoo.com.

Professional Liability Insurance

Are You Covered?

By Kathy Lewis, JD, PT

Insurance law is full of "hidden traps." Don't fall into them! A review of what to look for in professional liability coverage.

In 1987, a physical therapist began working as an employee, relying on the employer's blanket liability insurance policy for coverage. When she began practicing as an independent contractor in 1989, she purchased a claims-made professional liability policy. In 1991, she opened a private practice outpatient clinic in another state and wanted to purchase adequate professional liability insurance.

This hypothetical case suggests some typical liability insurance questions:

- Are there major differences between types of policies?
- Will a policy purchased in one state provide protection if the insured relocates to another state?
- When a therapist changes policies or insurance companies, are there gaps in the coverage?
- What other factors have an impact on the "adequacy" of coverage?
- Are there reasons not to rely solely on an employer's blanket policy?

Decisions about liability insurance are a serious matter and can be difficult to make. Insurance law is extremely complex. Dobbyn,[1] gave a colorful description of insurance law: "It is like a minefield, full of hidden traps.... Unlike peanut butter or light bulbs, it is so complex that the average consumer has very little idea of what he has actually bought (or what he has *not* bought) when he takes out a policy of insurance."

Entering into the Contract

When a physical therapist or an employer of physical therapists purchases insurance, as a policyholder he or she agrees with the insurer to be bound by the terms of the purchased policy; that is, the therapist or employer enters into a contract with the insurer (Fig 1). The policy and all written documents referenced in the policy are evidence of this agreement, and the precise language of the policy—not a retrospective perception of coverage—determines the insurer's responsibilities. Other documents that may be referenced within the contract include the application for insurance, binders, endorsements, and various documents describing the scope of practice (professional standards of practice, state practice acts, and other regulatory documents). The first page of the policy generally states the *type of policy* (eg, occurrence versus claims-made), *limits of liability* ("schedule of coverages," or the maximum amount of coverage provided by an insurance policy), *term of the policy, "First Named Insured,"* and *status of the insured* (group member, employee, or independent contractor).

Type of Policy

Blanket coverage. Under a blanket coverage policy provided by an employer, a physical therapist employee may have unexpected liability because the limits of liability coverage ("schedule of coverages") may be unclear or inadequate. Blanket policies generally do not specify individual limits of liability for each employee;

instead, the limits are stated as a total or aggregate amount for all employees and the practice. When employees are added to a policy, more people share the same amount of insurance. Furthermore, the doctrine of *respondeat superior* (a plaintiff's right to sue an employer for negligent acts of employees) does not prevent the plaintiff from suing an employed physical therapist instead of—or in addition to—the employer. Blanket coverage, then, may not be the best choice when the insurer's attorney represents both employer and employee as co-defendants (conflict of interest) or when the limits of liability already have been reached as a result of previous litigation. A personal policy may provide greater security. Most group policies provide coverage for activities "in the course of employment"; some specifically exclude "moonlighting activities." A physical therapist who "moonlights" especially should consider obtaining a personal policy.

Individual policies purchased by an entity other than the therapist. Although it is not a common practice, employers sometimes purchase individual policies for employed therapists. If an employer purchases individual policies for employees instead of blanket coverage, the therapist should find out who is the "First Named Insured" on his or her policy. The "First Named Insured" has the right to 1) request changes in the policy, 2) cancel the policy, and 3) receive all notifications pertaining to the policy from the insurance company. The corresponding *responsibilities* of the "First Named Insured" include 1) payment of all premiums (regardless of problems or disputes), 2) verification of or request for renewal of the policy, and 3) reporting of all claims. *Rights* may be assigned to a third party, but responsibilities may *not* be assigned to anyone other than the "First Named Insured." A common example of this principle is when a homeowner purchases homeowner's insurance and assigns the right to receive premium notices to a mortgagee: The homeowner always remains responsible for payment of the insurance premium.

When a physical therapist is the "First Named Insured," he or she is in control of the policy and is directly responsible to the insurer for payments and for all other responsibilities according to the policy terms. Even when the therapist assigns rights to his or her employer (eg, rights to request changes in the policy or to cancel the policy), the therapist still is responsible for meeting the policy terms and for any changes that the employer makes. When the entity that purchases the insurance policy (eg, the employer) is the "First Named Insured," the therapist does *not* have control of the policy; however, the therapist should keep informed about the status of the policy (eg, any changes in effective dates, type of policy, and coverage).

Disputes regarding timeliness of payment, reimbursement to the therapist for premium payments, or any other issues related to the employment contract should be resolved between the employer and therapist. Disputes that relate to the employment contract cannot be resolved with the insurer, because the insurer is not a party to that contract. Regardless of who the "First Named Insured" is, a therapist should seek legal counsel to review an employment contract.

Occurrence policies versus claims-made policies. Occurrence policies provide coverage for liability only when the incident in question occurs during the policy term; the claim itself can be made after the term. *Claims-made* policies, however, require both the incident and the claim to occur during the policy term. But these general definitions are not sufficient to understand coverage. To know when coverage is initiated and when reporting obligations begin, the therapist must understand the *specific definitions of terms as they are used in the policy.*

Different insurers, for example, may define "claim" differently. A claim may be defined as: 1) any report to the insurer, in writing, of an incident; 2) any report to an insurer, in writing, of a poor outcome of treatment; 3) any copies, sent to an insurer, of correspondence indicating a patient's intent to sue or the initiation of

---

Contracting Parties:
Insurer (source of insurance) and insured (policyholder)

Contract Elements:
Definitions
Premiums paid by policyholder
Length of policy period, or "term"
Limits of liability
Exclusions
Conditions
Endorsements
Deductibles
State statutes

Figure 1. Critical elements of the "contract" (insurance policy). The rights and responsibilities of the contracting parties (insurer and insured) are determined by the terms of the policy.

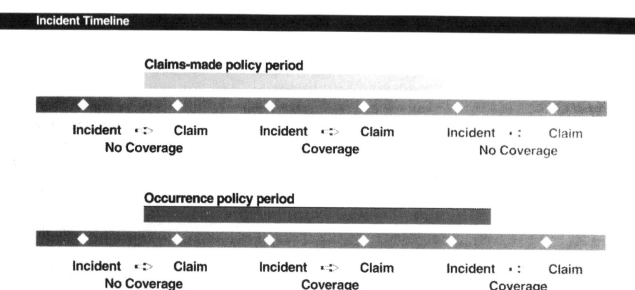

Figure 2. *When an incident occurs before the policy term is in effect and the claim occurs during the policy term, neither claims-made nor occurrence policies provide liability coverage. When both incident and claim occur during the policy term, both types of policies provide liability coverage. When an incident occurs during the policy term and the claim occurs after the policy term, occurrence policies provide protection; claims-made policies do not.*

a legal proceeding; or 4) any documentation, sent to an insurer, of a telephone call from an annoyed patient. The precise definition of "claim" as it appears in the policy is *the* controlling factor. This definition has an impact on both the reporting obligations of the therapist and the period of time for which the therapist is covered. Consider this scenario involving the therapist in the hypothetical case example described at the beginning of this article:

In 1991, when the therapist began a private practice in another state, she purchased professional liability insurance from a company other than the one from which her claims-made policy was purchased in 1989. In 1992, the therapist received notice that a lawsuit had been filed by a patient whom the therapist had treated in 1990. If the original, 1989-1990 claims-made policy had defined "claim" as "the initiation of a legal proceeding," the therapist would not be covered by that policy, because the claim was initiated after the term of the policy. However, if the policy had defined "claim" as "any poor outcome reported to the insurer in writing" and the therapist had notified the insurer in writing shortly after the incident in question, she would be covered by that original claims-made policy.

Gaps in Coverage Between Policy Periods

There are several situations in which a therapist may not have *any* insurance protection. One of the most common situations is described above: A therapist has a claims-made insurance policy and subsequently chooses to purchase insurance from a different company. Any claim filed after the termination of the claims-made policy will not be covered (Fig 2). Another common situation: A therapist is protected as a member of a group policy and then moves to another state in which the insurer is not licensed to do business. Other gaps may occur if provisions to continue insurance have not been made before the therapist retires, dies, or becomes disabled. It is possible for a therapist's estate to be sued. In these situations, "tail" coverage through the previous insurer or "prior acts" coverage through the current insurer can provide protection. Although the premiums for these types of insurance can be very high, having no protection or inadequate protection could result in an even higher cost to the therapist (see "In Practice," page 17).

Advance planning can help therapists avoid these precarious, potentially costly gaps in coverage. Prior to contracting for professional liability insurance, the therapist should ask the insurer or the party paying for the policy such questions as: Does the policy include "tail" coverage at the time of retirement, death, or disability (sometimes called "forgiving the tail")? Is a "tail" coverage option guaranteed at termination of the policy? What is the time limit for purchasing "tail" coverage (eg, 30 days, 60 days, or more than 60 days)? What are the optional lengths of coverage (6 months, 1 year, 5 years, or more than 5 years)? If an employer pays for insurance as a fringe benefit, ask whether "tail" coverage will be paid at the termination of employment. Does the insurer have reduced rates for "suspension" of a policy when the therapist might not be *actively* practicing?

What's Covered—and What Isn't?

Scope of practice. Although many of the activities performed by therapists—such as patient evaluation—are commonly accepted as being within the "scope of practice" of physical therapy, this designation may not be so clear when it comes to other activities, such as providing consultation services, serving as an expert witness, leasing equipment to others, or volunteering at athletic events. A therapist would be wise to include these less-common activities on the application for insurance with a request for coverage. If the therapist has an existing policy and plans to engage in activities that are *not* clearly covered by that policy, the insurer should be notified in writing with a request for written "endorsement" of those activities. (The only legal way to alter a policy, this type of written endorsement also can be called a "rider,"

a "policy change," or an "amendment"). The insurer should give written notice for any additional premium for such endorsement.

As previously stated, when a therapist is identified on a group policy as an "employee," coverage may be restrictive (eg, only for "on-site" activities). When a therapist identified as a "group member" engages in activities that are not specifically covered by the group policy—such as "moonlighting" or working in a health club—he or she should purchase additional insurance.

Exclusions. The policy exclusion section of the professional liability insurance contract lists activities or conditions that are not covered by the policy. Business contracts with employers or other third parties that include *"hold-harmless" clauses* (in which the therapist assumes responsibility for liabilities of the third party) may be specifically excluded by the liability insurance policy language. Even when there is no specific exclusion, the insurer has a strong defense for noncoverage because the insured does not have the right to contract with third parties about the insurer's liabilities. When a therapist is offered a contract for therapy services that contains hold-harmless clauses, he or she should 1) contact an attorney to review the contract, send a copy of the contract to the insurer for review, and request a response in writing before signing the contract or 2) negotiate to have the clause removed from the contract.

Actions that typically are listed in the policy exclusion section include assault and battery, criminal acts, violations of the law, slander, libel, sexual misconduct, punitive damages, and antitrust violations.

Defense costs. Therapists engaged in regulatory activities (eg, peer review and credentialing) may be especially vulnerable to liability for slander, libel, and antitrust violations if their actions or decisions are determined to be motivated by concern about their own economic benefit rather than by concern about quality of care. Most jurisdictions hold that an insurer's duty to defend must be stated in the policy.[2] The insurer *may* defend when the insured is charged with an excludable violation[3]; however, if the therapist is found liable, the insurer may not be responsible for awards to plaintiffs and may later recoup defense costs.[4]

The costs to defend these types of cases today average in the tens of thousands of dollars.[5] Defense costs are critical factors in determining adequacy of insurance coverage. Consider the following examples:

Therapist A has $200,000/$600,000 limits-of-liability coverage through Company Y. The policy states that defense costs are included in the total cost of a claim. The total cost to defend a claim made against Therapist A is $100,000, and the damages award to the plaintiff is $200,000 (total claim = $300,000). The insurer pays $200,000 of the $300,000 claim, and the therapist is personally responsible for the $100,000 balance.

Therapist B has $200,000/$600,000 limits-of-liability coverage through Company Z. Under that policy, defense costs are covered in addition to the per-occurrence limits. The total cost to defend a claim made against Therapist B is $100,000, and the damages award to the plaintiff is $200,000. The insurer pays the $200,000 damages award and the $100,000 defense cost. The therapist is not personally responsible for any of the costs.

To determine adequacy of coverage of defense costs, the therapist should ask the insurer a number of questions (Fig 3). The therapist also should ask whether the insurer provides reimbursement for the therapist's time spent defending the claim and for loss of income. If reimbursement is provided, are there caps or other limitations?

Conditions. The insurer's responsibilities to provide coverage are contingent on the insured meeting certain conditions. These conditions generally include accurate and complete application to purchase insurance, timely payment of premiums, reporting claims according to policy terms, cooperation throughout investigation and defense of claims, and reporting changes of practice.

Do You Need a Policy? Do You Need Additional Policies?

There are two critical stages in obtaining professional liability insurance coverage. The *negotiating period* is a time for the therapist or employer to gather information, identify risks, determine the amount of coverage needed, come to an understanding of policy terms, review state laws, identify the policy that best meets his or her needs, and accurately complete the application for insurance. It is important to note that neither high-cost insurance nor high limits-of-liability coverage

Stated Indemnity Limits, or Limits of Liability: $200,000/$600,000

- $200,000 is the maximum coverage amount allowed for each claim within a year.
- $600,000 is the maximum coverage amount allowed for the aggregate of all claims within that same year.

Factors that influence adequacy of coverage:

Deductibles
- Are there any deductibles? If so, how much are they?
- What circumstances trigger deductibles (eg, defense litigation)?
- If you are part of a group, are you personally responsible to pay the deductibles, or is there an adequate escrow account on behalf of all those insured?

Defense costs
- Are defense costs subtracted from the indemnity limits?
- Is the insured responsible for all or part of the defense costs?
- If defense costs are covered, is there a cap on defense coverage?
- Does the policy provide for the costs of defense even when the indemnity limits have been met—or for a claim that may not be covered by the policy?

Figure 3. Limits of liability. Insurance coverage may be greater or less than the stated indemnity limits.

necessarily equates to the best coverage. Decisions should be based on all information obtained during the negotiating period, and state laws should not be neglected. The state of Kansas, for example, has a statute that specifically excludes sexual misconduct from coverage by professional liability insurance. The state of Missouri and other jurisdictions have "joint and several liability," that is, the plaintiff can collect the *entire* damages award from one defendant, regardless of the percentage of fault that is determined. In these jurisdictions, a therapist who has extremely high limits of liability may be positioned at a higher risk for lawsuits than the therapist who has limits of liability that meet the average for claims against therapists (rather than the average for claims against physicians and other high-risk professionals) *in that particular jurisdiction.* Consider the following example:

In a jurisdiction that has joint and several liability, a plaintiff files a claim against a therapist and a physician or other co-defendant. The average claim against therapists in this hypothetical jurisdiction is $20,000. The therapist has $1,000,000/$6,000,000 limits-of-liability coverage, and the co-defendant has $500,000/$1,000,000 limits of liability coverage. The therapist is found to be 2% at fault, and the co-defendant is found to be 98% at fault. The plaintiff is awarded $1,000,000. The entire award may be collected from the therapist, regardless of co-defendant's percentage of fault. In this case, purchasing excessive limits of liability coverage was not a wise decision by the therapist.

After a policy has been purchased, the policyholder should comply with the terms of the policy; maintain all pertinent insurance records; notify the insurer of any changes in scope of practice; review the policy annually for adequacy of coverage; *obtain endorsements or additional policies, if necessary;* and keep informed about changes in the law and trends in risk (such as through the American Physical Therapy Association's Insurance and Member Benefits Department, colleagues, legal counsel, insurance carriers, and legislative activities). Start early with professional liability insurance coverage, and keep track of your anniversary dates!

Professional liability insurance is like a "delicate" bank account. It is an investment that will return benefits (in security or in coverage)—*if* it is understood and treated with precision. *PT*

Kathy Lewis, JD, PT, is Associate Professor, Physical Therapy Department, School of Allied Health, The Texas Tech University Health Sciences Center, Amarillo, Tex. She is a member of APTA's Risk Management Workshop Faculty.

References

1 Dobbyn J. *Insurance Law in a Nutshell.* St Paul, Minn: West Publishing Co; 1983.
2 Marick MM. Excess insurance: an overview of general principles and current issues. *Tort and Insurance Law Journal.* 1989;24:715-750.
3 Jorgenson L, Bishing SB, Sutherland PK. Therapist-patient sexual exploitation and insurance liability. *Tort and Insurance Law Journal.* 1992;27:595-614.
4 Pasich KA. Disappearing coverage: how to avoid being left high and dry by insurers. *American Bar Association Journal.* 1994; 80:68.
5 Johnson JD, Kirk B. *The Guide to Medical Professional Liability Insurance.* Chicago, Ill: American Medical Association; 1991.

Suggested Readings

Ashcroft CE. Your professional liability policy. *Clinical Management.* 1991;11(5):16-18.
Browning G. Doctors and lawyers face off. *American Bar Association Journal.* 1986;72:38-41.
Cartwright RE. The high cost of insurance: who's to blame? *The Brief.* 1987;Winter:14-18.
Ochs RD. What you should know about professional liability insurance. *The Journal of the Kansas Bar Association.* 1987;56:38-39.
Scott R. *Health Care Malpractice: A Primer on Legal Issues.* Thorofare, NJ: SLACK Inc; 1990.
St Clair JW. Those monstrous malpractice premiums. *Legal Economics.* 1987;March:24-26.

Deep Pockets

Are you purchasing too much professional liability insurance?

Physical therapists traditionally have been able to purchase large amounts of professional liability insurance coverage at a very reasonable rate. The choice of the amount of coverage to purchase typically has been based on the minimal cost difference between levels of coverage; for example, the premium payment for the minimum coverage policy of $100,000/$300,000 (amount per incident/amount per year) is only a fraction less expensive than the cost of the premium for the maximum coverage of $1 million/$5 million limits of liability. It therefore seems logical to ask: Why *not* pay a slightly higher premium payment per year and have "better" coverage? In fact, this may be one of those instances when, although having minimum coverage sounds like a negative, it can actually prevent you from becoming "the deep pocket" during a malpractice legal action involving multiple defendants.

Most malpractice suits are based on the legal theory of *negligence,*[1] that is, failure to provide care within the established standard of care for the profession for a patient for whom you have a duty to provide care, with injury to the patient as a result. There are four elements of negligence that must be proven by the plaintiff: duty, breach of duty, damages, and causation. With proof of these, the judge or jury may award a monetary judgment to the plaintiff for the damages suffered as a result of the care provided by the defendant.

Tort law recognizes that the responsibility for such damage frequently is the result of the actions of more than one individual.[1] One method of determining damage is the *doctrine of comparative negligence,* which determines the amount of responsibility of each party involved in the legal action—especially if the plaintiff can be shown to have some of the responsibility for the damage. Seldom, however, has the plaintiff been found to share in the responsibility for the damage from the negligence of a health care provider. A newer legal concept, *comparative fault,* now allows courts to apportion the plaintiff's damages between the negligent defendants.

Health care services typically involve a variety of providers. Therefore, most malpractice actions filed against health care providers involve more than one defendant. Many times, all providers of the plaintiff's health care are listed as defendants in the litigation because, in theory, all providers had an equal duty to protect the plaintiff from the harm that resulted from the care they assisted in providing.[1,2]

Joint and Several Liability

When the actions of two or more defendants have combined to produce a single, harmful result for the plaintiff, all of those defendants are considered to be liable for damages through the legal doctrine of *joint and several liability.* It seems reasonable to assume that each defendant would be limited to providing payment for the percentage of damages for which he or she had been found to be at fault; however, judgment actually can be awarded one of two ways:

- Judgment can be awarded as a combination of payments from each of the defendants involved in the litigation.
- The entire judgment can be sought from *any one* or more of the individual defendants.

This means that any defendant, even if he or she is only partially responsible for the plaintiff's injury, can be required to pay the full judgment awarded to the plaintiff if he or she is found to have either the assets or the insurance coverage to pay the awarded amount. Responsibility for paying judgments tends to be divided among the defendants who have the better insurance policy limits of liability through the concept of the deep pockets, or "whoever has the most pays the greater percentage of the award."[2]

Limiting Liability

During the course of tort reform legislation, many states have attempted to define a defendant's liability by the percentage of the fault for which that defendant had been found to be liable.[2] Several states have enacted legislation to limit a defendant's liability to only that percentage of the total dollar amount of damages equal to the percentage of the fault attributed to that defendant. In other words, if a defendant had been found to be 20% at fault for a judgment of $50,000, the payment from that defendant would be limited to 20% of the total award, or $10,000.

Other states have attempted to limit the percentage for which a defendant whose percentage of fault is found to be small can be held jointly liable for the damage awarded to the plaintiff. Still other states have suggested that joint liability payments can be made by one defendant only if that defendant was determined to be more than 50% liable for the damage.

What does this mean to you as a PT? There are several pieces of information that are critical for you to know in order to determine your appropriate liability limit and to prevent you from being in the position of becoming the deep pocket.

Legislation: Find out whether you practice in a state that follows the legal doctrine of joint and several liability. If you do, it is also critical for you to know what limitations your jurisdiction has placed on an individual defendant's responsibility for judgment in multiple-defendant cases. If there are no limitations, you could be held fully liable for a damage award, even if you are found to be only partly responsible for the damage to the plaintiff.

Even if there are limits on your liability, you still may be responsible for payment of a larger share of the judgment than that for which you were found liable. For example, if you practice in a state that limits the judgment against a defendant who is found to have less than 15% of the fault in a negligence action to four times that fault, you could still be responsible for up to 60% of the judgment. Accordingly, in a case in which you were determined to be 15% liable and the award to the plaintiff is $50,000, you could be responsible for payment to the plaintiff of a minimum of $7,500 (15%) up to a maximum of $30,000 (60%), which is four times your percentage of fault in the case.

Local limits: It also is critical for you to know the minimal limits of liability that

other health care professionals with whom you work are required to carry. Most physicians, for example, will carry only the minimum professional liability to allow them to maintain their staff privi-

~

If the hospitals in your area

require a minimum

of $100,000/$300,000 for a physician

to maintain staff privileges,

your decision to carry professional

liability limits

of $1 million/$5 million can make

you the deep pocket in any litigation

involving the physician

and you as defendants...

~

leges at the hospitals to which they want to admit patients. If the hospitals in your area require a minimum of $100,000/$300,000 for a physician to maintain staff privileges, your decision to carry professional liability limits of $1 million/$5 million can make you the deep pocket in any litigation involving the physician and you as defendants, with only a $100,000 liability limit for the physician and you carrying a $1 million limit per incident as your liability limit.

Personal limits: It is critical for you to analyze your own level of comfort and need when determining the limit of liability you want from your professional liability policy. Factors to consider include the professional liability limits required by any managed care or other contracting organizations with which you are involved, the dollar amounts of judgments awarded against other physical therapists in your area, the amount of joint liability your state allows, the

amount of coverage you want for all the incidences that could occur in 1 year, and your own peace of mind for financial security should you be involved in a professional liability legal action.

Once you have determined your own professional liability coverage need, purchase only that amount. Resist the temptation to have the most coverage you can purchase just because the cost differential is minimal. Don't allow yourself—and your insurance carrier—to become the *deep pocket!*

Barbara Melzer, PhD, PT, is Associate Professor and Academic Coordinator of Clinical Education, Department of Physical Therapy, Southwest Texas State University, San Marcos, Tex, and a physical therapy consultant with Ingram Physical Therapy and Rehabilitation, San Antonio, Tex.

References

1. Toth RS. Medical malpractice: physician as defendant. In: *American College of Legal Medicine: Legal Medicine, Legal Dynamics of Medical Encounters.* St Louis, Mo: CV Mosby Co; 1988
2. Pozgar GD, Pozgar NS. *Legal Aspects of Health Care Administration.* Gaithersburg, Md: Aspen Publishers Inc; 1996.

Malpractice

American Physical Therapy Association
Criteria for Standards of Practice
For Physical Therapy

The *Standards of Practice for Physical Therapy* are promulgated by APTA's House of Delegates; Criteria for the Standards are promulgated by APTA's Board of Directors. Criteria are italicized beneath the Standards to which they apply.

Preamble

The physical therapy profession's commitment to society is to promote optimal health and function in individuals by pursuing excellence in practice. The American Physical Therapy Association attests to this commitment by adopting and promoting the following Standards of Practice for Physical Therapy. These Standards are the profession's statement of conditions and performances that are essential for provision of high quality professional service to society, and provide a foundation for assessment of physical therapist practice.

I. Ethical/Legal Considerations

A. Ethical Considerations

The physical therapist practices according to the *Code of Ethics* of the American Physical Therapy Association.

The physical therapist assistant complies with the *Standards of Ethical Conduct for the Physical Therapist Assistant* of the American Physical Therapy Association.

B. Legal Considerations

The physical therapist complies with all the legal requirements of jurisdictions regulating the practice of physical therapy.

The physical therapist assistant complies with all the legal requirements of jurisdictions regulating the work of the assistant.

II. Administration of the Physical Therapy Service

A. Statement of Mission, Purposes, and Goals

The physical therapy service has a statement of mission, purposes, and goals that reflects the needs and interests of the patients/clients served, the physical therapy personnel affiliated with the service, and the community.

The statement of mission, purposes, and goals:

- *Defines the scope and limitations of the physical therapy service.*
- *Identifies the goals and objectives of the service.*
- *Is reviewed annually.*

B. Organizational Plan

The physical therapy service has a written organizational plan.

The organizational plan:

- *Describes relationships among components within the physical therapy service and, where the service is part of a larger organization, between the service and the other components of that organization.*
- *Ensures that the service is directed by a physical therapist.*
- *Defines supervisory structures within the service.*
- *Reflects current personnel functions.*

C. Policies and Procedures

The physical therapy service has written policies and procedures that reflect the operation, mission, purposes, and goals of the service, and are consistent with the Association's standards, policies, positions, guidelines, and *Code of Ethics.*

The written policies and procedures:

- *Are reviewed regularly and revised as necessary.*
- *Meet the requirements of federal and state law and external agencies.*
- *Apply to, but are not limited to:*
  - *Care of patients/clients, including guidelines*
  - *Clinical education*
  - *Clinical research*
  - *Collaboration*

- *Competency assessment*
- *Criteria for access to care*
- *Criteria for initiation and continuation of care*
- *Criteria for referral to other appropriate health care providers*
- *Criteria for termination of care*
- *Documentation*
- *Environmental safety*
- *Equipment maintenance*
- *Fiscal management*
- *Improvement of quality of care and performance of services*
- *Infection control*
- *Job/position descriptions*
- *Medical emergencies*
- *Personnel-related policies*
- *Rights of patients/clients*
- *Staff orientation*

D. Administration

A physical therapist is responsible for the direction of the physical therapy service.

The physical therapist responsible for the direction of the physical therapy service:

- *Ensures compliance with local, state, and federal requirements.*
- *Ensures compliance with current APTA documents, including* Standards of Practice for Physical Therapy and the Criteria, Guide to Physical Therapist Practice, Code of Ethics, Guide for Professional Conduct, Standards of Ethical Conduct for the Physical Therapist Assistant, *and* Guide for Conduct of the Affiliate Member.
- *Ensures that services are consistent with the mission, purposes, and goals of the physical therapy service.*
- *Ensures that services are provided in accordance with established policies and procedures.*
- *Ensures that the process for assignment and reassignment of physical therapist staff supports individual physical therapist*

responsibility to their patients and meets the needs of the patients/clients.

- *Reviews and updates policies and procedures.*
- *Provides for training of physical therapy support personnel that ensures continued competence for their job description.*
- *Provides for continuous in-service training on safety issues and for periodic safety inspection of equipment by qualified individuals.*

E. Fiscal Management

The director of the physical therapy service, in consultation with physical therapy staff and appropriate administrative personnel, participates in planning for, and allocation of, resources. Fiscal planning and management of the service is based on sound accounting principles.

The fiscal management plan:

- *Includes a budget that provides for optimal use of resources.*
- *Ensures accurate recording and reporting of financial information.*
- *Ensures compliance with legal requirements.*
- *Allows for cost-effective utilization of resources.*
- *Uses a fee schedule that is consistent with the cost of physical therapy services and that is within customary norms of fairness and reasonableness.*
- *Considers option of providing pro bono services.*

F. Improvement of Quality of Care and Performance

The physical therapy service has a written plan for continuous improvement of quality of care and performance of services.

The improvement plan:

- *Provides evidence of ongoing review and evaluation of the physical therapy service.*
- *Provides a mechanism for documenting improvement in quality of care and performance.*
- *Is consistent with requirements of external agencies, as applicable.*

G. Staffing

The physical therapy personnel affiliated with the physical therapy service have demonstrated competence and are sufficient to achieve the mission, purposes, and goals of the service.

The physical therapy service:

- *Meets all legal requirements regarding licensure and certification of appropriate personnel.*
- *Ensures that the level of expertise within the service is appropriate to the needs of the patients/clients served.*
- *Provides appropriate professional and support personnel to meet the needs of the patient/client population.*

H. Staff Development

The physical therapy service has a written plan that provides for appropriate and ongoing staff development.

The staff development plan:

- *Includes self-assessment, individual goal setting, and organizational needs in directing continuing education and learning activities.*
- *Includes strategies for lifelong learning and professional and career development.*
- *Includes mechanisms to foster mentorship activities.*

I. Physical Setting

The physical setting is designed to provide a safe and accessible environment that facilitates fulfillment of the mission, purposes, and goals of the physical therapy service. The equipment is safe and sufficient to achieve the purposes and goals of physical therapy.

The physical setting:

- *Meets all applicable legal requirements for health and safety.*
- *Meets space needs appropriate for the number and type of patients/clients served.*

The equipment:

- *Meets all applicable legal requirements for health and safety.*
- *Is inspected routinely.*

J. Collaboration

The physical therapy service collaborates with all disciplines as appropriate.

The collaboration when appropriate:

- *Uses a team approach to the care of patients/clients.*
- *Provides instruction of patients/clients and families.*
- *Ensures professional development and continuing education.*

III. Patient/Client Management

A. Patient/Client Collaboration

Within the patient/client management process, the physical therapist and the patient/client establish and maintain an ongoing collaborative process of decision making that exists throughout the provision of services.

B. Initial Examination/Evaluation/ Diagnosis/Prognosis

The physical therapist performs an initial examination and evaluation to establish a diagnosis and prognosis prior to intervention.

The physical therapist examination:

- *Is documented, dated, and appropriately authenticated by the physical therapist who performed it.*
- *Identifies the physical therapy needs of the patient/client.*
- *Incorporates appropriate tests and measures to facilitate outcome measurement.*
- *Produces data that are sufficient to allow evaluation, diagnosis, prognosis, and the establishment of a plan of care.*
- *May result in recommendations for additional services to meet the needs of the patient/client.*

C. Plan of Care

The physical therapist establishes a plan of care and manages the needs of the patient/client based on the examination, evaluation, diagnosis, prognosis, goals, and outcomes of the planned interventions for identified impairments, functional limitations, and disabilities.

The physical therapist involves the patient/client and appropriate others in the planning, implementation, and assessment of the plan of care.

The physical therapist, in consultation with appropriate disciplines, plans for discharge of the patient/client taking into consideration achievement of anticipated goals and expected outcomes, and provides for appropriate follow-up or referral.

The plan of care:

- *Is based on the examination, evaluation, diagnosis, and prognosis.*
- *Identifies goals and outcomes.*
- *Describes the proposed intervention, including frequency and duration.*
- *Includes documentation that is dated and appropriately authenticated by the physical therapist who established the plan of care.*

D. Intervention

The physical therapist provides, or directs and supervises, the physical therapy intervention consistent with the results of the examination, evaluation, diagnosis, prognosis, and plan of care.

The intervention:

- *Is based on the examination, evaluation, diagnosis, prognosis, and plan of care.*
- *Is provided under the ongoing direction and supervision of the physical therapist.*
- *Is provided in such a way that directed and supervised responsibilities are commensurate with the qualifications and the legal limitations of the physical therapist assistant.*
- *Is altered in accordance with changes in response or status.*
- *Is provided at a level that is consistent with current physical therapy practice.*
- *Is interdisciplinary when necessary to meet the needs of the patient/client.*
- *Documentation of the intervention is consistent with the Guidelines: Physical Therapy Documentation of Patient/Client Management (BOD G03-05-16-41).*
- *Is dated and appropriately authenticated by the physical therapist or, when permissible by law, by the physical therapist assistant.*

E. Reexamination

The physical therapist reexamines the patient/client as necessary during an episode of care to evaluate progress or change in patient/client status and modifies the plan of care accordingly or discontinues physical therapy services.

The physical therapist reexamination:

- *Is documented, dated, and appropriately authenticated by the physical therapist who performs it.*
- *Includes modifications to the plan of care.*

Glossary Standards and Criteria

Client. Individuals who engage the services of a physical therapist and who can benefit from the physical therapist's consultation, interventions, professional advice, health promotion, fitness, wellness, or prevention services. Clients also are businesses, school systems, and others to whom physical therapists provide services.

Diagnosis. Diagnosis is both a process and a label. The diagnostic process includes integrating and evaluating the data that are obtained during the examination to describe the patient/client condition in terms that will guide the prognosis, the plan of care, and intervention strategies. Physical therapists use diagnostic labels that identify the impact of a condition on function at the level of the system (especially the movement system) and at the level of the whole person.

Evaluation. A dynamic process in which the physical therapist makes clinical judgments based on data gathered during the examination.

Examination. A comprehensive screening and specific testing process leading to diagnostic classification or, as appropriate, to a referral to another practitioner. The examination has three components: the patient/client history, the systems review, and tests and measures.

Intervention. The purposeful interaction of the physical therapist with the patient/client and, when appropriate, with other individuals involved in patient/client care, using various physical therapy procedures and techniques to produce changes in the condition.

Patient. Individuals who are the recipients of physical therapy examination, evaluation, diagnosis, prognosis, and intervention and who have a disease, disorder, condition, impairment, functional limitation, or disability.

Physical therapist patient/client management model. The model on which physical therapists base management of the patient or client throughout the episode of care, including the following elements: examination, evaluation and reexamination, diagnosis, prognosis, and intervention leading to the outcome.

Plan of care. Statements that specify the goals and the outcomes, predicted level of optimal improvement, specific interventions to be used, and proposed duration and frequency of the interventions that are required to reach the goals and outcomes. The plan of care includes the anticipated discharge plans.

Prognosis. The determination of the predicted optimal level of improvement in function and the amount of time needed to reach that level.

Treatment. The sum of all interventions provided by the physical therapist to a patient/client during an episode of care.

F. Discharge/Discontinuation of Intervention

The physical therapist discharges the patient/client from physical therapy services when the anticipated goals or expected outcomes for the patient/client have been achieved.

The physical therapist discontinues intervention when the patient/client is unable to continue to progress toward goals or when the physical therapist determines that the patient/client will no longer benefit from physical therapy.

Discharge documentation:

- *Includes the status of the patient/client at discharge and the goals and outcomes attained.*
- *Is dated and appropriately authenticated by the physical therapist who performed the discharge.*
- *Includes, when a patient/client is discharged prior to attainment of goals and outcomes, the status of the patient/client and the rationale for discontinuation.*

G. Communication/Coordination/ Documentation

The physical therapist communicates, coordinates, and documents all aspects of patient/client management including the results of the initial examination and evaluation, diagnosis, prognosis, plan of care, interventions, response to interventions, changes in patient/client status relative to the interventions, reexamination, and discharge/discontinuation of intervention and other patient/client management activities.

Physical therapist documentation:

- *Is dated and appropriately authenticated by the physical therapist who performed the examination and established the plan of care.*

- *Is dated and appropriately authenticated by the physical therapist who performed the intervention or, when allowable by law or regulations, by the physical therapist assistant who performed specific components of the intervention as selected by the supervising physical therapist.*

- *Is dated and appropriately authenticated by the physical therapist who performed the reexamination, and includes modifications to the plan of care.*

- *Is dated and appropriately authenticated by the physical therapist who performed the discharge, and includes the status of the patient/client and the goals and outcomes achieved.*

- *Includes, when a patient/client is discharged prior to achievement of goals and outcomes, the status of the patient/client and the rationale for discontinuation.*

IV. Education

The physical therapist is responsible for individual professional development. The physical therapist assistant is responsible for individual career development.

The physical therapist, and the physical therapist assistant under the direction and supervision of the physical therapist, participate in the education of students.

The physical therapist educates and provides consultation to consumers and the general public regarding the purposes and benefits of physical therapy.

The physical therapist educates and provides consultation to consumers and the general public regarding the roles of the physical therapist and the physical therapist assistant.

The physical therapist:

- *Educates and provides consultation to consumers and the general public regarding the roles of the physical therapist, the physical therapist assistant, and other support personnel.*

V. Research

The physical therapist applies research findings to practice and encourages, participates in, and promotes activities that establish the outcomes of patient/client management provided by the physical therapist.

The physical therapist:

- *Ensures that their knowledge of research literature related to practice is current.*

- *Ensures that the rights of research subjects are protected, and the integrity of research is maintained.*

- *Participates in the research process as appropriate to individual education, experience, and expertise.*

- *Educates physical therapists, physical therapist assistants, students, other health professionals, and the general public about the outcomes of physical therapist practice.*

VI. Community Responsibility

The physical therapist demonstrates community responsibility by participating in community and community agency activities, educating the public, formulating public policy, or providing pro bono physical therapy services.

The physical therapist:

- *Participates in community and community agency activities.*

- *Educates the public, including prevention, education, and health promotion.*

- *Helps formulate public policy.*

- *Provides pro bono physical therapy services.*

HOD S06-03-09-10
Adopted by the House of Delegates
June 1980
Last amended June 2003

BOD S03-05-14-38
Adopted by the Board of Directors
November 1985
Last amended March 2005   A-3

American Physical Therapy Association
The Science of Healing. The Art of Caring. SM

Peer Review of Physical Therapy Services
HOD P06-04-16-15 [Initial HOD 06-95-32-19]

Peer review of physical therapy services is provided only by physical therapists who possess an active license without sanctions to practice physical therapy. This peer review shall be based on the following: American Physical Therapy Association (APTA) *Standards of Practice for Physical Therapy*; the *Guide to Physical Therapist Practice*; other pertinent APTA documents and supporting evidence-based literature, when available, state and other jurisdiction practice acts; and additional state, other jurisdiction and federal laws relevant to the physical therapist practice. APTA is opposed to any activities related to peer review that may adversely impact a physical therapist's plan of care or intervention without the involvement of a physical therapist peer reviewer. Adverse physical therapy patient/client management decisions made without the involvement of a physical therapist reviewer may constitute the unlawful practice of physical therapy.

Quality Assurance and Performance Improvement
HOD P06-98-13-13 [HOD 06-81-11-38]

The American Physical Therapy Association (APTA) is committed to excellence in physical therapy practice. Toward this effort, APTA is involved in monitoring systems and requirements aimed at improving quality and performance, facilitating distribution of information about activities of and requirements for performance improvement systems, and developing mechanisms to promote the use of physical therapists in performance improvement and peer review.

APTA advocates voluntary member participation in quality assurance and performance improvement activities which are incorporated into daily practice. The commitment to quality assurance and performance improvement is primarily a professional responsibility and is to be promoted and fostered by Association members through individual and collective efforts. APTA has adopted and maintains a *Guide for Professional Conduct* and *Code of Ethics* for the physical therapist, a *Standards of Practice for Physical Therapy*, and a *Standards of Ethical Conduct for the Physical Therapist Assistant*. Each APTA chapter shall create a means to promote quality assurance and performance improvement activities.

The Legal Standard of Care

The incidence of health care malpractice claims and lawsuits has increased steadily during the past few decades, prompting many health care providers and insurers to label the situation a "malpractice crisis." Although the greatest growth in litigation has involved allegations of physician malpractice, physical therapists also have been named as malpractice defendants in increasing numbers.

Malpractice traditionally has been defined exclusively as "negligence or legally actionable careless treatment resulting in injury to a patient." Today, more and more courts, legislatures, and scholars include other potential bases of liability in the definition of malpractice, such as intentional acts or omissions, breach of contract, and liability for injuries caused by defective products. As in the past, however, a simple adverse or "bad" outcome of patient treatment—without one of the above legal bases for liability—will not result in a malpractice verdict against a physical therapist.

Parameters of Negligence

Virtually all reported cases (those decided by appellate courts) of physical therapy malpractice involve allegations of negligence rather than allegations founded on any other bases of liability. For an injured patient to prevail against a physical therapist in a negligence lawsuit, the patient must prove—by a preponderance of evidence—the following four elements:

By Ronald W. Scott, JD, LLM, PT

1. The defendant-therapist owed a legal duty to care for the patient.
2. The therapist violated the duty owed.
3. The therapist's breach of duty was the direct cause of the patient's alleged injuries.
4. There were injuries that are legally cognizable to a judge or jury.

The Expert Witness: Establishing the Legal Standard of Care

Of the four elements involved in negligence, violation of the required standard of care most closely compares to the general public's perception of "negligence." In court, a patient-plaintiff cannot proceed unless he or she proves a breach of the standard of care.

How is the standard of care established in court? In the vast majority of cases, expert witnesses must testify as to the standard of practice that exists in one of the three relevant geographical frames of reference:

1. In a majority of states, the legal standard of care is that which passes as acceptable practice in the *same community or in communities similar to the community* in which the defendant-therapist practices.
2. The growing trend is to hold all health care providers, including physical therapists, to a *state or nationwide* standard.
3. A minority of states follow the traditional "locality" rule and require comparison of the therapist-defendant only to colleagues who practice in *the same locale*.

Regardless of the geographical frame of reference represented by the expert, he or she must testify as to whether a defendant-therapist acted as

a reasonable peer would have acted under the same or similar circumstances. Experts do *not* testify about what they *themselves* would have done under the circumstances. Experts testify whether therapist-defendant actions pass as minimally acceptable clinical practice.

An expert must establish the following qualifications in order to be legally "competent" to testify: 1) knowledge of the treatment procedure in question and 2) familiarity with the standard of practice that applied at the time of the alleged incident. Because the qualifications of the expert can be challenged by the opponent, the expert also must demonstrate how he or she obtained the specialized knowledge that makes him or her an expert (i.e., the expert must demonstrate that the knowledge was obtained through education, experience, or training). Depending on state law, the expert can base an opinion on authoritative textbooks, on the professional literature, on clinical practice guidelines, and even on practice that is customary in the community. When a court is faced with competing expert testimony about whether a provider met or breached the standard of care, the verdict often depends on which experts are most convincing.

Who can testify as an expert for or against a physical therapist on the legal standard of care? In the vast majority of legal cases that are reported, testifying experts have exclusively been physicians. In one case (Novey, 1988, which was overturned at the highest state level), an occupational therapist testified at trial as an expert on the physical therapy standard of care. The appellate court held that the occupational therapist was not competent to testify about the physical therapy standard of care. Although a strong argument can be made against chiropractors testifying on the physical therapy standard of care, this remains an open issue.

Impact of the Profession's Growth on Expert Testimony and the Legal Standard of Care

The parameters of the standard of care for any profession are ever evolving; this is particularly true of physical therapy. Fundamental changes in physical therapy practice made in the past few decades—including autonomous accreditation of education programs, postbaccalaureate entry-level education, clinical specialization certification, and practice without physician referral—have altered or will alter the legal standard of care to some degree. Physical therapists should be aware of the impact that these changes will have on the legal standard of care and on future therapist defendants in malpractice cases.

Autonomy. In effect since the 1970s, autonomous accreditation of education programs is evidence that the physical therapy profession now is controlled more by physical therapy practitioners and less by non-physical therapy practitioners. At the same time, however, physical therapists have largely ignored their responsibility to routinely establish the physical therapy standard of care in legal proceedings.

Advanced degrees. The evolution of entry-level physical therapy education from the bachelor's degree level to the master's degree level will affect the legal standard of care not only for those clinicians who have advanced degrees, but for all physical therapists. As more and more physical therapy clinicians obtain master's degrees and doctoral degrees, the standard of comparison will change. This likelihood raises a question: Can clinicians with bachelor's degrees testify on the standard of care for clinicians with higher degrees? Yes. Qualification as an expert is not necessarily based on formal education; rather, it is based on familiarity with the treatment procedure in question, whether that familiarity derives from formal education or informal training.

Clinicians who have advanced degrees and who find themselves testifying as experts should remember that the legal standard of care in a given community is not necessarily based on advanced-degree-level clinical skill (unless all practitioners in that community have advanced degrees), but on what is minimally acceptable practice for all practitioners in the community,

regardless of degree level or number of years in practice.

Clinical specialist certification. Specialist certification also has an impact on the legal standard of care. To date, there have been no reported legal cases involving certified clinical specialists. Predictions on how courts will treat cases involving specialists, therefore, must be based on cases involving physician specialists. If and when cases involving physical therapy specialists arise, the standard of care used for comparison probably will be a *national* standard, because certified clinical specialists take a standardized competency examination.

Will generalists be qualified to testify on the specialist standard of care? I believe so. The philosophy behind expert testimony by practitioners with levels of formal education different from that of the therapist-defendant also applies to expert testimony by non-specialist physical therapists on the specialist standard of care: Qualification as an expert is not necessarily based on formal education or credentials, but on proof of knowledge in court about the treatment procedure in question—whether that knowledge derives from formal or informal training.

Direct access. Direct access also may have a profound effect on the legal standard of care for clinicians practicing in jurisdictions in which practice without physician referral is legal. If a physical therapist practicing without referral engages in treatment that exceeds the legal scope of physical therapy practice, or if a physical therapist negligently fails to refer a patient to another provider when required and continues treatment, the physical therapist probably will be held to the standard of care of the health care practitioner to whom he or she should have referred the patient. In these cases, physical therapists probably will not be qualified to testify as experts on the applicable standard of care. The legal ramifications of misdiagnosis or failure to refer a patient, therefore, make it all the more imperative to practice within the parameters of state practice acts and individual scopes of

competency, whether in direct access or referral states.

Serving as an Expert Witness

Although professionals in medicine and law serve as expert witnesses for commercial gain, I do not recommend that physical therapists do so. Those who hold themselves out as "professional experts" often lose credibility in court when they are questioned about the amount of their fee and the number of times they have testified in the past. (The fee and the number of testimonies are not in themselves sufficient grounds for disqualification of a witness.) Attorneys normally prefer to seek out their own experts from university, practice, or other settings; however, all physical therapists should consider it their duty to testify as an expert when they are called to do so and when they are qualified to do so. If physical therapists do *not* assume this role, non-physical therapists will continue to define the physical therapy standard of care for us. **CM**

Ronald W. Scott, JD, LLM, PT, is a captain in the Army Medical Specialist Corps and chief physical therapist and legal advisor at Bayne-Jones Army Community Hospital, Ft. Polk, LA. He is the author of Health Care Malpractice: A Primer on Legal Issues for Professionals, *published by Slack, Inc.*

This article, adapted from a presentation given at the APTA Annual Conference in Nashville, TN, June 14, 1989, launches a series of five articles focusing on the legal standard of care; informed consent; Good Samaritan immunity from legal responsibility; vicarious or indirect liability for the negligence of employees, volunteers, and others; and other trends in health care malpractice law.

This series is not intended as legal advice for any specific practitioner. Legal advice can be given only by your personal legal counsel, based on the law of your state or on federal law, as applicable.

liabilityawareness

by Rita Arriaga, PT, MS

Stories from the Front:
Personnel Employment and Management

An examination of risk-management principles through the prism of case scenarios.

About this series: With physical therapy moving toward realization of the APTA Vision for Physical Therapy 2020, and in keeping with the goals that represent the 2004 priorities of the Association (see box on page 29), it is imperative that physical therapists (PTs) and physical therapist assistants (PTAs) recognize and appreciate that sound risk management is a hallmark of autonomous practice. APTA's Committee on Risk Management and Member Benefits uses "Stories from the Front," now in its sixth year, as a vehicle for conveying information about emerging and ongoing risk-management trends in clinical practice. Using a case-based format, the three columns in each year's series illustrate risk considerations identified by the committee through its review of claims data, and provide readers with references and documents that can assist them in making risk-reducing decisions.

An emerging issue of concern in physical therapy is the risk that surrounds personnel management and employment decisions. In addition to effectively managing the risks of clinical practice, physical therapy professionals must apply risk management principles when hiring and supervising employees and independent contractors who represent the practice. In this, the final column in the "Stories from the Front" series of 2004, two serious situations involving employee-related risk illustrate the profound importance this non-clinical area of practice holds for practice owners, managers/supervisors, and administrators.

The Cases

The first case involved a physical therapy practice that employed a certified athletic trainer (ATC) as an aide

and also engaged her as an independent contractor to provide athletic training services to a local high school's soccer team. The practice's professional liability insurance covered the ATC in both of her roles.

One of the soccer players was brought to the training room by a teammate following a game. The teenager told the ATC that he had sustained a blow to the head during the game, and he revealed that he had been involved in several practice- and game-related collisions over the previous 2 weeks. The blows, he reported, had left him with occasional dizziness, nausea, pressure behind the eyes, and headaches.

The ATC contacted the player's mother, expressed concern about the recurrent injuries and symptoms, and encouraged her to have her son examined by a physician and/or a neurologist. The mother took the ATC's advice and asked the family's physician to evaluate the teen. The physician did so and cleared him to return to practice and participate in the next scheduled match.

That decision concerned the ATC, who then contacted and briefed the soccer team's physician. That physician suggested the trainer conduct a daily functional exam of the teenager, but he added that the young man should be permitted to continue to participate in all team activities because the family's physician had cleared the youth to do so.

The trainer acted on those instructions, and each time she examined the teen he denied any return of his previous symptoms. His denials continued during an exam just prior to the start of

the next scheduled soccer match. Fifteen minutes into the match, the player collapsed on the sideline and died. Brain swelling and a subdural hemorrhage ultimately were listed as the causes of death.

A complaint of negligence, including careless monitoring, was brought against the ATC. Two ATCs for college teams subsequently told the defendant's counsel that the ATC's actions had met and perhaps exceeded the standard of care for an ATC, but the physical therapy practice's insurer felt the plaintiff's attorney could make a strong case that the ATC should have called the player's mother and family physician, not merely the team physician, after the family physician's evaluation to express her concerns and seek further discussion before the young man returned to the practice field.

Complicating matters were the facts that the family physician quickly settled separately and the team physician was protected from litigation by state law. This meant the ATC would have stood alone had the case gone to trial. The practice settled the claim for more than $300,000, which bought both the ATC and the practice that employed her full release from future prosecution.

The second case involved a PT who was employed by a physical therapy practice to provide treatment in patients' homes. The PT was sent to the home of 60-year-old woman who recently had had a stroke. In the course of providing an intervention, the PT asked the patient to undress and allegedly touched her inappropriately on her breast, stomach, and pubic area. A few days after the visit, the patient reported the incident to the police, who conducted an investigation that led to the PT's arrest. The PT ultimately pled no contest to the charges.

Allegations brought against the PT's employer included negligent hiring and negligent supervision. Practice officials responded that they had conducted a pre-employment background check on the PT that revealed no unethical or illegal behavior. A police investigation determined, however, that four prior accusations of sexual misconduct had been brought against the PT—three of them lodged by former patients. While it is possible that the person conducting the background check for the physical therapy practice was furnished with incorrect information, under the legal doctrine respondeat superior, the employer in this case nevertheless was deemed responsible for the actions of its employee. Given the nature of the allegations, the practice saw to it that the case was settled out of court—at a cost of approximately $100,000.

The Risks

These cases offer opportunities to consider how these physical therapy practices might better have prevented tragic outcomes for patients and also protected themselves from liability risk. It's important to note that, while outside observers can second-guess any decision to settle out of court, and while settling does not necessarily mean an individual or firm would have lost a case in court, the facts remain that in both of these cases, the practices involved and their professional liability insurers sized up the risks and deemed financial settlement the best option.

The first case points to the risks of using independent contractors and/or providing off-site services, and raises the following concerns for practices that enter into such arrangements:

❖ *Liability.* As part of the contracting process, physical therapy practices must consider whether they would be willing to have their liability insurance policy respond were a malpractice charge to be brought against an independent contractor with which the practice is working. Savvy contractors likely will raise this question as well, so it makes sense to be prepared. At the outset of any employment relationship, expectations in this area should be discussed and

liability awareness

employment contract language, if applicable, should be clear on the matter.

❖ *Employee orientation and oversight.* Just as proper orientation and oversight of onsite personnel is important, so, too, must employers sufficiently orient and oversee their offsite service providers. In this case, had the ATC been instructed during her orientation to report back to practice managers whenever she encountered difficult situations, and had a practice official maintained regular contact with her, the ATC may well have discussed the soccer player's situation with that individual—leading, perhaps, to more immediate and direct contact with the youth's family physician before the young man resumed regular activity with the team.

❖ *Vetting process.* It is unclear what steps, if any, the physical therapy practice took to vet the ATC before selecting her to represent the practice. While credentials are important, they don't ensure that a contractor is an appropriate representative of the practice. Conducting rigorous background and reference checks is important, as is engaging in a thorough interview process. There is evidence of thoughtfulness on the part of the ATC in this case, but perhaps another candidate for the job, properly vetted, might have performed better and prevented tragedy.

❖ *Legal protections.* This case highlights the need, before entering into any arrangements involving service provision to a school system, to determine whether any immunity or protection from liability is afforded under state law to health care professionals working with school athletic programs. If such protection is available, the next questions are which professions are covered and the extent of the protection (eg, complete immunity or a cap on damages).

The *second case* illustrates that a comprehensive risk management strategy must include effective personnel management practices and take into account professional and ethical considerations. These elements are key:

❖ *Human resources review.* A responsible practice examines its human resources processes and asks the following questions: Are applicant interviews conducted in a thorough manner? Does the practice seek several references for each applicant and insist on speaking with individuals who can substantively assess the applicant's abilities and professional behavior? Are those who conduct the reference checks for the practice properly trained to gather complete information and recognize "red flags"? Does the hiring process include contacting applicable physical therapy licensing boards and looking up the applicant in the National Practitioner Data Bank? (See resources box on page 37.) If answers to any of these questions falls short of a resounding "yes," the practice has work to do.

❖ *Employee orientation and oversight.* This case, like the first, illustrates the importance of properly orienting and overseeing all employees and contracted personnel. Responsible practices ask: How are employee competencies established—particularly those of people providing services offsite? Is there a mechanism for seeking patients' and clients' feedback on the care they have received? (Many general and physical therapy-specific resources are available to help ensure the effectiveness of orientation and oversight policies, processes, and

Resources

APTA. Core documents available at www.apta.org (click on "About APTA") include the APTA Vision for Physical Therapy 2020, the Code of Ethics, the Guide for Professional Conduct, and the Standards of Practice and the Criteria. Specific passages applicable to the cases profiled in this column include Principle 9 of the Code of Ethics ("A physical therapist shall protect the public and the profession from unethical, incompetent, and illegal acts") and Standards of Practice regarding administration of the physical therapy service (including establishment of written "personnel-related policies," position descriptions, and staff orientation procedures).

Additional resources from APTA include:

❖ Goals That Represent the 2004 Priorities of the American Physical Therapy Association. (Click on "APTA Governance" and "Goals and Mission" under "House of Delegates Policies.")

❖ **PT** articles. "Making the Match: A Look at the Many Aspects of Contracting" (November 2002) is available at www.apta.org. (Click on "Publications.") Other pertinent **PT** articles include "A Risk Consideration for Contract Staffing" (June 2000) and "Impacts and Implications of Employer Liability in a Physical Therapy Practice" (November 1998).

❖ Other APTA publications. These include *Business Skills in Physical Therapy: Legal Issues, A Normative Model of Physical Therapist Professional Education: Version* 2004, the *Guide to Physical Therapist Practice,* Revised 2nd ed, and *Risk Management for Physical Therapists: A Quick Reference.* (Click on "Store.")

❖ Ethics and Judicial Committee opinion. An opinion from April 2002 that is available by searching APTA's Web site covers reporting obligations with respect to "unethical, incompetent, or illegal acts."

❖ *Procedural Document on Disciplinary Action.* This document, BOD 03-04-11-23), is available on APTA's Web site.

❖ Legal aid. It may be helpful to consult an attorney familiar with state employment law and requirements. APTA members can get tips on connecting with a local attorney by searching membership benefits and services on the Association's Web site.

APTA chapters. Both the Health Policy and Administration Section and the Private Practice Section offer publications specific to business aspects of running a physical therapy practice. For additional information, visit www.aptahpa.org and www.ppsapta.org, respectively.

Federation of State Boards of Physical Therapy. Go to www.fsbpt.org and click on "Licensing Authorities" for contact information for each state board.

National Practitioner Data Bank. Go to www.npdb-hipdb.com for help in checking the background of prospective employees. The NPDB describes itself as "primarily an alert or flagging system intended to facilitate a comprehensive review of health care practitioners' professional credentials."

liability awareness

programs. See resources box.)

❖ **Disclosure.** It appears that the physical therapy practice in this case was the victim of poor background reporting by at least some of the PT's past employers, regardless of the ability or thoroughness of the person or people conducting the background checks. What is not clear is why this was the case. This scenario emphasizes the importance of keeping thorough employee records—including reasons for dismissal—and ensuring that those fielding background requests are sufficiently knowledgeable to do so and to reference all pertinent records. For guidance on ethical obligation to report unprofessional behavior, consult the April 2002 opinion of the APTA Ethics and Judicial Committee mentioned in the resources box on page 29. For information on legal obligation to report any such behavior, contact the Office of Counsel at APTA.

It is clear from these cases that properly managing non-clinical risk requires that owners, managers/supervisors, and administrators of PT practices of all sizes review and evaluate existing personal management plans and establish or modify paperwork, policies, and programs as necessary to maximize safety and minimize potential for incidents with serious human and economic consequences. Ⓟ

Rita Arriaga, PT, MS, is an associate clinical professor in the Graduate Program in Physical Therapy and the director of rehabilitation services at the University of California, San Francisco, and is a former chair of APTA's Committee on Risk Management and Member Benefits. She can be reached at 415/476-3453 or arriaga@itsa.ucsf.edu.

Do you have risk-management questions or concerns? Insights into what PTs need or want to know will help APTA educate members about the types of incidents occurring in the workplace and about appropriate risk-management techniques. Contact Jennifer Baker, director of APTA Risk Management and Member Benefit Services, at 800/999-2782, ext 3145, or jenniferbaker@apta.org.

The information presented here is not to be interpreted as specific legal advice for any particular provider or practice. Questions about the legal implications of matters related to personnel management—paperwork, policies, and programs—should be directed to legal counsel retained by the provider or practice.

liability awareness

by Rita Arriaga, PT, MS

Stories From the Front—
Part One: Burns

A real-life scenario illustrates some basic risk-management principles.

For the fourth straight year, **PT** is featuring a three-part Liability Awareness series presenting cases adapted from the APTA-endorsed professional liability insurance claims history. We pick up the series this month with the first of three case studies.

The following scenario illustrates the need for physical therapists (PTs) to manage risks up front in an effort to avoid burns, and to respond immediately and appropriately should burns occur, in order to minimize health consequences and professional liability.

As you read the scenario, consider these questions:

❖ What elements increase the PT's liability risk?

❖ What risk-management techniques could have been used to reduce that risk?

This case involved a 58-year-old retired US serviceman who presented with a tear of the medial collateral ligament of his left knee that he had sustained in a fall. The patient had a history of knee problems that had resulted in repair of the medial meniscus. On the date in question, the PT administered several interventions to the patient's knee, including a hot pack. After applying the hot pack the PT left the room to attend to other patients. He did not leave a bell or other signaling device with the patient, nor did he instruct a physical therapist assistant (PTA) to monitor the patient.

After approximately 15 minutes the patient began feeling discomfort and called out for assistance. Neither the PT nor any clinic personnel heard him, however. The PT returned 45 minutes after application,

removed the hot pack, and noted redness but expressed no particular concern to the patient about what he saw at any time during the remainder of the session. The PT completed the rest of his interventions and sent the patient home with instructions to return to the PT's office in three days.

Four hours after the visit, however, the patient returned to the physical therapy office with a persistent red mark on the knee to which the hot pack had been administered. The PT did not examine the knee, but did advise the patient to put ice on it and seek the attention of a physician. The PT did not follow up in any manner to ensure that the patient had taken this advice.

Two days after the incident the patient sought medical attention. He was running a low-grade fever and presented with a large open blister with swelling and erythema. The physician diagnosed cellulitis from a superficial burn that had become infected. She prescribed antibiotics and a salve.

Because the knee was sore, the patient cancelled the appointment with the PT that had been scheduled for the following day. The PT did not speak with the patient at the time of or subsequent to this cancellation. Over the course of the next 3 days the wound became more swollen and discolored, and the fever persisted. On the third day (5 days after the incident), the physician admitted the patient to the hospital. He remained in the hospital, on antibiotics, for 10 days.

After discharge from the hospital the patient continued to experience swelling and tenderness to palpation in the area of the burn. He was having difficulty with

activities of daily living such as bathing, sitting, sleeping, walking, and climbing stairs.

The patient filed a lawsuit against the PT, stating that the PT had failed to properly monitor the application of the hot pack, failed to respond appropriately upon removal of the hot pack, and subsequently failed to communicate appropriately with both the patient and the physician.

Investigation of the situation showed that, in addition to having left the hot pack on for too long and having failed to check on the patient or direct a PTA to do so, these factors were present:

❖ The PT had positioned the patient's knee on the hot pack (rather than laying the hot pack on the knee).

❖ The PT had not documented his initial examination of the sensation of the knee.

❖ The PT had failed to institute an effective system for monitoring and transmitting information about the water temperature in the hydrocollator, which was found to have been too hot.

Now, turn the page for commentary on this scenario from a risk-management perspective, including a table summarizing factors that created risk and some of the APTA House of Delegates (HOD) and Board of Directors (BOD) standards, policies, positions, and guidelines that specifically address them.

> The information here is not to be interpreted as specific legal advice for any particular provider. Personal advice can be given only by personal legal counsel, based on applicable state and federal law.

liability awareness

The PT failed to document the knee's sensation during the initial examination.

The *Guidelines for Physical Therapy Documentation* (BOD-03-00-22-54) instructs PTs to examine and document their findings.

The PT lacked good judgment and did not sufficiently serve the patient by failing to reexamine the knee.

Principle 4 of the *Code of Ethics* (HOD 06-00-12-23) states that, "A physical therapist shall exercise sound professional judgment." Further, the "Reexamination" section of *Standards of Practice for Physical Therapy* (HOD 06-00-11-22) states that "the physical therapist reexamines the patient/client as necessary during an episode of care," and that reexamination "identifies ongoing patient/client needs." In this case, reexamining the knee was a necessary aspect of sound practice. By failing to do so, the PT did not serve the patient's "ongoing needs."

The PT failed to properly communicate instructions to or concern for the patient, and to follow up with the physician.

The PT's apparent lack of concern for the patient, meanwhile, violates Principle 1 of the *Code of Ethics*, which states, "A physical therapist shall respect the rights and dignity of all individuals and shall provide compassionate care." Unintended accidents do occur, even when we have maintained good practice standards. When they happen, it is our duty to assist the patient in receiving appropriate care. In this case, the PT failed to demonstrate his concern for the patient's health by his lack of follow-up. Additionally, the PT's failure to communicate with the physician runs counter to *Professional Practice Relationships* (HOD 06-94-35-46), which states that APTA "endorses a collaborative, collegial practice relationship between PTs and all other health care providers."

The PT failed to properly instruct and monitor the patient during the hot pack application.

The "Provision of Services" section of *Standards of Practice for Physical Therapy* states that the information provided to patients/clients "clearly describes the proposed intervention." Obviously, however, the patient received little information about the hot pack procedure, because he wasn't even aware that he was free to remove it if it caused him discomfort.

Among the many APTA standards, policies, positions, and guidelines that are applicable here, in addition to the aforementioned Principle 4 of the *Code of Ethics*, are patient right number 10 under *Access To, Admission To, and Patients' Rights Within Physical Therapy Services* (HOD 06-93-12-22) which reads, "Expectation of safety in the provision of services and safety in regard to the equipment and physical environment"; and *Standards of Practice for Physical Therapy* provisions regarding intervention ("provided under the ongoing direct care of or under the supervision of the physical therapist") and policies and procedures ("the physical therapy service has written policies and procedures" that apply to "equipment maintenance" and "environmental safety"). In this case, equipment and safety procedures were not followed, and ongoing direct or supervised care was not provided—placing the patient at risk of injury and the PT at risk of liability.

This case exposes a variety of ways in which the PT created risk.

First, the thoroughness of the PT's initial examination and evaluation, in terms of checking the knee's sensation, could not be determined because the PT did not document those findings. When the case was examined, it was found that the PT had performed the appropriate systems review for practice pattern 4D in the *Guide to Physical Therapist Practice* (Impaired Joint Mobility, Motor Function, Muscle Performance, and Range of Motion Associated With Connective Tissue Dysfunction) and had checked peripheral nerve integrity, finding no deficit. By failing to document that finding, however, the PT left himself open to liability because the reviewer had no way of knowing whether sensation was examined.

Second, the PT lacked good judgment and did not sufficiently serve the patient by failing, both after removing the hot pack and when the patient returned 4 hours later, to reexamine the knee. Had he done so, he might have noted signs or symptoms that would have alerted him to a more serious problem.

The PT's third behavior that created risk was his failure to properly communicate instructions to or concern for the patient upon application and removal of the hot pack, upon examination 4 hours after the incident, or subsequently. If, for example, the PT had provided, and instructed the patient in the use of, a signaling device or had simply told the patient that he was free to remove the hot pack himself if it was giving him discomfort, the burn might well have been avoided. And what would have happened if the patient hadn't seen the physician as promptly as he did? The PT could have called the patient the day following the incident to find out if he had indeed seen his physician. By failing to follow up with the patient to emphasize the importance of seeking medical care, the PT might have contributed to making the incident worse.

The PT also would have been well-advised to have contacted the referring physician, both to inform her of the situation and to determine the patient's status. The PT would then have

continued on page 38 ▶▶▶

liabilityawareness

carefully documented in his records his instructions to the patient and his communication with the physician.

Finally, the facts that the patient was left alone with his knee on the hot pack for 45 minutes and that the water in the hydrocollator was too hot indicate serious issues of professional judgment and patient management, in that appropriate intervention and monitoring procedures of both patient and equipment were not performed. **(PT)**

Rita Arriaga, PT, MS, is an Associate Clinical Professor in the Graduate Program in Physical Therapy and the Director of Rehabilitation Services at the University of California, San Francisco, and is a former chair of APTA's Committee on Risk Management Services and Member Benefits. She can be reached at 415/476-3453 or arriaga@itsa.ucsf.edu.

Do you have risk-management questions or concerns? Insights into what PTs need or want to know will help APTA's efforts to educate members about the types of incidents occurring in the workplace and about appropriate risk-management techniques. Contact Jennifer Baker, director of APTA Risk Management and Member Benefit Services, at 800/999-2782, ext 3145, or jenniferbaker@apta.org.

Suggested Readings

American Physical Therapy Association. Board of Directors policies. Available at www.apta.org/governance/ governance_5/BODpolicies. Accessed November 29, 2001.

American Physical Therapy Association. Ethics and legal issues in physical therapy. Available at www.apta.org/ PT_Practice/ethics_pt. Accessed November 29, 2001.

American Physical Therapy Association. House of Delegates policies. Available at www.apta.org/governance/HOD/ governance_10. Accessed November 29, 2001.

A Normative Model of Physical Therapist Professional Education: Version 2000. Alexandria, Va: American Physical Therapy Association; 2000.

Guide to Physical Therapist Practice. 2nd ed. *Phys Ther.* 2001;81:9-744.

Risk Management for Physical Therapists: A Quick Reference. Alexandria, Va: American Physical Therapy Association; 2001.

LEGAL BRIEFS

Vicarious Liability

The term "vicarious liability" addresses the circumstances under which an employer bears indirect legal and financial responsibility for the negligence of another person, usually an employee. The concept of vicarious liability dates back to ancient times and in legal circles is often referred to by its Latin name, *respondeat superior* ("Let the master answer").

An employer's indirect responsibility for an employee's negligence does not excuse the party who is actually negligent from financial responsibility. The tortfeasor is always personally responsible for the consequences of his or her own negligent conduct. The concept of vicarious liability, however, gives the tort victim another party to make a claim against or sue. When an employer is required to pay a settle-

Second, the employer earns a profit from the activities of the employees and should bear responsibility for employees whose activities generate revenue. Third, the employer is better equipped than the patient to bear the risk of loss—through economic-loss allocation (i.e., purchasing insurance, pricing of services) as part of the cost of doing business.

Vicarious Liability for Nonemployees

An employer may be held vicariously liable for wrongdoing by those other than employees. In the relatively few cases addressing the issue, courts have imposed vicarious liability on hospitals for the negligence of volunteers, equating unpaid volunteers with employees. For this reason, hospitals and clinics using the services of volunteers should carry liability insurance for volunteers' activities. Another area of vicarious liability involves general

---

The basic rule of vicarious liability is that an employer is indirectly liable for the negligent conduct of an employee when the wrongdoer is acting within the scope of his or her employment at the time the act of negligence occurred. The wrongdoer is always personally responsible for the consequences of his or her own conduct.

The basic rule of vicarious liability is that an employer is indirectly liable for the negligent conduct of an employee when the wrongdoer ("tortfeasor") is acting within the scope of his or her employment at the time the act of negligence occurred. Therefore, when a hospital-based physical therapist or physical therapist assistant is alleged to have committed professional negligence in treating a patient, the hospital employing that physical therapist or physical therapist assistant may be required to pay a money judgement if negligence is proven in court.

ment or judgement for the negligence of an employee, the employer then has the legal right to seek indemnification from the employee for this outlay.

Is it fair to impose liability on an employer who is innocent of any wrongdoing? In balancing the equities between an innocent victim of negligence and an innocent employer of a negligent employee, the legal system weighs in favor of the victim of negligence. There are several good reasons for this. First, it is the employer, not the patient, who can control the quality of care rendered by the employees.

partnerships, wherein each partner is considered legally to be the agent of the other partners. Each partner is vicariously liable for the other partners' negligent acts when those acts are committed within the scope of activities of the partnership.

Exceptions

There are several important exceptions to vicarious liability. Although an employer may be liable for employees' negligence, the employer typically is not liable for intentional misconduct committed by employees. An example

---

By Ronald W. Scott, JD, LLM, PT

of intentional misconduct in the physical therapy setting would be commission of sexual battery on a patient by a hospital-based physical therapist.

Another exception to vicarious liability concerns independent contractors—for example, contract physical therapists working in a health care facility. The legal system distinguishes employees, for whom an employer is legally responsible, from contractors, for whom an employer generally is not legally responsible. This distinction is based primarily on the degree of the control the employer exercises over the physical details of the professional's work product. In some jurisdictions, courts hold employers vicariously liable for independent contractors' negligence under the theory of "apparent agency." When a contract physical therapist in a clinic is indistinguishable from an employee physical therapist in the eyes of patients, for example, the legal system may treat the contract therapist as an employee for purposes of vicarious liability. Therefore, in states in which apparent agency applies, the employer should consider taking steps to ensure that patients know when they are being treated by contract personnel rather than by employees (e.g., requiring contractors to wear name tags that identify them as contract personnel).

Direct Liability

A hospital or clinic in some instances may be directly or primarily liable for employees' or contractors' conduct. Such liability is independent of any vicarious liability that also might apply. An employer is directly liable under the legal concepts of negligent selection and retention, for example, for the wrongful actions of employees or contractors whom the employer reasonably should have 1) rejected for employment or 2) discharged from employment.

Under law, hospitals and private clinics have certain responsibilities that they may not attribute to employees or independent contractors, including monitoring the quality of patient care and ensuring patient and visitor safety in the facilities. Such responsibilities are termed "nondelegable duties."

Hospitals and health care clinics that employ physical therapists, physical therapist assistants, and contract personnel and that use the services of volunteers may be vicariously or indirectly liable for the negligent conduct of these persons. In addition, employers may incur primary responsibility (independent of vicarious liability for employees' wrongdoing) for their own negligent selection or retention of employees or for negligent failure to monitor patient care or to take reasonable steps to ensure patient safety on the premises. For state-specific advice, consult your facility or personal legal advisor. **CM**

Ronald W. Scott, JD, LLM, PT, is a captain in the Army Medical Specialist Corps and chief physical therapist and legal advisor at Bayne-Jones Army Community Hospital, Ft. Polk, LA.

This article is fourth in a series of five articles focusing on the legal standard of care; informed consent; Good Samaritan immunity from legal responsibility; vicarious or indirect liability for the negligence of employees, volunteers, and others; and other trends in health care malpractice law.

This series is not intended as legal advice for any specific practitioner. Legal advice can be given only by your personal legal counsel, based on the law of your state or on federal law, as applicable.

SUGGESTED READINGS

Ford, H.R. 1991. Effective delegation—Part II. *Physical Therapy Forum* March 22:8-10.

Pennsylvania adopts corporate liability for hospitals. 1991. *Health Care Facility Management* 27(July 11):1.

Scott, R. 1990. *Health Care Malpractice: A Primer on Legal Issues.* Thorofare, NJ, Slack Inc, pp. 68-73.

IN PRACTICE
by Gloria J Young, EdD, PT

Excellent Care is Not Enough

Some guidelines for avoiding malpractice exposure.

a physical therapist assistant (PTA) using cervical traction to treat a patient with chronic headaches left the treatment booth after set-up. When she returned, she discovered the patient had expired. Autopsy showed a massive heart attack.[1]

The physical therapist (PT) has a 1 in 10 chance of being sued by a patient for malpractice. As of 1990, 21% of physical therapy malpractice claims resulted from the actions of a physical therapy aide or PTA.[2] The above case—reported to a professional liability insurance company—is extreme, and whether it will result in a malpractice suit remains unknown; however, it underscores certain elements crucial to risk management.

Did the PTA and the supervising PT establish positive patient relations? Positive rapport, both with the patient and the patient's significant others, may be the best way to avoid malpractice exposure.[2,3] Guidelines include never leaving patients unattended; discussing procedures with patients and obtaining their consent; working within the scope of your skill, training, and expertise; always being accessible to your patients (eg, through an answering service or beeper); fostering realistic expectations ("under-promising" and "over-delivering"); ensuring that support personnel are supervised; and maintaining equipment.

If positive rapport had been established in this case, the family may have readily conceded that the actions of the PTA and the PT in no way contributed to the patient's death.

Was high-quality care ensured? APTA's *Standards of Practice for Physical Therapy* (1992) is viewed by many authorities as *the* tool for assessing the quality of physical therapy care. With the advent of specialist certification, the actions of PTs may be measured against the *specialist* level of care. Every department or practice should have a *written* plan for ensuring high-quality care.

Did the supervising PT communicate a well-documented history and precautions to the PTA? The medical record serves as evidence of the standard of care and may be a PT's best defense—or, if incomplete, a PT's worst enemy.

This patient's history may have revealed cardiovascular problems (eg, arrhythmias, aneur-

isms, blood clots, complaints of chest pain), indicating a need for close monitoring of pulse and blood pressure before, during, and after treatment. Did problems with other major organ systems exist? What medications was the patient taking? What types of diagnostic tests had been done? What were the results? What were the implications for physical therapy?

Of all malpractice claims against PTs, 10% involve "failure to refer" or "failure to diagnose."[4] If the medical background and patient questionnaire information are inadequate, consult with physicians and other colleagues. Do not be afraid to refer a patient to a specialist.

The initial physical therapy evaluation should establish quantifiable baseline data:[5]

Muscle strength. In this case, muscle weakness—especially in the sternocleidomastoid, trapezius, latissimus dorsi, and paravertebral muscles—may have indicated cardiovascular problems. The PT then may have prescribed deep-breathing exercises and a 12-minute walk test.

Range of motion (ROM). Weakness in the upper extremities and in the accessory muscles used in breathing typically limits active ROM; stiffness of the trunk typically affects breathing. Active ROM exercises or trunk extension exercises may have been indicated.

Function (eg, bed mobility, transfer ability, ambulation). Decreased exercise tolerance may have indicated cardiopulmonary deficiency. An appropriate exercise program, such as isotonic exercises for the lower extremities or a walking program or both, could have been designed.

Muscle tone, proprioception, and posture. Poor abdominal muscle tone may affect both inspiratory and expiratory abilities. Poor oral muscle tone may result in airway obstruction. Decreased proprioception may require neurological techniques and balance and gait training. In this case, posture screening may have indicated cardiopulmonary problems. Observation of the chest wall may have revealed abnormalities—kyphoscoliosis, asymmetry in levels of scapulae, flaring of the lower rib—the severity of which should have been documented.

Activities-of-daily-living (ADL) status. The patient's ADL status may have alerted the PT to

decreased exercise tolerance and to debility and shortness of breath.

Pain. Patient complaints of pain in the chest, shoulder, or back also may have indicated cardiopulmonary problems.

Using a thorough medical history and quantifiable assessment, the PT and the patient can set realistic long- and short-term goals with clearly expressed time frames (eg, "increase strength by one grade in right quads in 6 weeks").

Once the incident occurred, was everything done that could be done? All unusual incidents occurring during patient care must be immediately recorded and reported to the supervisor, administrator, and facility risk manager. Departmental policies and procedures, developed with input from support staff, should address when to write incident reports, what to include, and to whom reports should be submitted. To help ensure the defensibility of the provider's case, an early, thorough investigation should be conducted either by a risk manager or by outside counsel.

Physical therapy is delivered by humans, and humans make mistakes. Managing risks involves minimizing the adverse effects of these mistakes. If the PTA and the supervising PT established positive patient relations and used effective documentation techniques, they practiced not only good risk management techniques but good physical therapy. **PT**

Gloria J Young, EdD, PT, is President, Sunbelt Physical Therapy, PC, Birmingham, Ala. She is a member of APTA's Committee on Insurance and Member Benefit Services.

This column is not intended as legal or financial advice for any specific practitioner.

References
1 Hibbeler D. Brief narratives on open claims, interstate insurance group, actual examples. [Identity Removed.] Chicago Interstate Insurance Co; 1988.
2 Horting M. Understanding professional liability. *Clinical Management.* 1989;9(6):40-46.
3 Horting M. Understanding your professional liability insurance plan. *Risk Management Resource Guide.* American Physical Therapy Association; 1990.
4 Jones S. Medical malpractice and professional liability insurance: the need for physical therapists to be informed. *Orthopedic Practice.* 1992;4(4):11-13.
5 Lewis C. *Documentation: The PT's Course on Successful Reimbursement.* Professional Health Educators, Inc. Bethesda, Md; 1987.

by Ron Scott, MSPT, JD, OCS

Physical Therapy Malpractice Update II

PT *presents recent malpractice case reports and commentary on their outcomes and impact.*

This column summarizes three recently reported physical therapy malpractice legal cases. The cases address the management of patients and clients who are receiving care as a result of a workers' compensation claim and the processing of litigation documents by physical therapist-defendants in health care malpractice lawsuits. Legal terms are highlighted in *italics* and defined or described in lay terms in parentheses.

By way of brief review, the legitimate legal bases for imposition of health care/physical therapy malpractice liability include:

❖ *professional negligence* (objectively substandard care),

❖ intentional wrongful conduct (eg, sexual battery committed upon a patient or client),

❖ breach of an express contractual therapeutic promise made to a patient or client, and

❖ *absolute* or *strict liability* (without regard for culpability) for patient injuries emanating from dangerously defective care-related products (strict product liability) or abnormally dangerous clinical intervention activities.

To date, there have been approximately 30 physical therapy malpractice civil cases reported in the legal literature since 1960.[1,2] One reported physical therapy-related civil case dealt, not with alleged PT malpractice, but with legal *discovery* (the turning over of information to a party in a legal case) of a PT-initiated incident report by a product manufacturer in a case brought against the manufacturer by a patient under the therapist's care.[3]

In virtually every reported physical therapy malpractice case, the charges lodged against PTs by patients were grounded exclusively in alleged professional negligence, to the exclusion of all other potential bases of liability. Appellate courts ruled in patients' favor in half of these cases, either by affirming trial court judgments or by remanding cases to trial courts for further proceedings. No one knows the precise number of physical therapy malpractice legal cases, because the vast majority are settled, not appealed, or abandoned by plaintiff/patients prior to trial. Thus, the information is not disseminated to the general public.

The following section briefly summarizes three of the most recently reported physical therapy malpractice appellate cases and offers commentary on suggested clinical risk-management strategies and tactics to limit malpractice exposure based on the case holdings.

Moretto v Samaritan Health Systems. In this case,[4] a patient who had knee surgery after an industrial injury fell from a wheeled stool while undergoing physical therapy. The patient's PT allegedly directed him to sit on the stool while the therapist applied a knee brace and shoe to his involved leg. As a result of the fall, the patient sustained a lumbar disk herniation. He filed suit, claiming professional negligence on the part of the PT.

The attorney for the hospital where the PT worked won dismissal of the case at the pretrial stage of adjudication, successfully arguing that the patient failed to obtain *assignment* (ownership) of his potential claim against the therapist and hospital from his employer's workers' compensation insurance carrier, which was required because the back injury was part of a compensable workers' compensation claim (ie, the knee injury). The attorney also argued that the patient had failed to file his lawsuit in a timely manner under the state's *statute of limitations* (time frame for filing a formal lawsuit). The patient appealed.

The appellate court reversed the award of summary judgment in favor of the PT and hospital, concluding that a shortened statute of limitations for secondary injuries related to industrial injuries that are the subject of workers' compensation claims did not apply to this case. The shorter time clock was inapplicable, the court ruled, because the back injury did not aggravate the work-related knee injury, and the patient did not need to obtain permission from his employer to sue the PT and hospital for their independent alleged health care malpractice. The case was *remanded* (sent back) to the trial court for further proceedings.

This case raises the following practice issues: the nature of workers' compensation claims and attendant risks of liability exposure associated with caring for such clients; health care malpractice legal procedures, especially concerning summary judgment; and the statute of limitations for initiating legal action against a PT for alleged malpractice.

Greenberg v Orthosport Inc. In this case,[5] a patient who sustained a lumbar spine injury at work was undergoing a functional capacity evaluation for possible return to work. The patient claimed that she sustained a neck injury from the test and sued her PT for malpractice. The trial-level court awarded pre-trial *summary judgment* in favor of the PT on the grounds that the state workers' compensation system provided the exclusive remedy for patient's alleged evaluation-related neck injury.

The patient appealed the adverse decision against her. The appellate court reversed, opining that summary judgment is a drastic measure depriving a plaintiff of her right to redress at trial. The appeals court ruled that, because the alleged physical therapy malpractice was non–work-related, it could be pursued judicially by the plaintiff outside of the workers' compensation system.

Like the first case, this case raises concern about the management of a patient receiving care as a result of a workers' compensation claim or other litigation. Because the patient is involved in pursuing a claim, the PT has to be especially diligent with documentation. Oral statements made by such patients to professional and support personnel that typically would not be recorded should be documented in the patient's file.

Hebebrand v Arrien. In this case,[6] which involved an unspecified health care malpractice action brought by a patient against multiple primary care providers, including a PT, the patient asked the trial court to *strike* (remove from the case) the defenses pleaded by the PT for the alleged failure of the defendants to respond to the plaintiff's notice of intent to initiate litiga-

tion, a response required by the state's medical malpractice statute. The appellate court refused to strike the defendants' defenses to the plaintiff's case, as requested. However, the court did underscore the trial court's authority to strike the PT's response in the case and determined that the PT failed to comply with the requirement to conduct a "reasonable investigation" (prior to litigation) of the patient's claim.

This case illustrates the need to apprise attorneys immediately of possible legal claims, and to be responsive to legal documents, as required by law. Whenever a PT receives any legal document, he or she must carefully review it and consult with legal counsel to proceed. One cannot merely ignore legal papers.

Discussion

Although the number of reported and nonreported physical therapy malpractice cases remains relatively small compared to medical malpractice cases involving physicians and to civil litigation cases in general, it is still imperative for PTs'—and patients'—physical, mental, and financial well-being that prudent clinical risk management be practiced to limit malpractice exposure to the degree feasible. Effective risk-management skills must be introduced during entry-level health professional education and reinforced throughout clinicians' professional careers via continuing legal education or other appropriate means.

These recent physical therapy malpractice cases reinforce the need for PTs, physical therapist assistants, clinical managers,

liabilityawareness

and facility administrators to keep abreast of case law reports and changes in the legal status quo. In particular, it may be prudent for clinicians to maintain relatively formal professional relationships with patients and clients receiving care as a result of a claim or litigation, particularly workers' compensation cases. This includes the risk-management measure of always creating and maintaining accurate, comprehensive, objective, and timely documentation. Records should include both patient intervention documentation and non-care-related office memoranda or memoranda for record, as appropriate, to record *declarations against* (self) *interest* (ie, statements that adversely affect a patient's legal, business, or other interests) made by patients or clients regarding their conditions. Similarly, physical therapist-malpractice defendants must respond appropriately, and in a timely manner, to *legal process* (eg, summons or complaint) initiated by patients and others against them.

Through effective liability risk management, the interests of providers, health care organizations and systems, and patients and clients are best served, as is the compelling societal interest in minimizing health care malpractice litigation, with all of its attendant costs. ⓟ

Ron Scott, MSPT, JD, OCS, *is Associate Professor and Chair, Physical Therapy Department, Lebanon Valley College, Annville, Pennsylvania. He can be reached via e-mail at r_scott@lvc.edu.*

References

1. Scott RW. Malpractice update. *PT—Magazine of Physical Therapy.* 1996;4(4): 69-70.
2. Scott RW. *Health Care Malpractice: A Primer on Legal Issues for Professionals.* New York, NY: McGraw-Hill Inc; 1999.
3. *Community Hospitals of Indianapolis v Medtronic Inc Neuro Div,* 594 NE 2d 448 (Ind App 1 Dist, Apr 15, 1992).
4. *Moretto v Samaritan Health Systems,* No 1 CA-CV 97-0079 (C App Arizona, Oct 30, 1997).
5. *Greenberg v Orthosport Inc,* No 1-93-3379 (App C Ill, June 12, 1996).
6. *Hebebrand v Arrien,* No 95-3601 (Dist C App Fla, May 15, 1996).

by David W Clifton, Jr, PT

Legal Issues in Peer Review and Utilization Review—Part 1

To understand the legal debates surrounding the UR and peer review industry, you need to know some basic principles.

The development of a new industry is bound to raise issues for debate, many of which have to be decided in the legal arena. Legal cases tend to follow—and in many cases, shape—any industry's growth. The utilization review (UR) industry still is in its relative infancy; however, under managed care, payers' use of outside organizations for peer review and utilization review is certain to grow. Recent court decisions, such as the *Fox v Health Net of California* case in which a jury awarded nearly $90 million to the estate of a deceased enrollee of a health maintenance organization (HMO) that had rendered a denial decision for bone marrow transplant, have sent shock waves through the managed care industry and are certain to force many payers to rethink their current strategies for assessing claims. As UR evolves commensurate with the development of managed care, it also will be tested and shaped by legal challenges and precedents.

No Guarantee of a Risk-free Environment

There are many potential risks associated with attempting to ensure high-quality care *and* control costs. Determining whether care that is provided or proposed is medically necessary, reasonable, and appropriate—and thus, reimbursable—requires the best judgment of the reviewer and a delicate balance between economic rationality and humanitarian concern. Unfortunately, in today's litigious society, exercising extreme caution,

using common sense and appropriate review standards, and striving for fairness offer no guarantees.

In both peer review and UR, there are risks for all stakeholders. *Patients* may have to bear financial responsibility for payment for health care services for which reimbursement is denied. *Providers* may be denied reimbursement for services rendered. *Payers* may be subject to claims of acting in bad faith. And *reviewers* may be accused of making treatment decisions that are tantamount to practicing medicine.

Who is Responsible for What

To appreciate the basis for debate, it is necessary to understand the different contractual relationships between the parties involved. The patient (typically the insured), the provider, the payer (an insurer, a third-party administrator, or a self-funded employer), and the reviewer each may owe a duty or duties to one or more of the other parties. These duties include not only legal duties, but also professional and ethical duties. For example:

• *The provider* owes a number of duties to the patient. One is the professional and ethical obligation to provide care that meets the practice standards of the provider's profession and that "does no harm." Another is the legal duty to provide only care that the provider is authorized by law to perform. In addition, the provider may owe a duty to continue to provide care to a patient once he or

she has agreed to treat that patient, and violation of that duty may be considered patient abandonment.

The determination of whether a provider breached his or her duty to a patient frequently rests on whether care was rendered within the *legal standard of care*, which frequently is formulated by comparing the care provided with care that would be provided by a reasonable peer in good standing in the provider's community or in a community similar to the provider's, acting under the same or similar circumstances as that provider did.[1]

Another duty that the provider may owe to the patient can be viewed as a "business" duty that involves reimbursement issues (eg, providing only medically necessary and reasonable care as it is defined by the payer). Unfortunately, this duty sometimes may conflict with the duty to provide care within the legal standard. Numerous legal cases have arisen over this point, and one of these cases will be explored in the next installment of this column.

The provider also has a business responsibility to provide the payer and the reviewer with documentation (after obtaining the patient's consent to release of information) that supports the rationale for treatment and that documents outcomes that reflect the necessity and appropriateness of an intervention, given the diagnosis.

• *The insured* may be responsible for sharing financial risk for the cost of health care with the payer in the form of copayments and deductibles.

• *The payer* has a contractual (and thus, legal) obligation to the insured or the enrollee to finance (or to arrange financing for) the provision of medically necessary, reasonable, and appropriate medical services in accordance with the terms, conditions, and exclusions of the insurance policy or employee benefit plan. The payer also has a business obligation to the insured or enrollee (and a legal *right*) to investigate claims to ensure that only medically necessary and reasonable services are provided to the persons covered by its plan. Under this business obligation, the payer must make a good-faith attempt to protect the interest of the insured pool from extravagant costs that would be reflected in premium increases.

It is this effort to contain costs that in part has been responsible for the rise of managed care and, with it, peer review and UR. Gosfield[2] discussed payers' recent shift from simple cost containment to "value purchasing" and ensuring "effectiveness" of care, terms that signify a combination of attempts to control

costs, provide appropriate services, and obtain outcomes of an "acceptable" quality. She stated that this shift from retrospective to prospective management means that traditional arguments against "certain administratively burdensome programs," arguments that "focus only on the cost incurred in their implementation, fall on increasingly deaf ears." In fact, UR and utilization management (UM) have become the norm, not the exception.

• *The reviewer's* duties depend on the nature of the contract between the reviewer and the payer. Referrals for peer review and UR traditionally have been generated by insurance companies and employers. However, provider-generated requests for review are increasing at a rapid pace, thanks to the growth of independent provider associations, preferred provider organizations, and physician-hospital organizations. Many of these entities are responding to concerns (typically expressed by payers) that internal peer review provided by a network is akin to the fox not only guarding but designing the chicken coop. Providers increasingly seem to view independent review-

ers in the same "objective, outside party" light as does the payer community. In fact, many of the automated review criteria that are now available (see "Review Criteria: Cookbook Medicine or Professional Tool?", October) are used by both payers and providers.

The essential duty of the reviewer is to render an opinion, within reasonable medical or professional certainty, based on the facts of a case as he or she interprets and understands them. The reviewer may or may not have fiduciary responsibility for final disposition of claims (eg, the authority to make outright reimbursement or denial decisions). In circumstances in which final authority for reimbursement decisions rests with the payer, the reviewer's opinions are nonbinding; the payer may choose either to follow or to disregard the recommendations of the reviewer.

Some Sources of Debate

According to Gosfield,[2] a major source of contention with UR centers around the issue of determining what constitutes "medically necessary" care. The term "medically necessary," stated Gosfield, is "a woefully inadequate phrase to describe an appropriate standard of performance." This is a critical issue, because much of UR and UM focuses on ascertaining whether services proposed or rendered are medically necessary. And it raises the question of whether a reviewer who does not have the same educational or experiential background as the provider whose care is being reviewed is in a position to determine the "medical necessity" of that care.

Generally speaking, reviewers base their judgments on the clinical information and documentation provided by the insurer and the provider. The care that has been provided or proposed is then assessed according to review criteria, which may be based on regional or national practice standards or guidelines, and the reviewers draw conclusions regarding necessity and appropriateness of care. In the absence of any viable review criteria or standards (which, unfortunately, is extremely common), the reviewer's clinical experience, intuition, and common sense should prevail.

From a business standpoint, the reviewer's primary duty certainly is owed to the entity that requests the review, be it the payer or provider. But what about the *patient*? Does a health professional who is serving as a peer reviewer owe a duty—either business, professional, ethical, or legal—to the patient? And if the reviewer's contractual relationship with the payer gives that reviewer authority to approve or deny reimbursement for treatment, does that change the nature of any duty owed?

Questions such as these increasingly are being raised in legal and ethical debates to determine the scope of various parties' responsibilities under peer review, UR, and other areas of managed care. Part 2 of "Legal Issue in Utilization Review" will examine some of these cases and explore the impact that legal challenges are having on how UR and peer review is performed in this country.

David W Clifton, Jr, PT, is President, Disability Management Associates Inc, Springfield, Pa. He has 14 years of experience in the field of UR.

References

1   Scott R. *Health Care Malpractice*. Thorofare, NJ: SLACK Inc; 1990.

2   Gosfield A. Value purchasing and effectiveness: legal implications. In: Gosfield A. *Health Law Handbook*. Deerfield, Ill: Clark Boardman Company [Div of Thomson Legal Publishing Inc]; 1991:186.

Suggested Readings

Clifton D. Risk management in work therapy. *Orthopedic Physical Therapy Clinics*. 1992;J(1):168.

Melbinger M, Kalish G. Avoiding litigation over managed care decisions. *Risk Management*. 1994;October:19.

The information in this article should not be interpreted as specific legal advice for any particular practitioner. The author is not an attorney. Personal advice can only be given by personal legal counsel, based on applicable state and federal law. The reader is encouraged to seek qualified legal advice relative to the issues discussed herein.

UTILIZATION REVIEW

by   David   W   Clifton,   Jr,   PT

Legal Issues in Peer Review and Utilization Review—Part 2

Part 2 of an exploration of some of the legal issues surrounding the UR and peer review industry.

*i*n *"Legal Issues in Utilization Review and Peer Review Part 1" (December 1995), the author presented some basic principles of utilization review (UR) and peer review as an aid to understanding the legal debates that have an impact on the UR and peer review industry. To recap:*

There are risks for all stakeholders in UR and peer review. Providers may be denied reimbursement for services rendered. Payers may be subject to claims of acting in "bad faith." And reviewers may be accused of making treatment decisions that are tantamount to practicing medicine.

In addition, each of these parties may owe a number of professional, ethical, or legal duties to one or more of the other parties, including the provider's duties to provide medically necessary and reasonable care that is within legal standards, the payer's duty to finance the provision of that care, and the reviewer's duty to render an opinion based on the medical necessity and reasonableness of care. This month, those principles are applied to actual legal cases that have had an impact on how UR and peer review is performed in this country.

In a strange irony, as each new case shapes and reshapes the UR and peer review processes, the legal system serves in a quality assurance function for an industry that is itself involved in quality assurance! Ultimately, all stakeholders have something to learn from each case, and the review process is enriched by the experience. Below, two cases that are widely considered "watershed cases":

Wickline v California, 183 Cal App 3rd 1175, 231 Cal Rptr 560, 727 P2d 753 (1985)

This case ushered in a new era in terms of how UR companies view preauthorization of services. A patient with vascular disease was granted a 4-day stay in the hospital by the reviewer for the medical assistance program of the state of California. She then was discharged and developed complications leading to the amputation of a leg. The patient sued the medical assistance program and initially was awarded damages of $500,000 based on her premature hospital discharge. The case was appealed, however, and the court overturned the award, declaring that the determinations made by the reviewer were consistent with the community standard of care.

The court cautioned, however, that provider liability potentially could arise in situations in which the deprivation of care results in harm to the patient, and it emphasized the provider's responsibility for clinical decision making. The court stated:

> The physician who complies without protest with the limitations imposed by a third party, when his medical judgement dictates otherwise, cannot avoid his ultimate responsibility for his patient's care. He cannot point to the health care payor as the liability scapegoat when the consequences of his own determinative medical decisions go sour.

In other words, providers must aggressively appeal claims denials when their clinical judgment dictates that care is necessary and reasonable.

Traditionally, only medical providers (eg, physicians and surgeons) have been the targets of aggressive peer review or scrutiny. This has changed with the exponential growth of managed care and the demand by payers everywhere for the accountability of *all* health care providers.

Under managed care, payers increasingly use peer review and UR for services that are considered "carve-outs," such as psychiatry, substance abuse treatment, pharmacology, chiropractic, speech and language services, occupational therapy—and physical therapy. But the primary purpose of a review is to determine whether treatment procedures satisfy criteria for payment purposes; a reviewer is not typically in a position to terminate treatment. The reviewer's opinion is just that—an opinion and not a mandate. It remains the provider's responsibility to determine when to discontinue treatment. Even in cases in which reimbursement is not ensured, a provider still may have a duty to treat a patient. This raises the ethical (and possibly legal) issue of patient abandonment and recalls the concept introduced in part 1 of this two-part column: the provider's "business duty" to provide only medically necessary and reasonable care as it is defined by the payer and its health plan. Unfortunately, some circumstances do not give providers a clear sense of direction. When business, ethical, professional, and legal issues conflict, determining the right course of action can be like wrestling an octopus. A provider may be forced to make a personal choice regarding what is most important to him or her.

The postscript to the Wickline case is that the health plan changed its policy to allow for up to 8 days of hospitalization for the type of vascular disease that the patient had.

Wilson v Blue Cross of Southern California, 222 Cal App 3d 660, 271 Cal Rptr 876 (1990)

A patient was admitted to a hospital with multiple diagnoses: depression, drug dependency, and anorexia. The attending physician determined that the patient required 3 or 4 weeks of inpatient care. A nurse reviewer employed by an independent review organization subsequently determined that 1 week of care was reasonable, and a physician reviewer contracted by the same organization added 3 more days to that determination. Reimbursement through the patient's health plan ceased after 10 days, and the patient was discharged. Shortly thereafter, the patient committed suicide.

The patient's mother sued the insurer, the review organization, and the physician reviewer. This case introduced an interesting scenario of insurance coverage. The patient's coverage was underwritten by Blue Cross of Alabama, which did not require a concurrent review by a health care provider. But because the hospital was located in California, the hospital had assumed the patient's insurance was underwritten by Blue Cross of California, which at the time did require UR. The review organization was under contract with Blue Cross of California.

A lower court ruled in favor of the defendants, stating that any premature or inappropriate discharge was the treating physician's responsibility. The court of appeals reversed this decision, however, finding that the review had been improperly conducted. This case, predicated on the Wickline decision, was the first in which a court held that third-party payers may be liable for improper peer reviews.

Among the reasons for the court's finding was the fact that the reviewing physician was a neurologist, not a psychiatrist or psychologist. There are certain to be more legal disputes centering on the issue of "like review-

ing like" as a result of managed care's heavy use of primary care physicians in the review of specialty services. For example, primary care physicians, who frequently are the "gatekeepers" in the provision of health care services, typically are not equipped, from an educational or an experiential standpoint, to fully understand the scope of services rendered by physical therapists. *Wilson v Blue Cross of Southern California* reflects some of the problems that may result from health professionals of dissimilar backgrounds reviewing each other's care.

Lessons Learned

Physical therapists increasingly find themselves involved in peer review or UR, either as providers whose care may be subject to review or as peer reviewers themselves. It is important, therefore, to learn from others' mistakes as illustrated by existing legal challenges. Although there are risks inherent in almost anything professionals do, and many of those risks are beyond their control, there are precautions that can be taken by both providers and reviewers to protect their assets and ensure a fair review process.

More Legal Cases Involving Utilization Review

Egan v Mutual of Omaha, 24 Cal 3d 809, 157 P2d 452, 482 Cal Rptr 598 (1979).
The court held that an insurer's failure to consult with the insured's treating physicians or to have the insured examined by a physician of the insured's own choice may breach the covenant of good faith and fair dealing and constitute failure to properly investigate a claim.

Davis v Blue Cross of Northern California, 25 Cal 3d 418, 600 P2d 1060, 158 Cal Rptr 828 (1979).
An insurer's rejection of an insured's claim without advising the insured of the right to arbitration was held by the court to constitute a breach of the covenant of good faith and fair dealing.

Lockshin v Blue Cross of Northeast Ohio, 434 NE2d 754 (Ohio App 1980).
Utilization review was held to be a legitimate form of claims review because , as the court stated, "it is a function basic to an insurer's right to review claims that are submitted to it."

Lopez v Blue Cross of Louisiana, 397 So2d 1343 (La 1981).
Blue Cross was held liable for a claims denial involving a patient's hospitalization because 1) it based its denial on guidelines that were not provided to the treating physician or to the subscriber and 2) it failed to meet the reasonableness test in its investigation of the subscriber's claim.

Lavoie v Aetna Life Insurance Company , 470 So2d 1060 (Ala 1984).
The court found that the insurer did not follow its own procedures for

review because it never obtained the patient's medical records before rendering a denial decision.

Mordecai v Blue Cross/Blue Shield of Alabama, 474 So2d 956 (Ala 1985).
A patient's claim for home health benefits was rejected and the patient sued the insurer, arguing that the reviewer failed to consider a portion of the nurse's notes and failed to consult with the treating nurse and physicians. The court upheld that the process had been legitimate and that contact between the peer reviewer and the provider was not required.

Lithicum v Nationwide, 150 Ariz 326, 723 P2d 675 (1986).
A claim was reviewed four times by four different individuals. The court upheld retrospective denial of benefits and rejected the plaintiff's argument that multiple reviews constitutes a bad-faith practice.

Harcourt v General Accident Insurance Company, 615 A2 72 (Pa 1992).
A chiropractor's care of a patient who had been involved in a motor vehicle accident was reviewed by an osteopathic physician, and the chiropractor alleged that the peer review organization failed to adhere to the provisions of the state's Motor Vehicle Financial Responsibility Law, which stated that a "peer review organization (PRO) must include representation from same profession under review." The Superior Court held that the chiropractor was entitled to initial peer review by a member of his own profession.

If the care that a physical therapist provides is subject to UR or peer review, he or she should become familiar with the review process. Some steps that can help minimize the provider's risks in this area include:

- Requesting that a peer review be conducted by a practitioner of similar educational, licensure, or experiential background to that of the physical therapist—especially for appeal decisions.
- Requesting an appeal of adverse determinations.
- Requesting an explanation of the reasoning behind an adverse decision and asking for a description of the review criteria or standards used.
- Ensuring that critical clinical decision making continues to be based on the *provider's* clinical judgment—*not* on the determinations of a reviewer.

Before becoming involved in peer review, a physical therapist should make certain that the review procedures he or she follows offer some protection from liability. Both peer review and UR require a good-faith approach. Gosfield[1] asserted that "good faith demands a construction of medical review criteria consistent with community medical standards that will minimize the patient's uncertainty of coverage in accepting his physician's (or provider's) recommended treatment." The three elements Gosfield considered critical in supporting a good-faith review of a claim include:

- Determining the precise scope of a review.
- Applying an accepted standard of care.
- Having in place a fair appeals process.

In addition, it is important for health professionals who conduct peer review to ensure that their professional liability insurance covers any service provided within the scope of their education—including peer review.

The legal debates involving peer review and UR may increase for a time, as both consumers and providers of health care adapt to or challenge the many changes wrought by managed care. The jury is still out on many issues, and future legal cases are certain to shape the future of utilization management, managed care, and health care delivery in general.

David W Clifton, Jr, PT, is President, Disability Management Associates Inc, Springfield, Pa. He has 14 years of experience in the field of UR.

References

1   Gosfield A. Value purchasing and effectiveness: legal implications. In: Gosfield A. *Health Law Handbook.* Deerfield, Ill: Clark Boardman Company [a division of Thomson Legal Publishing Inc]; 1991.

Even when there's no negligence, the patient

may have a different perception. Review some risk

management basics with a checklist developed by a

PT who's "been there."

Can You Identify Risk? A Self-Test

by Sheila Reid, PT

Are you confident that you and your clinic are doing everything that can be done to avoid malpractice exposure? As former consultant to a lawyer defending a physical therapist colleague—and as a therapist who once was implicated in alleged malpractice—I know that the answer for most of us is "No."

What happened to me? Two experiences were key to raising my "risk awareness."

One Monday morning about 20 years ago, I was called into the office of my facility's medical director. It turned out that one of my patients with quadriplegia had been admitted to the emergency department of a general hospital during his weekend at home. Radiographs showed a fractured femur—and the patient was alleging that the fracture occurred during passive range-of-motion exercises in a physical therapy session.

In the presence of the facility's lawyer, the medical director asked me all sorts of questions about the treatment session I had conducted with the patient on the previous Friday. I consulted the patient's chart and found nothing out of the ordinary, with the exception that I had treated him on the ward instead of in the department that day because he had the flu. Twenty years ago, documentation standards were not what they are today; the patient's status at the end of the treatment session was not clearly stated.

The fracture was not going to affect the patient's life significantly except for possible transient hypertonicity, and it could have happened under any number of circumstances (including automobile transfers during the patient's weekend outing). And even though there was nothing out of the ordinary about the physical therapy he had received, I agonized over the case for a long time. The case never was pursued beyond a preliminary investigation, but I still remember every detail as though it were yesterday.

My second experience was less personal. I was practicing in a facility that specializes in the treatment of chronic pain. Many of our patients sustained injuries on the job and receive Workers' Compensation. One of these patients, who was nearing completion of her rehabilitation program, had an increase in back pain during repetitions on the back extension machine. The patient previously executed these particular repetitions with success. She had no new pain and no leg pain, but she reported an increase in her customary pain pattern. In that facility, the initial approach for dealing with increases in an existing pain pattern without peripheralization was to encourage the use of ice, gentle movement and stretching, and breathing and relaxation techniques. The patient was familiar with all of these techniques.

The patient's pain had not decreased when she returned for therapy the following day. One of the physical therapists examined her and found nothing to warrant a change in treatment, but he believed that the patient might feel more reassured if one of the facility physicians evaluated her. (Her treating physician was not available.) The physician found no reason for concern and encouraged her to continue applying the principles of her rehabilitation program. The patient completed the program that day and returned to her home.

In accordance with her insurance coverage, the plan was for her to continue with less intensive therapy closer to home to complete the transition to a home program. One of our occupational therapists followed up with her by telephone. The patient initially complained about increased pain. After several calls were made by the occupational therapist, the patient announced that she was going to see another physician and would not be returning to her treating physician at the facility. She refused to accept or return any more telephone calls from the occupational therapist.

The facility next heard from the patient 3 years later, when she brought suit. She alleged that a staff member had manually pulled back and released the weight on the back extension machine and that the momentum had forced her into flexion, thereby resulting in injury and increased chronic pain.

Although the staff were certain that they had not been negligent in any way, they had many hours of stress as a result of this lawsuit. They worried over what they said during the depositions and were concerned about how things would play out in court. They examined their documentation and wished that the information on events that had occurred 3 years earlier could have been more informative.

The story had a happy ending for us: The suit was dropped in the 11th hour, just before going to court—as is the case with many malpractice allegations. But even the possibility of being involved in a lawsuit can have a tremendous impact on a therapist's ability to practice with confidence—or to practice, period. Some young physical therapists are so traumatized by their implication in a lawsuit that they leave the profession even when the lawsuit never materializes.

"But It Can't Happen to Me— Can It?"

Whether we are experienced practitioners, new practice owners, or new graduates, we all like to think that "it can never happen to me." I learned from personal experience that it *can*. Even if a therapist isn't negligent, the patient may have a different perception of the care he or she received.

The following checklist (pages 50-56) was designed to help raise awareness about the importance of identifying and managing risk. It may be helpful to refer to APTA's *Managing Risk in Physical Therapy: A Guide to Issues in Liability*[1] as you adapt the checklist to your own needs.

Become more "risk conscious"—without becoming paralyzed by the fear of a lawsuit! *PT*

Sheila Reid, PT, is Care Site Leader, Spine Institute of New England, Fletcher Allen Health Care, UHV Campus, Burlington, Vt.

References

1 *Managing Risk in Physical Therapy: A Guide to Issues in Liability.* Alexandria, Va: American Physical Therapy Association; 1995.

Risk Management Checklist[a]

Item	Yes	No
1. a. Do you have a mission statement or treatment philosophy?		
b. If so, is it prominently displayed in your waiting area?		
2. If your state or clinic has "patient rights" statutes or guidelines, are they posted?		
3. a. Does your clinic have a clear definition of "patient responsibilities"?		
b. Is this definition distributed to patients early on in the course of treatment?		
4. Are the names of all clinic personnel, with their appropriate titles, posted?		
5. Has your clinic defined "standards of practice"?		
6. Do you have specific training or orientation in patient relations for new staff?		
7. a. Is the staff-to-patient ratio adequate to achieve the clinic's goals and mission?		
b. Are there adequate ancillary staff or systems to meet the clinic's goals and mission?		
8. Do you have contingency plans to deal with an increase in caseload volume because of a decrease in staff, an increase in referrals, or demands made by your managed care organizations?		
9. Do all staff have job descriptions?		
10. Are there clear policies and criteria for delegating treatment?		
11. If your clinic employs PTAs, are state and APTA regulations and standards being followed?		
12. Is there a structured staff orientation period?		
13. Are there clear guidelines for documentation of care?		
14. Are there regularly scheduled in-service programs and continuing education funds for clinical staff?		
15. Are there in-service programs for ancillary staff?		
16. Are there in-service programs on policies and procedures?		
17. Are there in-service programs on equipment use?		
18. Are admission/discharge criteria explicitly stated?		
19. Are referral mechanisms clear and known to all staff?		
20. Is there a regular schedule for inspection of the facility and its equipment?		
21. Do you adhere to Occupational Safety and Health Administration (OSHA) rules and regulations?		
22. Do you have a system for documenting complaints, incidents, and responses?		
23. Do you understand the reporting requirements and limits of your malpractice insurance policy?		
24. Does your clinic have emergency and safety plans?		
25. Do you have a method for dealing with after-hour emergencies?		

Item-by-Item Explanation: Risk Management Checklist[a]

Item	Yes	No
1. a. Do you have a mission statement or treatment philosophy? **b. If so, is it prominently displayed in your waiting area?** A mission statement or philosophy helps define and clarify the scope of your practice and highlights your areas of expertise. By defining what you do (eg, treatment of temporomandibular joint [TMJ] syndrome, sports injuries, or low back pain), you help set parameters so that patients have realistic expectations of you and your clinic. Setting limits on what you treat also may help you professionally. A physical therapist who has worked in a specialized spine clinic for the past 10 years may not be qualified to treat TMJ syndrome—and should recognize that.		
2. If your state or clinic has "patient rights" statutes or guidelines, are they posted? Post any existing patient rights statutes or guidelines in your clinic, and ensure that staff are familiar with them. You may want to consider posting other types of patient rights; for example, "The patient has the right to timely, high-quality treatment; to have all questions answered honestly; to be treated with respect at all times; and to be referred elsewhere if his/her care is beyond the expertise of the staff in this clinic."		
3. a. Does your clinic have a clear definition of "patient responsibilities"? **b. Is this definition distributed to patients early on in the course of treatment?** A handout on patient responsibilities officially informs patients that they are an integral part of the treatment team. This type of handout is especially important today in the managed care environment, with the reduction in the number of visits and the increased emphasis on patient education and home programs. Responsibilities might include participation with therapy, notification of appointment cancellation, and notification of changes in physical or medical status (those resulting from therapy and those that may affect therapy). Expectations regarding payment of services also should be clear. Patient responsibilities can be posted or can be listed for the patient in an information sheet or patient intake form.		
4. Are the names of all clinic personnel, with their appropriate titles, posted? A clearly displayed staff roster that includes titles (eg, "Physical Therapist" as opposed to "PT" or "MSPT") helps educate the patient about the staff's different qualifications. A brief definition of each discipline in a brochure or handout helps the patient appreciate that there are different areas or levels of expertise in the clinic. Being clear about these differences may prevent the unintentional misleading of the patient. Differences exist among PTs, physical therapist assistants (PTAs), exercise physiologists, and athletic trainers (ATCs), all of whom may work in the same clinic. The patients' own expectations form the basis for their evaluation of the care they have received, and a breach of those expectations—for instance, treatment by a PTA whom the patient assumed was a PT—could result in a lawsuit.		
5. Has your clinic defined "standards of practice"? Providing high-quality care is a source of professional pride. It also is an important part of the risk management program. Areas to consider include remaining within the scope of practice; spending high-quality time with your patients, that is, devoting full attention to them during treatment; showing a caring attitude through open, honest, and timely telephone and face-to-face communication; evaluating and reevaluating the patient and establishing a discharge plan; completing documentation; defining sexual impropriety; and obtaining informed consent. Documents that may be helpful in defining standards of practice include APTA's Core Documents (*Standards of Practice for Physical Therapy, Code of Ethics, Guide for Professional Conduct, Standards of Ethical Practice for the Physical Therapist Assistant*, and *Guide for Conduct of the Affiliate Member*)[1] and *A Guide to Physical Therapist Practice, Volume I: A Description of Patient Management*.[2] You may even want to post some of these documents or make them available in the waiting room.		
6. Do you have specific training or orientation in patient relations for new staff? Good patient relations are critical not only to patient care but to management of risk. Research has shown that patients are less likely to sue—even if negligence has occurred—when they feel they have a good relationship with their health care provider.[3] Good patient relations don't rely on giving technically competent care alone (although competent care certainly is something the patient has a right to expect). It hinges on making the patient feel as though the time spent with him or her is high-quality, undivided, uninterrupted time. The patient feels "heard"		

(continued)

Risk Management Checklist[a] (continued)

Item	Yes	No
and is an involved, informed, and active participant in the treatment plan. "Good patient relations" also means that cultural differences are known and respected and that patient complaints are dealt with in a manner that is acceptable—as much as possible—to the patient. If a patient indicates that he or she may be thinking of suing, the last thing you want to do is abandon care arbitrarily. Good patient relations do not necessarily come naturally, and you may need to provide specific training to new staff in this area. Connolly,[4] Payton,[5] and Scott[6] may be helpful resources.		
7. a. Is the staff-to-patient ratio adequate to achieve the clinic's goals and mission? **b. Are the ancillary staff or systems sufficient to meet the clinic's goals and mission?** There is no magic number for staff-to-patient ratio. Aspects to consider include whether the visit is for evaluation or treatment. Complexity of treatment also can dictate ratio. If patients don't need one-to-one supervision for all portions of their treatment, it may be feasible to have them exercise in a group setting that is supervised by a PTA (eg, bicycle riding or weight training). Written guidelines may help flag the times when you clearly are not meeting your own standards and when you may need to implement one of your contingency plans. (See Question #8.) Ancillary staff or systems can help the PT focus on the evaluation or treatment at hand. Running back and forth to the reception area to check in patients or answer telephones is a recipe for disaster. A potentially dangerous situation (eg, an unstable patient) may go unnoticed. "Failure to monitor the patient" is one of the most common reasons for which PTs are sued.[b] Interruptions during treatment can be extremely disconcerting to the patient and may create less-than-ideal therapist-patient rapport. If there is no receptionist, an answering machine or answering service is one solution. If you use an answering machine, make certain that you or a staff member return all calls on the same day. It is helpful to have a person who is knowledgeable about health care insurance available to answer billing questions (especially in today's confusing market). This person does not have to be on site; he or she can be part-time, and patients can be given a telephone number and times to call.		
8. Do you have contingency plans to deal with an increase in caseload volume because of a decrease in staff, an increase in referrals, or demands made by your managed care organizations? If the staffing pattern does not meet your own guidelines, you may have irate patients (who are more prone to sue) or more immediately dangerous situations, such as an unsupervised patient who is burned during a heat treatment or a patient who injures himself or herself on exercise equipment. Contingency plans may include prioritizing your waiting list, starting treatment at two times per week instead of three times per week, ensuring that patients are being reassessed and that the frequency of treatment is decreased as appropriate, hiring per-diem staff, and referring patients elsewhere. Although referral may not sound like a good idea when you're trying to cover overhead expenses, it takes only one lawsuit to prove that it isn't worthwhile to attempt to manage more patients than your system can handle. Depending on the results of the evaluation and the requirements of the insurer, you may decide to give some patients basic education on pain relief and resting positions and a basic home program and to schedule a follow-up visit. If so, remember to instruct patients to call the clinic if they have problems or questions. If the clinic is short-staffed, make the (potential) patient or the referring physician part of the solution: "I'm sorry, but we are short-staffed at present. Our waiting list is __ weeks. We want you to have high-quality care. I can evaluate you, give you some basic advice and education, and start you on a monitored home program in 1 week, with regular treatment starting __ week(s) after that, or I can recommend XYZ Clinic. Which would you prefer?"		
9. Do all staff have job descriptions? A job description that includes the title, a summary of job duties, a list of duties and responsibilities, education requirements, and training and supervisory requirements can help clarify whether a staff person is practicing within his or her scope of practice. It also can help clarify delegation of responsibility—who is supposed to be doing what, and when. Of course, any clinic with more than 15 employees must conform to the Americans With Disabilities Act (ADA) guidelines for job descriptions, including posting essential and marginal job functions.[7,8]		

	Yes	No

10. Are there clear policies and criteria for delegating treatment?

Sound, professional judgment concerning delegation of treatment is critical. This includes delegation to other PTs, PTAs, physical therapy aides, and other health care professionals. According to APTA's House of Delegates policy on Direction, Delegation, and Supervision in Physical Therapy Services (HOD-06-95-11-06), the PT is solely responsible for the following: interpretation of referrals; initial evaluation, problem identification, and diagnosis for physical therapy; development or modification of a plan of care based on the initial evaluation and including the physical therapy treatment goals; determination of which tasks require the expertise and decision-making capability of the PT and must be personally rendered by the PT and which tasks may be delegated; delegation and instruction of the services to be rendered by the PTA or other support personnel, including but not limited to specific treatment programs, precautions, special problems, or contraindicated procedures; timely review of documentation, reevaluation of the patient and treatment goals, and revision of the plan of care; establishment of a discharge plan and documentation of discharge summary and status.

You may want to identify "high-risk patients" who may not be suitable for delegation, such as the patient with an unstable medical condition, a known history of lawsuits, a tendency for questionable compliance, or unrealistically high expectations. Do not write these reasons in the chart, but keep them in mind when you are considering whether to delegate.

11. If your clinic employs PTAs, are state regulations and APTA standards being followed?

PTAs are required to work under the direction and supervision of a PT. Supervision does not always have to be direct or on site; regulations vary from state to state, and Medicare has supervision guidelines that vary according to setting. APTA's *Guide for Conduct of the Affiliate Member*[1] states that a PTA may not interpret referrals or conduct the initial evaluation, reevaluation, or discharge testing and may not modify treatment; however, with prior approval of the supervising PT, the PTA may adjust a specific procedure in accordance with changes in patient status. Supervision includes observation as well as case and chart reviews. Maintain records of supervision whenever possible.

12. Is there a structured staff orientation period?

Each facility should have its own policies and procedures. What may be done routinely in one clinic may not be done routinely in another. If a PT does not conform to the procedures of the clinic at which he or she practices, the PT could be liable for negligence in the case of a lawsuit. Consider implementing an orientation checklist, and have the supervisor and supervisee check off and initial each item covered or performed during the orientation period. The checklist may include items such as the mission of the facility, the infection control policy, and inventory guidelines. APTA's *Managing Risk in Physical Therapy*[3] offers specific suggestions for policies and procedures.

13. Are there clear guidelines for documentation of care?

From a risk management perspective, if it isn't documented, you didn't do it. If you check skin sensation before applying heat but don't document it, it becomes your word against the patient's word in a lawsuit, and the court may decide in favor of the patient. Document the status of the patient before and after treatment (eg, skin appearance prior to the application of a thermal modality). APTA's *Managing Risk in Physical Therapy*[3] devotes an entire chapter to "preventive recording." APTA's *Guidelines for Physical Therapy Documentation*[9] also may be helpful.

The evaluation should include a "physical therapy diagnosis" or state the "primary dysfunction." One of the most common reasons why PTs are sued is "failure to perform a physical therapy diagnosis."[b] Telephone calls—to patients, employers, and other health professionals—also should be documented. A brief note to indicate "who," "what," "when," "where," and "why" may be extremely helpful later on. Many lawsuits are initiated several years after treatment has stopped. Even when the staff have not changed, it can be extremely difficult to remember details of sessions and telephone conversations that occurred several years ago. If you give a patient advice over the telephone (as is increasingly likely to occur under managed care), jot down a brief summary of that advice, including photocopies of written material you send to the patient (eg, changes to a home exercise program).

All treatment cancellations and "no-shows" should be documented. If cancellations and no-shows happen repeatedly, the therapist should talk with the patient to find out the reason why and to allay any fears or concerns

(continued)

Risk Management Checklist[a] (continued)

Item	Yes	No
the patient may have. It is important that patients understand that it is their responsibility to attend treatment and that there is little likelihood of success unless they do. All documentation should be comprehensible and legible. Computer-generated documentation poses its own problems, such as potential lack of confidentiality[10] and possible loss due to system failure. Make certain that you have a backup plan. Patient confidentiality also applies to discussing cases in public places, including the clinic itself. Remember not to discuss a person's care when others are within earshot.		
14. Are there regularly scheduled in-service programs and continuing education funds for clinical staff? Continuing education shows commitment to high-quality care. If the continuing education budget is small, consider a journal club with readings from the current peer-reviewed literature. If a staff member takes a course, keep the course manual on hand in the clinic for easy reference. Documentation of all in-service programs is essential, as is a list of the attendees. This documentation does not have to be extensive. A notebook with listings for various in-service programs, including date, subject, and the list of attendees, should be sufficient. How often is "often enough" when it comes to giving in-service programs? Again, there is no magic number. Some clinics hold weekly in-service programs, with formal presentations on a monthly basis; others hold them only twice a year. A monthly in-service program, journal club, or presentation should be attainable for most clinics.		
15. Are there in-service programs for ancillary staff? Nonprofessional staff who have patient contact, especially those who assist with treatment, should have regular in-service trainings to ensure that proper techniques and clinic protocols are followed. These in-service programs ideally should be held at least annually or every 6 months, because people forget—especially the details. Professional staff should be involved in these programs so that they understand what ancillary personnel have been taught. In-service programs may be particularly necessary when there has been a turnover of staff, because use of techniques varies from clinic to clinic. Again, these in-service programs should be documented.		
16. Are there in-service programs on policies and procedures? At first glance, this may seem as though it's a waste of time because "everyone knows that stuff"; however, policies and procedures rarely remain static. Treatment techniques evolve, and methods can change as a result of one staff person attending a course. A year's worth of changes can add up—and if your practice differs from your policies and procedures manual, you may be held liable for the discrepancy. A manual that is current (with the date of the latest upgrade clearly indicated) is one of your best defenses in a lawsuit. Again, remember to document any in-service programs.		
17. Are there in-service programs on equipment use? All staff should be instructed on equipment—uses, precautions, indications and contraindications, and maintenance. Here, too, it's a good idea to have a review on a yearly basis. Staff change, and people often develop their own "styles" or "techniques," which may or may not be correct. Again, document the in-service training!		
18. Are admission/discharge criteria explicitly stated? These criteria should be indicated in your policies and procedures manual and may help reduce risk of liability for discrimination (eg, "This practice does not accept Medicaid") or overutilization. It may be helpful to document a priority system for new referrals and ongoing treatment, especially when staff and space are limited. Managed care, with its predetermined number of treatments, may pose a particular problem. You should determine what outcomes can be realistically expected with the approved number of visits and what additional goals might be reached with X more visits—and your determination should be made clear to the patient immediately after the evaluation. Of course, this information also should be sent to the referring physician, insurance company, and case manager.		
19. Are referral mechanisms clear and known to all staff? If your state requires physician referral for physical therapy, make certain to include the written referral in the patient's chart. Be sure to follow any outside agency regulations and requirements. Document all telephone calls to and from referring physicians and patients. If a telephone call to a physician results in a change of treatment to		

	Yes	No

which you both agree, send a brief letter to the physician outlining the change of plan. This letter can serve as written confirmation of the agreed-upon change.

"Failure to follow physician's orders" is one of the most common reasons why PTs are sued.[b] When physician referral is required, there is an obligation to contact the referring physician to discuss any proposed variation in treatment. Again, this contact should be documented. If the referring physician is not in agreement with the suggested changes, the PT may be in a difficult position, regardless of professional competency in evaluation and treatment. If no agreement can be reached, the therapist may decide to discharge the patient. This is an extremely delicate situation. The therapist must remain professional and must not malign the referring physician. The details of the "diverse opinion" should not be discussed with the patient; instead, the therapist might simply indicate that the treatment requested by the physician "cannot be provided at this clinic." A discharge note should be written, with documentation of what was explained to the patient. Include the patient's response and the patient's plans, and offer to refer the patient to another clinic with different expertise, or back to the referring physician. Remember that another common reason why PTs are sued is "failure to refer."[b]

As was suggested by Question #1, it may be helpful to define your clinic's limitations and guidelines for outside referral. Details of any disagreement with the referring physician should be kept in a separate record—similar to the way an incident report is recorded—and should include the rationale for the therapist's decision. References, literature citations, and advice or consultation from other professionals should be included as supporting documentation.

Because much of what we do as PTs still is being researched in randomized clinical trials, treatment options often are a matter of opinion or preference. This may be the case when a PT's and a referring physician's definitions of "optimal treatment" differ. If, however, the PT feels that the physician has made an incorrect diagnosis or has missed an important factor, the therapist is obligated to give the patient some guidelines or alternatives. Again, care must be taken not to interfere with a preexisting patient/physician relationship.

20. Is there a regular schedule for inspection of the facility and its equipment?

"Failure to maintain equipment and/or equipment failure" is yet another common reason why PTs are sued,[b] with patients most commonly injured while being treated with heat or electrical equipment (not always the fault of the equipment!) or during the performance of exercises with various types of equipment. A schedule of regular machine maintenance, along with documentation that shows it was done, helps alert staff to any potentially defective equipment (eg, loose parts, frayed wires) and shows that reasonable precautions have been taken to maintain equipment. Keep all manufacturer's repair and maintenance booklets on hand, and follow their instructions.

The facility itself needs regular inspections—from the parking area (if it is on clinic property) to the clinic entrance to the stairs, carpets, flooring, chairs, stools, wheelchairs, treatment tables, hotpack covers, and lighting. (This is by no means a complete list.) Are there loose or defective parts or worn or slippery areas? It may be difficult to see potential problems, such as a loose tile on the walkway, when you are so familiar with the setting. Is there anyone with an "unbiased eye" who could look for items that might not be obvious? Patient reports also are useful. When a patient comments, "There's a patch of ice on your front step," make certain that all staff pay attention and that, if they are unable to deal with the situation themselves, they notify someone who can.

If a piece of equipment seems to be defective, stop using it immediately, and place a visible "out-of-order" sign on it. If an area of the clinic is unsafe and nothing can be done about it at the time, make certain that the area is well marked, eg, "slippery floor." Any repairs to equipment or to the building and grounds should be made by qualified personnel (as opposed to "somebody's uncle who's very good with this type of thing"). All potential or real problems, along with their solutions, should be documented.

21. Do you adhere to Occupational Safety and Health Administration (OSHA) rules and regulations?

Each state must observe, at a minimum, OSHA federal standards; some states may impose even more stringent guidelines. Twenty-three states impose standards that are identical to those of the federal government. One regulation that is mandatory for all businesses (even when there is only 1 employee) is the posting of an OSHA poster explaining employee rights. Failure to post this information can result in a fine of $1,000. For businesses with 11 or more employees, there must be an OSHA log listing all on-the-job accidents and injuries. This log must be maintained for 5 years, and there can be a $1,000 fine for each year that the log has not been kept.[11]

(continued)

Risk Management Checklist[a] (continued)

Item	Yes	No
OSHA has rules and regulations concerning blood-borne pathogens, disposal of hazardous waste, documentation of all toxic substances kept on the premises (and you would be surprised at what may be considered a toxic substance!). OSHA's proposed ergonomic standards, which would have had far-reaching implications for many businesses, have been shelved.[12]		
22. Do you have a system for documenting complaints, incidents, and responses? Again, the patient's chart is not the place for this type of information. Keep a separate "complaints" file. A list of the complaints, along with your responses, helps demonstrate that you have tried to deal with the problem in as constructive and conciliatory a manner as possible. Keeping this information on file also helps refresh your memory should a problem arise several years later.		
23. Do you understand the reporting requirements and limits of your malpractice insurance policy? Every PT has some type of malpractice insurance, but not all PTs are cognizant of the details. What are your obligations concerning reporting of incidents? Do you need to send every incident report to the insurance company? What should you do with the complaints file that you've compiled? More important, do you know what is excluded by your policy? Many policies will not cover a professional for such items as sexual impropriety or the maligning of another professional. Know your policy's exclusions and requirements as well as its coverage limits. Know where your copy of the policy is kept, and consider purchasing your own policy if you are self-employed.		
24. Does your clinic have emergency and safety plans? What is the procedure in case of fire? Is the evacuation plan posted? Are emergency exits clearly marked? Are there adequate smoke detectors and fire extinguishers? Your local fire department will be glad to give advice. Checking smoke detector batteries and maintaining fire extinguishers should be part of the regular facility inspection. Emergency telephone numbers (for fire or ambulance) should be clearly posted by the phones. What happens if someone has a cardiac arrest in your clinic? All staff should be trained in cardiopulmonary resuscitation (CPR). This training, along with the annual update, should be documented on each individual's CPR card.		
25. Do you have a method for dealing with after-hours emergencies? Although there are not many life-threatening situations relating to physical therapy, there certainly are instances when a patient may have an adverse reaction to therapy, and this reaction may not become apparent until several hours after the visit. Make certain that your patients know what they are to do in case of an emergency, such as going to their local emergency department or contacting an answering service that will connect them to you or another therapist "on call." Having a system in place ensures that the patient does not feel abandoned. If your system does not involve having you speak directly with the patient right away, the patient should be encouraged to contact you as soon as possible the following day.		

[a]*This checklist was developed in association with Geraldine Amori, PhD, as a practicum for part of the author's course work for the master of science degree physical therapy program at the University of Vermont, Burlington, Vt. It is not intended to be a complete listing of every risk management item. Reid sent the first draft to 10 physical therapy clinics in Vermont, New Hampshire, and Georgia; their feedback helped refine and clarify the checklist.*

[b]*Personal communication, APTA's Insurance and Member Benefit Services Department.*

References Used in the Checklist

1 APTA Core Documents. *PT—Magazine of Physical Therapy.* 1996;4(1):93-99.
2 A Guide to Physical Therapist Practice, Volume I: A Description of Patient Management. *Phys Ther.* 1995;75:707-764.
3 *Managing Risk in Physical Therapy: A Guide to Issues in Liability.* Alexandria, Va: American Physical Therapy Association; 1994.
4 Connolly JB. Power of positive patient relations. *Clinical Management.* 1991;11(2):12-13.
5 Payton OD, Nelson CE. Involving patients in decision making. Habits of Thought. *PT—Magazine of Physical Therapy.* 1995;3(12):74-76.
6 Scott RW. Informed consent. *Clinical Management.* 1991;11(3):12-14.
7 *Americans With Disabilities Act Handbook.* Washington, DC: Equal Opportunity Commission and the US Department of Justice; 1990.
8 Connolly JB. Understanding the ADA. *Clinical Management.* 1992;12(2):40-45.
9 *Guidelines for Physical Therapy Documentation.* Alexandria, Va: American Physical Therapy Association; 1995.
10 Hughes C. "What did you say?" Tapping Technology. *PT—Magazine of Physical Therapy.* 1995;3(2):70.
11 OSHA Instruction. CPL 2.103. September 1994. Washington, DC: US Department of Labor.
12 Hunter S. Using CQI to improve workers' health. Sidebar on *OSHA Ergonomics Program Guidelines 3123. PT—Magazine of Physical Therapy.* 1995;3(11):65.

"Reality Sets In"

Editor's note: In 1992, the At Risk column will follow a physical therapist—"Pauline"—throughout her career, from her first job as a new graduate to her ownership of a private practice. Pauline will cope with the types of sensitive and at times potentially dangerous situations that may result in compromised patient care, malpractice claims, and other legal claims against a practice. In starting her own business, she also will face the challenges of developing the policies and procedures, quality improvement mechanisms, and customer services programs that help manage risk.

Creating these scenarios: insurance and risk management experts who will cover issues such as failure to monitor the patient, failure to maintain equipment, and failure to treat properly. The column will serve both as an introduction for newly graduated physical therapists and as an education tool for physical therapy managers who want to raise staff awareness about risk management. In the first scenario, Pauline has begun working in a hospital setting, where "reality sets in."

Pauline is typical of many physical therapists who graduated and became licensed this year. She is 26 years old. She financed her education through a combination of student loans, full-time summer employment, and part-time work during the school year as a nursing aide. She graduated from the physical therapy program with honors. Her curriculum was demanding. Late at night and every weekend she studied her course notes. She was intrigued by the variety of treatment approaches for the patient problems identified both in the classroom and in the clinic. The only course she found less than exciting was administration, which she took during her last year. The issues discussed in that class

seemed far away, separate from what she understood to be the reality of physical therapy practice.

Pauline now is one of three physical therapists at an acute care general hospital with a skilled nursing unit. This is her second full week in her first position as a *health care professional.* Today, before Pauline settles in to the daily routine, the hospital operator relays a message from Linda, one of Pauline's coworkers, who will be out for the week because her child has chicken pox. No sooner has Pauline finished with the operator when Betty, her boss, calls her to say that she has been called to court on a case against the hospital and Jerry, the therapist whom Pauline replaced.

"The case was filed by the family of a former patient in the skilled nursing unit," explains Betty. The family alleges that Jerry severely

bruised their mother during a bed-to-chair transfer, causing her severe physical pain and suffering, and that the rib fractures that were diagnosed three days later also were caused by the transfer incident. Pauline doesn't understand it. She had heard that Jerry was always very gentle with his patients.

"The sad thing is," Betty adds, "he had no individual malpractice insurance and was relying entirely on the hospital's policy." Pauline can tell from the tone of Betty's voice that Betty thinks Jerry should have known enough to take out his own malpractice insurance. How could a therapist practicing in today's environment be so naive?

Changing the subject, Pauline informs Betty about the physical therapy department being short-staffed. After Betty assures Pauline that Pauline can handle the situation, their conversation ends. She can't get Jerry off her mind, however; he may have personal losses that exceed $250,000. She knows he's a good practitioner. How could this happen? Pauline thinks about the fact that she doesn't have her own individual malpractice insurance. How can she protect herself from getting into the same situation? Her thoughts are interrupted when the first outpatient enters the clinic.

The patient is a 54-year-old roofer who had fallen in the neighborhood grocery store 15 months ago and bruised his coccyx. He currently is suing that store and its parent corporation for $800,000 for alleged severe pain and suffering and loss of work and for medical expenses. Pauline has never treated this patient before, but his initial comments give her the strong sense that he is angry and dissatisfied with all of his medical care. He complains about everything but she feels confident that she can handle him.

By Susan H. Abeln, PT, ARM

The treatment described in the patient's record seems straight forward: ultrasound therapy, deep friction massage, exercise—and micro-amperage electrical stimulation. This worries Pauline; she's never used it before.

Pauline had been sick when this modality was discussed in class and had never encountered it during her practical examinations or when on clinical affiliation. What should she do now? If she "fakes" her way through it, the patient may realize it—and he already has one lawsuit pending. Pauline decides not to use a modality with which she is unfamiliar. As she waits for him to change into his gown, she recalls the course in administration that had seemed so irrelevant. She remembers the professor expounding on the traditional definition of malpractice: *negligence or legally actionable careless treatment resulting in injury to a patient*. The professor had gone on to say that, for litigation to succeed, an injured patient must prove 1) that the physical therapist owed the patient a duty of care, 2) that the physical therapist breached that duty of care, 3) that the patient was injured, and 4) that the patient was injured as a result of the physical therapist's breach of duty of care (i.e., that the patient suffered *legally cognizable damages*).

Pauline remembers that the first item seldom is at issue because the therapist, as a health care provider, owes a legal duty to patients under his or her care; it's the second item that often is the crux of a malpractice action. The question is, How can she—as a newly graduated and newly licensed physical therapist—tell whether she is meeting or failing to meet the legal standard of care that she owes the patient? She knows that under the law she is required to use the same degree of

professional skill and judgment that any other competent physical therapists acting under the same or similar circumstances would use. Failure to use that degree of professional skill and judgment, her professor had emphasized, may constitute *legally actionable professional negligence*—negligence that could result in a malpractice claim.

The standards of care of the physical therapy profession—as found in judicial decisions and state statutes and regulations and as supplemented by the APTA's *Standards*

---

*T*he question is, How can she— as a newly graduated and newly licensed physical therapist—tell whether she is meeting or failing to meet the legal standard of care that she owes the patient?

---

of Practice for Physical Therapy— mandate that treatment must be provided at a level "consistent with current physical therapy practice." Can she provide micro-amperage electrical stimulation at that "level"? She answers her own question: No.

Pauline decides she will tell the patient about this and offer him the promise that she will be prepared to treat him using the modality when he returns for his next treatment— but she won't tell him until she has provided the other treatments first.

She begins applying ultrasound. The last treatment notes indicated a dosage of up to 1.2 W/cm². When the patient states he doesn't feel anything, Pauline—who already feels bad about not being able to provide the treatment that he's used to—increases the dosage to 1.5 W/cm². The patient does not complain, but does say "it feels a bit warm." She notices that his skin is pink as she begins friction massage. After treatment, the patient begins to complain about a dull, deep aching pain, which she assumes is a natural consequence of friction massage.

After the patient exercises, Pauline begins to explain that she won't be able to provide his usual treatment. As she explains, he becomes more and more angry. His original discontented demeanor develops into rage. As he dresses, he screams at her from behind the curtain, accusing her of not knowing what she is doing, of burning him with the ultrasound machine, and of not being a competent therapist. He slams the door when he leaves the clinic.

Pauline is anxious. What has she done? She can't reach Betty to ask her what to do, so she calls Shirley, the hospital risk manager, whom Pauline had met during her orientation. Shirley tells Pauline that the best thing to do is to complete an occurrence or incident report immediately. "The purpose of this report," explains Shirley, "is to monitor potentially compensable incidents at the hospital and prepare the insurance carrier for a potential liability exposure." She also explains that this may mean a possibility of financial loss to Pauline.

Pauline fills out the incident report describing not only the reddening of the patient's skin after the ultrasound treatment and his complaints of unusual dull aching pain

OCCURRENCE REPORT

HOSPITAL: Your Hospital
CITY: Anytown STATE: USA

OCCURRENCE TRENDING REPORT FOR PATIENTS AND VISITORS

PRIVILEDGED AND CONFIDENTIAL
PREPARED FOR USE BY HOSPITAL ATTORNEY

NAME: R. Rodney
ADDRESS:
PHONE #:
M.D.:
M.R. #: ROOM #:

SECTION I. GENERAL INFORMATION—INSTRUCTIONS: Complete all areas by writing in information and by checking applicable item. If information asked for is not applicable, so indicate. Forward OCCURRENCE REPORT to Risk Manager within 24 hours of incident. (Check all that apply.)

1. GENERAL INFORMATION
A IDENTIFICATION
___ Inpatient ✓ Outpatient ___ Visitor

CATASTROPHIC EVENT/SERIOUS OCCURRENCE—RISK MANAGER MUST BE NOTIFIED IMMEDIATELY
001 Anaphylactic Shock
002 Apgar Score 5 and Below
003 Brain Damage
004 Paralysis
005 Severe Burn
006 Unanticipated Damage/Loss of Organ
007 Unanticipated Death
008 Unanticipated Loss of Limb
009 Unanticipated Loss of Vision
010 Other

B. UNIT/DEPT. REPORTING OCCURRENCE: Physical Therapy
C. OCCURRENCE DATE: Jan 12, 19XX
D. DATE REPORTED: Jan 12, 19XX

E. OCCURRENCE
SHIFT 1st ✓ 2nd ___ 3rd ___
TIME AM 8:35 PM

2. LOCATION OF INCIDENT
011 Emergency Department
012 OR/Recovery
013 Labor & Delivery/Post Partum
014 Skilled Nursing
015 Psych
016 ICU
017 Nursing Unit (specify)
018 Public Areas
019 Radiology
020 Laboratory
021 Physical Therapy
022 Other

3. INDIVIDUAL(S) DIRECTLY INVOLVED
01 RN 12 Volunteer
02 Pool Nurses 13 Student
03 LVN/LPN 14 Physician
04 CRNA 15 Consultant
05 Graduate Nurse 16 Podiatrist
06 Patient Care Att. 17 Resident
07 Therapist 18 Intern
08 Technician 19 Physician Asst.
09 Dietician 20 Dentist
10 Pharmacist 21 Visitor
11 Social Worker 22 Other:

SECTION II. NATURE OF OCCURRENCE (Check all that apply.)

4. COMMUNICATION
023 PANIC, STAT
024 Lab/X-rays Not Called
025 MD Not Notified/No MD Response
026 Missing Record/Significant Portion
027 Consent Problems
028 Overlooked/Mislabeled/Misread order
029 Physician Coverage Related
030 Inappropriate Medical Record Documentation
031 Other

5. NATURE OF INJURY (MARK ONE)
032 Abrasion
033 Adverse Effect; Medication/Treatment
034 Aggravated Pre-Existing Condition
035 Aspiration/Anoxia
036 Bruise/Hematoma
037 Burn
038 Code/Arrest
039 Dental Related
040 Fracture/Dislocation
041 Head Injury
042 Infection
043 Internal Injury
044 Laceration
045 Sprain/Strain
046 No Known Injury
047 Needle Puncture/Sharp Injury
048 Self-Inflicted Injury/Suicide
049 Caught In/On/Between
050 Sexual Misconduct
051 Suspected Child Abuse
052 Injury Self/Others
053 Handling and/or exposure to Hazardous Waste
054 Other

6. SAFETY OCCURRENCE (Physical Plant and On-Grounds Internal/External)
Location (Be Specific):
Police Report Taken: ___ Yes; ___ No
File #
Officer's Name
DL # Exp.

7. SAFETY/PROPERTY
055 ___ Patient ___ Visitor ___ Emp-Own ___ Physician
056 ___ Fall With Injury ___ Wet Floor?
057 ___ Fall Without Injury Why?
058 While Ambulating
059 From Bed
060 From Chair
061 From Commode
062 From Stretcher
063 From Wheelchair
064 From Exam Table
065 Found On Floor
066 Assisted to Floor in Bathroom
067 Patient States
068 Other

8. OTHER SAFETY ISSUES
069 Suspected Child Abuse
070 Injury to Self
071 Injury to Others
072 Handling/Exposure
073 Hazardous Waste
074 Other

9. MEDICATIONS
075 Narcotics
076 Psychotropics
077 Diuretics/Laxatives
078 Anti-Hypertensives
079 Other

10. MEDICATION VARIANCES
080 Wrong Patient
081 Wrong Dose
082 Wrong Route
083 Wrong Time
084 Wrong Medication
085 Transcription Error
086 Reaction
087 RX Incorrectly Dispensed
088 Delay in Dispensing
089 Ordered, Not Given
090 RX Incorrectly Compounded
091 Expired Drug
092 Contraindication/Allergies
093 Controlled Substance
094 Variance
095 Other

11. DISSATISFACTION/NON-COMPLIANCE
096 Irate/Angry
___ Patient/Family
___ Nursing
___ Physician
097 ✓ Other Therapist / Perceived Patient Dissatisfaction
098 AMA
099 Refused Prescribed Med. TX
100 Left W/O Service
101 Disregarded Instructions
102 Other

SECTION II. NATURE OF OCCURRENCE (Continued)

12. PERINATAL
103 Infant Injury/Complications Requiring Medical Intervention
104 Resuscitation of NB
105 Delivery Not Attended by Physician
106 Maternal Injury/Complication
107 Maternal/Infant Transfer to ICU
108 Fetal Distress
109 4th Degree Laceration
110 Post-op Bleed/Requiring Transfusion or Surgical Intervention
111 Other

13. SURGERY/ANESTHESIA
112 Instrument/Sponge/Needle Count Discrepancy
113 Cardio/Respiratory Arrest
114 Unplanned Return (removal/repair/bleeding)
115 Foreign Object
116 Adverse Results of Anesthesia
117 Post-Op Neuro Deficit
118 Unplanned Removal or Repair of Organ
119 Intubation Resulting In Injury
120 Unplanned Surgical Cancellation
121 Other

14. IV
122 Wrong Solution
123 Infusion Rate Wrong
124 Patient Action
125 Equipment Malfunction
126 Transcription Error
127 Wrong Additive
128 Multiple Sticks (>3)
129 Contraindications/Allergies
130 Labeling Errors
131 Wrong Patient
132 Reaction
133 Incorrect Administration/Consent
134 Other

15. IV Complications
135 Infiltration
136 Phlebitis
137 Other

16. EQUIPMENT
138 Failure/Malfunction
139 Equipment Unclean
140 Availability
141 Crash Cart Variances
142 Other

17. DIAGNOSIS/TREATMENT/PROCEDURE
143 Performed on Wrong Patient
144 Improper Prep of Patient
145 Specimen (Delayed/Lost/Mishandled)
146 Omission of Procedure
147 NPO Not Maintained
148 Break in Technique/Policy Variances
149 Repeats
150 Timeliness of Procedure
151 Test Incorrectly Done or Read
152 Unplanned Repeat Diagnostic Procedure
153 Multiple (>3) Attempts of one Procedure-Tubes-Drains-Needles
154 Unplanned return to ER for Same or Related Problem
155 Unplanned Transfer to ICU
156 Code Blue If Applicable
157 Adverse Outcome
158 Patient Incorrectly ID'd
159 Pt. Related Complication
___ Removal of Tubes/
___ Drains/
___ IV's
160 Contraindicated
161 Other

18. PROPERTY LOSS
162 Prosthesis (Dentures, glasses, contact lens, hearing aid, etc.)
163 Jewelry Loss
164 Clothing Loss
165 Money Loss
166 Vehicle Loss
167 Theft
168 Fire/Smoke
169 Explosion
170 Collision
171 Cash over/short
172 Auto Accident
173 Vandalism
174 Water/Plumbing
175 Electrical
176 Vehicle
177 Violent Act
178 Other

SECTION III. SUPPLEMENTAL INFORMATION (Check all that apply)

19. PATIENT FACTORS PRIOR TO INCIDENT—CIRCLE/CHECK ALL THAT APPLY
179 Alert/Normal
180 Agitated
181 Unconscious
182 Refuses to Cooperate
183 Confused
184 Sedated
185 Senile
186 Depressed
187 Disoriented
188 Anesthetized
189 Substance Abuse
190 Handicapped
191 Other

20. WAS THE PERSON SEEN BY A PHYSICIAN?
YES ___ NO ✓ NOT APPLIC. ___
If 'yes' Time Seen ___ AM ___ PM
Physician's Name (Print)
Physician's Comments:

21. ENVIRONMENTAL FACTORS THAT APPLY TO SLIP OR FALL—CIRCLE ALL THAT APPLY
BED LEVEL
192 Bed Up
193 Bed Down
194 Not Applicable
BED RAILS
195 Up-How Many
196 Down-How Many
197 Not Applicable
ACTIVITY ORDERS
198 Strict Bed Rest
199 OOB in Chair
200 OOB With Help
201 OOB Ad Lib
202 BRP Only
203 No Orders
204 Not Applicable
205 Call Bell in Reach
206 Patient Instructed in Use
207 Restraints Ordered
208 Restraints Not Ordered
209 Restraints On
210 Restraints Off
211 Other

22. NAME OF EMPLOYEE-OWNER INVOLVED IN OCCURRENCE:
(print name & title) Pauline P.T.
(sig & title) Pauline P.T.

WHO DISCOVERED THE OCCURRENCE?
(print name/date) Pauline PT, 1/12/XX
(sig & title) Pauline PT

SUPERVISOR:
(print name/date) Betty PT 1/12/XX
(sig & title)

NAME OF REVIEWER:
(print name/date)
(sig & title)

15. FOR RISK MANAGEMENT USE ONLY
212 Injury Code
213 E-Code
214 Other

23. FACTUAL DESCRIPTION OF INCIDENT
Patient states that after ultrasound administered at 1.5 w/cm² over his gluteal muscle approximating coccyx bilaterally, he experienced a dull aching pain. This complaint was voiced after 10 minutes of friction massage to same area. Patient then completed prescribed exercises correctly. Therapist then informed patient that e-stim would not be provided. At which time, the patient became angry and left clinic without home program.

Figure 1. Pauline fills out the incident report...in such a way that only objective findings are stated and no conclusions are made.

after treatment, but also his reaction to Pauline's decision not to use micro-amperage electrical stimulation. Following the risk manager's instructions, Pauline writes the report in such a way that only objective findings are stated and no conclusions are made (Figure 1). Shirley takes the report and says that after immediately notifying the hospital's insurance carrier, she will call the patient to see if there is anything she or the hospital can do to address his complaints. She tells Pauline that this risk management technique—called "loss reduction"—both helps meet the patient's needs and helps mitigate the hospital's losses. Using a loss reduction technique simply means working to decrease any possible cost associated with a claim resulting from an incident. As Shirley leaves the physical therapy department, her last words remind Pauline of administration class.

"There are a lot of medical injuries caused by negligence, but research shows that only one claim makes its way to the court system for every eight cases of injury caused by medical negligence. On the other hand," Shirley warns, "I just got a mailing on study results reported by the Robert Wood Johnson Foundation that show a large number of claims arise from cases in which there has been no injury and no negligence. These are claims that may have been filed *solely* because the patient became dissatisfied with the treatment, with the provider, or with the end result" (Figure 2).

On the way home, Pauline thinks about malpractice and why people sue despite the fact that there has been no breach of duty, no negligence, and no harm. What effect do those suits have on her profession and on her insurance coverage as a therapist? Pauline wonders. She again thinks of Jerry being without malpractice coverage of his own. Is *she* covered by the hospital policy? Even if the hospital's malpractice insurance policy

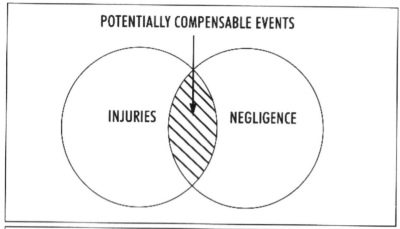

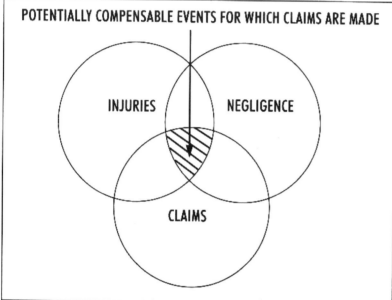

Figure 2. "There are a lot of injuries caused by negligence, but research shows that only one claim makes its way to the court system for every eight cases of injury caused by medical negligence. On the other hand...a large number of claims arise from cases in which there has been no injury and no negligence; claims that may have been filed solely because the patient became dissatisfied with the treatment, with the provider, or with the end result." (Figure adapted from Abridge—A Selected Summary of Recently Published Research by Grantees *[1991] with permission from the Robert Wood Johnson Foundation, Princeton, NJ.)*

covers her conduct as an employee acting within the scope of employment, should she obtain individual malpractice insurance?

Will Pauline's patient make a malpractice claim against her? Find out in the next issue, when claims-by-reason coding will be discussed.

Susan H. Abeln, PT, ARM, is president of Strategic Healthcare Alternatives (SHA). An Associate in Risk Management (ARM) as awarded by the Insurance Institute of America, Abeln is a member of APTA's Insurance and Member Benefits Committee. At CSM 1992 in San Francisco, she will present "Physical Therapy and Risk Management: Managing Your Exposures" with George Head, PhD, CPCU, ARM, CSP, CLU, Vice President of the Insurance Institute of America.

This article is not intended as legal advice for any specific practitioner. Legal advice can be given only by your personal legal counsel, based on the law of your state or on federal law, as applicable.

SUGGESTED READINGS

Abridge—A Selected Summary of Recently Published Research by Grantees. 1991. Princeton, NJ, Communication Office of the Robert Wood Johnson Foundation.

Brennan, T.A., L.E. Hebert, N.M. Laird, et al. 1991. Hospital characteristics associated with adverse events and substandard care. *JAMA* 265:3265-3269.

Brennan, T.A., L.L. Leape. 1991. Incidents of adverse events and negligence in hospitalized patients: Medical practice study 1. *N Engl J Med* 324:370-376.

Harker, R. C. 1990. Malpractice and other bases of potential liability for the physical therapist. In: *Risk Management, An APTA Malpractice Resource Guide.* Alexandria, VA, American Physical Therapy Association, Inc.

Scott, R.W. 1991. The legal standard of care. *Clinical Management* 11(2): 10-11.

Standards of Practice for Physical Therapy. 1991. Alexandria, VA, American Physical Therapy Association, Inc.

"I'm in Good Hands"

In the January/February issue, this column introduced Pauline, a physical therapist beginning clinical practice. She had just learned about Jerry, a former employee who was involved in a malpractice trial, when she experienced an adverse event herself during a patient visit. She wondered about the costs of malpractice both to her as a therapist and to a physical therapist like Jerry, who had no individual malpractice coverage. She also wondered whether her hospital's policy provided adequate coverage for her. If not, how should she choose coverage?

Two weeks have passed since Pauline's patient, Mr. Walker, stormed out of the clinic, accusing her of not knowing what she was doing, of burning him with the ultrasound machine, and of not being a competent therapist. Pauline finally has a chance to talk with her boss, Betty, about the malpractice coverage provided through the hospital to all employees. She discovers that the hospital policy covers a maximum of $100,000 per incident and $300,000 in aggregate for any and all claims made against her during one calendar year. She remembers that Jerry, the physical therapist whom she replaced, is being sued for $250,000 for a single incident.

Pauline wonders what has happened with the incident report she had filled out about Mr. Walker's reaction to treatment. She decides to take time during her lunch

By Susan H. Abeln, PT, ARM

Jerome B. Connolly, PT

break to visit Shirley, the hospital's Risk Manager, to ask advice. Shirley greets Pauline with an enthusiastic smile; Pauline's incident report fortunately had been a false alarm. When Shirley had talked with Mr. Walker, he had been very cooperative and almost apologetic for becoming angry; the man who had had vague complaints of pain after treatment—and who was so notably upset—later noticed improvement that he attributed to Pauline's care. Shirley says she will monitor the situation and communicate with the patient, but she has minimal concerns about the possibility of a malpractice suit.

"In the hospital setting, the most frequent and most severe types of incidents that result in claims involve obstetrics and gynecology cases," Shirley remarks. "Do you know which procedures, techniques, and situations place physical therapists at the most risk of a malpractice claim?"

"Well ... I remember my administration professor saying that 'the highest frequency and cost per claim is for failure to treat properly with modalities.' He was emphatic about that. He even had a special handout [Figure 1]. I remember thinking at the time, How can I use this information to prepare for practice? It didn't seem relevant."

"I bet it seems more relevant now," says Shirley. Pauline nods—but she still doesn't quite understand what she can do as a physical therapist to reduce malpractice claim statistics.

Although she's relieved that the situation with Mr. Walker has not become an 'incident,' Pauline knows it still is an important lesson for her. She asks Shirley's advice about how to purchase malpractice insurance in case a future incident later becomes a claim. Shirley explains that the American Physical Therapy Association has offered some suggestions for therapists who want to purchase malpractice insurance (Ashcroft 1991):

"First, contact your professional organization and request information on sponsored products. Ask for detail on the type and limits of coverage, in terms of both the incident and the aggregate. The usual maximum in physical therapy is $1 million per incident and $3 million in aggregate. Ask for the Best rating of the company who is underwriting the insurance policy—the rating shouldn't be less than A-. And ask for the current and projected pricing for the next five years, 'within consistent environment and limits.' If you're an APTA member, you can request the same kind of information about coverage products endorsed by your chapter or section."

"But how do I *really* know which company is right for me?" asks Pauline.

"Ask questions about each company's customer service. Take note of how long each company takes to answer the phone, whether all your questions are answered, how quickly your application could be processed. Ask them if the company advises clients on what to do immediately after an incident occurs. If you ever do have to deal with a claim, you'll want a company that helps you through the legal process and allows you to be involved in settlement decisions. A company that gives sound advice on courtroom presentation if you're actually sued.... Be sure to check with physical therapists in the hospital or in your district who are insured by each company you're considering."

"Sounds like a lot to do," says Pauline, feeling overwhelmed.

"Yes," Shirley agrees, "but it's important. Choosing your coverage is a long-term decision that could have a financial impact on you that lasts a lifetime. You need to think about what your career goals are going to be for the next 7 to 10 years."

"Seven to 10 years!" Pauline exclaims. "I've only been in practice for a few weeks."

Shirley sympathizes and urges her to talk with Betty. "I know that risk management seems complicated, but it really is based on common sense. Why don't you come to the risk management and liability inservice I'm giving for the nurses?" Shirley asks. "Thursday at 3. See you there."

Both Pauline and Betty decide to attend the risk management inservice on Thursday. Shirley begins with a discussion of risk management basics.

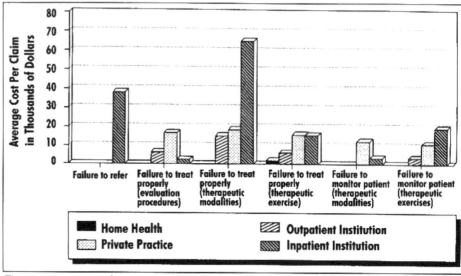

Figure 1. Average total cost incurred per claim by cause-of-loss code, sorted by setting for physical therapist claims reported after July 1989 through September 1991, regardless of policy year, with APTA endorsed programs (data compiled by APTA, 9/15/91).

"Risk management—'RM'—is a logical decision-making process, a specialty area within the general field of management. The Insurance Institute of America, or the IIA [1985], defines it as 'the process of planning, organizing, leading, and controlling the resources and activities of a hospital or a physical therapy practice to minimize the adverse effects of actual and potential accidental losses to that practice.'

"As with all areas of management, risk management is concerned with making decisions about how to allocate resources to best fulfill the goals of your facility. That means risk management also has to do with meeting patient needs for safety and high-quality care.

"According to the IIA [1985], the risk management decision-making process involves 1) identifying and analyzing the exposures, 2) formulating alternative solutions to the problem, 3) choosing the apparent best solution, 4) implementing the chosen solution, and 5) monitoring the results to detect and adapt for error or changes." Shirley hands out a flow chart [Figure 2] that summarizes the process.

"I've found that the best RM methods are risk-control techniques designed either to reduce the frequency or severity of accidental losses or to make them more predictable. These techniques include *exposure avoidance, loss prevention, loss reduction, segregation of loss exposures,* and *contractual transfer.*"

"Here's a definition list [Figure 3] I've developed for all the hospital staff. Review these, and think about how they relate to what you do each day."

At the end of the inservice, Betty leaves for another meeting, and Pauline walks toward the clinic, reading over the definition list that Shirley has just handed out: "Loss prevention aims to reduce the frequency of a particular activity or asset...." It still sounds a little abstract to me, she thinks to herself. Suddenly she realizes that Julie, the physical therapy aide, is calling her name.

"I was setting up Mr. Young for heat and electrical stimulation," says Julie, "and the stimulator suddenly turned on. Mr. Young got shocked!"

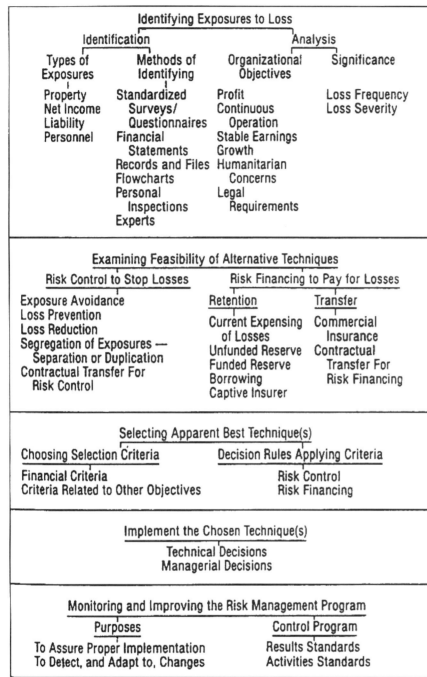

Identifying Exposures to Loss

Identification
- **Types of Exposures**
  - Property
  - Net Income
  - Liability
  - Personnel
- **Methods of Identifying**
  - Standardized Surveys/ Questionnaires
  - Financial Statements
  - Records and Files
  - Flowcharts
  - Personal Inspections
  - Experts

Analysis
- **Organizational Objectives**
  - Profit
  - Continuous Operation
  - Stable Earnings
  - Growth
  - Humanitarian Concerns
  - Legal Requirements
- **Significance**
  - Loss Frequency
  - Loss Severity

Examining Feasibility of Alternative Techniques

Risk Control to Stop Losses
- Exposure Avoidance
- Loss Prevention
- Loss Reduction
- Segregation of Exposures — Separation or Duplication
- Contractual Transfer For Risk Control

Risk Financing to Pay for Losses

Retention
- Current Expensing of Losses
- Unfunded Reserve
- Funded Reserve
- Borrowing
- Captive Insurer

Transfer
- Commercial Insurance
- Contractual Transfer For Risk Financing

Selecting Apparent Best Technique(s)

Choosing Selection Criteria
- Financial Criteria
- Criteria Related to Other Objectives

Decision Rules Applying Criteria
- Risk Control
- Risk Financing

Implement the Chosen Technique(s)
- Technical Decisions
- Managerial Decisions

Monitoring and Improving the Risk Management Program

Purposes
- To Assure Proper Implementation
- To Detect, and Adapt to, Changes

Control Program
- Results Standards
- Activities Standards

Figure 2. Shirley hands out a flow chart that summarizes the risk management decision-making process. (Reprinted with permission of the Insurance Institute of America from The Essentials of the Risk Management Process, *vol. 1, ed. 1, by G.L. Head and S. Horn II, 1985, Malvern, PA).*

Pauline asks Julie to take her immediately to Mr. Young, whom Pauline had met two days ago when she performed his initial examination. Pauline remembers that during that evaluation, she had made a conscious effort to

develop a warm but professional relationship with Mr. Young, establishing eye contact and using voice fluctuations, phraseology, and body-language mirroring to help make him feel comfortable. She had spent time getting to know

him, being open enough to disclose a little about herself. She also had been careful to identify the patient's expectations of physical therapy, to explain the roles of the physical therapy staff, and to obtain his informed consent using the hospital's simple consent form. After the evaluation, Pauline had pointed out the objective findings to avoid the possibility that Mr. Young might harbor unrealistic expectations. She discussed the treatment plan goals, soliciting his input. Pauline feels proud that she had communicated so well with him. She approaches Mr. Young, who is sitting on the edge of a treatment table.

"Mr. Young, Julie tells me there was a problem with the stimulator. I came right away. Are you all right?"

"It was very uncomfortable! It really spooked me," Mr. Young replies, visibly shaken.

"Let me take a look to make sure everything is okay. We want to make sure nothing interferes with your progress and recovery," Pauline reassures him.

"You sure are on top of things around here. I can't believe how much everybody cares."

"We try to be as thorough as possible. Obviously, we have one machine that needs a little therapy as well."

Pauline nods to Julie. "Let's get a new stimulator in here, Julie. Mark this one for a maintenance check."

"I'm sure I'll be all right," says Mr. Young, who seems to be feeling much better. "If you have to take care of the equipment as well as patients, you have a lot of responsibility."

"Our number one responsibility is getting you back to normal

MEMO

TO: ALL HOSPITAL STAFF
FROM: Shirley Newcomb, Risk Manager
RE: RISK-CONTROL TECHNIQUES YOU NEED TO KNOW

Exposure avoidance eliminates entirely the possibility of loss. It is achieved by either abandoning or never undertaking a particular activity or asset. In others words, you eliminate the possibility of malpractice by never providing the service in the first place.

Loss prevention aims to reduce the frequency of a particular loss. A common example of this technique is the use of preventive maintenance procedures to prevent equipment malfunction that may harm a patient.

Loss reduction, on the other hand, strives to reduce the severity, the extent, and the financial consequences of the loss. One aspect of this technique also is called 'mitigating' our losses. Efforts such as providing free care to remedy an injury sustained as a result of treatment can be used as a loss reduction technique.

Segregation of loss exposures involves arranging an organization's activities and resources so that no single event can cause simultaneous loss to all. Segregation can take two forms: separation or duplication. A perfect example is backing up your computer documents on a floppy disk and storing the disk in a place other than right next to your computer.

Contractual transfer occurs when the organization to which you are transferring assumes all the financial and legal responsibility for loss that the transferring party typically would assume. Leasing of property and subcontracting are common examples.

Figure 3. "Here's a definition list I've developed.... Think about how they relate to what you do each day."

Pauline: Mr. Young, Julie informed me there was a problem with the stimulator ...
Mr. Young (interrupting): Problem? I'd say it's more than a problem! I was electrocuted.
Pauline: Well, I came right away to check on you and make sure you were okay.
Mr. Young: Well, you're a little late. You're the therapist, aren't you? You should be here doing my treatment instead of that "candystriper" aide. Maybe this wouldn't have happened if you'd have been doing your job!
Pauline: All our staff are trained and qualified to perform their duties.
Mr. Young: Well, if that's training and qualifications, I'm not sure I want any more treatment. I might be better off without therapy!
Pauline: That's up to you. As a patient you certainly have the choice of what kind of care you receive ...
Mr. Young: You're darn right I do and you can be sure I don't want anymore of this. You will be hearing from my lawyer on this one.

Figure 4. Pauline wonders what might have happened if she had not developed rapport with Mr. Young during the initial evaluation.

function, Mr. Young. We want to do everything we can to make that happen as quickly as possible."

"I feel like I'm in good hands. It was just a small shock. It just surprised me. Thanks for showing your concern."

As Pauline walks back to the charting area, she begins to tie incidents and information together. Although her primary goal had been to take care of Mr. Young, she actually had used rapport to reduce the severity of an incident—as a loss-reduction technique in risk management! She wonders what might have happened if she had not developed rapport [Figure 4] with Mr. Young during the initial evaluation. She bends down to pick up Shirley's definition list, which she had dropped while hurrying down the hall to find Mr. Young. The

second item on the list—loss prevention—includes preventive maintenance procedures to avoid equipment malfunction. She remembers that failure to to maintain equipment is the most frequent and most expensive malpractice claim for physical therapy. Mr. Young's shock certainly falls into that category.

Pauline feels good that she has been able to defuse the incident; however, she knows that to prevent a future claims occurrence, she needs to do something else. Pauline resolves to talk to Betty about arranging a more comprehensive preventive maintenance schedule for all equipment. **CM**

In the next issue, Pauline embarks on the creation of a comprehensive risk management program designed specifically for the physical therapy department. She also plans for a career move toward independent contracting. What will that mean in terms of risk management strategies?

Susan H. Abeln, PT, ARM, is president of Strategic Healthcare Alternatives (SHA). An Associate in Risk Management (ARM) as awarded by the Insurance Institute of America, Abeln is a member of APTA's Insurance and Member Benefits Committee.

This article is not intended as legal advice for any specific practitioner. Legal advice can be given only by your personal legal counsel, based on the law of your state or on federal law, as applicable.

REFERENCES
Ashcroft, C.E. 1991. Guaranteed protection. *Clinical Management* 11(6):56-57.
Head, G.L., S. Horn II. 1985. *The Essentials of the Risk Management Process, vol. 1, ed. 1.* Insurance Institute of America, Malvern, PA.

"I'm Ready"

Editor's note: *In the last issue, Pauline learned important lessons about the need for personal liability coverage and risk management. Using effective patient relations and thorough evaluation—treatment techniques that also serve as loss-reduction techniques in risk management—Pauline defused an incident involving a physical therapy aide and a patient who had received an electric shock. In this issue, Pauline helps develop a risk management program, handles a difficult situation with a physical therapist who is providing temporary coverage, and begins to think about her own future as a private practitioner.*

On Friday morning, Linda—one of three physical therapists in Pauline's department—receives some bad news. Only two weeks after her son has recovered from his bout of chicken pox, her daughter needs to have a tonsillectomy. This means that Linda will need to take at least two more weeks off from work.

With a full caseload of inpatients from the hospital and the skilled nursing unit and with outpatients scheduled throughout each day, Betty, the department director, knows she needs to arrange for short-term staff coverage right away. She contacts Megan, a self-employed physical therapist, who agrees to provide six hours of coverage daily during the two weeks when Linda is out.

Pauline feels relieved that she will have some assistance during Linda's absence. She also begins to wonder what it would be like to be a self-employed physical therapist like

By Liz Gaynor, MS, PT

Gloria J. Young, EdD, PT

Megan, practicing within her own schedule and at her own pace—something she hasn't thought about since graduation. But what about liability? What about exposure to risk? She drops by the office of the hospital risk manager, who pulls *Essentials of Risk Control* (Insurance Institute of America 1985) from her bookshelf:

"The IIA defines *contractual transfer* as 'a shifting [transferring], as through a subcontract, to another entity, the responsibility for a particular activity, thus also shifting both the legal and financial responsibility for any accidental losses,' " the risk manager explains. "In this case, Megan would be the 'entity' and patient care is the 'activity.' 'Accidental losses' would be Megan's own work-related injury or the injury of a patient arising out of the activity—when a court has decided that both the hospital and the 'entity'—Megan—are responsible."

As a self-employed physical therapist providing services to facilities, would Pauline become the "entity" for those facilities? Pauline had never thought about that part of contractual responsibility before; she had thought only about the fact that she would be an owner of her own practice.

When the physical therapy staff gather for their weekly Friday meeting, Pauline puts aside these thoughts of independent practice. Betty and she are presenting a new plan for preventive maintenance to the physical therapy staff. The incident in which Mr. Young received a shock from the electrical stimulation equipment made Pauline realize the importance of preventive maintenance programs and staff education.

"The latest data from the APTA indicate that the highest frequency and cost per claim for physical therapists is for failure to treat properly with modalities," Betty begins. On a flip chart, Pauline writes down several ideas on how to help avoid these types of claims.

✓ Update dept. equipment inventory list
✓ Organize manufacturer info. and operating manuals in 1 file
✓ Design/implement hazard surveillance program
✓ Each of us is RESPONSIBLE for regular review of equipment condition!
✓ What is role of hospital bldg. engineering dept. in regular maintenance checks of electrical/battery-run equipment?
✓ Establish safety guidelines for equipment at higher risk of malfunction
✓ Document risk mgnt. efforts in manual
✓ Establish policies/procedures when equipment isn't functioning and when it's repaired but not yet returned to service

"What does a typical hazard surveillance program involve?" asks Julie, the physical therapy aide who had been attending Mr. Young during the electrical stimulation incident.

"Well, for example, we might develop a checklist for a brief walk-through inspection of the department," explains Pauline. "In addition," continues Betty, "all staff would be assigned duties, such as inspecting hot-pack covers for worn or bald spots or making sure that footstools have adequate tips; wheelchairs and stretchers have functional locks; and paraffin baths, hot-pack units, and whirlpools have accurate thermometers."

"Why don't we make our equipment checks right before our last weekly meeting of the month?" offers Linda. "We could present our results to the group."

Everyone agrees to this plan. As the meeting breaks up, Linda says goodbye to the staff and begins her leave.

An Impatient Patient

On Monday morning, Megan arrives on time to begin her first day. She signs a contract in the personnel department, providing a copy of her license and proof of her malpractice insurance coverage. Megan has nine years of practice experience in a variety of settings and excellent references, and Betty is confident she will provide high-quality care in Linda's absence.

Betty takes Megan on a tour of the physical therapy department, introduces her to the staff, and shows her the day's schedule. The appropriate patient records are pulled and given to Megan. Betty must attend a meeting of local physical therapy directors at a nearby facility and leaves Pauline in charge in her absence. Pauline wants to ask Megan about how she established her business, but there

---

***The** physical therapy aide has observed physical therapists set up patients on the isokinetics unit; she has never set up the patient herself. "But if a physical therapist is asking me to do it," she asks herself, "doesn't that mean I'm qualified to do it?*

---

is a long schedule ahead of them and her questions will have to wait.

Several hours (and patients) later, Peter J. arrives for his appointment and is told by the receptionist that Megan is covering for Linda, his regular therapist. Peter J. is a 34-year-old mechanical engineer who injured his knee skiing last winter. He underwent arthroscopy two weeks ago when his orthopedic surgeon diagnosed a minor tear in the left medial meniscus. After surgery, Peter J. was referred for physical therapy; Linda had performed the physical therapy evaluation last week. Peter J.'s treatment plan includes ice, high-voltage electrical stimulation, isokinetics, active range-of-motion (ROM) exercises in the clinic, and a home program for ROM and strengthening exercises.

Megan initiates Peter J.'s treatment with ice and electrical stimulation. While he is undergoing this treatment, she starts working with another patient. Because Megan already is running a little late and Pauline is busy teaching an inpatient to use crutches on the stairs, Megan asks Julie to help Peter J. onto the isokinetics unit. Megan recently had worked in an office in which the physical therapy aide regularly performed this task, so she assumes Julie also is trained to perform it. Megan also assumes Julie understands that she is to help the patient sit on the unit seat—not initiate the treatment itself.

Although Julie has observed physical therapists set up patients on the isokinetics unit several times, she has never set up the patient herself. But if Megan is asking me to do it, Julie asks herself, doesn't that mean that I'm *qualified* to do it?

Peter J. notices Julie's hesitation and looks anxiously at his watch.

"Julie, I'm in kind of a hurry today—I've got a big meeting back at the office," he says. "I used the isokinetics unit last time. I already know how it works. I don't need to wait for Megan."

He says he thinks the unit was set on "low" during his last session. Julie turns on the unit. "Let me know when the speed feels the way it did last time," she says. As Peter J. extends his knee with full force, he feels increased pain. He reports this, and Julie immediately turns off the unit and calls for Megan and Pauline.

As Pauline walks over to Peter J., she remembers her discussions with Shirley and follows the steps she has learned to follow when this type of incident occurs.

"I hear that you're having worse pain, Peter," Pauline begins. "Can you tell me what happened?"

"I know I should have waited for Megan before starting these exercises," Peter says. "It's just that I have this big meeting, and I can't be late...."

Pauline is warm and sympathetic and allows Peter J. to talk about his role in creating the problem. She knows that when he shares the responsibility for turning on the unit, he is helping protect the facility. She also knows that patient compliance—or lack of it—is an important behavior to document.

Julie is upset after the incident, and Peter J. does not want Julie to get in trouble. After ice is applied to his knee, he reports that it feels much better. He is instructed to apply ice again that evening, forego his home exercise program, and return tomorrow as scheduled. Pauline suggests that Megan telephone Dr. Kelly to inform him about the incident.

Even though it appears that there will be no malpractice claim, Pauline asks Julie to complete an incident report.

"Be sure to write only objective findings and leave out any speculation," Pauline explains, remembering her own experience with the patient who had accused her of burning him with ultrasound treatment [*CM*, January/February 1992, Vol. 12, No. 1, pp. 18-21]. Pauline also calls Betty at her meeting to let her know the situation. Megan and Julie feel bad that the incident occurred, but they continue with the rest of their day, and Pauline reviews with Megan the appropriate documentation in the patient record.

Experience is No Substitute for a Thorough Orientation

When Betty gets back to the department later that morning, Pauline meets with her to discuss what happened.

> ## "Megan has several years of clinical experience," says Betty, "but she still needed a thorough orientation to this department's policies and procedures. She should have been told exactly what Julie could and could not do."

"Megan has several years of clinical experience," says Betty, "but she still needed a thorough orientation to this department's policies and procedures. She should have been told exactly what Julie could and could not do."

"We should have had her take more time to review patient records, too," sighs Pauline, "especially when there was such a full caseload of unfamiliar patients."

"And Julie showed poor judgment when she didn't consult with Megan and allowed Peter to encourage her to start the isokinetics unit," adds Betty.

Agreeing that staff awareness of the need for risk management is not what it should be—and that incident reporting and documentation guidelines need to be reviewed and included in an orientation manual—Betty and Pauline retrieve the physical therapy policy and procedure manual from Betty's office. They

find that the manual lacks detailed information on the orientation of staff, the setting of priorities when staffing is limited, and the role of the physical therapy aide. In addition, the manual includes none of the preventive maintenance procedures identified during their Friday meeting—procedures essential to an effective risk management program.

"Risk management is an ongoing planning and organizing process," Betty says. "What happened today shows us that the process is never really finished. We've got to make it a part of our everyday practice. It's even more critical when staffing is short; nowadays, every time someone is out for a few days, we need to call on a physical therapist who provides temporary services, and usually that person is unfamiliar with our department and our patients."

A Team Process

To write a more thorough description of the role of the physical therapy aide and the on-the-job training required for that position, Betty enlists Julie's help. Together they develop a list of Julie's activities and patient-related tasks and expand the role of the aide in a preventive maintenance program. Because Pauline has shown so much interest in risk management, Betty also asks her help in revising and updating the manual. Pauline enthusiastically agrees—after all, involvement in this type of planning can only prepare her for the time when she decides to start her own business. Even though she knows that what happened with the isokinetics unit probably will not become a claim, she wants to avoid the possibility of ever being in that situation herself—regardless of whether she is self-employed or employed by someone else.

One of the first policies and procedures that Betty and Pauline revise focuses on the orientation of new physical therapists, including physical therapists providing short-term coverage. Based on her experience with Megan, Pauline identifies some of the information that should be reviewed by a new physical therapist before beginning work in the department:

1. General information about the facility and the physical therapy department
2. Staff job descriptions and roles
3. Procedures to help ensure employee and patient health and safety
4. Procedures for emergencies such as cardiac arrest and fire
5. Procedures for infection control
6. Office management procedures
7. Caseload expectations and mechanisms to help deal with excessive caseloads
8. Supervisory relationships
9. Employee responsibilities and contract therapist responsibilities
10. Quality improvement and risk management programs
11. Modalities
12. Protocols used by the department

Pauline thinks specifically about the preoperative and postoperative knee protocol for Peter J., which should have been discussed with Megan before Megan began Peter J.'s treatment.

Betty and Pauline take three weeks to think through the policies and procedures. Before they present the revised manual to Shirley for her comments, they ask the physical therapy staff to review the content as part of the staff's regular inservice education.

As the staff share their suggestions for the manual during the monthly meeting, Pauline reflects that the adverse—and potentially dangerous—event involving Peter J. has a positive side: It has inspired

them to improve the overall quality of patient care and to limit the department's exposure to risk.

Going Solo

Betty and the physical therapy staff continue to monitor the results of the revised policies and procedures, orientation program, and preventive maintenance program and find that adverse events are reduced and defused through the use of those policies and procedures—and that no malpractice claims are made. Pauline continues to develop her clinical skills in general acute care, and, as a result of her experiences in the hospital's skilled nursing unit, she is becoming increasingly interested in geriatrics.

When Pauline passes her second anniversary in the department, she decides it is time for her to move on to another physical therapy setting. Her reputation as a conscientious, highly skilled physical therapist results in an opportunity to provide services to three skilled nursing facilities in her area. Although she feels ready to become a private practitioner, she is uncertain about contracts.

Pauline contacts her friend Michael, who has been in private practice for several years, to ask him for some advice about being self-employed. They meet for dinner the next evening.

"Really, every physical therapist should have a contract," says Michael. "Not just therapists who are self-employed, but those who are employed by, say, a hospital."

"I suppose that's true," says Pauline. "After all, we're all independent practitioners in the sense that we're responsible for our patients' physical therapy care."

"Every contractual arrangement is different," explains Michael, "but there are some general items that a therapist who provides temporary

services should consider. When it comes to patient records, for instance, you'll need to spell out in the contract who develops the treatment plans and under what conditions those plans may be altered. What evaluation forms, progress notes, verbal orders, and discharge forms should you use? Who supplies the forms? To whom are significant changes in a patient's condition reported? To the referring physician? To the PT department head?"

"And how are 'significant changes' defined?" interjects Pauline.

"Right," Michael agrees. "You'll also need to know the time constraints for submitting paperwork....These are just some of the things you may want to include in the contract. And you'll need to iron out things such as terms of termination—How many days of notice are required by the facility that you're contacting with?"

Pauline feels overwhelmed by the legal and administrative detail that obviously is involved in "going out on your own." She also knows there is much to consider in terms of malpractice liability. She will never forget the "close call" she had during her first weeks in practice when a patient said she had burned him with the ultrasound machine. And she remembers when Mr. Young received an electric shock from the electrical stimulation equipment that Julie was setting up.

"What about equipment? If a facility requires me to provide my own equipment—for instance, an ultrasound machine—would I be liable for its failure? Would I be responsible for preventive maintenance and for biomedical checks for power surges, or would the facility be responsible?"

"When it comes to who provides the equipment—and who's liable when that equipment fails—you need to have everything spelled out in the contract," explains Michael. "You should offer a choice to the administrator. If the facility opts to have you provide the equipment, the facility should provide you with adequate space, and you should build into the contract the monthly costs of preventive maintenance and liability coverage for claims that might arise as a result of equipment failure."

"What about malpractice insurance? Who pays for it? What limits are acceptable? Do I assume all the responsibility? Do I have to agree to indemnify and 'hold harmless' the facility from any lawsuits or damages that could arise as a result of my acts or my employees' acts?"

"I could tell you what I do in my practice, but you need to tailor your coverage to *your* needs. The best thing to do is to retain an insurance agent who will go out and find the different insurances that you need. And make sure that your agent has had plenty of experience with putting together insurance packages for health care professionals— preferably for PTs. Will you be using your own car for your business? Are you going to have additional insureds—like a PTA or a PT aide?"

Pauline shakes her head. "I don't know."

"Well, these are the things you'll need to discuss with your insurance agent. You also can contact the APTA. They can give you some toll-free numbers to call for information."

Pauline thanks Michael as they leave the restaurant and heads home. She makes a mental list of the basic items she needs to research, including professional liability insurance, personal health insurance, disability coverage, Workers' Compensation laws and unemployment insurance obligations for staff she might hire, automobile insurance, medical exam-inations for staff, policies and procedures, quality improvement programs, and risk management programs.

It's a lot to do, she says to herself, but I'm ready. **CM**

Next issue: Pauline begins a new phase in her career as a physical therapist working in skilled nursing facilities, hires her first employee, and, with her business booming, establishes a new practice.

Liz Gaynor, MS, PT, is in independent practice in Westchester County, NY, and currently chairs the APTA Committee on Practice. Gloria J. Young, EdD, PT, is president of Sunbelt Physical Therapy, Birmingham, AL.

This column is coordinated by Susan H. Abeln, PT, ARM, president of Strategic Healthcare Alternatives (SHA). An Associate in Risk Management (ARM) as awarded by the Insurance Institute of America, Abeln is a member of APTA's Insurance and Member Benefits Committee.

This column is not intended as legal advice for any specific practitioner. Legal advice can be given only by your personal legal counsel, based on the law of your state or on federal law, as applicable.

SUGGESTED READINGS
Abeln SH. Reality sets in. *Clinical Management* 1992;12(1):18-21.
Abeln SH. 1992. I'm in good hands. *Clinical Management* 1992;12(2):20-23.
Gaynor L. 1991. High quality, low risk. *Clinical Management* 1992; 11(3):16-19.
Head GL, Horn S II. *The Essentials of the Risk Management Process*, vol. 1, 1st ed. Malvern, PA: Insurance Institute of America; 1985.
Scott RW. *Health Care Malpractice.* Thorofare, NJ, SLACK, Inc; 1990.

A T R I S K

"This Is Just What I Wanted"

In the fourth installment of a risk management series following a physical therapist throughout the stages of her career, Pauline musters her clinical, administrative, and risk management experience to go out on her own.

"This is just what I wanted for my career," muses Pauline as she surveys the small physical therapy department equipped by the nursing facility in which she is contracting services. "To provide the best care possible—and to have responsibility for and control over my own practice."

Pauline spent her first two years of practice in an acute care setting. She knows the experience was extremely beneficial in enhancing her evaluation and treatment skills. Although she misses the staff with whom she worked those two years, she is anxious to develop her own company. She already has begun the second phase of her career working as an independent contractor for three skilled nursing facilities (SNFs).

At the suggestion of her friend Michael, who already owns a private clinic, Pauline contacts his insurance agent for advice about insurance coverage. She also contacts APTA for information about the many insurance programs available to members of the Association. Before beginning her contracting duties, she receives her professional liability coverage and health insurance. She also enrolls in the APTA-sponsored disability insurance program because she is ineligible for Worker's Compensation coverage

By Barbara A. Melzer, PhD, PT

as a "single owner" and knows she needs to protect her income-producing ability in the event she becomes unable to work either temporarily or permanently.

In establishing contracts with the three nursing facilities, she insists that each facility be responsible for equipping and maintaining an area in which she will treat her patients. Each facility also agrees to provide the support personnel she will need to assist her during treatment time. As a condition of her contract with each facility, she agrees to participate in quality improvement programs. She also agrees to assist the facilities with any appeals of denials of reimbursement for physical therapy services provided by her or by her future employees.

It isn't very long before Pauline is so busy that she is working a minimum of six days a week to meet the demands of her growing caseload. She realizes that it is time to hire an employee. Because she has facility personnel to assist with transportation and provide aide duties, she decides to hire a physical therapist assistant. At first, the administrators of the facilities are concerned that services provided by a physical therapist assistant will not be reimbursed. "After all," one facility director tells Pauline, "the services of the restorative aides to whom you discharge your patients when the physical therapy goals have been met are not 'reimbursable services' through Medicare or other insurance carriers."

To reassure the facility administrators, Pauline attends several facility meetings, sharing information she has received from APTA and from the local physical therapist assistant education program. This material helps the administrator and nursing personnel recognize that the physical therapist assistant is a licensed practitioner who can serve Pauline's needs—as well as the needs of the patients—better than the additional nonlicensed personnel supplied by the facility or through her own contract can serve those needs.

Pauline's First Hire

Pauline hires Betsy, a physical therapist assistant who has recently graduated from a local physical therapist assistant program. Prior to Betsy's first day of employment, Pauline contacts the professional liability carrier to arrange insurance for Betsy. Pauline also contacts the health insurance carrier to determine how best to have Betsy insured for health coverage. Health care insurance coverage will be one of the agreements in the employment contract that will be drawn up between Pauline and Betsy. Pauline also realizes that it is necessary to have Workers' Compensation insurance and contacts her insurance agent to obtain that insurance for Betsy, informing Betsy of the pending coverage.

On Betsy's first day of employment, Pauline spends a long time orienting her to the facility's requirements. Knowing that Betsy is anxious to begin meeting the facility staff as well as her assigned patients, Pauline tells her about the contract employee at the hospital at which Pauline had previously been employed and the malpractice incident that could have arisen because of the poor orientation that had been provided for that employee. Because it had been Pauline's responsibility to refine the "Orientation" section of the policy and procedures manual after that incident, Pauline is acutely aware of the need for an appropriate orientation. She requires Betsy to thoroughly read the practice's policy manual and sign a statement that she has read and understood the manual. Only when Pauline is confident that Betsy understands both the facility's and Pauline's requirements is Betsy allowed to begin treating patients.

Policy in Practice: A Fall Prevented

During the second month of employment, Betsy is treating Mrs. Harding at one of the SNF's. Mrs. Harding has a repaired fracture of the right hip. During the second day of gait-training activities in which weight bearing is not to be more than 50 percent of her body weight, Mrs. Harding is slightly agitated and distracted: Her family has not visited her in three weeks. She is having difficulty remembering the proper gait sequence and steps down on her right leg without proper weight transferred to the assistive device. She immediately begins to scream in pain. Betsy attempts to comfort Mrs. Harding, who is hysterical, continues to scream in pain, and begins to fall to the floor.

As required by Pauline's policy, Betsy had placed a gait belt around Mrs. Harding's waist before the session began and now uses it to lower her to the floor. Several nurses and aides from the adjacent wings of the facility rush to the scene. They help Betsy lift her from the floor to a stretcher so she can be taken back to her room for further evaluation. On the way, Mrs. Harding repeats "She doesn't like me. She let me fall." The nurses contact the physician, and an ambulance takes Mrs. Harding to the nearby hospital for evaluation.

Betsy immediately telephones Pauline, who is at one of the other facilities evaluating a new patient. Pauline reassures Betsy and instructs her to consult the policy and procedures manual for the correct form to use to report the incident.

Betsy completes an incident report with objective data and waits for Pauline to arrive before she continues to treat any more patients. Pauline talks to the director of nurses at the SNF to determine whether the individuals who assisted Betsy also will write an incident report. She then finds Betsy so they can review the completed incident form together and sign it. On the way to the director's office to drop off the report, Pauline passes the copy room and decides to make two copies: one for her own records and one to send the liability carrier as notification of potential suit.

Named as Defendants

One day a few weeks later, Pauline and Betsy receive notice that Mrs. Harding's family has filed a malpractice suit in which both Betsy and Pauline have been named as defendants. Pauline informs her professional liability carrier about the pending legal action and sends a copy of the notification of suit. She also contacts the facility administrator to inform her of the pending legal action.

Later that day, Pauline asks her friend Michael whether he knows how other physical therapy practices have handled this type of situation. He is sympathetic, citing several similar situations that have occurred in the local physical therapy community. He recommends that Pauline contact his attorney, who either should be able to help or recommend someone who can.

Pauline contacts Michael's attorney and meets with her that afternoon. She brings copies of Mrs. Harding's completed physical therapy evaluation, treatment notes, the incident report, and the physician's orders. Because this lawyer's specialty is business law, she recommends Pauline see one of the firm's other attorneys, who agrees to contact her professional liability carrier for permission to be the attorney of record for both Pauline and Betsy. He says he'll inform her as the suits progress.

The next few months are a flurry of activity as Pauline's contract business continues to grow. She decides to take the first vacation she has had since she set up her own company and contracts with a self-employed physical therapist who will provide evaluation, treatment, and supervisory services in Pauline's absence. This physical therapist works with her for several days before Pauline leaves for vacation so that he is oriented to the responsibilities required in each facility.

Relief. The day before leaving for her vacation, Pauline receives a call that Mrs. Harding's pending malpractice suit has been dropped based on the findings of the "discovery" phase of the legal process (in which the documentation and incident report, as well as the medical record, had been reviewed). Because of the multiple factors involved in the refracture, the family is convinced the incident was not Betsy's fault and in fact has decided that their infrequent visits to their mother had precipitated the situation. They certainly no longer want to pursue the legal action against Pauline or Betsy.

"This is just what I wanted for my career," muses Pauline. "I want to be able to provide the best care possible and have responsibility for and control over my own practice. Maybe it's time to have a 'home base' from which to provide other types of patient services. I wonder what Michael would think about having some competition or about taking on a partner..." **CM**

Next issue: *Pauline considers purchasing a facility.*

Barbara A. Melzer, PhD, PT, is owner of Ingram Physical Therapy and Rehabilitation in San Antonio, TX, and is an Associate Professor of Physical Therapy at Southwest Texas State University, San Marcos, TX. She is Secretary of the APTA Board of Directors and is a member of APTA's Insurance and Member Benefits Committee.

This column is coordinated by Susan H. Abeln, PT, ARM, President, Strategic Healthcare Alternatives(SHA). She is an Associate in Risk Management (ARM) (Insurance Institute of America) and is a member of APTA's Insurance and Member Benefits Committee.

This column is not intended as legal advice, which can be given only by your personal legal counsel, based on the law of your state or on federal law, as applicable.

"The Effort Is Worth It"

Editor's note: *In 1992, the At Risk column has followed a physical therapist throughout the stages of her career, from new graduate to independent contractor. In July/August, Pauline established herself as a provider of contract physical therapy services. In this final installment of the series, Pauline leases her own facility and learns how to reduce her exposure to liability as the owner of a business.*

For almost a year now, Pauline has provided contract physical therapy services to three skilled nursing facilities (SNFs). She's enjoyed being an independent contractor and wonders whether it's time to establish a "home base" for her contract business—and time to expand her services. Her first thought turns to forming a business association with her long-time friend and colleague, Michael, and their initial discussions about this go smoothly. However, because of differences in clinical interest and expertise—and because Pauline is not ready to risk personal liability exposure for a partner's actions—they decide that a business partnership is not appropriate at this time. Michael does offer to assist Pauline in the planning of her new business, outlining the steps she needs to take.

Step 1: The City Planning Office

Pauline visits the city planning office to obtain demographic information. She plots the statistics on an area map to create a visual display of the important demographic aspects of the city and its suburbs, identify-

By Barbara A. Melzer, PhD, PT

ing the population areas that currently may be lacking in physical therapy services. She realizes that the development of her "home base" will be a slow, painstaking process—especially if she is going to continue her contract business while planning and implementing the new project.

Step 2: The Bank

Pauline's next contact is with a bank located in the area in which she has decided she would like to set up her practice. At Michael's suggestion, she has prepared a summary of her demographic study as well as a preliminary business plan and pro forma budget. "Bankers always need to see plans and goals as well as projected income and expenses before granting a loan," he says.

Pauline is amazed at the banker's lack of knowledge about the benefits of physical therapy and is concerned when she learns that a small loan could be approved only if she had a cosigner. This experience drives home the need to "educate the public" about the physical therapy profession as part of her marketing strategy.

Refusing to allow her disappointment with the first banker to stop

her from reaching her goal, Pauline discusses her business plan with several other area banks, at the same time introducing herself to area physicians and dentists. To allow herself more time for laying this groundwork, she contacts Megan, an independent contractor Pauline had met on her first job and with whom Pauline had contracted to provide vacation coverage earlier in the year. All the patients and physicians at the SNFs had given Megan enthusiastic reviews for her professional approach, rapport, and techniques. Megan's quality of care (as measured through Pauline's quality improvement program) had exceeded expectations. Because Megan is a temporary "contract" employee with her own malpractice insurance, Pauline does not provide malpractice insurance for her. Under most circumstances, Megan as a contract employee would be responsible for her own torts ("wrongful acts"), including malpractice.

Pauline interviews five bankers before she decides that the loan terms and the working relationship proposed by the third banker are the most acceptable and that continued investigation is unnecessary. Not only will she be the independent guarantor for the loan, but the loan also will serve as a line of credit to which she may have access as needed. The bank also will provide her with other necessary financial services, including a merchant card for accepting patients' charge cards.

Step 3: The Space Planner

Although Pauline originally wanted to purchase a facility, during her interviews with bankers she realized that she is not ready to make that type of financial commitment. After making some initial inquiries about offices for lease, it quickly becomes obvious to Pauline that she does not have time to look for rental space if she also is to meet the demands of her continually growing contract business. She contacts several real estate agents who refer her to a space planning consultant to help her determine space needs, plan a safe environment, and find appropriate locations. Because the space planner has assisted other physical therapists in developing their facilities, he is able to make several useful suggestions for Pauline's clinic—suggestions that are also excellent loss-prevention strategies.

"There are some very simple, but very important, things you should be sure to do," explains the planner. "For example, all the electrical outlets should be placed approximately at waist level to reduce the incidence of back injuries among your employees as they bend over to plug in machines."

"That would reduce my Workers' Compensation exposure, too," Pauline adds.

"You also want to avoid equipment losses," continues the planner. "Adding outlets to each treatment cubicle helps prevent circuit overload and equipment damage."

Pauline's dream of shiny hardwood floors is replaced with the reality of flooring that is easy to clean and textured to resist skidding and help prevent falls. "I also suggest that at least one of your treatment cubicles have solid walls instead of partitions, so that initial evaluations can be made with more privacy," says the planner. Pauline agrees: Solid walls would help ensure the kind of privacy required for the development of rapport and trust between patient and therapist—which in turn would help enhance treatment outcomes and reduce malpractice exposure. The planning consultant fee is definitely worth it. The clinic is taking shape.

Step 4: Equipment Suppliers

While the space planner develops plans for the clinic and locates potential sites, Pauline contacts physical therapy equipment suppliers and a leasing company that has been highly recommended to her. After Pauline and her accountant discuss the merits of leasing versus purchasing, she decides to purchase only the most necessary, basic equipment and to lease the less-essential equipment, which she will purchase in a few years.

As she speaks with each leasing supplier, Pauline remembers an incident that took place earlier in her career: Because of equipment malfunction, a patient received a shock while a physical therapy aide was preparing him for heat therapy and electrical stimulation [*CM*, Vol. 12, No. 2, March/April 1992, pages 20-23]. Pauline spends much time and energy reviewing the suppliers' reputations for prompt service and trouble-free maintenance, asking to see the biomedical checks and preventive maintenance performed on each piece of equipment.

Step 5: Transportation Issues

Pauline contacts several automobile leasing companies to discuss the possibility of leasing vehicles for herself and her contract staff rather than continuing to pay mileage for personal vehicles used in traveling to patients. Pauline realizes that a commercial automobile policy may be necessary to protect her growing business and her employees if travel between the new office and contract locations continues. She decides to require all her traveling therapists to successfully complete a defensive driving course within the next 30 days to protect them on the road. After all, automobile accidents are one of the largest Workers' Compensation exposures that Pauline's business has.

Step 6: The Site

Several months pass before appropriate space plans are finalized and several properties are located. When Pauline has reviewed all the sites and made her choice, she delegates the negotiation of the lease to the space planner and her attorney. The "build out" costs are assigned as the responsibility of the building owner; however, the additional electrical work—installing ground fault interrupter circuits (GFIs) for the whirlpool area and additional outlets in each treatment cubicle—are assigned as Pauline's responsibility.

Anticipating new risks. As the time to open her facility grows closer, several new risks become apparent. One physical therapist in the community recently faced a situation in which a visitor had injured herself in the clinic; another local therapist's patient records and business records had been destroyed in a fire. How can Pauline protect her visitors against injury and protect her business against these types of losses?

The destruction of business records should be easy to prevent, she reasons; she must not only back up her hard drive each day but also take backup disks home with her or lock them in a fireproof safe. But what about her patients' charts? What if there was a fire? What if there was a hurricane like the one that recently hit southern Florida, and her office was flooded? Pauline's mind races ahead. What if an employee is in the file room when a fire breaks out? Is there more than one way out?

Pauline reviews in detail the space planner's final drawings and is relieved to see that both the file room and the front office will have sprinklers in the ceiling and at least two exits; however, for the computers in the front office, sprinklers would not help. Pauline writes herself a note to check on which extinguishers may be the least toxic and the least destructive to the circuitry and plastics in the main computer area. She also contacts her insurance agent and the APTA Insurance and Member Benefits Department to obtain information about additional insurance coverage. She finally decides she needs liability insurance coverage not only for the premises but for "business overhead."

Step 7: Office Staff

Rather than interviewing a large number of individuals for the position of office manager, Pauline takes advantage of a placement service to provide the initial screening of applicants. She has difficulty narrowing her decision to only one of the final three candidates recommended by the placement service, but finally hires Maria, Pauline's first nonprofessional staff member. This decision is based on Maria's excellent references, strong financial background—and her strong interpersonal skills.

Thinking back over the years, Pauline remembers an early lesson in her professional life: Although a number of injuries are caused by negligence, research shows that of every eight cases of injury resulting from medical negligence, only one claim makes its way into the court system. And many claims arise solely because the patient becomes dissatisfied with the treatment or the provider (Brennan and Leape 1991). Maria's interpersonal skills will be critical in making certain each and every patient who comes into the office is as satisfied as possible with the quality of care he or she receives.

As a condition of employment, Pauline adds Maria to the health plan. Because Pauline knows that there may be some situations (e.g., an emergency) in which Maria may be asked to help with patients, Pauline has required Maria to attend an eight-week certification program to become a physical therapy aide. This means that Maria, like other permanent staff, must be covered by the clinic's malpractice liability policy.

Office procedures. It becomes Maria's responsibility to develop the policies and procedures of the office (including the maintenance of patient files and the procedures for billing). She also creates an intake form and patient satisfaction survey as part of Pauline's ongoing effort to control losses and reduce the new clinic's malpractice exposures. Pauline delegates the accounts payable management responsibility to Maria, who also sets up a petty cash system to cover incidental office and clinic expenses. Both Maria and Pauline agree to procedures suggested by Pauline's accountant for providing the necessary safety checks for handling of cash receipts. Maria researches collection agencies, billing and collection services, and computerized billing and management programs available for the physical therapy office.

Step 8: Policies and Procedures

When Pauline sets out to develop a policy and procedure manual for the clinic, she delegates a revision of her existing manual to Megan and the physical therapist assistant; this manual will be used in the "contract side" of the business. To both the clinic manual and the contract services manual, Pauline adds the procedures required by the new Occupational Safety and Health Administration (OSHA) safety standard for blood-borne pathogens.* She also makes certain that her procedures meet the Americans with Disabilities Act (ADA) standards that relate to her business.†

Pauline adds a new section to her manual on informed consent so that

---

For information, contact the Health Standards Office, OSHA, U.S. Department of Labor, 202/523-7157.

†*See "The ADA and You" by R. W. Scott, CM, Vol. 12, No. 1, January/ February 1992, pages 16-17, and "Understand the ADA," by J. Connolly, CM, Vol. 12, No. 2, March/April 1992, pages 40-45.*

she and her therapists will be certain to incorporate the informed consent procedures that meet APTA professional standards. These procedures can help Pauline avoid litigation resulting from a lack of "professional disclosure." Also added is a section outlining the quality improvement process to be followed in the clinic and the philosophy and plan for continuing education and inservice training to maintain the skills of current and future staff.

Step 9: Patient Education Strategies

Pauline's last project: The development of a strong patient education policy. She develops a tentative plan for a videotape education center for patients that would be used to educate patients about their conditions and about the advantages and the risks of their treatment options. Pauline knows that when a local multispecialty physician's office developed a videotape education center, the number of patient complaints dwindled, patient compliance increased, and malpractice exposure was reduced.

Step 10: Marketing

Before opening her new facility, Pauline develops a marketing package that Maria delivers to all area medical and dental offices while introducing herself to the office staff. Maria also places advertisements in several local newspapers; arranges to have area bus benches painted with information about the clinic; and sends individual letters to the administrators of all nursing facilities, retirement centers, and commercial businesses in the area. In all written materials, extra care must be taken to provide accurate information not left open to misinterpretation. Misinterpretation may result in tort liability for *negligent misrepresentation.* Pauline must make it clear that she cannot provide *all* physical therapy services. She has limitations both because of the types of equipment she has in her facility and because of her area of clinical expertise.

A Slow Start

The first few days of business are disheartening. Only four new patients are treated during the first week. Although Michael assures Pauline that this is normal, it isn't until the clinic is treating more patients that Pauline begins to relax and enjoy herself. Following the official open house and ribbon-cutting ceremony, which is reported in the local business journal in an article accompanied by photographs, Pauline's caseload begins to grow.

At the end of the first and second business quarters following the clinic's opening, Pauline reviews her balance sheet and profit-and-loss statements with her accountant. Her contract business continues to exceed expectations, and the clinic business is beginning to meet projections. Pauline and her accountant discuss the need to hire additional professional and nonprofessional staff both for the clinic and for the continually increasing contract services. They also discuss the potential of adding other therapeutic services and pursuing the plan to become a Medicare-certified agency.

As Pauline leaves her accountant's office, she reflects on the fact that there are risks involved in nearly every aspect of her business. She realizes she has progressed only a short distance on what will be a long, hard climb, but she knows the effort will be worth it. **CM**

Barbara A. Melzer, PhD, PT, is owner of Ingram Physical Therapy and Rehabilitation, San Antonio, TX, and is Associate Professor of Physical Therapy, Southwest Texas State University, San Marcos, TX. She is Secretary of the APTA Board of Directors and a member of APTA's Insurance and Member Benefits Committee.

This column is coordinated by Susan H. Abeln, PT, ARM, President, Strategic Healthcare Alternatives (SHA). She is an Associate in Risk Management (ARM) (Insurance Institute of America) and is a member of APTA's Insurance and Member Benefits Committee.

This column is not intended as legal advice, which can be given only by your personal legal counsel, based on the law of your state or on federal law, as applicable.

REFERENCES
Brennan TA, Leape LL. Incidents of adverse events and negligence in hospitalized patients: Medical practice study 1. *N Engl J Med*. 1991;324:370-376.

Malpractice Update

*a*s politicians, jurists, and legal scholars continue to debate implementation of expansive tort reform legislation to stem the flood of civil litigation in the United States, patients continue to bring new legal actions against health care professionals for treatment-related injuries. The bases for these health care malpractice cases include professional negligence (ie, substandard care), intentional wrongs (eg, sexual battery), breach of contractual promises, and injury from defective products used in treatment.

There have been 27 physical therapy malpractice civil cases reported in the legal literature since 1960, eight of which were tried after 1990.[1,2] (One reported case, related to physical therapy but not alleging physical therapy malpractice, dealt with whether a physical therapist's incident report about alleged patient injury could be used to aid in the defense in a products-liability suit.[3]) No one knows what the total number of physical therapy malpractice claims is, because most cases are either settled out of court, abandoned by plaintiffs before trial, or not appealed beyond the initial trial court-level, and therefore are not disseminated to the public.

One note of interest: In virtually every reported case, allegations of malpractice lodged against physical therapists by patients have been grounded in professional negligence. Appellate courts have ruled in the patient's favor in 48 % (13) of these cases, either by affirming trial court judgments or by remanding cases to the trial court-level for reconsideration.

This report summarizes the three most recently reported physical therapy malpractice cases. Not included in this report are descriptions of two recent criminal cases (one state, one federal) in which physical therapists were convicted of having committed felonious sexual battery on patients.

Flores v Center for Spinal Evaluation, 865 SW 2d 261 (Tex App 1993)

A patient with a work-related shoulder injury received physical and occupational therapy treatment at a rehabilitation center. During his discharge evaluation from the center, the patient allegedly strained back muscles. A follow-up visit to his referring physician resulted in the patient being sent back to the rehabilitation center for reevaluation and continued care.

During subsequent care at the center, the patient complained of worsening back pain symptoms with activity. The center's director referred the patient to a psychologist for an evaluation. Based in part on the psychologist's assessment, the center discontinued therapy and discharged the patient.

The patient then saw another physician, who diagnosed the patient as having preexisting, multilevel lumbar spondylolysis. A lumbar diskectomy and fusion ensued. The patient subsequently filed suit against the center, alleging professional negligence (substandard care).

The trial court granted a pretrial "summary judgment" in favor of the rehabilitation center, concluding as a matter of law that the patient did not have sufficient evidence of professional or ordinary negligence to proceed to and prevail at trial. The patient appealed, claiming in part that alleged discrepancies in the defendant physical therapist's affidavit (sworn statement) and pretrial deposition "created" material issues that made summary judgment for the center inappropriate. The appellate court disagreed with the patient and affirmed (upheld) the trial court verdict in favor of the center. Specifically, the appellate court ruled that the defendant-physical therapists and their assistants were not negligent in instructing the patient in his exercises.

One additional point is noteworthy in this case. In *dicta* (remarks not directly related to the decision), the appellate court conceded that there is very little case law on record, either statewide or nationwide, concerning physical therapy malpractice. The judge writing the opinion went on to say that physical therapy malpractice actions should be treated exactly the same as physician malpractice actions.

Hodo v Basa, 449 SE 2d 523 (Ga App 1994)

The patient/plaintiff had a double amputation as a result of complications of diabetes mellitus. After her second amputation, the patient was referred by her surgeons for physical therapy evaluation and gait training, using her new prosthesis. During the evaluation, the patient fell while turning inside parallel bars. She sued the hospital for vicarious liability, alleging ordinary negligence on the part of the physical therapist and claiming physical injury and pain and suffering.

The trial court rendered its judgment in favor of the defendant (the hospital), based on the technicality that the patient's lawsuit was a professional negligence malpractice case and the patient's attorney had failed to include an expert opinion supporting professional negligence with the pleadings in the case. The appeals court rejected the patient's argument on appeal that her case should have been labeled an ordinary negligence case, which would have obviated the requirement for an expert opinion.

While her case against the hospital was on appeal, the patient filed a separate lawsuit against the physical therapist in charge of her postamputation care, alleging professional negligence. Both the trial judge and the court of appeals denied this latter suit on the grounds of *res judicata*, meaning that a final judgment had already been rendered regarding this incident.

Spence v Todaro, No 94-3757 (ED Pa, Oct 14, 1994)

A patient sued her physical therapist for failure to obtain informed consent, alleging reinjury of a previously surgically repaired rotator cuff muscle lesion while undergoing rehabilitation. The federal district court, interpreting Pennsylvania state law, dismissed the patient's case on the ground that Pennsylvania does not require health care providers to obtain patient informed consent before treatment, except for "surgical or operative procedures." Because of this procedural, pretrial dismissal, the trial judge never addressed the substantive issues of whether the defendant physical therapist had in fact obtained patient informed consent to treatment or whether the therapist's care met or breached professional standards.

This is the second recently reported Pennsylvania case to hold that state law does not extend the legal and ethical doctrine of informed consent to routine, nonsurgical health care.[4] Pennsylvania is the only jurisdiction to expressly rule that patient informed consent applies only to surgical cases. However, PTs in Pennsylvania who are members of the American Physical Therapy Association still are required by the *Guide for Professional Conduct*, Section 1.4, to obtain the patient's informed consent to treatment. The ethical obligation to obtain informed consent before physical therapy treatment stems from respect for patient autonomy regarding treatment-related decision making.

Although the number of reported physical therapy malpractice cases remains relatively small compared to physician malpractice cases (and civil litigation cases generally), it is imperative that clinicians practice prudent risk management. As Clement shows in "Liability Concerns in Aquatic Physical Therapy" (pages 63-68), risk management planning requires a detailed analysis of potential liability concerns related to practice and a knowledge of applicable laws and standards. Be aware!

Ronald W Scott, JD, PT, OCS, is Associate Professor and Interim Chair, Department of Physical Therapy, School of Allied Health Sciences, The University of Texas Health Science Center, San Antonio, Tex. He is a member of PT's Editorial Advisory Group, incoming chair of the APTA Judicial Committee, and a member of the legal faculty for APTA's risk management seminars.

References

1　Scott RW. *Health Care Malpractice: A Primer on Legal Issues for Professionals.* Thorofare, NJ: Slack, Inc; 1990:47-49.
2　Scott RW. Malpractice update. *PT—Magazine of Physical Therapy.* 1993;1(12):62-64.
3　*Community Hospitals of Indianapolis v Medtronic Inc Neuro Div,* 594 NE 2d 448 (Ind App 1 Dist Apr 15, 1992).
4　*Friter and Friter v Iolab Corp,* 607 A 2d 1111 (Pa Sup Ct 1992).

Liability and Loss Trends

One of the best tools for protecting against liability is information. PTs need to be aware of the trends in physical therapy claims and litigation.

Physical therapists and physical therapist assistants face significant liability exposure related to their clinical practice duties. Patients might lodge claims or file lawsuits against PTs for anything from the patient's subjective perception of an unsatisfactory treatment outcome to personal injury sustained while the patient is under the PT's care. In this era of general litigation crisis, the fear of liability exposure has led, on the positive side, to prudent, systematic clinical risk management, and, on the negative side, to expensive and wasteful defensive clinical practices such as attempted exculpatory contractual clauses and overutilization of services.

A patient who is simply dissatisfied with the intervention provided cannot win a malpractice lawsuit against a PT solely on that basis. Even in cases where patients sustain injury incident to the PT's evaluation, treatment, or professional advice, liability can only attach where there is a recognized legal basis for imposing it. The four recognized bases for imposing physical therapy malpractice liability include:

- Professional negligence or substandard care.

- Intentional conduct resulting in patient injury.

- Patient injury from dangerously defective treatment-related products sold to patients by clinicians or from abnormally dangerous treatment activities.

- Failure to achieve an express therapeutic promise made to a patient.

As previous columns have stated, there have been approximately 27 physical therapy civil legal cases involving patient injury reported in the legal literature since 1960, eight of which were tried after 1990,[1-3] possibly showing evidence of a growing trend in physical therapy claims and litigation. Of those cases, most were malpractice cases, and all of them were grounded in allegations of professional negligence, that is, substandard care. Several of those cases involved issues of defective treatment-related products, but product liability was not alleged by patients/plaintiffs against physical therapists/defendants.

A substantial minority of the 27 physical therapy legal cases involved allegations or findings of "ordinary negligence," which is not malpractice. Ordinary negligence is legally actionable, alleged carelessness on the part of an owner or occupier of physical premises; an example of an ordinary negligence case would be a patient falling on a wet surface in a patient dressing room. Unlike malpractice findings, a finding of ordinary negligence does not result in the provider's name being recorded in the National Practitioner Data Bank,[4] a federal data base maintained by the Department of Health and Human Services to store malpractice data, which is routinely accessible to health care employers and licensure entities. (The Databank is accessible to practitioners who want to check their own records; for more information, call 800/767-6732.)

Professional Liability Claims

Before adverse patient incidents (also known as potentially compensable events, or PCEs) such as injury or serious dissatisfaction with care can ripen into formal lawsuits, they frequently are dealt with as claims, either by employers and their professional liability insurers or by providers and their individual professional liability insurers. PTs are served by a small number of professional liability underwriters (agents) and an even smaller number of actual insurance companies (as underwriters may write policies for the same insurers).

Sources for one large insurance underwriter reported a claims frequency rate (ie, total number of claims for a given period, usually 1 year) of 376 claims for the period from 1993 to 1995. Claims involved the following allegations of malpractice (ranked by the percentage of total claims that allegations in each category represent; note that the total of percentages exceeds 100 because multiple allegations may be lodged for a single PCE):

- Negligent evaluation: 23%

- Negligent treatment involving exercise or activities of daily living (ADLs): 23%

- Negligent treatment involving modalities: 20%

- Negligent failure to monitor patients during exercise or ADLs: 10%

- Negligent failure to monitor patients during modality treatments: 9%

- Miscellaneous allegations: 9%

- Negligent failure to refer to other providers: 7%

- Sexual misconduct: 2%

Another major underwriter of PTs (using slightly different PCE categories from the other carrier) reported the following causal data for the same time period, ranked in descending order by numbers of claims:

- Miscellaneous allegations

- Improper performance of tests

- Improper patient positioning/failure to monitor/injury during manipulation

- Failure to supervise treatments or procedures

- Improper management of the course of treatment

- Inappropriate clinician behavior

- Failure to diagnose

- Failure to instruct patients on equipment use

Clinicians, clinic managers, and practice owners need to be aware of these trends and of how to maintain the fine balance between optimizing the quality of patient care and practicing effective liability risk management. This balance has been made even harder to maintain under managed care, where patient delivery may seem more businesslike and dollar-focused. Clinicians and managers should be proactive: Consult with your facility's risk management expert—or a contracting risk management expert—and health care attorneys and involve them regularly in inservice education.

The author wishes to express appreciation to Holly Moore of Maginnis & Associates and Christie Susko of APTA's Insurance and Member Benefits Department for their contributions to this column.

Ronald W Scott, JD, PT, OCS, is Associate Professor, Department of Physical Therapy, School of Allied Health Sciences, The University of Texas Health Science Center, San Antonio, Tex. He is a member of PT 's Editorial Advisory Group.

References

1   Scott RW. *Health Care Malpractice: A Primer on Legal Issues for Professionals.* Thorofare, NJ: Slack, Inc; 1990:47-49.
2   Scott RW. Malpractice update. *PT—Magazine of Physical Therapy.* 1993;1(12):62-64.
3   Scott RW. Malpractice update. *PT—Magazine of Physical Therapy.* 1995;3(4):69-70.
4   Health Care Quality Improvement Act of 1986, 42 USC 11101.

Practicing Across State Lines –Part 2

Could a PT be sued for malpractice in a state he or she has never entered? Maybe.

Last month's installment of this column addressed the topic of practicing across state lines and licensure requirement as it relates to activities such as supervision, expert witness testimony, utilization review, education, and "telemedicine." This month's column explores some malpractice risks and professional liability insurance concerns related to practice across state lines.

Malpractice/Licensure Relationship

Malpractice litigation is a means by which the legal system regulates health care providers and protects people from incompetence. In a malpractice lawsuit, the plaintiff must show that the defendant practitioner failed to live up to the applicable standard of professional care and that the defendant's failure to do so was the cause of injury to the patient.

A noteworthy aspect of the relationship between licensure requirements and malpractice is that a PT's compliance or noncompliance with licensure law is quite irrelevant to liability for malpractice. That is, the fact that a PT was engaged in the unlicensed practice of physical therapy (which typically would be a criminal act) ordinarily is not relevant to the question of whether he or she was practicing negligently. A good illustration of this principle is a Kentucky case in which a patient with an above-knee amputation sued a clinic, claiming that the PT's negligence in flexing her leg caused a fracture of the neck of the femur. The PT happened to be a recent graduate who was not licensed at the time of the incident. The appellate court, in remanding the case for a new trial, admonished the trial court not to admit into the record any evidence that the PT was unlicensed, as follows:

> Whether or not she was licensed had no relevance to the question of her negligence. If she was negligent, the Center is liable; if not, the Center is not liable based on her conduct.[1]

The same reasoning would have applied if, for example, the PT had been unlicensed at the time of the incident owing to an inadvertent failure to pay the license renewal fee on time. For purposes of malpractice litigation, an individual's failure to comply with an applicable licensure requirement is neither a sword nor a shield. Noncompliance with the requirement is not itself evidence of negligence, but this does not relieve the therapist of the duty to exercise a professional level of care.

Standard of Care

In a malpractice case, the defendant practitioner will be held to the applicable standard of care, ordinarily defined by reference to what a competent practitioner, exercising the level of knowledge and skill generally exercised by competent practitioners, would have done under circumstances comparable to those faced by the defendant.

This formula does not specify whether a court should look to the level of care provided on a local, statewide, or national basis, and the rule as to the proper geographic scope may vary from state to state. For example, the law of one state might look to the level of practice by PTs in the "same or similar localities,"[2] the "actual or a similar community,"[3] or the "general locality,"[4] whereas another state might look to the statewide level[5] or even the regional or national level (for example, Delaware has a statutory provision that serves to make the relevant standard statewide, unless evidence in the record indicates a regional or national standard[6]).

Therefore, in a malpractice suit, a PT based in one state who treats a patient in another state might be held to a standard of care that is different from the one applicable in his or her home state. Whether the difference would help or hurt the PT would depend on the circumstances.

Long-Arm Jurisdiction

The trial courts of every state may hear malpractice actions—in legal parlance, they have *subject matter jurisdiction* over such lawsuits. A separate question, however, is whether the courts of a state are entitled to exercise jurisdiction over a particular nonresident defendant—in legal parlance, whether they have *personal jurisdiction* over the individual.

Every therapist obviously will be subject to the personal jurisdiction of the courts of any state in which he/she dwells or in which he/she regularly practices. For example, a therapist who lives in Connecticut and practices physical therapy from an office in New York will be subject to the jurisdiction of the courts of both states. In such a case, the plaintiff could choose to sue in Connecticut or New York, based upon strategic considerations such as comparative geographic convenience, the speed of processing in the two jurisdictions, and perceived differences in the willingness of jurors to award generous verdicts.

If a physical therapist who was sued in a neighboring or distant state simply ignored the proceeding, the court typically would enter a default judgment, and the plaintiff could seek to enforce the default judgment in the courts of the PT's home state (eg, by attaching the PT's property or garnisheeing wages). Under the US Constitution, the courts of one state generally must enforce the valid judgments of courts of another state. Therefore, a party who simply ignored a lawsuit brought outside his or her home state would do so at his or her own peril. A default judgment generally would be enforceable in the home state courts unless the defendant persuaded the home state court that the other court's attempt to exercise jurisdiction over him or her was in violation of the US Constitution's Due Process guarantee.

Every state has a law, commonly known as a "long-arm" statute, that authorizes the courts of the state to exercise personal jurisdiction over nonresident defendants in certain circumstances. For a PT who has contact with patients from a state other than the one where the PT resides or regularly practices, the procedural question is whether the PT will be subject to the jurisdiction of the courts of the second state in addition to those of the PT's own state. The answer to that question depends on the limitations on long-arm jurisdiction imposed by the Due Process clause of the Fourteenth Amendment to the US Constitution. (Strictly speaking, whether a nonresident is subject to the jurisdiction of a state's court depends in the first place on the terms of that particular state's long-arm statute. A sizable number of states take the position that their long-arm statute reaches as far as the US Constitution permits, so this article focuses on the federal limitation on long-arm jurisdiction.)

The US Supreme Court has recognized that each state has a legitimate interest in providing its residents with a convenient forum for redressing injuries inflicted by out-of-state actors, and that it would be unfair to allow individuals who "purposefully derive benefit" from their interstate activities to escape having to account in other states for the consequences of their activities.[7] Due process is essentially a matter of fairness, and the constitutional question is whether a person's "conduct and connection with the forum State are such that he should reasonably anticipate being haled into court there."[8] The Supreme Court has said that "it is essential ... that there be some act by which the defendant purposefully avails itself of the privilege of conducting activities within the forum State, thus invoking the benefits and protections

≈

Under the US Constitution, the courts of one state generally must enforce the valid judgments of courts of another state. Therefore, a party who simply ignored a lawsuit brought outside his or her home state would do so at his or her own peril.

≈

of its laws."[9] If it is determined that a defendant did purposefully establish "minimum contacts" with the forum state, the court must then consider the factors relevant to fair play, such as the burden on the defendant of having to defend in the forum state, the state's interest in adjudicating the matter, and the plaintiff's interest in obtaining convenient and effective relief.

The Due Process limitation that long-arm jurisdiction may not violate notions of "fair play and substantial justice"[10] is a rather vague standard with which courts have had to grapple in numerous medical malpractice actions.[11] Unfortunately, the case law provides very few clear-cut rules as to long-arm

jurisdiction over medical practitioners, because the decision depends on the totality of the circumstances of the particular case. In general, when a patient travels out of state for treatment (particularly to a distant state) the courts are slow to find that the patient's home state has long-arm jurisdiction over the practitioner, even though the injury caused by any malpractice will be felt in the patient's home state.[12-18] For example, one court ruled that Idaho lacked jurisdiction over a South Dakota physician who sent a prescription to Idaho after a patient moved there.[19] In another case, a Texas court was found not to have jurisdiction over a nationally prominent Ohio surgeon who did not have Texas licensure or hospital privileges and treated a patient only in Ohio.[20]

Courts are more likely to find long-arm jurisdiction in cases where the practitioner solicits and obtains out-of-state patients or otherwise engages in interstate "marketing" activities.[21-23] For example, a California urologist who wrote a nationally distributed book was held subject to jurisdiction in Texas in a case brought by a Texas resident whose own physician referred her. The patient had traveled to California for one consultation, and the California urologist recommended that she participate in an experimental program he was conducting, for which the urologist mailed her the drugs.[24] In another case, an ophthalmologist who performed surgery in Utah was subject to Montana jurisdiction based on allegedly giving negligent postoperative advice in a phone call to Montana.[25]

Many PTs hold licenses in multiple states, so the question of whether licensure in a state confers long-arm jurisdiction has some practical importance. The mere fact of being licensed to practice physical therapy in a certain state, by itself, most likely would not be enough to make the therapist subject to the state's long-arm jurisdiction in a malpractice action. In a case involving a Maryland podiatrist who was licensed in the District of Columbia but did not practice there, the court held that the podiatrist was not subject to the long-arm jurisdiction of the District.[26] Similarly, in a case involving a New Jersey physician who was licensed in Pennsylvania (and listed in Pennsylvania phone directories), the court held that he was not subject to Pennsylvania's long-arm jurisdiction, saying, "It is the actual practice of a profession ... and not the possession of the right to practice that brings a person within the jurisdiction of a ... court."[29]

Professional Liability Coverage

Physical therapists typically obtain malpractice liability insurance to protect them against claims of professional negligence. An insurance policy is a contract, and the question of whether a PT's policy covers a claim arising out of activities that somehow cross state lines is essentially a matter of contract interpretation. *In any particular case, the answer will depend primarily on the precise language of the policy, not on any general "legal" rules.* A policyholder must look first to the portions of the policy that grant coverage and then to the policy's exclusions.

Affirmative coverage. A professional liability insurance policy ordinarily will provide for coverage of claims arising out of the holder's practice of his/her profession. For example, the professional liability policy endorsed by APTA provides:

> The **injury** or **damage** must be caused by a **medical incident** arising out of the supplying of or failure to supply **professional services** by **you** in the practice of the profession described in the Declarations or anyone for whose professional acts or omissions **you** are legally responsible. [Emphasis in original; the emphasized terms are defined by the contract.][28]

If any policy covers liability arising out of a PT's "professional services" (or a similar category), the scope of the coverage will depend on the contractual definition of the term, if there is one. Ordinarily, a professional liability policy would identify the profession (eg, "physical therapy") but would not define it. In the case of a physical therapy policy, unless the policy itself contains a definition (which would be possible, but unlikely), a court construing the policy presumably would look to the ordinary meaning of the term.

No single definition of "physical therapy" is authoritative for all purposes. Each state defines "physical therapy" in its practice act, but insurance policies typically do not make the scope of coverage dependent on any state's practice act. The most suitable source of guidance for a court likely would be the definition adopted by APTA. APTA's *Model Definition of Physical Ther-*

~

An insurance policy is a contract, and the question of whether a PT's policy covers a claim arising out of activities that somehow cross state lines is essentially a matter of contract interpretation.

~

apy for State Practice Acts[29] should carry great weight because it is the only national definition. This model definition is quoted in *A Guide to Physical Therapist Practice, Volume I: A Description of Patient Management*, which APTA's Board of Directors adopted in 1995. APTA also has a related policy, *Guidelines for Defining Physical Therapy in State Practice Acts*,[30] as well as a Philosophical Statement on Physical Therapy, which says, in part, "Other professional activities that serve the purpose of physical therapy are research, education, consultation, and administration."[31]

An insurer would be prudent to refer to APTA's definition in any situation that raises a question as to the scope of coverage under a policy issued to a PT.

In general, the question of whether a particular claim arises out of the practice of "physical therapy" (within the meaning of a professional liability policy) is unrelated to whether the PT's activities in some fashion crossed state lines. For example, if a PT regularly traveled to and treated patients in a neighboring state in which he or she was licensed, a malpractice claim brought by one of those patients undoubtedly would be covered, because the claim would arise out of the policyholder's practice of his or her profession.

Exclusions. A professional liability insurance policy ordinarily will contain various exclusions from the coverage granted affirmatively in the coverage clause(s). Such exclusions, which vary from company to company and from policy to policy, often refer to very high-risk items, such as antitrust damages and punitive damages. In addition, policies frequently seek to exclude liability attributable to the policyholder's intentional wrongdoing. For example, the policy endorsed by APTA provides:

> We will not defend or pay, under this Coverage Part, for:
> F. **injury** or **damage** resulting from a **medical incident** which is also a willful violation of a statute, ordinance or regulation imposing criminal penalties. We will defend any civil suit against **you** seeking amounts which would be covered if this exclusion did not apply. In such case, we will pay only the **claim expenses** related to such defense. [Emphasis in original.]

An exclusion such as this could conceivably apply to a claim arising out of services provided by a PT who, at the time of providing the care, was engaged in the unlicensed practice of physical therapy in violation of an applicable practice act. A therapist who simply ignored an applicable licensure requirement and blithely treated patients while unlicensed would be at some risk of losing insurance coverage (whether the treatment occurred in state or out of state) if the policy had an exclusion extending to willfully illegal behavior. Whether the insurer would be justified in denying coverage in such a case would be a matter of contract law (not licensure or malpractice law). Moreover, even if the insurer had the contractual right to deny coverage, the choice whether to do so would be a business decision.

....

John J Bennett, Esq, is APTA's General Counsel.

References

1   *Meiman v Rehabilitation Center, Inc*, 444 SW2d 78, 81 (Ky 1969).
2   *Emig v Physicians' Physical Therapy Service, Inc*, 432 NE2d 52 (Ind App 1982).
3   *Novey v Kishwaukee Community Health Services*, 531 NE2d 427, 430 (Ill App 1988).
4   *McAvenue v Bryn Mawr Hospital*, 369 A2d 743, 745 (Pa Super 1976).
5   *Wade v John D Archbold Memorial Hospital*, 252 Ga 118, 311 SE2d 836 (Ga 1984).
6   *Sweeny v Medical Center and Lamb v Hall*, 1989 Del Supe. LEXIS 517.
7   See *Burger King Corp v Rudzewicz*, 471 US 462, 473-474 (1985).
8   See *Burger King Corp v Rudzewicz*, 471 US 462, 474 (1985), quoting *World-Wide Web Volkswagen Corp v Woodson*, 444 US 286, 297 (1980).
9   See *Burger King Corp v Rudzewicz*, 471 US 462, 475 (1985), quoting *Hanson v Denckla*, 357 US 235, 253 (1958).
10 See *Burger King Corp v Rudzewicz*, 471 US 462, 476 (1985), quoting *International Shoe Co v Washington*, 326 US 310, 320 (1945).
11 See Annotation, In Personam Jurisdiction Under Long-Arm Statute, Over Nonresident Physician, Dentist, or Hospital in Medical Malpractice Action (1983), 25 ALR.4th 706.
12 *Prince v Urban*, 49 Cal App 4th 1056, 57 Cal Rptr 2d 181, (Cal App 1996).
13 *Mullen v Glick*, 1994 U.S. Dist. LEXIS 16020 (D NH 1994).
14 *Walters v St Elizabeth Hosp Medical Center*, 543 F Supp 559 (WD Pa 1982).
15 *Lebkuecher v Loquasto*, 255 Pa Super 608, 389 A2d 143 (Pa Super 1978).
16 *Cambre v St Paul Fire & Marine Insurance Co*, 331 So2d 585 (La App 1976).
17 *McAndrew v Burnett*, 374 F Supp 460 (MD Pa 1974).
18 *Gelineau v New York University Hospital*, 375 F Supp 661 (D NJ 1974).
19 *Wright v Yackley*, 459 F2d 287 (9th Cir. 1972).
20 *Clark v Noyes*, 871 SW2d 508 (Tex App 1994).
21 *Kennedy v Freeman*, 919 F2d 126 (10th Cir 1990).
22 *Phelps v Kingston*, 536 A2d 740 (NH 1987) .
23 *Cubbage v Merchent*, 744 F2d 665 (9th Cir 1984), *cert denied* 470 US 1005 (1985).
24 *Bullion v Gillespie*, 895 F2d 213 (5th Cir 1990).
25 *McGee v Riekhof*, 442 F Supp 1276 (D Mont 1978).
26 *Ghanem v Kay*, 624 F Supp 23 (D DC 1984) .
27 *Lebkuecher v. Loquasto*, 255 Pa Super 608, 389 A2d 143, 145 (Pa Super 1978).
28 *Professional Liability Coverage*. Chicago, Ill: CNA Financial Corporation; 1992.
29 APTA BOD 03-95-24-64.
30 APTA BOD 03-96-16-49.
31 APTA HOD 06-83-03-05.

Medical Devices/Medications

Pharmacology in Physical Therapist Practice
HOD P06-04-14-14 [Initial HOD 06-89-43-89]

Physical therapist patient/client management integrates an understanding of a patient's/client's prescription and nonprescription medication regimen with consideration of its impact upon health, impairments, functional limitations, and disabilities. The administration and storage of medications used for physical therapy interventions is also a component of patient/client management and thus within the scope of physical therapist practice.

Physical therapy interventions that may require the concomitant use of medications include, but are not limited to, agents that:

- Reduce pain and/or inflammation.

- Promote integumentary repair and/or protection.

- Facilitate airway clearance and/or ventilation and respiration.

- Facilitate adequate circulation and/or metabolism.

- Facilitate functional movement.

Electrophysiologic Examination and Evaluation
HOD P06-96-20-04 [Initial HOD 06-85-37-63; HOD 06-85-34-62]

Electrophysiologic examinations and evaluations as practiced by physical therapists encompass both the professional and technical components of the observation, recording, analysis, and interpretation of bioelectric muscle and nerve potentials, detected by means of surface or needle electrodes, for the purpose of evaluating the integrity of the neuromuscular system.

Electrophysiologic evaluations include, but are not limited to, clinical electromyography, motor and sensory nerve conduction studies, and other evoked potential procedures.

Independent, safe, effective, and efficient electrophysiologic examinations and evaluations by physical therapists include the following:

- Establishing appropriate rapport with each patient/client.

- Conducting a history and systems review in order to plan an appropriate electrophysiologic examination and evaluation.

- Documenting the electrophysiologic examination results.

- Analyzing and interpreting the findings of the electrophysiologic examination.

- Communicating examination procedures and results of evaluation to the appropriate individuals.

The professional education of the physical therapist includes gross anatomy, neuroanatomy, muscle and nerve physiology, clinical neurology, myology, pathology, physical and clinical sciences of electrophysiologic examination and evaluation, clinical practice experience, and provides the knowledge base for the independent performance of electrophysiologic examinations and evaluations.

By Marlene Tandy, MD, JD,
and Ed Waldron, PhD

The Basics of Medical Device Classification and Labeling

*J*ust as your patients might ask you about your education, licensure, and experience, you have the right to ask manufacturers about the research, development, safety, and effectiveness of medical equipment. If you're involved in purchasing decisions for your facility, you probably know to ask the manufacturer if a device is Food and Drug Administration (FDA) approved. But the answer can often come back in industry jargon. Here are the basics of medical device classification and labeling, intended to give you an understanding of the FDA approval process.

The Medical Device Amendments of 1976 amended the Federal Food, Drug, and Cosmetic Act (FFDCA) to create three classes of medical devices, based on possible risk to the patient. How a device is classified determines the level of supporting information and rigor of review required for the product to receive approval from the FDA.

Classification

Class I devices are low-risk devices for which the general statutory controls of the FFDCA are sufficient to provide reasonable assurance of safety and effectiveness. Manufacturers must comply with all of the following: adulteration and misbranding provisions (ie, a device must not be adulterated—made in an unsafe manner using unsafe components—and must not be misbranded—labeled in a false or misleading manner); registration and listing require-

How a device is classified determines the level of supporting information and rigor of review required for the product to receive approval from the FDA.

ments at the FDA; applicable premarket notification (510[k]) requirements; notification, repair, replacement, and refund provisions; good manufacturing practices requirements; record-keeping and reporting requirements; and provisions related to an FDA determination to ban a device from commerce.

Class II devices are medium-risk devices for which, in addition to general controls, special controls are required to provide reasonable assurance of safety and effectiveness. Special controls include performance standards, postmarket surveillance, patient registries, guidelines, recommendations, or other appropriate FDA action.

Class III devices are higher-risk devices that must meet the same requirements of the

previous two classes, as well as complete a pre-market approval application (PMA) process by FDA prior to marketing. Under the law, Class III devices that were already on the market at the time of the 1976 Medical Device Amendments and Class III devices introduced to the market after the 1976 Amendment, but that are substantially equivalent to a legally marketed Class III device, may be on the market legally without an approved PMA in place, until such time as the FDA calls for those PMAs to be submitted and approved. (The law requires the FDA to call for these PMAs by 1995.)

Two examples of pre-amendment physical therapy Class III devices are the stair-climbing wheelchair and the rigid pnuematic structural orthosis, which is a pressurized suit that provides whole-body support to help people with thoracic spine paraplegia walk.

The FDA issues a determination of substantial equivalence through a premarket notification (510[k]) submission that a manufacturer files with the agency in advance of commercial marketing. Class III devices that are marketed after the 1976 Amendments and that are not substantially equivalent as defined above must have, prior to marketing, a PMA approved by the FDA.

Most of the devices used in physical medicine and physical therapy are Class I and Class II devices. Class I devices include prosthetic and orthotic accessories, splints, limb orthoses, daily activity assist devices, manual patient rotation beds, nonmeasuring exercise equipment, and nonpowered sitz baths. Class II devices include immersion hydrobaths, paraffin baths, powered patient rotation beds, powered exercise equipment, and some powered patient transports. Also included under Class II are electrical muscle stimulators, transcutaneous electrical nerve stimulators (TENS), and diagnostic electromyography equipment.

The classification of medical devices is not always as clear-cut as it might seem. A mechanical wheelchair is Class I, but a powered wheelchair is Class II, as are special-grade wheelchairs, standing wheelchairs, and wheelchair elevators. Stair-climbing wheelchairs are Class III devices. Sometimes

> I can be helpful for consumers to ask if a device has been cleared through the 510(k) process and, if so, what the scope of that FDA clearance is. Also, is the device being promoted beyond its clearance level?

different uses of the same device are classified into different levels. Microwave diathermy, shortwave diathermy, and ultrasonic diathermy, for example, are considered Class II devices for some uses and Class III devices for others. These modalities are cleared for marketing as Class II devices when their intended use is for deep heating.

Other intended uses may require an investigational device exemption for clinical effectiveness studies. Iontophoresis may also be considered Class III when used in conjunction with a drug that has not been approved for use with iontophoresis devices.

Labeling

All medical devices, regardless of class, must comply with certain labeling and promotional requirements. Labeling includes the actual label on the product as well as any written, printed, or graphic matter on the container or wrapper or accompanying the device. Labeling must not be false or misleading. Labeling can be false or misleading by including statements that fall into that category or by failing to reveal material facts. In addition, comparative claims that are false or misleading are prohibited by the FDA.

Promotion by manufacturers of intended uses that are outside the scope of the intended uses approval in a PMA is prohibited. Similarly, a manufacturer is not permitted to promote a product beyond the scope of the 510 (k) substantial equivalence determination.

In addition, promotion of an investigational device (ie, a device still under study by a manufacturer to determine safety and effectiveness) is prohibited. This means that a company may not take sales orders for an investigational device and may not represent an investigational device as safe and effective.

Even though a device may be cleared for marketing, it is illegal for the labeling or advertising of a device to state or suggest that the device is FDA approved. In addition, no representation of approval is permitted through suggesting that a 510(k) has been cleared for the product or through the use of the FDA registration number for the device.

In dealing with labeling and advertising issues, the users of the device may want to inquire from the manufacturer whether the device is investigational. An investigational device cannot be marketed or sold commercially. It can be helpful for consumers to ask if a device has been cleared through the 510(k) process and, if so, what the scope of that FDA clearance is. Also is the device being promoted beyond its clearance level? It is also appropriate for a device user to ask the manufacturer to provide information that substantiates the claims made in labeling and advertising. *PT*

Marlene Tandy, MD, JD, is senior analyst and counsel in the Technology and Regulatory Affairs Department of the Health Industry Manufacturers Association (HIMA). Before joining HIMA, Dr Tandy served as a food and drug attorney with a Washington, DC, law firm.

Ed Waldron, PhD, is senior writer and editor for HIMA. Prior to joining HIMA, Dr Waldron taught medical ethics at the University of North Dakota School of Medicine. He also wrote and edited a quarterly publication for the UND Medical Center Rehabilitation Hospital.

Moderator Charles D Ciccone, PhD, PT, is Associate Professor, Department of Physical Therapy, School of Health Science and Human Performance, Ithaca College, Ithaca, NY. He served as editor of *Physical Therapy*'s special series on pharmacology (May and June issues). "The goal of the series," explains Ciccone, "is to provide some critical insights into how physical therapy and pharmacology are interrelated." Ciccone is Associate Editor—Abstracts and Reviews for the journal and is a member of *PT*'s Editorial Advisory Group.

ROUNDTABLE

Medications and the PT's Role

WHAT IS YOUR RESPONSIBILITY

WHEN IT COMES TO PATIENTS AND

THEIR MEDICATIONS?

Meg Barry, MS, PT, is Research Physical Therapist, Department of Neurosurgery, Children's Hospital, Pittsburgh, Pa. She currently is investigating the effects of intrathecally administered baclofen and selective dorsal rhizotomy, primarily in patients with cerebral palsy.

Lawrence P Cahalin, MA, PT, CCS, is Cardiopulmonary Physical Therapy Transplant Coordinator and Assistant Professor, Massachusetts General Hospital and Institute of Health Professions, Boston. In "Pulmonary Medications" (*Physical Therapy*, May), Cahalin and H Steven Sadowsky, RRT, PT, CCS, discussed medications commonly used in the treatment of pulmonary disorders.

Donna El-Din, PhD, PT, is Distinguished Professor and Chair, Department of Physical Therapy, Eastern Washington University, Cheney, Wash. She has published and presented papers on ethics and documentation and currently is a member of the *Journal of Physical Therapy Education* editorial board.

Margaret Schenkman, PhD, PT, is Associate Professor, Graduate Program of Physical Therapy, and Co-Director, Claude D Pepper Older Americans Independence Center, Duke University Medical Center, Durham, NC. In "Pharmacological and Nonpharmacological Interventions in the Treatment of Parkinson's Disease" (*Physical Therapy*, May), Schenkman and coauthors Toni Cutson, MD, MHS, and Kathryn Cotter Laub, PT, emphasized the collaboration of multiple disciplines in patient management.

Ciccone: If we had to come up with one word to characterize physical therapy practice, it probably would be "diversity." This roundtable panel certainly represents that diversity. Our areas of expertise range from pediatrics to geriatrics to sports to orthopedics to cardiopulmonary to neurology. But we have a unifying theme: Most of our patients are taking some type of medication. What should every PT—regardless of setting—know about drugs?

El-Din: Every PT should recognize that patients generally are unaware of the actions of the drugs they take.

Cahalin: I may be biased, but of all the drugs that patients take, cardiopulmonary and cardiovascular medications may be the most common and have the most dramatic side effects—and be the least understood. If patients don't know about the potential effects, they can be in real jeopardy.

Barry: It's also essential that patients' *families* understand drug effects. In pediatrics, for example, antispasticity medications are commonly prescribed, but the people who are primarily responsible for monitoring the use of these medications—the caregivers in the home—often don't understand how they work.

Schreck: Many prescribing physicians either don't have or don't take the time to educate patients and families about drugs. Education therefore becomes the PT's responsibility, especially with geriatric and pediatric patients.

Barry: But so many PTs don't understand the effects of drugs.

Ciccone: Do PTs typically receive a formal course on pharmacology in school?

El-Din: Some PT education programs do provide formal courses. Others are beginning to include pharmacology in the curriculum as an adjunct to each area of study, which may be a more effective method because it encourages students to view drug effects as one more factor in the clinical decision-making process.... The profes-

sion is moving toward a professional postbaccalaureate degree because we want PTs to develop the skills to be lifelong learners—skills that are difficult to develop at the undergraduate level, such as listening, careful observation, and consultation. And nowhere are those skills more important than in the area of drug effects.

Ciccone: Why is that?

El-Din: Drug effects have an impact on every aspect of the patient's medical treatment. All of the health care providers working with the patient need to know—and have a responsibility to share—that information. It *can* be a matter of life or death.

Schenkman: Is knowledge of pharmacology specifically included in the accreditation standards, and, if not, should it be?

Ciccone: The accreditation standards do not explicitly state what courses must be taught. They state only that the curriculum must consist of a combination of didactic, clinical, and research experiences that are reflective of contemporary practice and include instruction in basic and clinical sciences. This certainly could include pharmacology. It's up to the schools to decide. Participants in the national 1993 IMPACT conference on postbaccalaureate entry-level [professional] curricula came to the consensus that students should be expected to understand pharmacokinetics and the ways in which drugs may affect physical therapy.

Thein: But physical therapy education—like medical education—can address only so much. If PTs need to know about drug effects to help educate patients and to understand patients' reactions to therapy, PTs have to take the responsibility to educate themselves through reading, attending continuing education courses, and communicating with physicians.

Schreck: The US Army-Baylor University Graduate Program in Physical Therapy emphasizes the PT's role as evaluator and manager of patients with neuromusculoskeletal conditions, and that includes not just understanding drug effects but pre-

Richard C Schreck, COL, SP, USA, MS, PT, OCS, is Chief, Physical Therapist Section, US Department of the Army, Office of the Surgeon General. In *Physical Therapy* (May), Schreck and coauthors Cindy J Benson, LTC, SP, USA, PT, Frank B Underwood, LTC, SP, USA, PhD, PT, and David G Greathouse, COL, SP, USA, PhD, PT, described the credentialing process and the expanded clinical privileges that allow military PTs to order certain medications. Schreck was featured in "More than a Uniform: The Military Model of Physical Therapy" (*PT*, March).

Ronald W Scott, JD, PT, OCS, is Assistant Professor and Interim Chair, Department of Physical Therapy, The University of Texas Health Science Center at San Antonio, Tex. A retired major in the US Army, Scott is a practicing attorney, serves on APTA's Risk Management Faculty and on APTA's Judicial Committee, and is a member of *PT*'s Editorial Advisory Group.

Lori A Thein, MS, PT, SCS, ATC, is Physical Therapist and Associate Lecturer, Department of Kinesiology, Physical Therapy Program, University of Wisconsin Sports Medicine Center, Madison, Wisc. With coauthors Jill M Thein, PT, ATC, and Gregory L Landry, MD, Thein discussed ergogenic aids in *Physical Therapy* (May).

"MANY PRESCRIBING PHYSICIANS EITHER DON'T HAVE OR DON'T TAKE THE TIME TO EDUCATE PATIENTS AND FAMILIES ABOUT DRUGS. EDUCATION THEREFORE BECOMES THE PT's RESPONSIBILITY."

—Dick Schreck

scribing certain medications. Once our PTs accept this role, they are responsible for their own continuing education. When their credentials are reviewed, they must be able to verify completion of continuing education in pharmacology.

Ciccone: How do military PTs obtain the continuing education they need?

Schreck: Military physicians and pharmacists willingly provide in-service and continuing education programs locally, at the individual military facility. In the civilian sector, there are very few continuing education courses offered just on pharmacology; however, many physical therapy continuing education courses do address it as one part of the course.

Ciccone: When adequate continuing education opportunities are unavailable, are there other avenues?

Scott: It's perfectly acceptable for the PT to engage in a "self-education" process *with* the patient. When I review a patient's record and notice that the patient is taking medications with which I'm not familiar—such as a new NSAID [nonsteroidal anti-inflammatory drug] or a new muscle relaxant prescribed by an orthopedist—I look up the mechanism of action, indications, contraindications, and potential interactions so I'll be prepared to go over them with the patient during the initial visit. I often read

the *Physicians' Desk Reference* out loud with the patient. But I'm always careful to let the patient know that I am not interpreting the information, because interpretation is beyond my scope of practice as a therapist. I also inform the physician that the patient didn't have adequate knowledge of the drug and its effects.

Ciccone: Ron has touched on the PT's scope of practice. We'll get back to that. Are pharmacists a good education resource?

Cahalin: I get a great deal of information from pharmacists, sometimes more than I do from physicians or other health care providers.

Schreck: Pharmacists are a good educational resource for the Army PT. Again, as part of the credentialing process, they provide lectures and on-the-job training.

El-Din: The relationship with the pharmacist is key. It's an example of the kind of professional liaisons we need to pursue with all of the health professions.

Ciccone: Like PTs, pharmacists have had to change their focus from being service providers only to also being consumer educators. In my experience, they're very willing to talk with PTs.

Barry: In the pediatrics setting, I primarily work on a team with physicians and nurses. Nurses also are a great source of information.

Ciccone: How might a nurse's perspective on drugs differ from that of a physician or a pharmacist?

Barry: Nurses see firsthand the effects of drugs on patients and have experience with the relevant medical and social issues. In the acute care and rehab settings, nurses may be very familiar with the patient and may have insight into how a medication could affect physical therapy goals and treatment. Nurses also can be helpful in coordinating the medication schedule with the physical therapy schedule, especially for patients who need an analgesic before therapy, for instance.

Drug Effects Versus Disease Effects

Ciccone: Drug effects may mimic some of the symptoms of the disease for which the patient is being treated. How can PTs help distinguish between the two?

Schenkman: First things first: Learn about potential drug effects. Second, keep up with the literature. For example, Berg et al[1] showed that the side effects of medication for Parkinson's disease include dystonia and dyskinesia—both of which also can occur as a consequence of the disease itself. There is increasing evidence that drug therapies can retard recovery from neurological insults such as stroke.[2] PTs are the health professionals who work daily and intimately with patients on the functional problems that drugs typically affect. PTs therefore may have the best opportunity to sort out what's symptomatic of the disease and what's symptomatic of the medications. But this requires good clinical decision making and analysis, because there are very few situations in which symptoms are clearly one or the other.

Cahalin: Because of advancements in medical technology, PTs are treating patients who are sicker than ever before—patients who may have multisystem failure. Just as we need to identify the primary disease that may affect processes related to the physical therapy problem, we need to identify the primary drug that may be having an impact—beneficial or detrimental—on our physical therapy interventions. [See "Cardiopulmonary Case in Point," page 60.]

Barry: In pediatrics, for example, PTs need to be alert to patientss who take seizure medications and who may become lethargic as a result. In children, cardiac medications may cause tremors, and chemotherapy may result in tremors or in neurotoxicity. There also may be changes in sensation or changes in motor control, such as foot drop.... It's essential for PTs to document these drug effects.

El-Din: PTs are notorious for their ability to note change! They document impaired

"PTs MAY HAVE THE BEST OPPORTUNITY TO SORT OUT WHAT'S SYMPTOMATIC OF THE DISEASE AND WHAT'S SYMPTOMATIC OF THE MEDICATIONS. BUT THIS REQUIRES GOOD CLINICAL DECISION MAKING AND ANALYSIS, BECAUSE THERE ARE VERY FEW SITUATIONS IN WHICH SYMPTOMS ARE CLEARLY ONE OR THE OTHER."

—Margaret Schenkman

mobility, balance, stability, weakness, stiffness, and pain. But they don't always document what may be the *potential causes* of these problems. Pharmacologic agents may cause weakness, for example, or they may change a patient's perceptions of pain. In addition, we have to consider the potential effects of other substances. After all, the definition of "drug" has expanded to include alcohol. Is the patient a heavy coffee-drinker? If so, does that have an effect on physical therapy treatment? If an elderly patient is incontinent, we can't assume the cause is "just old age." There are so many factors.

Schenkman: Because PTs see patients regularly, they should be especially aware of the signs and symptoms of overmedication or undermedication for common problems. For example, patients may be hypertensive or have orthostatic hypotension because of miscompliance with drug therapy involving diuretics or calcium channel blockers. If the diet, exercise, and medications of patients with diabetes are

not well controlled, those patients may become diaphoretic, confused, or orthostatically hypotensive. And if elderly patients have atypical confusion or somnolence, the PT should be aware that they may be misusing drugs or adding sleeping or antianxiety drugs such as the benzodiazepines. The PT is in a good position to counsel the patient and to refer the patient back to the physician.

El-Din: We shouldn't forget that there are some very common, overall effects of drugs, such as sedation and euphoria or nausea and vomiting, which may be confused with disease effects. These are symptoms that PTs screen on a daily basis. It's also important to distinguish between the effects of drugs and the effects of social and cognitive factors. Among the elderly, for example, these factors may include living alone or being intellectually impaired. Elderly people who feel isolated often show behavioral changes, such as depression, which may mimic drug effects.

Ciccone: What should PTs know about drug interactions?

Scott: Dealing effectively with drug interactions requires an interdisciplinary process, with pharmacists as the primary technical consultants. I recently questioned whether to use phonophoresis with hydrocortisone for a patient who was undergoing anticoagulant therapy. The physician didn't think there would be any contraindications, but he wasn't certain. Nor was the pharmacist. It took a computer software decision tree program to reach the conclusion that there might be a contraindication! These types of decisions can't be made by a PT or a nonphysician provider learning pharmacology through on-the-job training. We need training at the professional education level and beyond.

Communicating With Families and Physicians

Ciccone: How can PTs help families with children who are taking medications?

Barry: The PT can explain drug effects and the signs that families should monitor. For instance, telling the family of a child taking baclofen that "his movement disorder may improve" probably would mean very little to them. The possible benefits should be described in such a way that the family can determine whether a medication is effective: "Adducting the hips to change a diaper may become easier." The PT also can explain how a drug may affect a child's function: "If, as a result of using this medication, your child no longer 'scissors' when he attempts to walk, he may be able to walk a greater distance with less effort."

Ciccone: So parents don't usually know what to expect?

Barry: No. That's why it's important for the PT to describe the usual course of events. If parents see what seems to be greater weakness in their child, they may assume that the medication is detrimental. They may not realize that physical therapy for strengthening is necessary before any functional improvement can be facilitated by the medication. [See "Pediatric Case in Point," page 66.] Families also need to be reminded of possible adverse effects—such as drowsiness in the case of baclofen—and what to do about them. Because PTs may have frequent contact with the family, they have the opportunity not only to monitor the effects of the drug on a regular basis but to discuss the parents' observations and to communicate this information to physicians.

Cahalin: A PT's documentation of changes over time can result in adjustments to the medical routine that ensure a better response to medical treatment—but only if the PT communicates those changes *appropriately* to a physician, a nurse, or a pharmacist.

Ciccone: This brings us to Donna's [El-Din] earlier point about the PT's role as consultant. What specific strategies can a PT use to communicate adverse side effects to other members of the health care team?

Schenkman: When we don't try to speak beyond what we know—when we are able to identify what we *think* versus what we know from the literature—we have more credibility with other health professionals.

Schreck: Once you've established that credibility, just do what PTs do best: Describe changes in patient status and monitor symptoms and response to care. Then ask how those changes may be related to the medication.

Barry: If you feel a medication would be beneficial to your patient, don't hesitate to send physicians copies of journal articles that describe drug effects or the relationship between drug effects and physical therapy. In describing the patient, offer both objective and subjective information. Patients often are willing to tell PTs things that they won't tell physicians. They may complain about pain for weeks to the PT, but when they go to the physician, they say, "I feel fine."

Cardiopulmonary Case in Point: Communicating Drug Effects

Physical therapists treat many patients who are taking multiple drugs that can have profound side effects and interactions. As is illustrated in the case below, therapists often are in the best position to note these effects and interactions—and to provide the physician with critical information about the patient's status.

Three years ago, Ms R, now 56 years old, received an isolated right-lung transplant as a result of alpha-1 antitrypsin–deficiency-associated emphysema. She developed symptoms of increasing dyspnea and fatigue 2 months ago after a routine visit to her primary care physician, who at that time prescribed 50 mg of Tenormin® once per day for the uncontrolled hypertension that had resulted from obesity (she weighs 235 lb) and from immunosuppressive therapy (125 mg of cyclosporine twice daily, 75 mg of Imuran® once daily, and 15 mg of prednisone once daily). Table 1 lists other medications being taken by Ms R.

Because of continued dyspnea and fatigue, Ms R has been referred to outpatient physical therapy by her primary care physician for exercise evaluation and exercise conditioning. She is brought to the physical therapy department via wheelchair and is observed to be in mild respiratory distress while seated and receiving 2 L/min of supplemental oxygen through a nasal cannula. Resting vital signs include a very low heart rate, blood pressure, and oxygen saturation level, with a modestly elevated respiratory rate (Tab 2). A single-lead electrocardiogram and then a 12-lead electrocardiogram confirm a sinus bradycardia of 40 bpm, without heart block.

Ms R is instructed to perform 10 knee extension exercises bilaterally while seated in the wheelchair. The physical therapist notes that although this exercise does not increase heart rate or blood pressure, it does increase the respiratory rate while decreasing the oxygen saturation level slightly. After exercise, Ms R's vital signs return to baseline and ambulation is attempted, during which she is observed to have a hypoadaptive systolic blood pressure response, an unchanged heart rate, an elevated respiratory rate, and a marked reduction in the oxygen saturation level. Ms R is able to walk only 6 feet, at which point she complains of severe dyspnea, fatigue, and dizziness. After sitting with her legs elevated for several minutes and receiving increased supplemental oxygen, her vital signs return to baseline.

The physical therapist discusses these changes with Ms R's primary care physician, who decides to replace Tenormin® with another antihypertensive agent, Cardizem® (60 mg, three times daily). Within 1 week, Ms R's symptoms and blood pressure control markedly improve.

What has happened here? Prednisone helps reduce the severity of Ms R's immune system attack on the transplanted lung; however, it is at the cost of morbid obesity and skeletal muscle wasting. Obesity and inactivity—in addition to the effects of cyclosporine and Imuran®—have resulted in hypertension. Tenormin®, which was prescribed to control that hypertension, unfortunately has its own side effects, which are more than this patient with lung disease can tolerate: It lowers not only blood pressure but heart rate.

Although Tenormin® is beta₁-specific (ie, blocking only beta₁-adrenergic receptors that decrease heart rate and force of contraction), in some patients and at higher doses it also can block beta₂-adrenergic receptors (ie, inhibiting bronchodilation in the lungs). Tenormin® therefore produces a modest degree of bronchoconstriction, which further decreases oxygenation, produces more profound dyspnea and fatigue, and increases respiratory rates. It is likely that the observed hypoxia resulted in an increased amount of vasoconstriction in the lungs, which in turn increased the work of the right heart and resulted in a transient degree of right-sided heart failure and in the hypoadaptive blood pressure response noted during ambulation. Use of a non-beta-blocking antihypertensive agent (Cardizem®) apparently has allowed for greater bronchodilation and has increased heart rate and blood pressure so that adequate oxygenation can occur, resulting in reduced symptoms and improved vital signs. Cardizem® has its own interactive effects, however. It is known to increase cyclosporine levels; Ms R's dose of cyclosporine therefore is reduced to 100 mg.

Not all cases are as complicated as those involving lung transplantation, of course. But many of our patients are taking multiple medications for more common neurological, orthopedic, and cardiovascular conditions, and physical therapists can be the key observers and communicators of effects that indicate potentially dangerous drug actions and interactions.

—*Lawrence P Cahalin, MA, PT, CCS*

Table 1. Ms R's Medications

Medication	Purpose	Some Possible Adverse Effects
Cyclosporine	Immunosuppression.	Kidney and liver damage, hypertension, muscular cramping or tremor or both, possible muscle mitochondrial dysfunction, excessive hair growth, and increased susceptibility to infection.
Imuran®	Immunosuppression.	Bone marrow suppression with associated decrease in white blood cells or platelets or both, hepatitis, mouth sores, and increased susceptibility to infection.
Prednisone	Immunosuppression.	Muscle wasting, osteoporosis, obesity, hyperlipidemia, glucose intolerance, fluid retention, increased susceptibility to infection, and mood swings.
Tenormin®	Treatment of hypertension.	Bradycardia; hypotension; bronchospasm; heart failure; heart block; and possible central nervous system symptoms of dizziness, lightheadedness, and fatigue.
Lasix®	Treatment of edema and hypertension.	Profound diuresis with water and electrolyte depletion.
Potassium	Treatment of potassium depletion caused by use of Lasix®.	Muscle cramping and cardiac dysrhythmias.
Atrovent®	Used as a bronchodilator for maintenance treatment of bronchospasm associated with emphysema.	Possible central nervous system stimulation and associated symptoms (nervousness, dizziness, headache).
Azmacort®	Oral glucocorticosteroid used to maintain bronchodilation and to treat bronchial asthma.	Oral infections and a dry, irritated throat and mouth.
Aspirin	Prevention of thrombosis.	Gastrointestinal disturbances.
Bactrim™	Prevention of pneumonia and other infections.	Gastrointestinal disturbances and allergic skin reactions.
Clotrimazole	Treatment of fungal and yeast infections of the mouth and tongue.	Edema, stinging sensations, and erythema of mouth and tongue.
Questran®	Reduction of elevated serum cholesterol levels.	Constipation and other gastrointestinal disturbances.

Table 2. Ms R's Vital Signs

Vital Signs	At Rest	During Knee Extension Exercises	During Ambulation
Heart rate (bpm)	40	40	40
Blood pressure (mm Hg)	90/60	90/60	70/46
Respiratory rate	28	34	40
Arterial oxygen percent saturation (SaO_2 [%])[a]	88	86	78

[a]While receiving 2 L/min of supplemental oxygen.

Pain and Undermedication

Ciccone: Meg has brought up the issue of pain. Is pain undermedicated in this country?

El-Din: With the elderly population, there are two extremes. One is the "start low, go slow" approach commonly advocated by pharmacists, which may result in undermedication. The other is the strategy of medicating patients so that they will be manageable in the nursing home setting, which may result in overmedication. Fortunately, the latter approach is falling to the wayside. The complex issue of pain perception plays a big role in undermedication. As people age, for example, they lose certain neurons within the spinal cord, which may cause them to have a heightened pain threshold. In addition to physiological changes, there are social factors that affect how people perceive pain, regardless of age. We need knowledge not just of the drugs involved but of the patient's cultural background. People of southern European cultures, for instance, are thought to feel free to express their emotions, whereas people of certain Asian cultures are thought to feel less free to do so.

Thein: In outpatient orthopedics, patients tend to fall into two categories: Those who are undermedicated because a physician believes that most pain related to orthopedic conditions is "tolerable," and those who are undermedicated because they were prescribed an antiinflammatory agent that has an analgesic component, which they choose not to take because they think it's only for pain and they don't want to become addicted to painkillers. It all goes back to patient education.

Barry: It also goes back to physician education. Many physicians are afraid to prescribe narcotics out of a fear of addiction. In reality, addiction to narcotics is very rare.[3] In pediatrics, physicians are especially apprehensive. Undermedication for pain is a problem, particularly in children who are unable to communicate. However, infants and children do feel pain, and narcotics can be a safe way to manage that pain.[4,5] At our facility, for example, we use epidural morphine for pain control post-rhizotomy, and the children generally do very well. Because their pain is relieved, they are mobilized more quickly, reducing the risk of cardiopulmonary complications and reducing the length of stay.

Ciccone: Are families fearful about the use of narcotics in the treatment of their children?

Barry: In my experience, the parents' primary concern is for the pain to be taken away from their child. They generally don't worry about addiction unless a prolonged use of narcotics is necessary.

Scott: Physician perceptions of addiction in part led to the clinical practice guidelines for acute pain management that were promulgated by the Agency for Health Care Policy and Research [AHCPR].[6,7] It was found that physicians often undermedicate. The most important statement of the guidelines may be this: "The institutional process of acute pain management begins with an affirmation that patients should have access to the best level of pain relief that may safely be provided."[6]

El-Din: Under managed care, however, addiction *may* become an issue. Patients are being discharged from the hospital earlier and may become more dependent on pharmacologic agents to be able to function at home.

> **"WHEN THE PATIENT IS AT THE CENTER OF GOAL SETTING BY THE TEAM, THE PT CAN ALWAYS REFER THE PHYSICIAN TO THOSE GOALS... THE KEY IS TO REMOVE YOURSELF FROM THE SITUATION."**
> **—Lori Thein**

Ciccone: What are some specific strategies for PTs who feel that their patients are undermedicated?

Thein: Over the course of several months of therapy, a PT may hear patients with chronic pain complain about a general decline in their ability to take part in daily activities, about lack of sleep, or about an inability to get out of bed. The PT may believe that antidepression medication or a referral to a pain clinic is needed. It can be a challenge to communicate these types of recommendations and observations, especially to an orthopedic surgeon who may not necessarily be comfortable prescribing antidepressants. Rather than saying, "I think the patient needs medication," the PT can say, "These are the signs and symptoms I've seen over this period of time. I'm concerned that the patient may be _____. What do you think?" Initiate the conversation about what might be done, but allow the physician come to the conclusion.

El-Din: We're emphasizing the PT's role as consultant, but we need to remember that it isn't just a matter of whether the PT is inclined to function in this type of role. It's also a matter of whether the health care environment allows or encourages the PT to function in this way. The overall climate is not necessarily conducive to collaboration.

Thein: On the other hand, in many facilities and hospitals undergoing reorganization, "patient focused care" and "care teams" are the models for professional interaction. When the patient is at the center of goal setting by the team, the PT can always refer the physician to those goals: "The pain is interfering with the achievement of the goals that we, the treatment team, set for this patient." The key is to remove yourself from the situation. Focus on the patient.

Barry: Sometimes when we communicate with physicians about pain medication, we approach them as though we're asking for a personal favor. Focusing on the goals avoids the power play.

Scott: Team meetings to review the AHCPR pain guidelines may be necessary

> **"IN ADDITION TO PHYSIO-LOGICAL CHANGES, THERE ARE SOCIAL FACTORS THAT AFFECT HOW PEOPLE PERCEIVE PAIN, REGARDLESS OF AGE. WE NEED KNOWLEDGE NOT JUST OF THE DRUGS INVOLVED BUT OF THE PATIENT'S CULTURAL BACKGROUND."**
>
> **—Donna El-Din**

so that everyone is up to speed on the need to adequately medicate these patients.

Cahalin: My communication strategy is three-pronged. First, I discuss the patient's care with the physician; second, I send copies of progress notes; and third, and perhaps most important, I let the *patient* know that he or she has a right to ask the physician to prescribe pain medication.

Thein: I've used that technique selectively with physicians. I've had limited success, depending on the type of relationship that the patient and physician have. The physician may feel that the PT "coerced" the patient or that the PT went beyond the scope of physical therapy practice.

Schenkman: It's almost as though there are two different conversations going on within this roundtable.

Ciccone: And within our profession!

Schenkman: One conversation advocates approaching the physician "obliquely," with our focus on the patient's goals, as described by Lori [Thein] and Meg [Barry]. The other conversation advocates developing the knowledge base to speak directly on the issue of drugs. The reality for most PTs

today is that they have to approach the issue obliquely unless they have a particular kind of relationship with a physician. To approach the physician directly, we as a profession would need to change our perception of our role on the health care team and to increase our knowledge base to communicate effectively.

Schreck: Here's where we may want to consider another alternative. As are PTs in the military, PTs in the civilian sector could be privileged to write prescriptions for medications to assist with the rehabilitation program. It would improve efficiency if PTs didn't have to go back to a physician for certain medications. Not only would we as a profession have to change our perception of the role we play on the team, but we as a profession would need to change our education programs, state licensing laws, and credentialing processes.

The Privilege to Prescribe

Ciccone: We've arrived at an important question! *Should* PTs be able to prescribe certain drugs?

Scott: As Dick [Schreck] indicated, it would require changes in the medical, physical therapy, and pharmacy practice acts of 50 states!

Schreck: Military PTs do have an advantage. For them, federal government regulations and policies guide medical practice, regardless of the state in which the treatment facility is located.

Ciccone: How did the PT prescription-writing privilege come about in the military?

Schreck: Twenty years ago, as a result of a physician shortage, PTs projected themselves into the role of primary musculoskeletal screeners at a direct access level. From that role evolved the limited ability to prescribe medications such as analgesics and NSAIDs. We developed the necessary training, monitoring, physician review, and credentialing process to do this; pharmacology was incorporated into our musculoskeletal screening evaluator course. The

most important factor was that we had physician support.

Scott: In the Army, the individual PT applies for the privilege based on the specific areas in which he or she would like to prescribe, such as orthopedics. The application goes through the Pharmacy and Therapeutics Committee and is reviewed by a separate interdisciplinary credentials committee. The PT then must receive approval for prescription privileges by the administrator of the individual medical facility or hospital. These credentials are reviewed every 2 years. [For more on pharmacology and physical therapy within the military model, see the May issue of *Physical Therapy*.]

Ciccone: Would a specific credentialing process benefit civilian practice?

Schenkman: Not unless the civilian health care system evolves in the same way that the military health care system did.

Scott: But that may happen. Under managed care, PTs in the civilian sector may expand into a primary care provider role for patients with neuromusculoskeletal problems. That's certainly a move that APTA has taken up with the Institute of Medicine's Committee on the Future of Primary Care.[x]

Thein: If the need did exist in the civilian sector, and if we were able to build pharmacology into the professional education process, the ability to prescribe could be linked to specialization.

Schreck: Which would be very similar to the military model.

Ciccone: Is pharmacology currently included as a competency in specialist certification examinations?

Thein: According to Patti Tice, APTA Director of Specialist Certification, pharmacology is included as a knowledge area in the examinations, with varying degrees of emphasis. I'm a member of the Sports Specialty Council of the American Board of Physical Therapy Specialties, and the sports specialist certification examination does test for specific pharmacology knowledge.

Ciccone: Ron, what do the state practice acts say about PTs prescribing drugs?

Scott: The medical practice acts of several states allow a physician to delegate certain "medical acts" to nonphysicians, such as prescribing drugs with a physician's countersignature. In some cases, nurses and physician assistants can prescribe a limited formulary *without* a physician's countersignature; such prescription must be allowed under all of the applicable state practice acts.

Pharmacists in a few states, such as Florida and California, also can prescribe certain drugs without physician countersignature. But prescription is a moot point for us, because, to the best of my knowledge, physical therapy practice acts do not address drug prescription by PTs.

Ciccone: What about recommending over-the-counter [OTC] drugs?

El-Din: In the United States, people assume that if a drug is OTC, it's safe.

Scott: And that's not necessarily true! OTC

drugs can be very powerful, especially in the way that they may interact with other drugs. It's been said that if aspirin were introduced today, it would have to be introduced as a prescription drug.... The medical practice acts I just cited do not disallow nonphysicians from recommending OTC drugs without a physician's countersignature. Pharmacists recommend OTC drugs all the time; even work-study clerks in student health services—including clerks who aren't students of the health professions—reportedly do. In some states, such as Texas, the medical practice act allows nonphysicians to give nutritional advice but remains silent

Pediatric Case in Point: Evaluating Drug Effects

As this case shows, physical therapists also have an integral role in helping to determine the therapeutic effects of drugs.

Lee is a healthy, 17-year-old boy with spastic diplegic cerebral palsy. He is evaluated in the spasticity clinic of a children's hospital by an interdisciplinary team that includes the disciplines of neurosurgery, orthopedics, physical therapy, occupational therapy, physiatry, social work, and nursing. Lee states that his goal is to "walk better," and his mother is supportive of any intervention that may improve his functional ability and allow him more independence.

Lee uses an anterior rolling walker and hip-knee-ankle orthoses (HKAFOs), with a major amount of upper extremity weight bearing. When he walks without the orthoses, he has adduction and flexion of the hip and flexion of the knee, and he walks on his toes. There is very little lower extremity dissociation. He has contractures resulting from hip and knee flexion and ankle plantar flexion.

Lee had hamstring and heel-cord lengthening at 7 years of age. Using the Ashworth scale,[1] his spasticity level is graded as 4/5 throughout the lower extremities and 1/5 throughout the upper extremities. The spasticity team recommends a trial of intrathecally administered baclofen to reduce spasticity and improve ease of movement. The team explains to

both Lee and his mother that risks may include infection, drowsiness, nausea, and headache. Lee is admitted for a trial of single intrathecal baclofen injections (25 μg). Because this is a double-blind trial, he also receives placebo. Using the Ashworth scale, the physical therapist assesses lower extremity muscle tone each morning preinjection and every 2 hours postinjection for 8 hours.

The response to baclofen is considered positive when the average lower extremity score drops by 1 point.[2] Lee responds positively and is offered a programmable implanted pump for continuous intrathecal baclofen infusion (CIBI). The team explains the risks, which include infection, overdose, drowsiness, headache, and catheter or pump problems. Physical therapy is recommended at a rate of three times per week for 3 months to build strength before surgery. The pump is implanted; Lee's hospital stay is 11 days. At discharge, the physical therapist reports that Lee is able to perform transfers more easily than he was able to do before surgery and that Lee has had no adverse side effects from the drug. The CIBI dosage is 200 μg/day.

After 1 month of outpatient physical therapy for stretching, strengthening, and gait training, Lee's therapist documents that his spasticity still is interfering with function. As a result, the physician increases the dosage to 240 μg/day. At his 5-month postoperative visit, Lee is

walking with ankle-foot orthoses (AFOs) instead of HKAFOs. At 6 months, the dosage is increased to 268 μg/day. Through physical therapy, Lee has gained enough strength to tolerate this higher dose, which means that he is relying less on extensor spasticity to walk. Lee is able to walk with Lofstrand crutches at 7 months postsurgery.

Two years after pump implantation, Lee walks independently with AFOs and Lofstrand crutches. The daily dosage of 268 μg/day seems to be optimal for him. Lee's mother is very pleased and feels the benefits are worth the 10-hour drive for pump refills every 3 months. Lee reports that he feels the combination of CIBI and physical therapy has allowed him to gain independence and meet his goal of "walking better."

This case is an example of the need for research protocols, as Campbell et al[3] stated, "to clarify [baclofen's] effects on control of voluntary movement, functional limitations, and quality of life."

—*Meg Barry, MS, PT*

References

1 Ashworth B. Preliminary trial of carisoprodol in multiple sclerosis. *Practitioner.* 1964;192:540-542.
2 Albright AL, Cervi A, Singletary J. Intrathecal baclofen for spasticity in cerebral palsy. *JAMA.* 1991;265:1418-1422.
3 Campbell SK, Almeida GL, Penn RD, Corcos DM. The effects of intrathecally administered baclofen on function in patients with spasticity. *Phys Ther.* 1995;75:352-362.

about giving OTC drug advice. In my opinion, that silence should not necessarily be interpreted as permission to recommend OTC drugs to patients.*

Ciccone: What, then, is the PT's liability?

Scott: If a PT were to recommend aspirin to a teenager, for example, and that teenager were to develop Reye syndrome, the PT could be liable civilly for professional negligence and could even be challenged for practicing medicine without a license.

Thein: In the sports specialization area, PTs often can evaluate and treat teenage athletes without physician referral; however, we cannot recommend OTC analgesics. It's public school policy that not even school nurses can recommend or give OTC drugs. Lori Thein, next-door neighbor, can say to a teenager, "Take some aspirin." But

Susan Abeln, PT, ARM, chair of APTA's Committee on Risk Management Services and Member Benefits, reports that the committee to date knows of no complaints or legal actions involving the recommendation of OTC drugs by physical therapists.

> **"DRUG PRESCRIPTION BY PTs WOULD REQUIRE CHANGES IN THE MEDICAL, PHYSICAL THERAPY, AND PHARMACY PRACTICE ACTS OF 50 STATES!"**
> **—Ron Scott**

Lori Thein, PT—given the body of physical therapy knowledge and the scope of physical therapy practice—can't. It's frustrating.

Ciccone: But we *can* let patients know that certain OTC drugs may be helpful in certain situations. We should urge patients to see

their physician first, however. As Ron [Scott] pointed out, there may be a medical reason why a patient shouldn't take a particular OTC drug.

Schreck: Our limitations regarding OTC drugs is especially frustrating because you know where patients *do* get their information about drugs—by word of mouth or through the media.

Thein: A study published in 1990 in *American Journal of Diseases of Children*[9] showed that physicians were at the bottom of the list in terms of where people obtain their information about drugs such as anabolic steroids. But the problem isn't just where people get their information. It's also where they get the actual drugs. Ergogenic aids such as anabolic-androgenic steroids, used illegally by athletes to increase energy production and enhance performance, can be easily obtained on the black market. Sports PTs sometimes are in the uncomfortable position of suspecting the use of black-market drugs and being unable to overcome the underground information and hype about the benefits of these drugs.

Cahalin: Anabolic steroids are illegal in this country, and yet athletes can obtain them; meanwhile, our patients who have muscle-wasting diseases—patients who, as shown in several European studies,[10,11] could therapeutically benefit from anabolic steroids—cannot obtain them.

Medications and the PT's Role: The Bottom Line

Ciccone: We've covered a lot of ground. What have we concluded?

Cahalin: Our profession is varied, and many medication issues are patient-specific and drug-specific. Is the ability to *prescribe* really the most important thing?

Thein: Even if PTs *could* prescribe certain drugs, the health professions still would need to answer the question, "Where does the buck stop?" Someone has to have the ultimate responsibility for coordinating and monitoring the patient's medications. Would it be the physician, the pharmacist, the physical therapist?

Schenkman: The physical therapy profession should avoid trying to do *everything*. We need to make legitimate decisions about how far it's appropriate to go. In a complex world, we need to become knowledgeable so that we can be effective contributors. And we need to realize that being effective contributors doesn't mean being the final decision makers in all arenas.

Ciccone: Do we agree on what the PT's responsibility is?

Barry: We've identified the need to educate ourselves—and then the patient and family—about the drugs they take. But we also should help ensure that our patients are informed about all of the possible treatment options. For example, the PT has a responsibility to make certain the parent knows that an injection of botulinum-A toxin in the gastrocnemius muscle could delay or preclude the need for a heel-cord lengthening in a child with cerebral palsy.[12,13]

Cahalin: Through documentation of drug effects, many PTs already have made an important difference in the patient's medical care—even though physicians may not have thought to tell them about it. Of course, specific responses observed during serial therapy sessions also may be our best defense for physical therapy care.

El-Din: Many of us think research is removed from the realm of daily practice, but in this health care environment, we can no longer have that attitude. We must document the way drugs affect physical therapy outcomes as we modify our treatment strategies—not only to improve our own practice, but to help other care providers improve theirs.

Schreck: PTs need to approach patients directly about the abuse of nontherapeutic drugs and the misuse of therapeutic drugs. We have a key role in identifying when a

"WE'VE OUTLINED PRACTICAL STRATEGIES THAT PTs IN ANY SETTING CAN USE TO HELP ENSURE THE BEST OUTCOMES."
—Chuck Ciccone

patient is using a drug for too long or at too high a dosage. If a patient has a continued need for medication, our role may be to show the patient that there are alternative methods of pain management, such as modalities, mobilization, or exercise.

El-Din: Iatrogenesis will be an increasingly important area for which PTs need to take some responsibility. It's been estimated that among people over the age of 70, as many as 12% to 17% of acute hospital admissions are due to drugs—and that over half of those are the result of self-medication.[14] In general, overdose admissions are climbing, according to the medical literature.

Scott: In a 1993 Louisiana court case, *Gassen v East Jefferson General Hospital*, the court held that nurses had a responsibility to correct obvious medication errors made by physicians and pharmacists. It hinted that this responsibility may lie with other providers, too. The case lends support to the PT's enhanced role in pharmacology. If there is an incorrect prescription, PTs may have the responsibility to try to correct the error.

Thein: A similar precedent—not specifically in terms of drugs but in terms of correcting others' errors—has been set in sports. In a 1976 court case, *Lowe v Texas Tech University*, certified athletic trainers and student athletic trainers were found to be responsible for faulty equipment. The court decided that the physician held the ultimate responsibility, but it also decided that—as components of care for that athlete—the other health care team members were responsible for identifying problems and notifying the responsible party.

Ciccone: This roundtable makes it clear that pharmacology can have a big influence on how we practice as PTs. There's a consensus that we must have a fundamental knowledge of medications to recognize the beneficial actions and detrimental effects of drug therapy. This knowledge can enable us to educate patients and their families—and empower us to communicate with physicians and other members of the health care team about how drug therapy is affecting the patient's ability to reach specific rehabilitation goals. We also must consider the legal implications that may affect our ability to recommend and administer medications in certain situations. There are no formulaic answers to most questions about drugs and their effects. Here, we've outlined some of the practical strategies that PTs in any setting can use to help ensure the best possible outcomes for their patients. *PT*

References

1 Berg MJ, Ebert B, Willis DK, et al. Parkinsonism—drug treatment part I. *Drug Intelligence and Clinical Pharmacy.* 1987;21:10-21.
2 Goldstein L. Basic and clinical studies on pharmacologic effects on the recovery from nervous system injury. *J Neural Transplant Plast.* 1993;4:175-192.
3 Porter J, Jick H. Addiction rare in patients treated with narcotics. *N Engl J Med.* 1980;302:123.
4 Koren G, Maurice L. Pediatric uses of opioids. *Pediatric Clinics of North America.* 1989;36:1141-1156.
5 Berde CB. Pediatric postoperative pain management. *Pediatric Clinics of North America.* 1989;36:921-940.
6 *Acute Pain Management in Adults: Operative Procedures. Quick Reference Guide for Clinicians.* Rockville, Md: Agency for Health Care Policy and Research; 1992.
7 *Acute Pain Management in Infants, Children, and Adolescents: Operative and Medical Procedures. Quick Reference Guide for Clinicians.* Rockville, Md: Agency for Health Care Policy and Research; 1992.
8 Dininny P. APTA presents testimony at Institute of Medicine meeting on the future of primary care. *PT—Magazine of Physical Therapy.* 1995;3(1):20.
9 Terney R, McLain LG. The use of anabolic steroids in high school athletes. *American Journal of Diseases of Children.* 1990;144:99,103.
10 Schols AMWJ. The effects of nutritional support and anabolic steroids on body composition and physiologic function in patients with COPD. A placebo controlled randomized trial. Abstract. *Am J Respir Crit Care Med.* 1994;149:A313.
11 Martins I, Jardim J, Verreschi J, et al. The influence of anabolic drug on body mass of COPD patients. Abstract. *Am J Respir Crit Care Med.* 1994;149:A138.
12 Koman LA, Mooney JF, Smith B, Goodman A, Mulvaney T. Management of cerebral palsy with botulinum-A toxin: preliminary investigation. *J Pediatr Orthop.* 1993;13:489-495.
13 Cosgrove AP, Corry IS, Graham HK. Botulinum toxin in the management of the lower limb in cerebral palsy. *Dev Med Child Neurol.* 1994;36:386-396.
14 Kart CS, Dunkle RE, Lockery SA. Self-health care. In: Bonder BR, Wagner MB, eds. *Functional Performance in Older Adults.* Philadelphia, Pa: FA Davis Co; 1994:141.

LIABILITY AWARENESS
by Elaine Selle, Esq

The Safe Medical Devices Act of 1990

Awareness of the legal requirements for reporting patient injuries due to equipment malfunction is a must for health care providers who use medical devices in treatment.

*t*he Safe Medical Devices Act (21 CFR Part 803) of 1990 (SMDA) amended various sections of the Food, Drug, and Cosmetic Act of 1938. This legislation reflected Congressional intent to increase protection for the public related to the use of medical "devices," defined in the Act as any instrument, apparatus, machine, or contrivance (including any component parts or accessories) intended for use in the diagnosis, cure, mitigation, treatment or prevention of a disease or intended to affect the structure or any function of the body.

Among other provisions, the SMDA defines specific responsibilities and reporting requirements related to the use of medical devices. Of particular interest to physical therapists are the responsibilities of the "device user facilities," which include hospitals, ambulatory surgical facilities, nursing homes, or any outpatient treatment facilities that are not private offices. (Health care professionals who see patients in private offices or at home have no reporting obligations under the SMDA, even if they believe a patient's injury or death was due to a medical device.)

What must be reported, and when?

Under the SMDA, a facility must report to the US Food and Drug Administration (FDA) any information it receives or becomes aware of that reasonably suggests that there is a probability that a medical device caused or contributed to the *death of a patient* of the facility not later than 10 working days after the facility becomes aware of the information. In addition, if the identity of the manufacturer of the device is known, the facility must also report such information to the manufacturer.

If the facility receives or becomes aware of information that reasonably suggests that there is a probability that a device caused or contributed to a *serious injury or serious illness of a patient*, the facility must report this information either to the FDA or to the device manufacturer within 10 working days. The SMDA defines "serious illness or injury" as a condition that either (1) is life threatening; (2) results in permanent impairment of a body function or permits damage to a body structure; or (3) necessitates immediate medical or surgical intervention to preclude permanent impairment of a body function or permanent damage to a body structure.

A facility is deemed to have received or become aware of such reportable information when medical personnel employed by or otherwise formally affiliated with the facility receive or otherwise become aware of that information in the course of their duties in the facility. The SMDA broadly defines "medical personnel" to include all professional staff, as well as "biomedical engineers, technologists, and risk managers."

Under the SMDA, facilities are required to submit to the Secretary of Health and Human Services a semi-annual report (due January 1 and July 1 of each year) summarizing incidences of deaths, injuries, and illnesses attributed to medical devices. This requirement puts the facility and its medical personnel in the position of determining whether or not a "probability" exists that a medical device caused or contributed to the death, serious illness, or serious injury of a patient.

In addition to these reporting requirements, device user facilities are required to maintain "device incident files." These files must contain all information stemming from investigations undertaken by the facility to determine whether or not a device caused a death, serious injury, or serious illness, including records of any related oral or written communications received by the facility. The SMDA requires that facilities maintain these files for 2 years after the date of submission of the report to the FDA and the manufacturer, and these data must be made available for inspection by authorized the FDA employees upon request.

Are reports to the FDA kept confidential?

Reports submitted to the FDA typically are not subject to public disclosure. Federal regulations state that the FDA will not disclose the identity of a device user facility that complies with the federal reporting requirements. However, the SMDA *does* provide for three exceptions under which the facility's identity can be disclosed. These are:

1 Reports made in connection with an action on the FDA's part to enforce the reporting requirements of the SMDA.

2 Reports involving communication between the FDA and the manufacturer of the device that is the subject of the user facility's report.

3 Reports to representatives of the Department of Health and Human Services or Department of Justice.

Although such broad exceptions greatly dilute the status of "confidentiality" ostensibly afforded by the statute, the names of patients are not included in the facility's reports. If the FDA later requests specific patient information, it is required to protect such information from public disclosure. The only identifier that appears on the facility's

Final rule publication of Medical Device User Facility and Manufacturer Reporting, Certification and Registration; Delegations of Authority; Medical Device Reporting Procedure (*Federal Register*, December 11, 1995;60:63577-63606) is available through the Federal Food and Drug Administration's World Wide Web pages at **http:www.fda.gov.**

report is the name of the person authorized to submit the report on behalf of the facility.

What happens once the report has been submitted?

If the Secretary determines, based on a "reasonable probability," that a device caused adverse consequences or death, then the Secretary will order the "appropriate person" (manufacturer, importer, or distributor) to immediately cease distribution of the device. This person will immediately notify health care providers of the Secretary's order and will instruct professionals and facilities to cease using the device. No later than 10 days following the order's issuance, the manufacturer, importer, or distributor will have an opportunity for a formal hearing with the Secretary, who may amend the order.

What are the penalties for noncompliance?

In addition to recalling the product from the market, the FDA also can impose civil and/or criminal penalties upon both the manufacturer and the device user facility. Under the SMDA,

facilities that engage in prohibited acts or fail to comply with the regulations can be subject to penalties that previously were applicable only to device manufacturers and distributors.

The Prohibited Acts and Penalties section of the SMDA provides for a variety of circumstances under which civil and/or criminal penalties can be imposed, including refusal to allow the FDA access to records, failure to register or submit reports to the FDA, failure to retain reports or allow required FDA inspections, and other fraudulent and misleading actions. Other federal regulations prohibit the submission of any report required under the SMDA that is false or misleading in any material respect.

In addition, the failure to establish or maintain any record, failure to make any required report, or failure to provide information required by the SMDA can result in criminal liability.

Under the SMDA, penalties for criminal liability can include imprisonment from 1 to 3 years and fines from $1,000 to $10,000, or both. Civil penalties include injunctive relief and penalties in an amount not to exceed $15,000 for each violation and not to exceed $1,000,000 for all violations adjudicated in a single proceeding where such violations constitute a "significant or knowing departure" from the SMDA's requirements or create a risk to public health.

What steps can aid facilities in complying with the SMDA?

First, it is absolutely critical that all device user facilities review and evaluate their procedures for compliance. Facilities must establish a written protocol for identifying incidents or circumstances covered by the SMDA and reporting them. Facilities also must train their "medical personnel" as defined by the SMDA in the filing of such reports, and they should specifically designate an individual to accept responsibility for this task.

User facilities also must be aware that their own classification of documents as "confidential" is not necessarily legally sufficient to protect information from disclosure. Therefore, utmost scrutiny must be given to the content of reports to the FDA. These reports must contain only factual, accurate descriptions of circumstances related to product use. The reports should appropriately document only objective facts as they have occurred and should never assign fault or contain accusatory language that could be used against the manufacturer or facility should a lawsuit be filed. Subjective comments and personal opinions or conclusions have no place in a report to the FDA (or in any facility-generated report involving a medical device).

Facilities also must review their policies and procedures related to the requirement to maintain device incident files and have them available for FDA inspection for 2 years after the date of FDA submission. The facility should have in place a document retention policy to comply with the Act's requirements. Emphasis also must be given to procedures related to the facility's investigations of medical device user problems requiring FDA reporting.

Compliance with the reporting and information retention requirements specified in the SMDA undoubtedly creates some problems for device user facilities, who may experience increased paperwork, higher administrative costs, and risk management dilemmas. The price for inattention to any of these details, however, could be a liability that would outweigh these comparatively minor inconveniences.

Elaine Selle, Esq, is an attorney practicing with Locke, Purnell, Rain, and Harrell, New Orleans, La. She concentrates in medical malpractice litigation, defending a wide range of health care providers, and is a faculty member of the National Institute for Trial Advocacy, APTA's risk management team, and the Joint Commission on Accreditation of Healthcare Organizations (JCAHO).

Patient Relations

Access to, Admission to, and Patient/Client Rights Within Physical Therapy Services
HOD P06-03-16-13 (Initial HOD 06-86-12-26)

In providing physical therapy services, the physical therapist is accountable first and foremost to the individual receiving physical therapy. The physical therapist is also accountable for abiding by professional standards and ethics and the laws governing the practice of physical therapy in the jurisdiction where the service is rendered.

The physical therapist shall ensure services regardless of race, creed, color, gender, age, national or ethnic origin, sexual orientation, disability, or health status. The physical therapist respects the rights of individuals referred or admitted to the physical therapy service. The individual referred or admitted to the physical therapy service has rights which include but are not limited to:

1. Selection of a physical therapist of one's own choosing to the extent that it is reasonable and possible.

2. Access to information regarding practice policies and charges for services.

3. Knowledge of the identity of the physical therapist and other personnel providing or participating in the program of care.

4. Expectation that the referral source has no financial involvement in the service. If that is not the case, knowledge of the extent of any financial involvement in the service by the referring source.

5. Involvement in the development of anticipated goals and expected outcomes, and the selection of interventions.

6. Knowledge of any substantial risks of the recommended examination and intervention.

7. Participation in decisions involving the physical therapy plan of care to the extent reasonable and possible.

8. Access to information concerning his or her condition.

9. Expectation that any discussion or consultation involving the case will be conducted discreetly and that all communications and other records pertaining to the care, including the sources of payment for treatment, will be treated as confidential.

10. Expectation of safety in the provision of services and safety in regard to the equipment and physical environment.

11. Timely information about impending discharge and continuing care requirements.

12. Refusal of physical therapy services.

13. Information regarding the practice's mechanism for the initiation, review, and resolution of patient/client complaints.

Complementary and Alternative Therapeutic Interventions
HOD P06-01-26-26

The American Physical Therapy Association supports the continued integration of evidenced-based complementary and alternative therapeutic interventions into practice consistent with the patient/client management model, education, and research.

PTs Respond to HIPAA:

By Thomas G Dolan

The Real World Experience

The privacy regulations of the Health Insurance Portability & Accountability Act became effective 3 months ago. PTs share their experiences in bringing their practices into compliance with the new rules.

— ❧ —

As the April 14, 2003, implementation date approached for the privacy regulations contained in the Health Insurance Portability & Accountability Act (HIPAA), some health care providers compared their concern to another deadline they faced 3 years earlier. David O Lane, PT, MHS, president of CBL Solutions Inc in Oviedo, Florida, recalls, "The feeling among some physical therapists (PTs) was that the impact of these regulations on health care would be more damaging than what was once expected from Y2K" ["Year 2000": the fear that computer systems would crash on January 1, 2000].

However, Y2K generally proved to be a non-event, thanks to thorough preparation by information technology professionals. Similarly, the April 14 deadline for HIPAA privacy compliance has come and gone without major disruptions. Physical therapists who are familiar with the HIPAA regulations credit the profession for having done its homework. They also acknowledge that the Centers for Medicare & Medicaid Services (CMS), which developed the rules, modified or clarified some of the provisions that threatened to present major problems. (See sidebar "Debunking the Urban Myths.") And some PTs suggest that the panic may not have been completely justified. "I read that if Chicken Little were alive today, he would be a HIPAA consultant," says Ann York, PT, PhD, compliance officer and coordinator, Crawford Memorial Hospital & Health Services, in Robinson, Illinois.

Nevertheless, as many PTs became familiar with HIPAA in the months leading up to April 14, they say their anxiety levels did increase. For example, Carolyn Bloom, PT, says, "Since I've never transmitted patients' records electronically, I thought the law might not apply to me. I had a false sense of security. But

I've since found that there are other features [that do apply], such as the privacy notice and having a security contract with outside business partners as well." Bloom, owner of Bloom & Associates Therapy in Topeka, Kansas, is past president of APTA's Section on Health Policy and Administration.

Joseph A Lucca, PT, PhD, of Newark, Delaware, associate professor in the Department of Physical Therapy, University of Delaware, describes a similar experience. "I don't have to worry about the electronic transfer part, since I don't do that. But I'm still trying to clear up where my other liabilities might be."

As PTs have discovered, the HIPAA regulations affect many aspects of practice. The final privacy regulations require that "covered entities"—including health care providers who conduct certain health care transactions electronically—take five basic steps:

❖ Notify patients about their privacy rights and inform them of how their information can be used,

❖ Adopt and implement privacy procedures,

❖ Train employees so they understand the privacy procedures,

❖ Designate an individual who is to be responsible for ensuring that privacy procedures are adopted and followed (a "designated privacy officer"), and

❖ Ensure that patient records containing individually identifiable health information are secure.

Previous columns in *PT Magazine* have provided detailed guidelines on what the regulations require.[1,2] In this article, PTs describe how they have modified their practices and procedures to comply with the new rules and offer suggestions for other PTs.

As noted in the sidebar "Debunking the Urban Myths," CMS has clarified some of the more troublesome issues. However, areas of uncertainty remain.

Office Security and Patient Privacy

Gayle Lee, APTA's associate director for federal regulatory affairs, says, "We've been getting a lot of calls regarding safeguards in the office. Should there be a solid door so other people can't see a PT talking to a patient? What about a shared bathroom with another facility? Or people coming to the facility to practice and seeing information about other patients? There have been issues relating to getting referrals, having people in the waiting room, and talking on the phone."

PTs are required to establish procedures to verify a patient's identity similar to those used by a financial institution (eg, social security number, address, zip code, mother's maiden name, or preassigned code words). Yet even if a PT has been treating a patient for 20 years and recognizes his voice instantly, the PT may be liable if he or she fails to verify the patient's identity.

Some experts advise against overreaction to the privacy rules because this, too, might lead to trouble. For instance, Lee points out, if a patient requests that you send all of his mail to a post office box rather than a street address, you are *not* required to comply with his request. But if you *do* agree to the request, then fail to do so, you open yourself to liability.

A number of those interviewed stressed that, in many cases, existing patient privacy considerations simply will be formalized to comply with HIPAA. For example, Richard W Rausch, PT, regional manager for Physiotherapy Associates (PA) in Illinois and Wisconsin, says the new regulations won't require PA to make major alterations. "Our layouts won't change to a great extent in light of the HIPAA regulations. We may add a few more private rooms, but we won't lose our basic gym layout. And we may need to buy a few new file cabinets with stronger locks. We'll also ensure that our open reception areas are arranged in such a way that phone conver-

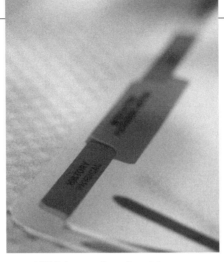

HIPAA requires health care providers to secure patient records containing individually identifiable health information so that they are not readily available to those who do not need them.

sations regarding patients cannot be overheard. This is really just a fine-tuning of practices already in place."

One change that the PA clinics will initiate may have an effect on time management. "We used to walk our pediatric patients out of the gym into the waiting area, to consult with their parents there. We'll now need to bring the parents back into the gym for the consultation. Getting the families out of the gym on time may prove to be a challenge," Rausch says.

The HIPAA regulations require health care providers to secure patient records containing individually identifiable health information so that they are not readily available to those who do not need them. Douglas M White, PT, OCS, co-owner of Milton Orthopaedic and Sports Physical Therapy, PC, in Milton, Massachusetts, explains, "A PT cannot look at another PT's patient records unless he or she has a

well-justified reason, such as during a peer review process. And support staff and clerical staff cannot access records unless the information is necessary to perform their jobs—and even then, they should be accessing only the limited information they need." Therefore, he says a facility should have at least one room where therapists can work privately on patient charts, make patient-related phone calls, and consult on patient issues. [See "Building a Practice with Hammer and Nails" in the May issue of **PT** for more information on designing a private area for PTs.[3]]

"With the new HIPAA laws, you have to protect the chart from being *heard* as well as being *seen*," J W Rusinowski, Jr, PT, MBA, says. "Make sure that your front office area has a window that can be shut for soundproofing, so that patients in the waiting room can't hear private billing and insurance information being discussed on the phone." Rusinowski is director of Therapeutic Resources Inc in Parkland, Florida, and a consultant on clinic design.

On the other hand, CMS points out that the HIPAA privacy rule does not specifically require offices to be retrofitted. "The department does not consider facility restructuring to be a requirement under this standard," according to CMS.[4] It says the privacy rule does not mandate the following types of structural or system changes:
❖ Private rooms
❖ Soundproofing of rooms
❖ Encryption of wireless or other emergency medical radio communications that can be intercepted by scanners
❖ Encryption of telephone systems

Lane and Lee agree that modifications to and clarification of HIPAA regulations have moved in the direction of

"Make sure that your front office area has a window that can be shut for soundproofing, so that patients in the waiting room can't hear private billing and insurance information being discussed on the phone."

J W Rusinowski, Jr, PT, MBA

PTs Respond to HIPAA

Debunking the Urban Myths

As the HIPAA regulations were being developed, confusion arose about what the rules might require. Over time, some rumors and misunderstandings took on a life of their own, in some cases resembling urban legends. PTs wouldn't be able to leave messages on patients' answering machines. They wouldn't be able to use sign-in sheets. PTs would need to execute a business associate contract with janitorial services. And so on. Here are some of the rumors and excerpts of CMS's response to them. For more information, go to http://answers.hhs.gov.

May PTs leave messages for patients at their homes, either on an answering machine or with a family member, to remind them of appointments? May providers continue to mail appointment reminders to patients' homes?

Yes. The HIPAA Privacy Rule permits health care providers to communicate with patients regarding their health care. This includes communicating with patients at their homes, whether through the mail or by phone or in some other manner. In addition, the Rule does not prohibit covered entities from leaving messages for patients on their answering machines. However, to reasonably safeguard the individual's privacy, covered entities should take care to limit the amount of information disclosed on the answering machine. For example, a covered entity might want to consider leaving only its name and number and other information necessary to confirm an appointment, or ask the individual to call back. See 45 CFR 164.510(b)(3).

May PT offices use patient sign-in sheets or call out the names of their patients in their waiting rooms?

Yes. Covered entities, such as physicians' offices, may use patient sign-in sheets or call out patient names in waiting rooms, so long as the information disclosed is appropriately limited. The HIPAA Privacy Rule explicitly permits the incidental disclosures that may result from this practice, for example, when other patients in a waiting room hear the identity of the person whose name is called, or see other patient names on a sign-in sheet. However, these incidental disclosures are permitted only when the covered entity has implemented reasonable safeguards and the minimum necessary standard, where appropriate. For example, the sign-in sheet may not display medical information that is not necessary for the purpose of signing in. See 45 CFR 164.502(a)(1)(iii)

Can a provider's office fax patient medical information to another health care provider's office?

The HIPAA Privacy Rule permits physicians to disclose protected health information to another health care provider for treatment purposes. This can be done by fax or by other means. Covered entities must have in place reasonable and appropriate administrative, technical, and physical safeguards to protect the privacy of protected health information that is disclosed using a fax machine. Examples of measures that could be reasonable and appropriate in such a situation include the sender confirming that the fax number to be used is in fact the correct one for the other provider's office, and placing the fax machine in a secure location to prevent unauthorized access to the information. See 45 CFR164.530(c).

Is a business associate contract required with organizations or persons where inadvertent contact with protected health information may result—such as in the case of janitorial services?

A business associate contract is not required with persons or organizations whose functions, activities, or services do not involve the use or disclosure of protected health information, and where any access to protected health information by such persons would be incidental, if at all. Generally, janitorial services that clean the offices or facilities of a covered entity are not business associates because the work they perform for covered entities does not involve the use or disclosure of protected health information, and any disclosure of protected health information to janitorial personnel that occurs in the performance of their duties (such as may occur while emptying trash cans) is limited in nature, occurs as a by-product of their janitorial duties, and could not be reasonably prevented. Such disclosures are incidental and permitted by the HIPAA Privacy Rule. See 45 CFR 164.502(a)(1).

"what is reasonable in terms of practice." For instance, the sign-in sheet, a key element in office management, for a time was considered a potential HIPAA privacy violation because it allowed certain patient information to be viewed by other patients. The government clarified its position, allowing sign-in sheets when accompanied by reasonable safeguards and when requiring the minimum necessary information. Similarly, the rules draw a distinction between what someone might overhear outside a curtained treatment area and what one might hear discussed in the waiting area.

The key, according to CMS, is that covered entities must implement "reasonable" safeguards "to limit incidental, and avoid prohibited, uses and disclosures." The rule does not require that all risk of protected health information disclosure be eliminated. CMS advises, "Covered entities must review their own practices and determine what steps are reasonable to safeguard their patient information. In determining what is reasonable, covered entities should assess potential risks to patient privacy, as well as consider such issues as the potential effects on patient care and any administrative or financial burden to be incurred from implementing particular safeguards."

Nevertheless, some PTs express concern about the vagueness of the word "reasonable." Peggy Grey, PT, MA, ACT, CEO/owner, Integrated Rehabilitation Services, LLC, Enfield, Connecticut, says, "I've been working with an attorney for over a year. Yet CMS keeps making changes, and my biggest fear is that they will say we've misinterpreted something, that their definition of 'reasonable' is not the same as mine."

A Heavy Burden

Some PTs say that the burden to ensure patient privacy is unevenly distributed. Grey, who is responsible for compliance for her entire organization, of which the physical therapy department is a relatively small part, says, "For the smaller or medium-size private practice this will be more of a challenge, for

CMS has limited the scope of a "business associate" to those persons or organizations whose functions or services involve the use or disclosure of protected health information. Therefore, signing an agreement with a trash service doesn't elevate the trash service to the level of a "business associate" for the purposes of HIPAA.

they won't have people like me writing policies and practices."

"I've seen all levels of response," says Lane. "Many PTs have no idea what to do—not just employees of small clinics or hospitals, but practice owners as well. They're just not sure what's going on. I see providers looking for the simplest approach, looking to vendors for off-the-shelf privacy plans. Many are turning to the APTA-endorsed Internet interactive tool [HIPAA*steps*PT, a do-it-yourself product that includes gap assessment tools, risk mitigation documentation, a policy document creator, online staff training, and physical therapy orientation. See "HIPAA Resources on the Web" on page 56]. At a higher level, some are hiring a lawyer at a cost of $20,000 to $50,000."

Associate Relationships

HIPAA requires that when PTs talk to prospective business associates—including physicians, health care facilities, vendors, insurance or collection agencies, and con-

tracted services—the PTs must inquire about *their* HIPAA compliance plan, obtain a copy, request the educational and other background experience of the party's employees, ask how those associates perform background checks and training, provide a copy of their training materials, and more. And just as PTs are required to request this information from their business associates, those health-related business associates will make the same requests from PTs.

CMS has clarified these regulations by limiting the scope of a "business associate" to those persons or organizations whose functions or services involve the use or disclosure of protected health information. Therefore, signing an agreement with a trash service doesn't elevate the trash service to the level of a "business associate" for the purposes of HIPAA.

In addition, if a facility uses contract PTs or occupational therapists (OTs), a business associate contract with them isn't needed either, according to Bloom. She says, "I learned that my contracted PTs and OTs function as employees for the purposes of this law, so I didn't have to have a business associate contract with them."

Another often-raised subject is the fax machine. According to CMS, faxing is permitted so long as covered entities have "reasonable and appropriate administrative, technical, and physical safeguards" to protect the privacy of protected health information. CMS says such measures could include the sender confirming that the fax number to be used is in fact the correct one for the other health care provider's office, and placing the fax machine in a secure location to prevent unauthorized access to the information.

A PT who is careless in his or her use of faxes will still be liable under the privacy measures. But even if you take "reasonable" measures, such as receiving faxes in and sending them to secured areas, the laws of unintended consequences don't stop here. Grey says that the physicians she deals with interpret the use of faxes differently. One will not fax anything with the patient's name, assuming that "you'll know who he is." Another refuses to transmit or receive any faxes at all, delaying what previously was immediately available and necessary information for a week to 10 days.

The Impact on Education

Although the general perception may be that the HIPAA regulations affect only practicing health care professionals, the fact is that the regulations also reach into the educational system.

As an educator, Lucca says, "We know that all schools will be including these regulations in their curriculums, and we are starting on this trek." As the regulations were being developed there was some concern that the HIPAA privacy rule's "minimum necessary requirements" might prohibit PT and PTA students from accessing patient medical information in the course of their training. CMS insists that this is not the case: "The definition of 'health care operations' in the privacy rule provides for 'conducting training programs in which students, trainees, or practitioners in areas of health care learn under supervision to practice or improve their skills as health care providers.' Covered entities can shape their policies and procedures for minimum necessary uses and disclosures to permit medical trainees access to patients' medical information, including entire medical records."

The Solution

CMS notes, "Health care providers have a strong tradition of safeguarding private health information." As a result, some of HIPAA's requirements simply codify and require documentation of practices already in place. Furthermore, these standards create a minimum "floor" of protection. They do not preempt any state law that establishes more stringent protections for the privacy of health information.

Nevertheless, the regulations have required changes in PT operations and documentation procedures.

For office security, Grey suggests, "Think about what you need to do to ensure privacy, and then document it. Think about your office, your file cabinets, your waiting room, your fax, and so on. Make it simple, and easy on yourself. If you have a fax in the waiting room, put it in a back administrative office. If it is already there, leave it there. But, in either case, document it. Show you've thought about it, and put it in writing. Go through your entire office in this way, looking for possible privacy holes, close them, and document same." Maureen Kavalar, PT, vice president of program and provider services for Easter Seals, Chicago, agrees. "One of the things I tell people when they get bent out of shape about it is, 'Use your common sense.'"

To further simplify the process for PTs, York describes what her facility has done. "We work very closely with our medical records department. We set up a procedure with that

department so PTs do not have to make any decisions about records. This minimizes the amount of paperwork PTs have to do," York says.

Even if you aren't yet subject to HIPAA's regulations, Mary R Daulong, PT, of Business & Clinical Management Services Inc, Houston, has a suggestion. "While you may not be a covered entity, you will appear negligent to your patients if you do not embrace the privacy regulations. My recommendation is to take the opportunity now to do a gap analysis. See what information goes in and goes out, and who has access to it. Develop a sound compliance notice and privacy procedure. If your practice grows or if payers require you to submit electronically, then you will be ready for the privacy part of the regulations."

It's also important to understand that, unlike Y2K, compliance with HIPAA standards is not an event with a defined ending. On a continuing basis, new patients must be informed about their privacy rights. New employees must be trained so that they understand the privacy procedures. And health care providers must ensure that privacy procedures are being followed.

Rather than viewing these ongoing responsibilities as chores, Daulong suggests, "We will see privacy adherence that probably should have been in place a long time ago. For both patients and providers, it will be a good thing." **PT**

Thomas Dolan is a freelance writer. Additional material supplied by freelance writer Ellie Kuykendall.

REFERENCES

1. Ravitz K. The HIPAA privacy final modified rule. *PT—Magazine of Physical Therapy*. 2002; 10(11);21-25.

2. Lee G. PTs face new federal privacy requirements. *PT—Magazine of Physical Therapy*. 2003; 11(3);28-30, 76.

3. Coyne C. Building a practice with hammer and nails. *PT—Magazine of Physical Therapy*. 2003; 11(5);42-47.

4. Questions & Answers. Available at http://answers.hhs.gov/cgibin/hhs.cfg/php/enduser/std_alp.php. Accessed April 22, 2003.

HIPAA Resources on the Web

❖ www.apta.org/Govt_Affairs/regulatory/privatepractice/hipaa
  HIPAA information on APTA's Web site

❖ www.hhs.gov/ocr/hipaa/finalreg.html
  The regulations' actual language

❖ www.apta.org/products_services/product_highlights/hipaastepspt
  Information on HIPAAstepsPT, an online HIPAA solution for physical therapists

❖ www.apta.org/Govt_Affairs/regulatory/privatepractice/hipaa/HIPAA_Privacy/HIPAA_websites
  Helpful HIPAA Web sites

government affairs

By Gayle Lee, Esq

PTs Face New Federal Privacy Requirements

New federal standards for protection of health care information are requiring physical therapists to think about how they use patient records and what procedures they have in place to ensure confidentiality.

Despite a looming deadline and widespread concerns of health care providers about the privacy requirements of the Health Insurance Portability and Accountability Act (HIPAA), compliance with these requirements should not pose a significant problem for most physical therapists (PTs). Once PTs understand the basic standards, most physical therapy practices will be able to establish and implement with relatively little difficulty or expense privacy policies and proce-dures that demonstrate compliance with HIPAA requirements.

PTs and other providers face a host of complex compliance issues related to the imposition of a new level of administrative steps and expenses to ensure compliance with federal rules designed to safeguard the confidentiality of patients' medical infor-mation, which must be implemented by April 14 of this year. This column will attempt to address three areas related to disclosure of protected health information that are of particular concern to PTs—the "minimum necessary" standard, incidental disclosures, and the notice of privacy. (These and many other topics are addressed in more detail on APTA's Web site. Go to www.apta.org and click on "Government Affairs," "Private Practice," then "HIPAA Regulations.")

Do These Requirements Apply to Me?

In general, most PTs will be included in the HIPAA privacy rule's definition of "covered entities," which includes health plans, health care clearinghouses, and health care providers that conduct certain health care transactions electronically (billing, funds transfers, etc). The US Department of Health and Human Services' (HHS) Office for Civil Rights—HIPAA (www.hhs.gov/ocr/hipaa), which is charged with implementing the privacy standards, offers guidance that providers and health plans can use to help determine if they are a covered entity.

The final privacy regulations require that health care plans and providers do five basic things:

❖ Notify patients about their privacy rights and inform them of how their information can be used,

❖ Adopt and implement privacy procedures,

❖ Train employees so that they under-stand the privacy procedures,

❖ Designate an individual who is to be responsible for ensuring that privacy procedures are adopted and followed (a "designated privacy officer"), and

❖ Ensure that patient records containing

individually identifiable health information are secure.

Many physical therapists already have taken these steps. Again, those who haven't can find helpful guidance on APTA's Web site, as well as other sites on the Internet. (See the "HIPAA Resources" box on page 30.)

The HIPAA privacy requirements are likely to have the most severe impact on PTs practicing in states that have no, or weak, state laws regarding privacy of health care information. Federal privacy standards create a minimum "floor" of protection that patients must be afforded. The HIPAA statute, however, does not preempt any state law that establishes more stringent protections for the privacy of health information. PTs practicing in states that have privacy statutes may already be affected by HIPAA because many states have reacted to HIPAA by putting more stringent state standards in place. The Washington, DC-based Health Privacy Project (www.healthprivacy.org/info-url _nocat2304/info-url_nocat.htm) can provide helpful information on current state privacy laws.

How Private Is "Private"?

The HIPAA standards require covered entities to make reasonable efforts to limit the use or disclosure of, and requests for, "protected health information"—which includes individually identifiable health information communicated in any form, including orally, in writing, and electronically—to the "minimum necessary" to accomplish the intended purpose, as defined in the regulations. In addition, covered entities are required to establish and implement appropriate administrative, technical, and physical safeguards to reasonably safeguard protected health information from any intentional or unintentional use or disclosure that would violate the standards.

This requirement initially raised substantial concern among health care providers who feared that they could no longer engage in confidential conversations with their patients or other providers if there was any possibility that the substance of the conversation could be overheard. Could covered entities be required to prevent any incidental disclosure—such as those that could occur if a visiting family member or some other person not authorized to have access to protected health information just happened to walk by a report or some material containing individually identifiable health information, or if a patient signed in on a clinic log-in sheet and saw the names of other patients?

HHS has clarified that the HIPAA privacy standards are not intended to prevent customary and necessary health care communication or practices from occurring. Thus they do not require that all risk of incidental use or disclosure be eliminated in order for PTs to comply with the standards. Rather, the privacy regulations permit uses or disclosures that occur as a byproduct of a use or disclosure otherwise authorized under the rule, provided that the covered entity has applied reasonable safeguards and implemented the minimum necessary standard, where applicable.

A physical therapy practice or other covered entity must have appropriate administrative, technical, and physical safeguards in place to limit incidental uses and disclosures—although these safeguards are not expected to guarantee the privacy of protected health information from any and all potential risks. For example, the HIPAA rule recognizes that

government affairs

HIPAA Resources on the Web

❖ www.apta.org/Govt_Affairs/regulatory/privatepractice/hipaa
(HIPAA information on APTA's Web site)

❖ www.hhs.gov/ocr/hipaa/finalreg.html
(the regulations' actual language)

❖ www.hss.gov/ocr/hipaa/privacy.html
(guidance from the Office for Civil Rights)

❖ www.cms.hhs.gov/hipaa/hipaa2/
support/tools/decisionsupport/default.asp
(tools for determining if you are a "covered entity")

❖ www.healthprivacy.org
(HIPAA information from the Health Privacy Project)

oral communication often must occur freely and quickly in treatment settings. Safeguards are expected to vary from covered entity to covered entity depending on such individual factors as the entity's size and the nature of its business. Covered entities also should inquire about and consider the steps other professionals are taking to protect patient privacy.

HHS has offered some specific examples of privacy applications for PTs and other health care providers:

❖ Providers will not be required to retrofit their offices, provide private rooms, or soundproof walls to avoid any possibility that a conversation will be overheard. In areas where multiple patient-PT communication routinely occurs, the use of cubicles, dividers, shields, or curtains (rather than separate rooms) may constitute reasonable safeguards.

❖ Providers can leave messages for patients on telephone answering machines, although they should take care to limit the amount of information disclosed (eg, leave only the patient's name and the general date-and-time information needed to confirm an appointment). Providers also can leave a message with a person other than the patient, but, again, should use professional judgment in limiting the amount and type of information disclosed.

❖ Providers can use patient sign-in sheets

or call out patient names in waiting rooms as long as the information disclosed is appropriately limited. For example, a patient sign-in sheet should not include the reason for the visit.

❖ Providers can maintain patient charts at the bedside or outside of exam rooms, but steps should be taken to safeguard access to these areas, such as ensuring that the area is supervised, escorting non-employees who enter the area, and facing the chart down or toward a wall.

PTs and other health care providers also are generally permitted to disclose protected health information to a family member or other person involved in the patient's care. In situations in which the

patient is present, the PT or provider may disclose protected health information if it is reasonable to infer from the circumstances that the patient does not object to the disclosure.

Revealing the Minimum Necessary

As noted previously, the HIPAA regulations require PTs and other health care providers to make reasonable efforts to limit the use or disclosure of, and requests for, protected health information to the "minimum necessary" to accomplish the intended treatment or purpose.

The regulations provide some specific exceptions, however, for which the "minimum necessary" requirements do not apply:

❖ Uses or disclosures that are required by law,

❖ Disclosures to the individual who is the subject of the information,

❖ Uses or disclosures for which the provider has received an authorization that meets the appropriate requirements,

❖ Disclosures to or requests by a health care provider for treatment purposes (eg, a PT is not required to apply the minimum necessary standard when

APTA Resources

APTA provides a number of resources to help its members keep abreast of the changing regulatory environment. In addition to the HIPAA information available on the Association's Web site, APTA offers a complete online HIPAA solution that is easy to use and understand. HIPAAstepsPT enables you to determine your current level of compliance with HIPAA privacy regulations, establish a record of your compliance efforts, create necessary documentation, and train online at your own pace. (For more information, go to www.apta.org, "Products and Services," "Online Shopping," then "New HIPAA Tool Walks You Through the Compliance Process"). Also, you have until March 14 to register for the last of three "Get Hip to HIPAA" workshops, to be held in Dallas on March 28. (There's more information on APTA's Web site; click on "Calendar.") Finally, APTA is planning seminar presentations on current issues in HIPAA implementation and fraud and abuse compliance at PT 2003 in Washington, DC (again, go to "Calendar" on APTA's Web site).

discussing a patient's plan of care with a physician), and

❖ Uses or disclosures that are required for compliance with the regulations implementing the other administrative simplification provisions of HIPAA, or disclosures to HHS for purposes of enforcing the rule.

PTs and other covered entities are required to develop and implement policies and procedures that reasonably minimize the amount of protected health information used, disclosed, and requested. For routine or recurring requests and disclosures, the policies and procedures may be standard protocols. For example, policies and procedures concerning disclosure to accrediting organizations could be set forth in advance. For non-routine requests, each request must be reviewed individually—

with the most likely person to do that being the designated privacy officer.

In some circumstances, the regulations allow a PT or other covered entity to reasonably rely on the judgment of the party requesting the disclosure as to the minimum amount of information that is needed. This reliance is permitted for requests made by a public official or agency, another covered entity, a business associate, or a researcher. The PT or entity is obligated to instruct its business associates to request only the minimum amount of information necessary.

The minimum necessary standard permits a PT or covered entity to disclose protected health information to comply with workers' compensation or similar programs established by law that provide benefits for work-related injuries or illnesses

without regard to fault. Specifically, the information should be shared to the full extent permitted by state law.

Patients' Rights to Privacy

The HIPAA privacy regulations give every individual the right to adequate notice of how his or her protected health information may be used or disclosed by a covered entity. This notification should explain the individual's rights and the entity's obligations with respect to protected information. The privacy notice must be made available to any person who requests it, and it must be posted prominently at the entity's location and made available on any Web site it maintains. (To view a sam-

continued on page 76 ▶▶▶

government affairs

continued from page 31

ple privacy notice, go to the HIPAA resources on APTA's Web site.)

The provider is required to give the privacy notice to the individual on the date that services are first provided—meaning the date that a treatment relationship with the patient is initiated. Furthermore, the provider must make a good-faith effort to get the individual's written acknowledgment that the notice was received. The regulations allow a provider to have patients sign a separate sheet or list, or simply to initial a cover sheet of the notice. However, having the patient's signature directly on the privacy notice will reduce the likelihood of any dispute about whether notice was received.

If a patient refuses to sign an acknowledgment, the provider should document his or her efforts to obtain the signature and the reason it was not signed. Failure to obtain the patient's acknowledgment is not a violation of the regulations if a good-faith effort to do so is documented.

Providers may form organized health care arrangements (OHCA) that would allow one joint privacy notice to cover a number of affiliated providers as long as certain requirements are met. For example, a PT or physician could enter into an OHCA with a hospital. If the patient goes to that hospital and gets a notice of privacy, when the PT or physician comes to the hospital to meet with the patient there would be no need to give additional notice. If, however, the patient should leave the hospital and go to the office of the PT or physician to receive services, that office should give the patient its notice. Also, if a provider does not include a clause in the original privacy notice stating that he or she reserves the right to change privacy practices at some future date, the provider is obligated to give the new notice to every patient if a change in privacy procedures is made.

More Rules, More Help

These are only three of the areas in which the HIPAA privacy standards have an impact on physical therapy practices. Rules governing the use and disclosure of protected health information for activities related to treatment, payment, and health care operations also will affect many practices. And, as noted previously, these privacy standards are part of a constantly changing network of federal and state legislation and regulations related to the use of patient information. PTs must be aware of and in tune with this developing regulatory environment or risk serious penalties and costs for failing to adhere to the requirements. **PT**

Gayle Lee, Esq, is associate director of APTA's Government Affairs Department. She can be reached at 800/999-2782, ext 8549, or gaylelee@apta.org.

liabilityawareness

by Fran Welk, PT, MEd

Managing the Hostile Patient

Every practice should have a protocol for dealing with angry patients.

It's a typically busy Monday afternoon in your outpatient physical therapy clinic when a member of the billing department interrupts your treatment session with a patient to say, "We need you in the waiting room now!" With apologies to your patient, you excuse yourself and make your way to the unusually crowded waiting room. There, an agitated man is leaning over the receptionist's desk demanding a refund for all of the copayments he made on his previous visits. In a tone audible to everyone in the waiting area, he says he feels justified in his request because he has discovered that some of his previous care was rendered by a student, and, if he is paying, he deserved to be treated by licensed individuals "who know what they are doing."

Every physical therapy practice needs to have a strategy in place to ensure that the scenario described above can be resolved with a high level of customer satisfaction and, more importantly, without an escalation in behavior that could lead to litigation or even personal harm. An effective communication system, coupled with established operational procedures, can protect the practice, its personnel, and the patient when aggressive behavior evolves from patient dissatisfaction.

Three key areas of risk need to be addressed in order to manage these types of situations effectively: individual patient personalities, the physical layout of the practice, and operational procedures.

Patient Personalities

Individual patient personalities are the most difficult to identify or control. If you were to ask PTs how many difficult patients they face in a day, that number would probably be lower than the number reported by front-office staff, who routinely deal with patients who are frustrated about missed appointments, prolonged waiting times, or billing concerns. It is frequently those in the front office who also will be the first to identify patients who are disgruntled or displeased with the organization or its care, or who have the potential to become confrontational.

Although it is not necessary to compile a personality profile on every patient, being alert to certain behaviors can help the practice be aware of potential problems or difficult patients. Staff should share their observations with one another to alleviate the chance of being caught by surprise if a problematic situation arises.

Physical Layout

Environmental factors need to be reviewed not only for clinical efficiency but also for protection of patients and staff. Clinical areas such as large, open gym areas afford easier direct supervision of patients and avoid potential situations in which staff may be alone with a patient who is dissatisfied or displays inappropriate behavior. However, this type of arrangement can make protection of patient confidentiality and modesty difficult, and patients who do not feel comfortable in such an open setting may become dissatisfied. Maintaining a mix of both open and private treatment areas provides clinicians and patients the choice of a venue in which both are comfortable.

The business areas of the practice, such as the reception and waiting areas, also should have spaces that both protect patient confidentiality during intake interviews or discussion of patient concerns or billing issues and provide office staff with a barrier between them and patients. The business areas also should be designed to ensure that office conversation, communication, and documentation are out of range of those in the waiting area.

Operational Procedures

Within the practice, operational procedures for managing difficult or hostile patients should be established. Just as staff are aware of operational procedures in case of a fire, they should know the protocol to be followed and what role they may need to play in the event of a hostile patient interaction. Included in these operational procedures should be guidelines for terminating a practitioner-patient relationship. (See Bennett[1] for more on this topic.) A health care attorney with knowledge of local jurisdictional issues should be consulted for assistance with both the policy and letter of notification.

Ideally, the director of the practice should take the lead in a confrontation with an agitated patient; however, another individual may be designated as having sufficient authority and interpersonal skills to manage the situation. The interaction should be redirected to a private area rather than be allowed to develop in the clinic, waiting room, or reception area, where it is within earshot of other patients. However, staff must take care to ensure that the environment is safe for both the patient and the staff.

Alcohol or drug usage can significantly increase the volatility of a confrontational situation. Staff must determine if such incidents can be handled by the available staff in a safe and effective manner. If there is concern about injury or harm, it may be necessary to involve either institutional security or local police. A prearranged password or sign can indicate to coworkers that the situation requires external support, signaling another employee to contact the appropriate authorities.

When dealing with an angry patient one-on-one, there are certain proven communication techniques that may help. Following are some tips for communicating with a hostile patient:

❖ Introduce yourself and clearly state your position in the practice.

❖ If possible, sit down, and invite the other person to do so also.

❖ Maintain a safe distance from the patient and avoid any physical contact.

❖ Stay calm, show respect, maintain eye contact, listen attentively, and, most importantly, control your own behavior and tone of voice.

❖ Clarify for the patient that you are going to work with him or her to identify the problem and then address the problem specifically, not the patient's behavior.

❖ Engage the patient to work with you in identifying goals or solutions to the problem.

❖ Avoid touching on emotional topics such as religion, race, or politics.

❖ If multiple issues are identified, don't attempt to solve them all. Start with the

liability awareness

issue that is of the most immediate concern to the patient and work with him or her to resolve it before moving on to the others.

❖ If an issue cannot be resolved immediately, come up with a concrete plan that outlines what steps will be followed and when and who will communicate a response back to the patient.

Appropriate and timely follow-up to the meeting may not only resolve the issue, but also, by showing the commitment to patient satisfaction, convert a dissatisfied individual into a repeat customer.

Effective communication with patients can go a long way in preventing many incidents of dissatisfaction. For example, in the opening scenario, if the patient had been made aware on the first visit that part of his care would be rendered by a student, and the involvement of the PT and PTA had been outlined, the confrontational situation could have been avoided. Informed patients who are actively involved in the clinical component of their care are more likely to have a satisfactory clinical outcome.

Don't allow yourself or your staff to be caught off guard in an escalating situation. Take the time to review the risks in your work environment and implement all necessary procedures and physical layout adjustments to address them.

Fran Welk, PT, MEd, is Owner of Susquehanna Physical Therapy and Director of Physical Therapy at the Bloomsburg Hospital in Bloomsburg, Pennsylvania. He is a member of the APTA Risk Management and Member Benefits Committee as well as APTA Treasurer and a member of APTA's Board of Directors.

Reference

1. Bennett JJ. APTA examines patient abandonment. *PT—Magazine of Physical Therapy.* 1999;8(7):24-28.

Navigating a Web of Opportunities and Risks

by Kathleen Lewis, PT, MAPT, JD

Maintaining a Web site and communicating with patients electronically pose a variety of legal risks. Be aware of the dangers and take proper precautions!

In the first quarter of this year, 40.9 million adult Americans used the Internet to access health information, an 18% increase from the last quarter of 1999.[1] By January 2000, there were more than 17,000 health-related Web sites,[2] and 21% of patients were communicating via e-mail with their health care providers.[3]

It is expected that 115 million adult Americans will be seeking health information online by 2010;[4] that, by 2003, health care commerce will reach $70 billion between business and consumers and $170 billion from business to business;[5] and that there will be a 40% annual increase in use of "telehealth" over the next 10 years.[6] (A section of a recent bill[7] that revised Kentucky's physical therapy practice act defines telehealth as "the use of interactive audio, video, or other electronic media to deliver health care" and states that it "includes the use of electronic media for diagnosis, consultation, treatment, transfer of health or medical data, or continuing education.")

Still unconvinced that health care is "going cyber"? A study[8] conducted earlier this year by the American Association of Medical Colleges asserted that 70% of outpatient care will be provided electronically by 2010. And there is evidence that patient demand will force lagging health care providers onto the Internet. In a survey[9] conducted by Cyber Dialogue, a firm that does Internet market research, 14.8 million adult Americans expressed interest in switching to doctors who have Web sites, and 11.9 million expressed interest in switching to doctors who use e-mail. These studies and others show how important it is for health care practitioners to be savvy about this ongoing revolution and the opportunities and challenges it poses.

Cyberspace offers a variety of outlets for telehealth, including Web sites, newsgroups, listservs, and chat rooms. *Web sites* provide general health information and often accommodate requests for advice by allowing the viewer to send questions via e-mail. (Some Web sites have begun charging a fee when viewers submit questions.) *Newsgroups* are online discussion forums, categorized by subject, where people read and post messages. *Listservs* distribute e-mail messages to a list of subscribers. *Chat rooms* allow "real time" communication between two or more individuals.

But just as these cyberspace outlets offer consumers new opportunities, they also carry dangers for the general public. The quality of health information on the Internet is unreliable, according to a study of

health care Web sites[10]: 99% do not disclose conflicts of interest, 82% do not give the dates on which information was posted or last updated, 69% do not give the author's name, 80% do not give the author's credentials, and only 1% provide evidence-based resources. Independent organizations such as the Internet Healthcare Coalition (www.ihealthcoalition.org), the Health on the Net Foundation (www.hon.ch/home.html), and Health Internet Ethics (www.hiethics.org) have arisen to address "e-health" ethical issues.

The Digital Millennium Copyright Act,[11] signed into law on October 28, 1998, amended copyright law to address online concerns, and the Department of Justice and other government agencies are receiving increased funding and manpower to combat cyber crime. In a speech delivered earlier this year to the schools of law, medicine, and pharmacy at the University of Buffalo, John Bentivoglo, who was then the Justice Department's chief privacy officer, noted that "the same factors that make information technology useful in the health care industry—low barriers to entry, relative anonymity, the elimination of geographic boundaries—also provide new opportunities for unscrupulous providers and new incentives to trample on the legitimate."[12]

Points to Consider

Each of the following Web site features or characteristics presents ethical and legal issues that must be addressed:

❖ Pictures scanned from a textbook.

❖ Copies of published articles.

❖ Links to other Web sites.

❖ Consumer information about wellness with no disclosure of the author or his or her credentials.

❖ Financial support from advertising or undisclosed financial support from other sources.

❖ Listing of "physical therapy" among a variety of medical services offered.

❖ Opportunities for the user to communicate about individual problems via e-mail, listservs, newsgroups, or chat rooms.

Navigating a Web of Opportunities and Risks

Many professional organizations are developing guidelines for information dissemination and interaction with patients via the Web. Here are some basic things to keep in mind:

Copyright laws. Compliance with copyright laws is essential. Copyright protects original works that are creative and in a fixed medium (ie, written work, drawings, photographs, etc). An exception to the rule of copyright infringement is the concept known as "fair use," which permits the reproduction of small amounts of copyrighted material—such as excerpts from a book for purposes of illustration or comment, or reproduction by a teacher or student of a small part of a work to illustrate a lesson—when the copying will have little effect on the value of the original work. In an educational content, fair use generally involves a particular audience, a limited period of time, and a limited amount of copyrighted material. College faculty, for example, may be able to meet fair use standards for distance education if only students who are enrolled in the course have access to the course material.

Anyone posting copyright-protected material in cyberspace should proceed carefully. An excellent "Crash Course in Copyright" is available on the University of Texas system's Web site at www.

utsystem.edu/ogc/intellectualproperty/cprtindx.htm. To view the copyright/trademark notice on APTA's Web site, go to www.apta.org/Home/Copyright_notice.

If your Web site was designed by a third party as an independent contractor, the designer most likely has the copyright, unless the original contract transfers copyright to your health care organization. If the copyright is not transferred to your health care entity, you may have to limit future changes to and uses of the site to avoid being cited for copyright violation(s).

Another touchy copyright area involves linking to another Web site. Laws in this area are unsettled, but violations are more likely to occur when you link without permission to a Web site that has posted a notice requiring that such permission be obtained. Violations also can occur when you design your Web page in such a way as to bring *content* from another site to your site, rather than allowing the visitor to navigate directly to the linked site. This is called "framing" by using "multi-pane" Web page design, and it can prevent viewers from seeing advertising and other revenue-generating mechanisms at the linked site.

A common myth about copyright is that violations do not constitute criminal offenses. In fact, the Digital Millennium Copyright Act[11] poses the threat of criminal prosecution for reproducing or distributing one or more copies of one or more copyrighted works that have a total retail value of more than $1,000.

Credentials. The *Guide to Physical Therapy Practice*,[13] licensure laws, the profession's *Code of Ethics*,[14] and other professional documents state that physical therapy is provided by licensed physical therapists. Some Web sites that list physical therapy as a service, however, either do not identify the credentials of those providing physical therapy services or list individuals who lack those credentials. Issues tied to the unlawful practice of physical therapy, inappropriate advertising, and aiding and abetting the unlawful practice of physical therapy arise on such sites.

Nature of relationship to the consumer. Consumers who seek information online potentially receive poor or inaccurate information and may subsequently experience harm. Health care providers, for their part, who give information to a stranger who is subsequently harmed risk malpractice suits and licensure disciplinary actions.

Exchanging online information is more hazardous when a therapist-patient relationship can be established. Prescribing without first seeing and examining the patient subjects physical therapists (PTs) and physical therapist assistants (PTAs) to licensure disciplinary actions, not to mention malpractice lawsuits. In March 2000, the Oregon Medical Board disciplined a physician for unprofessional and dishonorable conduct when the physician claimed to have examined a patient by reviewing a form the client had completed online. State attorneys general have filed civil actions against companies for distribution of drugs by physicians and pharmacists who are not licensed in the states where patients received the care.

PTs should be particularly wary that a therapist-patient relationship might be established when one or more of the following characteristics apply:

❖ There is a fee for communication.
❖ The communication occurs via e-mail, implying a confidential nature.
❖ The consumer receives advice specific to his or her particular situation.

Navigating a Web of Opportunities and Risks

Privacy issues. Another potential hazard for consumers is disclosure of personal information. Although Web site users might believe their visits to be anonymous, health care Web sites can gain a remarkable amount of personal information from surveys, registration forms, and other means, including not only name and address but health concerns and purchasing interests.

On many Web sites, the privacy policies are inadequate, or there are inconsistencies between stated policies and actual practices. By reviewing Web sites' HTML code for security status information and using a special computer program called a "pocket sniffer" to identify data leaks, researchers for government and nonprofit advocacy organizations such as the Federal Trade Commission and the California Health Care Foundation have found that many health care Web sites carelessly or intentionally disclose personal information.

Protection of health information is highly regulated, however. The Health Insurance Portability and Accountability Act of 1996[15] and other federal laws include provisions for the privacy and security of health information, and accreditation groups such as the Joint Commission on Accreditation of Healthcare Organizations require confidentiality and security measures. In addition, electronic ventures that provide financial incentives for directing potential clients to the venture's Web site may violate various state and federal anti-kickback and self-referral regulations.

What You Can Do

Here are some basic tips to help you avoid making costly mistakes in disseminating health information via the Internet.[16, 17]

The following points pertain specifically to Web design and management:

Seek legal counsel early in the planning process. Laws are changing and there are multiple legal and ethical issues to be considered from the outset. Have counsel review your remuneration agreements with ownership investors or advertisers to avoid violating federal and state self-referral and anti-kickback laws.

Guard against copyright infringement. Get written permission from copyright owners whenever you use their content, images, graphics, sound, and animation. Be judicious in linking to other sites —link only to credible sites and only after receiving permission to do so. If you anticipate modifying the design of your own site at a later date, make sure any contract you sign with another party to design your Web page states that you hold the copyright to the Web page design.

Protect your interests and ensure compliance with your standards when other parties are involved with your Web site. Clear, specific written agreements are easier to enforce in the event that a disagreement or a harmful situation arises. Written agreements with Web site management companies or advertisers on your site should specify that your privacy policies will be honored, that Health Insurance Portability and Accountability Act (HIPAA)[17] Internet security requirements will be met, and that you will be indemnified for breach of contract or adverse effects from equipment failure or other transmission problems. (The HIPAA requires the use of encryption software, technologies that authenticate the identities of senders and recipients of health information, software that gives only authorized people access to certain information, unique IDs and software that track appropriate and authorized access to health information, and oversight procedures to ensure compliance.)

Apply the principles of the profession's Code of Ethics[14] to your Web site. Generally, health information should be provided only by health professionals, and the author's credentials should be clearly displayed. Include a notice that the health information provided at the site is not intended to replace care by the visitor's health care providers. Clearly display a listing of your Web site's funding resources. Make sure advertising material is easily identifiable as promotional. Do not, however, use disclaimers merely as a ploy to circumvent liability. Assign a review committee or editorial board to ensure that your Web site's material is always of high quality, accurate, current, and understandable to the reader.

Other good sources of guidance regarding Internet ethics issues include the Health Internet Ethics coalition, which lists "Ethical Principles For Offering Internet Health Services" at www.hiethics.org/Principles/index.asp; the Health On the Net Foundation, which provides its "HON Code of Conduct for Medical and Health Web Sites" at www.hon.ch/HONcode/; and the American Medical Association, which gives "Guidelines for Medical and Health Information Sites on the Internet" at

Navigating a Web of Opportunities and Risks

http://jama.ama-assn.org/issues/v283n 12/full/jsc00054.html. In addition, the Federation of State Boards of Physical Therapy may approve new telehealth guiding principles at its December 2000 board meeting. When those principles are finalized, they will be available at www.fsbpt.org.

Make sure you comply with state licensure laws and other federal, state, and local regulations. A notice to visitors to your Web site should list the jurisdictions in which PTs affiliated with your site are licensed, and it should state explicitly that care cannot and will not be provided to visitors from other jurisdictions. When a Web site visitor and a health care practitioner communicate, the practitioner should state his or her intent not to enter into a therapist-patient relationship. Similarly, the visitor should be required to verify that his or her intent is not to enter into a provider-patient relationship, nor to substitute the receipt of information for a care provider-patient relationship. If the PT and the visitor intend to enter into a provider-patient relationship, both parties should expressly agree, and subsequent services—including a face-to-face examination of the client prior to providing any intervention—should be provided in compliance with the *Guide to Physical Therapist Practice*[13] and licensure laws.

Be alert to changes in practice acts: As noted earlier, Kentucky's recently revised physical therapy act[7] specifically regulates the provision of physical therapy and continuing education via telehealth. Also, keep apprised of federal anti-fraud efforts such as the Federal Trade Commission announcement "Operation CureAll Targets Internet Health Fraud" at www.ftc.gov/opa/1999/ 9906/ opcureall.htm.

Take care not to violate visitors' privacy and confidentiality rights. Web site visitors should have the express right to decide what kind of personal information about them—if any—may be collected and how that information may be used. Don't collect personal data such as names and addresses unless visitors voluntarily provide it. Back up

Navigating a Web of Opportunities and Risks

your written agreements with advertisers and other third parties to your site regarding adherence to your privacy and confidentiality policies by monitoring their compliance. Review privacy and confidentiality recommendations from special interest groups; one excellent resource is the HealthKey Privacy Advisory Group's report, *The HealthKey Program: A Frame-work and Structured Process for Developing Responsible Privacy Practices.*[5]

The World Wide Web isn't the only Internet medium to pose risks to health care providers. The following tips pertain specifically to management of e-mail communication with patients and clients:

Develop policies and procedures regarding the purpose, objectives, and appropriate and inappropriate uses of e-mail communication. These detailed plans serve as road maps for educating staff and patients, implementing risk management,

and ensuring effective communication. Recently, an HMO sent e-mail correspondence meant for 858 customers to the wrong enrollees! The HMO minimized the potential for subsequent errors, however, by immediately revising its e-mail protocols to address the problem and ensure that it wasn't repeated.[18]

Lay ground rules for message content. Since e-mail communication always carries the risk that the wrong party will receive or intentionally gain access to a confidential message, it's generally best to avoid addressing matters that are of an urgent, sensitive, or emotional nature when writing e-mail messages to patients.

Develop strict confidentiality procedures for all electronic communication. You may consider requiring staff to sign a statement that they have read, understand, and agree to abide by your confidentiality protocols.

Navigating a Web of Opportunities and Risks

Ensure that confidential information is secure. Methods of doing this may include using password-protected screen savers, placing computer monitors only in a secure location, and instituting access protocols. Make sure you have the necessary hardware, software, and technical support to ensure security.

Ensure that all electronic medical record information is properly archived. Add hard copies of all e-mail communications regarding appointments and patients' care plans to patients' paper records. Back up electronic files weekly to guard against any loss of information.

Educate staff and patients about privacy issues and the measures you've instituted to protect patients' rights, and tell staff what disciplinary actions will be taken if they violate privacy and confidentiality policies.

Give new employees an orientation to your privacy policies and review those policies annually with all staff. Give patients verbal and printed instructions on: 1) informed consent policies for e-mail use; 2) the importance of using discreet subject headings (provide examples); 3) the need to immediately confirm receipt of e-mail; 4) the desirability of using nonelectronic communication methods for urgent, sensitive, and emotional matters; 5) the necessity of including a confidentiality statement with each e-mail message; and 6) the need to give patients a time frame for staff response.

The following tips pertain to compliance with documentation standards, the APTA Code of Ethics, and state practice acts:

Obtain the patient's written consent to communicate via e-mail.

Include a confidentiality statement in all your e-mail messages to patients/clients. Consider this wording, which features elements of various policies: *This message is confidential. If you are not the intended recipient, you may not disclose, print, copy, or disseminate this information. If you have received this mes-*

sage in error, please inform the sender of this and delete the message. [Institution name], its subsidiaries, and affiliates claim all applicable privileges related to this communication.

Put discreet subject headings on all e-mail messages. Instruct patients/clients to do the same.

Review each message prior to sending it to ensure that the correct message is being sent to the appropriate patient.

Configure your e-mail software to send an automatic reply to all incoming messages from patients. This reply should inform patients that their messages have been received, give them a timeframe for your response, and tell them what to do if they require immediate assistance.

Require the patient to acknowledge receipt of your e-mail message. Set your computer to automatically inform you when your messages have been received.

As health care in cyberspace continues to mature, providers will have new opportunities to educate, communicate, and improve health care service delivery. Regulations will change, and consumers will present their own new demands. As a profession, we must respond to these developments in a way that will best serve the public interest and our own future. **PT**

Kathleen Lewis, PT, MAPT, JD, an Associate Professor in the physical therapy department at Wichita State University in Kansas, is a member of the APTA Risk Management Member Benefits Committee and the APTA Editorial Advisory Group. She can be reached at 316/618-5430 or via e-mail at dknlewis@worldnet.att.net.

This information should be viewed as general and limited within the scope of this article. Consult legal counsel and skilled technical support personnel for answers to specific questions.

References

1. Cleary M. Survey: net health sector growing. *Inter@ctive Week* [online]. August 28, 2000. Available at http://www.zdnet.com/intweek/stories/news/0,4164,2620299,00.html. Accessed September 7, 2000.
2. Goldman J, Hudson Z. *Privacy: Report on the Privacy Policies and Practices of Health Web Sites*. Oakland, Calif: California HealthCare Foundation; 2000:98. Available at http://admin.chcf.org/documents/ehealth/privacywebreport.pdf. Accessed March 28, 2000.
3. *5th HON Survey on the Evolution of Internet Use for Health Purposes*. Geneva, Switzerland: Health on the Net Foundation; 1999. Available at www.hon.ch/Survey/ResultsSummary_oct_nov99.html. Accessed March 28, 2000.
4. CyberDialogue and The Institute for the Future. *Ethics Survey of Consumer Attitudes About Health Web Sites*. Washington, DC: California Healthcare Foundation and The Internet Healthcare Coalition; 2000:22. Available at http://admin.chcf.org/documents/ehealth/surveyreport.pdf. Accessed March 28, 2000.
5. HealthKey Privacy Advisory Group. *The HealthKey Program: A Framework and Structured Process for Developing Responsible Privacy Practices*. Princeton, NJ: Robert Wood Johnson Foundation; 2000:21. Available at www.healthkey.org. Accessed June 1, 2000.
6. Telemedicine to grow 40% annually over next 10 years, says pundit. *Telemedicine Today*. 1999. Available at www.telemedtoday.com/website99/news_items.htm. Accessed March 10, 2000.
7. An act relating to the use of information technology in the delivery of health services. Kentucky Legislature. HB 1777. Available at www.lrc.state.ky.us/RECORD/00RS/HB177.htm. Accessed September 13, 2000.
8. Proctor J. Delphi study makes predictions for the future. *AAMC Reporter* [online]. February 2000. Available at www.aamc.org/newsroom/reporter/feb2000/delphi.htm. Accessed October 2, 2000.
9. Chin T. E-health firms fail to fulfill promise. *American Medical News* [online]. August 21, 2000. Available at http://ama-assn.org/sci-pubs/amnews/pick_00/te110821.htm. Accessed July 3, 20000.
10. Hersh W, Gorman P, Sacherek L. Applicability and quality of information for answering clinical questions on the Web. *JAMA*. 1998;280:1307-1308.
11. *Digital Millennium Copyright Act*. PL 105-304.
12. Bentivoglio JT. Telemedicine: evolving legal and regulatory issues for the health professions. Presented at: University of Buffalo; July 2000; Buffalo, NY.
13. *Guide to Physical Therapist Practice*. Alexandria, Va: American Physical Therapy Association; 1999.
14. *APTA Code of Ethics and Guide for Professional Conduct*. Alexandria, Va: American Physical Therapy Association; 2000.
15. *Health Insurance Portability and Accountability Act of 1996*. PL 104-191.
16. Winker M, Flanagin, A, Chi-Lum B, et al. Guidelines for medical and health information sites on the Internet: principles governing AMA Web sites. *JAMA*. 2000;283:1600-1606. Available at http://jama-assn.org/issues/v283n12/ffull/jsc00054.html. Accessed June 25, 2000.
17. Kane B, Sands DZ. Guidelines for the clinical use of electronic mail with patients: a white paper. *Journal of the American Medical Informatics Association*. 1998; 5(1):104-111. Available at www.amia.org/pubs/pospaper/positio2.htm. Accessed February 19, 2000.
18. Health notes. *Health Lawyers News*. 2000;4(9):18.

liabilityawareness

by Carol R Schunk, PT, PsyD

Responding to Patient Complaints

Proper preparation and skillful handling can improve patients' and clients' satisfaction and decrease the potential for liability.

Complaints by patients and clients can arise no matter how well you practice. Receiving a complaint is never a pleasant experience, but you do have considerable influence over the outcome. The way a complaint is handled often is just as important to determining the outcome as is the nature of the complaint itself.

A complaint is any action taken by an aggrieved party. In a physical therapy context, complaints may be related to:

❖ **Clinical intervention.** A man may write to a physical therapist (PT) to complain that he does not think the PT's plan of care for his elderly mother is effective or meets her needs.

❖ **Billing.** A patient or client may leave a PT a voicemail message stating that she is very upset because she was charged for a service she does not believe she received.

❖ **General customer service.** On her way out the door after a visit to the clinic, a client may tell the receptionist she is very annoyed because her session started 20 minutes late and she now is tardy to pick up her children at school.

Complaints may be delivered informally or formally, directly or indirectly, orally or in writing (on paper or via electronic media). They can be brought to the PT's attention by various individuals or entities—patients and clients, family members, colleagues, and referral sources.

Consider These Steps

Whatever the nature of the complaint or the channel of communication by which it is received, you as a PT can increase your chances of defusing the problem by taking the following steps:

Take every complaint seriously. Do not consider frivolous any complaint a patient or client brings to your attention. The fact that someone feels strongly enough about the matter to share it with you is reason enough for an earnest response. Your subsequent investigation may reveal that there is a logical explanation for what has occurred, a misunderstanding that you can clear up with relative ease, or a misperception that you can quickly correct. Don't assume from the outset, however, that any complaint is groundless or insubstantial.

Your clinic or facility's administrative policies and procedures should include an action plan for responding to complaints so that you are prepared to act in a prompt and caring manner. The plan should include having someone within your practice designated as the point person for handling complaints. Sometimes those who are rendering care can be somewhat defensive when responding to a complaint, because they may take it personally. This is a good reason to consider having the department or clinic director be the one to respond.

To illustrate each of the next three steps, let's use the example of a patient who sent you an e-mail message in which she stated that a physical therapy aide assisted her and that she refuses to pay for the services she received from the aide.

Acknowledge the complaint. First, let the patient know that you have received the complaint and that you will investigate and respond to it in a timely fashion. Making a complaint can be uncomfortable

and scary for the patient, so if he or she does so, the effort should be noted. This does not mean you should agree with the patient or concede any wrongdoing. It simply means you should thank the person for taking the time to alert you to the concern and indicate when you will provide a more thorough response.

The worst thing you can do is to minimize or ignore a complaint. Reacting in a defensive or demeaning way, or not addressing the complaint at all, may very well cause the situation to escalate. The patient may feel the need to take more drastic action—such as retaining an attorney, calling the state physical therapy licensing agency, or requesting an outside investigation into your business practices—in order to ensure that his or her concerns are addressed.

Instead, acknowledge all patients' and clients' complaints quickly and sensitively. If at all possible, try to acknowledge receipt of complaints in person or by phone. Always keep in mind that any voicemail messages you need to leave should omit all confidential details. Ask only that the patient or client call you back. For example, here's an incorrect response to the patient who sent the e-mail message stating that a physical therapy aide assisted her and that she refuses to pay for services: "I'm so sorry that happened; don't worry about the bill." Another incorrect and inappropriate response would be, "That is impossible. You must be mistaken."

The correct response would be: "I've received your e-mail message. Thank you for taking the time to write. We are looking into the matter now and will get back to you in 5 to 10 business days."

In some cases, it may not be clear what issues lie at the heart of a complaint. In these instances, take the opportunity during the acknowledgement contact to ask some clarifying questions. All such questions should be factually oriented and should never commit you to any course of action. Questions such as, "I want to be sure I fully understand your concern—what more can you tell me about this situation?" or "How can I best help you with this concern?" may help get to the bottom of things.

If the complaint mentions a lawsuit or the problem seems serious enough to lead to a claim, immediately inform your malpractice insurance carrier and your attorney. In such a case, let your attorney guide the investigation. If litigation actually occurs, you might be entitled to withhold from the patient or client notes, reports, and other records created by or at the direction of the attorney. Records you prepare on your own initiative would not be subject to such protection, so you should be cautious about creating new records in a potentially serious case without your attorney's guidance or go-ahead.

Investigate the complaint. In a situation in which there is no evident threat of litigation or liability, it is important that you gather and review all of the facts before responding to the patient or client. Investigate each complaint immediately and thoroughly to determine what actually happened. The investigation can include but is not necessarily limited to reviewing the documentation in the patient's or client's file, pulling bills for evaluation, interviewing all clinical and/or administrative staff who can shed light on the situation, and doing a safety check on any pieces of equipment referenced in the complaint. The goal of your investigation is to pull together an objective picture of the circumstances related to the complaint. This portrait will help you ascertain the validity of the complaint and any remedial actions you can and should take.

In the case of the patient who sent an e-mail message stating that a physical therapy aide administered care to her and that

liabilityawareness

Sample Complaint-Response Letter

[Salutation: Do not be informal with the patient/client unless an informal relationship already has been firmly established.]

Dear Ms. Brown:

[Part I: Thank the person again for bringing the complaint to you and convey the value your facility puts on patient/client/customer (use whatever term is right for your setting) satisfaction. If you have customer satisfaction data, cite it briefly.]

Thank you again for your e-mail message expressing your dissatisfaction with your visit to our facility on September 1, 2003. As I mentioned in my initial response, we take our clients' satisfaction very seriously. It is our goal to meet or exceed expectations in all cases, and I am pleased to say that, per a recent satisfaction survey of our clientele, we are meeting this goal more than 95% of the time.

[Part II: Identify the complaint as stated by the patient or client, including any additional information you gained when you originally acknowledged the complaint. Then state your response/solution.]

You had stated that during the visit in question you received care from a physical therapy aide. In response to that statement I reviewed your chart. I found that on that date Ms Peggy Wilson administered your care. Ms Wilson is a licensed physical therapist assistant, not a physical therapy aide. She is licensed by the state and works in compliance with all practice standards. In speaking with Ms Wilson and Ms Angela Hanley, your physical therapist, it is clear that they were in communication regarding your case and that Ms Wilson played a proper role in your plan of care.

In the future, we will ensure that all of our clients are aware of the credentials of those providing their care. To assist in this effort, we are preparing short staff biographies that can be provided to our clients upon request (Ms Wilson's is enclosed). We have held a staff meeting to remind everyone to ensure that proper and full introductions take place whenever a new staff member becomes involved in a patient's or client's plan of care.

[Part III: Wrap it up and tell the patient/client who he or she can contact with any additional concerns.]

In light of our findings, we believe that your bill is correct and that changes are not warranted. I hope this response addresses your concern. If you find that you need any further assistance please feel free to contact me directly. I can be reached by phone at 422/322-1212 or via e-mail at bjones@xyzPT.com.

[Closing: Thank the person again, and sign off.]

Thank you again for taking the time to alert us to your concern. We do appreciate your business.

Sincerely,

Betty Jones, PT, OCS
Clinical Director
XYZ Physical Therapy

the patient or client refuses to pay for those services, you should review the documentation in the patient's file and interview all clinical staff who rendered the care. During this investigation you may find that the staff person treating the patient was actually a physical therapist assistant (PTA), but that this fact was not evident to the patient or client because proper introductions were not made, and the patient was not informed about the role of the PTA (as opposed to that of an aide). Such a finding would suggest that you may want to reevaluate your communication policies so that staff clearly communicate to patients and clients the roles of those who are administering care and assures them that their PT is abreast of their progress at all times.

Alternatively, investigation may find that the PT assigned to this case was swamped and decided to have a physical therapy aide supervise the patient's or client's strengthening exercises. If so, improper delegation has occurred. Appropriate remedial steps might include meeting with the PT individually to review all relevant practice standards related to delegation and supervision, as well as instituting staff training on this topic. Also, review your billing and eliminate the codes in which the aide participated.

Respond to the complaint. It is important to remain objective, focus on facts, and address only the issue at hand when responding to any complaint, whether orally or in writing. There is no hard and fast rule that dictates that you must use the telephone to respond to complaints received via telephone, e-mail to respond to complaints received via e-mail, and so forth. Rather, you should consider all your format options and then use your best judgment based on the specific circumstances of each individual complaint. If you are unsure what format is most appropriate, it may be helpful to consult with a risk management professional or an attorney familiar with applicable state and federal law.

Often, a thoughtfully worded response can turn things around. If your investigation reveals that a complaint is founded and has the potential for litigation, take the time to consult with a risk management professional or an attorney familiar with applicable state and federal law for guidance on the best way to proceed before getting back to the patient or client.

On the other hand, if you find that a complaint is unfounded, craft a response that outlines your findings. If you have decided to make changes in clinic policy or taken other remedial action, state this in general terms to assure the patient/client that you have attempted to see to it that they and others will not have the same experience in the future. (See the sample complaint-response letter elsewhere on page 24.)

Additional Considerations

Anonymous complaints and carbon copies. You have no obligation to respond in instances in which complaints are lodged anonymously. In fact, it may be risky to do so, precisely because the source of the complaint is unknown. There also may be instances in which a complaint is lodged (anonymously or not) and other parties are copied on it (the "cc" on e-mail, for example). While it probably is wise to take note of who else has seen the complaint, you are under no obligation to respond to any "carboned" party—and again, it actually may be risky to do so.

Documentation. Accurate and complete documentation of all patient/client records is a hallmark of good practice. Per APTA's Guidelines for Physical Therapy Documentation[1] (BOD 02-02-16-20), documentation is required for every visit or encounter with a patient or client. Documentation of each visit or encounter must include, among other elements, adverse reaction(s) to interventions, if any, as well as communication/consultation with providers/patient/client/family/significant other. Documentation can be a valuable resource for a facility, but it is use-ful if the facility or practice has in place a documentation policy that staff consistently follows.

Such a policy should require that:

❖ Each physical therapy visit is documented.

❖ Information is recorded only on proper forms, with all entries including the date and time of the session and including the PT's signed first initial, last name, and professional designation.

❖ Information is recorded as close as possible to the time that care is delivered; no documenting in advance or leaving important notations for the end of the day.

❖ All abbreviations in documentation are common ones approved for use by the facility or practice.

❖ Any changes in documentation are

continued on page 27 ▶▶▶

liabilityawareness

continued from page 25

denoted in such a manner as to eliminate any questions about their authenticity.

* The patient's symptoms are described as they are elicited and offered, with quotations recorded accurately.
* All documentation is objective and factual, never opinionated.
* The facts are reported in an organized and systematic manner, in sufficient detail and in chronological order.
* All telephone calls involving pertinent patient/client information are documented. This includes cancellations and conversations with other care providers or referral sources.
* Both internal protocol and external regulations and policies relative to patient's or client's confidentiality are followed. These regulations and policies may come from the federal, state, or local government and/or reimbursement sources or other entities. It is important to be mindful of this issue when handling incoming calls related to a patient's or client's condition and/or when using electronic documentation.
* When using electronic documentation, steps are taken to protect records' confidentiality and to alert authorized users of their responsibility to maintain the confidentiality of a patient's or client's record at all times.
* All attempts to contact referral and/or payment sources (eg, the insurer) are documented.

Confidentiality. However cavalier the patient or client may be with personal information when communicating a complaint, you should be careful to maintain confidentiality in all stages of your response.

Money. Sometimes a patient or client is so upset that he or she wants his or her money back or his or her expenses covered. This course of action may be appropriate in some cases if it is "the right thing to do" and will satisfy the patient or client and resolve the dispute. In health care, however, to return money, or to offer to pay for or actually pay expenses associated with a complaint, may be construed as an implication that wrongdoing did take place. Under the rules of evidence, offering to pay for or actually paying medical expenses is not by itself sufficient to prove liability. One must realize, however, that such a gesture may raise questions down the line if a complaint escalates to the level of a lawsuit or other investigation.

We all want our patients and clients to be happy customers, and we all aim for 100% satisfaction, but the reality is that complaints can and do happen. The good news is that a prompt and professional response can not only minimize the potential for a complaint to escalate but also actually turn things around 180 degrees and create a customer who is impressed with your attention to his or her concerns and is prepared to recommend you to others in your community. **PT**

Carol R Schunk, PT, PsyD, a member of APTA's Committee on Risk Management and Member Benefits, is a consultant with Northwest Rehab Alliance and TAOS (Therapeutic Associates Outcomes System). She also works at home health and rehabilitation facilities for PT on Call. In addition, Schunk is editor of GeriNotes, a publication of the APTA Section on Geriatrics. She can be contacted via APTA's Risk Management and Member Benefits Department at insfinsvcs@apta.org.

Reference

1. Guidelines for Physical Therapy Documentation (BOD 02-02-16-20). Available at www.apta.org/Pdfs/governance/bodPoliSec1.pdf. Accessed August 18, 2003.

Power of Positive Patient Relations

Your relationship with your patients is the backbone of your practice. A warm, professional relationship not only helps your patients through the healing process, it helps you avoid miscommunication and misunderstandings that might result in malpractice suits.

High patient expectations coupled with poor therapy results may lead to allegations of malpractice. Because many of your patients may never return to their full functional level (no matter how sound the therapy is), you must reconcile any differences that exist between your understanding of reality and your *patient's* understanding of reality. Developing positive patient relations, and formalizing office procedures to facilitate those relations, are the first steps in reconciling those differences.

To develop positive patient relations and reduce the likelihood of malpractice claims, you first must understand what patients expect—both of you and of therapy. You also must recognize that not every patient is a good candidate for your practice. Patients must be chosen and managed skillfully to lower the risk of poor results and subsequent liability allegations.

Meeting Basic Patient Expectations

Today's patients have high expectations of health care. They are more knowledgeable about health care, and they are not afraid to ask questions. With this knowledge and attitude comes a tendency to challenge the provider about quality of care. You can best lay the groundwork for positive patient relations by communicating your intentions to meet their basic expec-tations of

By Jerome B. Connolly, PT

competence, safety, caring, and a positive outcome at a reasonable cost.

Competence. Patients expect you to be properly trained and licensed, to make an accurate evaluation of their condition, and to properly implement the treatment plan. They expect you to be up-to-date in your field. They also expect you to consult with peers and other practitioners for additional information or assistance when necessary.

Patients have the same expectations of your staff. Because you are ultimately responsible for the actions of those to whom you delegate authority, your selection, training, and supervision of employees are essential. In a recent Chicago Insurance Company survey of malpractice claims against physical therapists, 21% of the claims reviewed resulted from the actions of an aide or an assistant. Consider this actual case: Claimant had been receiving physical therapy for a torn meniscus and a patellar malalignment syndrome. When the physical therapy aide had trouble starting the stimulator and began twirling the setting dial, the machine turned on and shocked the claimant.

Safety. You should provide for patient safety from the moment patients step onto your facility's property. The building and grounds should be in good repair and routinely examined. Special care should be taken to ensure that all equipment is functioning at an optimal level and that manufacturers' servicing requirements have been met.

Be aware of how patients perceive these physical aspects of your office. They quickly sense if a clinic or department is disorganized. You may be a genius at rehabilitating the knee, but if

your facility is not clean, safe, and orderly, patient distrust and anxiety may persist.

Written policies and procedures to protect patients from injury and to facilitate patient recovery are reasonable patient expectations. Safety systems must be defined, and compliance must be enforced.

Caring. Many practitioners may have become targets of malpractice allegations because they perceived patients as body parts to be fixed, rather than as individuals with problems that affect daily life. Never forget the importance of one-to-one caring relationships with patients.

Patients expect to be treated with respect and dignity and to be kept informed about their treatment. Those who feel that they have been treated fairly and professionally may hesitate to sue, even when they may have sustained injuries while under therapist care. Those who feel neglected—who were kept waiting on a regular basis for appointments or who did not receive answers to telephone calls—may be much more inclined to sue.

Case Scenario

For several months you treat a patient who sustained injuries in an automobile accident. Therapy begins prior to a knee reconstruction and continues postsurgery. Patient makes slow but steady progress, even though she frequently misses appointments and does not cooperate with the treatment plan. When you talk with her about this, she is very defensive and makes it clear that your lack of skill—not her lack of cooperation—is impeding her progress. Patient never returns for therapy; all attempts to contact her fail. What follow-up actions should you take?

Action 1. Send patient a letter stating that you believe continued treatment is necessary and that you would be happy to refer her to another physical therapist.

Action 2. If patient insists on terminating treatment, notify the referring practitioner, the patient, and the insurance carrier, stating that patient has terminated treatment of her own accord and that you believe continued treatment is necessary.

Choosing Patients

Accept only those patients who have conditions within your area of expertise. Physical therapy is becoming increasingly specialized. In a malpractice suit, you would be held to a standard of care that is applicable to your peers. If you are not up-to-date on current technology and techniques in the area in which you treat the patient, you may be considered negligent. Patients with conditions that are not within your scope of expertise or specialization should be referred to appropriate medical personnel.

Managing Patients

Set realistic patient goals. Successful retail businesses subscribe to a philosophy that also applies to physical therapy practice: To live up to your client's expectations, do not offer that which cannot be delivered.

To give yourself and the patient a benchmark to measure progress, communicate therapeutic goals from the outset. Success or failure becomes the joint responsibility of the patient and the therapist. Ask yourself these questions: Are the proposed goals realistic? Are they consistent with your expectations as well as those of the patient? If achieved, will the goals satisfy the patient's needs? Encourage difficult patients to articulate their understanding of the goals. Note their response in the patient record. If appropriate, patients should sign off on a written copy of the goals.

Establish a support system. Patients should have your home phone number or the number of an answering service that can get in touch with you in the event of an emergency. Have another physical therapist available at all times to talk to patients, even if it is just to refer the patient to an emergency department or to the treating physician.

Develop a protocol for handling each patient. All cases should be thoroughly documented. Include the physician's referral when necessary. A protocol for securing the patient's informed consent to treatment should be defined and followed by all staff members.

Exercise sound judgment in decisions involving patient treatment. In develop-

ing treatment plans, you must always think in terms of the patient's best interests. Undertreating due to insurance limitations and overtreating to maximize revenue are unacceptable.

Terminate treatment in a responsible fashion. If a therapist accepts a patient and needs to return that responsibility to the physician or transfer it to another therapist, the rationale and the implementation process must be clearly explained to the patient.

Avoid improper conduct. The APTA's *Guide for Professional Conduct* provides very specific guidelines on matters of professional conduct involving responsibilities, referral relationships, remuneration, and confidentiality.

Clarify all situations that may appear to be improper, illegal, or unethical. Signing insurance bills for patients treated by other physical therapy practitioners in your facility may facilitate reimbursement, but it could present problems if in conflict with your state law.

Resolve problems quickly. Problems with treatment, patient progress, or payment should be addressed with the patient and all involved parties. When necessary, the patient's family should be involved. Thorough documentation is essential. **CM**

Jerome B. Connolly, PT, is a member of the APTA Board of Directors and Executive Committee and chairs the APTA Committee on Member Benefit Insurance. He is president of a private practice in Billings, MT.

First in a series of articles adapted from the workshop syllabus entitled, Risk Management: An APTA Malpractice Resource Guide, *this article is not intended as legal advice for any specific practitioner. Legal advice can be given only by your personal legal counsel, based on the law of your state or on federal law, as applicable.*

SUGGESTED READINGS
Brief Narratives on Open Claims. 1988. Interstate Insurance Group, actual examples, identity removed.
Code of Ethics and *Guide for Professional Conduct.* 1987. American Physical Therapy Association.
LeVoy, R. 1984. *Course Notes—Practice Building Principles, Building Patient Rapport.* Private Practice Section, Denver, CO, November 1984.
Scott, R.W. 1990. *Health Care Malpractice: A Primer on Legal Issues for Professionals.* Thorofare, NJ: Slack, Inc.

Starting Off on the Right Foot

Your relationship with the patient begins the moment an appointment is made. Do everything you can to allay patient anxieties. To ensure that customer service personnel uphold a service-oriented image, routinely listen in to their conversations with patients. Be accommodating; extend office hours into the evenings or to include Saturdays. Be considerate; too much delay makes patients feel that their time is not valuable to you. On the first visit, you may wish to introduce yourself to the patient in the waiting room, give a short tour of the facility, and personally escort him or her to the treatment area. Hand out brochures that describe your background and services; create a slide show or videotape about the facility.

Pay particular attention to developing rapport with children and their parents. Show parents that their child will be cared for by a competent professional. Personally escort the child to therapy and to his parents after therapy. Approach the child at the child's eye level; don't let your eye contact be too intense or intimidating.

Let patients know that you and your staff keep up-to-date on techniques. Post staff biographies and notices of the continuing education courses that you attend or sponsor.

"Inform before you perform." The importance of communication cannot be overemphasized. Explain exactly what you are going to do and why. Leave no room for misinterpretation. Avoid statements that might have a dual meaning, especially when treating a member of the opposite sex. If there is any potential risk, discuss it. Failure to do so may increase patient anxiety, apprehension, and tension that could lead to injury during treatment. Even when a condition is routine and minor, don't make light of it—but don't unnecessarily alarm the patient, either. Remember that patients who have had bad experiences may be more likely to find fault with you, which could lead to a malpractice suit.

Reaching Our Potential

Positive patient relations—the cornerstone of effective practice and sound risk management—require sophisticated cognitive skills that transcend physical limitations.

Charlotte is a 29-year-old physical therapist who was injured in a ski accident 1½ years ago. She is paraplegic. After spending 6 months in a rehabilitation center, she learns to adapt to what seems to be an inordinate number of architectural barriers in both public and private settings. She never relents in her home therapeutic exercise program.

Charlotte also becomes reflective. She wonders why she still exists and what she should do with her life. She eventually concludes that she can—and should—continue to promote healing in others. She also concludes that most human beings want the same thing: to be respected.

Charlotte resumes her physical therapy career, accepting a new job with a local hand rehabilitation center. She and the human resources manager develop her job description, focusing on essential functions of the job and discussing reasonable accommodations that would allow Charlotte to perform those tasks (eg, modifications to the desk at which Charlotte would prepare her documentation). A ramp is installed on the lower level of the clinic, and three handicapped parking spaces are reserved adjacent to that ramp.

Charlotte's first patient is Ms Harris, a 35-year-old secretary who had sustained third-degree burns to 35% of the palmar surface of her left hand while lighting a fire in her fireplace. Charlotte introduces herself to Ms Harris in a warm, professional, and friendly manner. At first, Ms Harris shows some discomfort when she sees that her physical therapist is in a wheelchair, and she avoids eye contact; however, Charlotte

Whether it is the patient or the therapist who has a disability, establishing positive patient relations is integral to minimizing risks.

continues to behave in a professional, thorough manner, focusing the discussion on the patient's injury.

Ms Harris expresses great concern about the scars that may remain on her hands "when all this rehabilitation is over." Charlotte reassures Ms Harris that she will receive caring, competent service. She reviews Ms Harris's medical history and asks her if there is any other information she should know. After receiving the patient's verbal consent, Charlotte then performs an initial evaluation, instructing the physical therapy aide how to assist the patient on the isokinetic/isometric testing machine. After gathering all necessary data, Charlotte identifies some problems, including slight contracture of the metacarpal phalangeal, proximal interphalangeal, and distal interphalangeal joints and contracture of the flexors of the fingers

on the left hand. She then asks Ms Harris to identify what *she* perceives as problems. Charlotte listens and reserves value judgments when Ms Harris explains she is afraid that her injured hand will contract further, resulting in permanent disability. Ms Harris also says she is afraid she will be a burden to her husband and her 6-year-old daughter. Because of her own experiences, Charlotte relates to the fear of becoming dependent on others, but allays Ms Harris's fears by emphasizing that hard work, compliance with the rehabilitation program, and perseverance can help alleviate current—and help prevent future—weakness and limitations in active range of motion.

Charlotte communicates with attentiveness; with a relaxed, "open" posture; and with facilitating gestures, such as head nodding. She responds to Ms Harris's concerns in an empathetic manner. Charlotte is an *"active listener,"* restating and repeating the patient's statements as she hears them and trying to *reflect* both the content and the implied feelings. Charlotte also *"clarifies,"* summarizing or simplifying Ms Harris's thoughts and feelings and converting confused verbalizations into clear, concise statements.

Charlotte assesses Ms Harris's desires and expectations. Charlotte and Ms Harris then develop mutual goals and expectations for therapy. Trust and respect begin to emerge as a result of this shared experience. Because she has been involved in the decision-making process from the beginning, Ms Harris feels that Charlotte has confidence in her ability as a patient to make wise and appropriate decisions when given the facts and the options. When Charlotte and Ms Harris have set clear boundaries and expectations for therapy, Ms Harris signs informed consent forms, and the treatment plan is implemented.

• • • •

Whether it is the patient or the therapist who has a disability, establishing positive patient relations is integral to minimizing risks. And disability or no disability, the therapist must practice the standard of care as defined by state, local, and federal laws and adhere to the standards of care established by the profession.

When physical therapy students with a disability begin careers or when physical therapists with a disability resume already-established careers, they are advocating, through their actions, the rights of their patients, many of whom also have disabilities. In addition, the therapist with a physical limitation may be more able to empathize with patients, which is a primary component of the communica-

> A therapist who has personally experienced the rehabilitation process—and the introspection that typically accompanies the process—may have already resolved the value conflicts that sometimes can be an obstacle in patient relations.

tions required to establish positive patient relations. Positive patient relations involve *facilitating* the patient's decision making, *not* controlling it. A therapist who has personally experienced the rehabilitation process—and the introspection that typically accompanies the process—may have already resolved the value conflicts that sometimes can be an obstacle in patient relations.

What else contributes to positive patient relations? Rapport. To establish rapport, therapists must have a clear sense of "self" and their own personal inadequacies. Therapists also must try to discover how the world seems to the patient. What are the patient's expectations? What does the patient think are the problems? Each patient should have the opportunity to help plan, implement, and evaluate the learning experience that physical therapy really is.

A therapist also must be introspective enough to develop a working philosophy about adult learners. Do you believe all adults can learn or are "educable"? Do you believe all adults are responsible for their own actions and should have input into decisions that affect their lives? Do you believe that all adults should participate equally in society? When physical therapists provide opportunities for patients to identify their own goals, they automatically place these patients in a position of equality and shared leadership.

We are all physically limited to one degree or another, but, as Davis[1] wrote,

> ...if we are to realize our potential, the adult learning process must become a creating, releasing experience rather than a dull series of passively attended indoctrination exercises.

By helping ourselves reach our own potential as professionals, we help our patients reach their potential as participants in their own rehabilitation. *PT*

References

1 Davis C. *Patient/Practitioner Interaction.* Thorofare, NJ: SLACK Inc; 1989.

Suggested Readings

Combs AW, Avila DL, Purkey VV. *Helping Relationships—Basic Concepts for the Health Professions,* ed 2. Boston, Mass: Allyn and Bacon Inc; 1971.

Head G, Horn S II. *The Essentials of Risk Management,* ed 2. Malvern, Penn: Insurance Institute of America; 1991.

Risk Management: An APTA Malpractice Resource Guide. Alexandria, Va: American Physical Therapy Association; 1990.

Gloria J Young, EdD, PT, is President, Sunbelt Physical Therapy, PC, Birmingham, Ala. She is a member of APTA's Committee on Insurance and Member Benefit Services.

liabilityawareness

by Rita Arriaga, PT, MS

Stories from the Front:
Fitness, Wellness, and Alternative Medicine

An examination of risk-management principles through the prism of a case scenario.

About this series: With physical therapy moving toward realization of the APTA Vision for Physical Therapy 2020, and in keeping with the goals that represent the 2004 priorities of the Association (see box on page 35), it is imperative that physical therapists (PTs) and physical therapist assistants (PTAs) recognize and appreciate that sound risk management is a hallmark of autonomous practice. APTA's Committee on Risk Management and Member Benefits uses "Stories from the Front," now in its sixth year, as a vehicle for conveying information about emerging and ongoing risk-management trends in clinical practice. Using a case-based format, the three columns in each year's series illustrate risk considerations identified by the committee through its review of claims data, and provide readers with references and documents that can assist them in making risk-reducing decisions.

Many PTs feel that integrating methods into their practice from alternative medicine and the health, fitness, and wellness arena can improve patient and client outcomes. This, the second "Stories from the Front" column of 2004, looks at some of the risk management issues of such integration. Before incorporating any new methods, PTs must carefully research each and understand their appropriate use within a physical therapy program. PTs in such circumstances also must be able to determine what constitutes a professional service, versus a general one, as risk management strategies may differ.

The Case

A 52-year-old woman had experienced recurrent, nonspecific neck and back pain that a physician had determined was pos-

tural and soft tissue in nature. She was referred to a PT for treatment and, after a few physical therapy sessions over the course of 4 weeks, noted significant reduction in her symptoms.

At that point in her care, the PT recommended yoga as part of the patient's physical therapy program. The PT told the patient she could attend yoga classes the PT was teaching at a nearby gym—and that if she did, the classes could be billed to the patient's health insurance as part of the physical therapy plan of care.

The patient began the yoga classes and progressed in her physical therapy goals over the course of several sessions. During the fifth yoga class, the patient, at the PT's instruction and under his supervision, lost her balance and fell over while attempting to achieve a shoulder stand position. Her left hip and side hit the floor. Though an examination detected no fractures, the patient did sustain significant soft tissue injuries. She subsequently claimed that the accident had made her "fully disabled."

The patient brought suit against the PT and the gym in which the yoga classes were taught. She accused the PT of providing physical therapy—including the yoga instruction—in a negligent and reckless manner. Specifically, she charged that: the PT asked her to engage in yoga positions that were beyond her physical ability and strength; the PT should not have asked her to attempt the shoulder stand position at all, or at least should

have advised her of the risks and then spotted her more effectively during the attempt; and the PT provided inadequate equipment and facilities for the yoga positions being taught. The suit also charged that the owners of the gym failed to: sufficiently train their yoga instructors or ensure adequate standards of instruction, supervise the yoga techniques taught by the PT, and provide adequate equipment and space for yoga instruction.

This case eventually was settled through mediation with a judge. The PT's liability insurance share of the settlement costs was more than $100,000.

The Risks

What risks did the PT in this case incur, and how might they have been avoided? Which APTA documents and instructional materials serve as guides to best practice? Let's take a closer look.

Patient/client safety. Regardless of venue or intervention used, a PT engaging in the practice of physical therapy always must meet professional standards of care, exercising sound judgment and ensuring patient/client safety.

In this case, the patient-provider relationship clearly had been established prior to the patient beginning yoga classes. That relationship was extended to the yoga class when the PT recommended yoga as part of the patient's plan of care and said it would be included in the physical therapy bill sent to the insurance payer. There is no question, therefore, that the PT needed to provide for the patient's safety in both the clinic and the gym setting.

Even though the PT clearly felt the yoga position that precipitated the injury was within the patient's physical capacity, he should have employed appropriate guarding techniques to protect the patient should she lose her balance attempting to achieve the position. If the PT was unable to provide that level of one-on-one assistance, the PT should not have allowed the patient to make the attempt. Whether an intervention is rendered in a physical therapy clinic or a more casual setting such as a gym has no bearing on the PT's responsibility to exercise sound risk management and employ appropriate practice behaviors and procedures.

The Guide to Physical Therapist Practice[1] defines physical therapy as including, in part, "restoration, maintenance, and promotion of optimal physical function, optimal fitness and wellness, and optimal quality of life as it relates to movement and health." The Code of Ethics[2]—which is "binding on all physical therapists"—states that PTs shall "act in a trustworthy manner toward patients/clients" (Principle 2), "exercise sound professional judgment" (Principle 4), and "provide and make available accurate and relevant information to patients/clients about their care" (Principle 8).

The PT in this case also failed to meet the provisions in the Standards of Practice and the Criteria[3] regarding patient/client collaboration and intervention. That document states that, "Within the patient/client management process, the physical therapist and the patient/client establish and maintain an ongoing collaborative process of decision-making that exists throughout the provision of services." It also dictates that all interventions be "provided at a level that is consistent with current physical therapy practice."

As noted in the APTA booklet *Risk Management for Physical Therapists: A*

APTA Vision Statement for Physical Therapy 2020 [HOD 06-00-24-35]

Physical therapy, by 2020, will be provided by physical therapists who are doctors of physical therapy and who may be board-certified specialists. Consumers will have direct access to physical therapists in all environments for patient/client management, prevention, and wellness services. Physical therapists will be practitioners of choice in clients' health networks and will hold all privileges of autonomous practice. Physical therapists may be assisted by physical therapist assistants who are educated and licensed to provide physical therapist-directed and -supervised components of interventions.

Guided by integrity, life-long learning, and a commitment to comprehensive and accessible health programs for all people, physical therapists and physical therapist assistants will render evidence-based service throughout the continuum of care and improve quality of life for society. They will provide culturally sensitive care distinguished by trust, respect, and an appreciation for individual differences.

While fully availing themselves of new technologies, as well as basic and clinical research, physical therapists will continue to provide direct care. They will maintain active responsibility for the growth of the physical therapy profession and the health of the people it serves.

Goals That Represent the 2004 Priorities of the Association [HOD 06-03-07-09]

Goal I: Physical therapists are universally recognized and promoted as the practitioners of choice for persons with conditions that affect movement, function, health, and wellness.

Goal II: Academic and clinical education prepares doctors of physical therapy who are autonomous practitioners.

Goal III: Physical therapists are autonomous practitioners to whom patients/clients have unrestricted direct access as an entry point into the health care delivery system and who are paid for all elements of patient/client management in all practice environments.

Goal IV: Research advances the science of physical therapy and furthers the evidence-based practice of the physical therapist.

Goal V: Physical therapists and physical therapist assistants are committed to meeting the health needs of patients/clients and society through ethical behavior, continued competence, and advocacy for the profession.

Goal VI: Communication throughout the Association enhances participation of and responsiveness to members and promotes and instills the value of belonging to the American Physical Therapy Association.

Goal VII: American Physical Therapy Association standards, policies, positions, guidelines and the *Guide to Physical Therapist Practice; Normative Model of Physical Therapist Education and Evaluative Criteria;* and the *Normative Model of Physical Therapist Assistant Education and Evaluative Criteria* are recognized and used as the foundation for physical therapist practice, research, and education environments.

continued on page 37 ▶▶▶

liabilityawareness

continued from page 35

Quick Reference,[4] "The first and most important thing that you can do to manage your own risk is to be ever mindful of the risks associated with the care you provide and take proactive steps to mitigate the potential for harm." A "Risk Management Checklist for the Office" within that publication is an excellent tool for identifying and avoiding risks such as those taken in this case.

Documentation. While the PT maintained adequate documentation of the care provided in his clinic, he did not fully document the yoga classes as an additional intervention within the physical therapy plan of care. Rather, he merely noted that yoga had been recommended and that the patient was taking classes he was teaching. Integration of traditional physical therapy methods and methods from alternative

medicine and/or the health, fitness, and wellness arena—when based on evidence and sound clinical reasoning—can be beneficial to patients. In this case, however, the PT did not document subjective or objective information that described the patient's response to or tolerance of yoga. Nor did he outline the progression of yoga positions the patient was attempting.

Thus, there was no strong evidence to support the PT's decision to ask the

patient to perform the shoulder stand, or his determination that there was no need for close guarding. Neither had the PT provided specific documentation of the yoga session in question. This lack of documentation not only was a deviation from clinical practice standards, but it also made things problematic for the PT when he subsequently was faced with the patient's allegations. At that time, he disputed the patient's version of the incident.

APTA core documents, policies, and positions are available on the Association's Web site (www.apta.org). Click on "About APTA" for the links.

Also, consult these publications: *A Normative Model of Physical Therapist Professional Education: Version 2004, Guide to Physical Therapist Practice, Revised 2nd ed,* and *Risk Management for Physical Therapists: A Quick Reference.* Descriptions and ordering information are available on APTA's Web site. Click on "Online Shopping," then "Order From Online Catalog."

continued on page 39 ▶▶▶

liabilityawareness

continued from page 37

Because he had not thoroughly documented all of the care he had rendered to the patient, however, he did not have the written record he needed to support his contention that the patient's account was incorrect. Good risk management requires meticulous documentation of all the physical therapy care a patient receives, from initial evaluation to discharge.

Documentation is the focus of an entire section of the Standards of Practice and the Criteria. That section spells out that the PT "communicates, coordinates, and documents all aspects of patient/client management," including interventions and response to interventions. *Risk Management for Physical Therapists: A Quick Reference* features a section titled "Documentation as a Defense" that directs PTs to "report the facts in an organized and systematic manner, with adequate detail and in chronological order." That publication also advises PTs to consult APTA's Guidelines for Physical Therapy Documentation[5] and refer to the documentation template in the *Guide to Physical Therapist Practice*.

Reimbursement. Some insurers provide coverage for alternative medicine and even some health, wellness, and fitness activities. Still, it may or may not be appropriate for a PT to bill for those services. How a PT is paid for his or her services generally is not a salient factor in professional liability claims, but there are other risks involved in submitting claims, such as the possibility of being audited, or investigated for fraud and abuse. Specific questions about appropriate reimbursement practices for interventions adopted from alternative medicine and/or the arena of health, fitness, and wellness should be directed first to the patient's insurer. APTA members also may contact the Association's Department of Reimbursement for assistance or, if the matter pertains to Medicare or Medicaid, APTA's Department of Government Affairs.

Gray Matters

It is important to note that there are not always black-and-white answers to risk management questions. In this case, it was clear that the PT had established a patient-provider relationship with the claimant and was practicing physical therapy when the incident occurred. But what if the PT also had been a certified yoga instructor, and had been conducting yoga classes at the gym apart from his practice as a PT? What if the person who claimed injury had been a gym member who had signed up for one of those yoga classes? Could the PT have been deemed to have been practicing physical therapy, making him vulnerable to a malpractice claim brought against him as a PT—as opposed to being considered a yoga instructor or an employee of the health club? Would the answer be different if the yoga class had been advertised as being led by a PT—suggesting, perhaps, that the instructor, as a health care professional, had great expertise in wellness and injury prevention?

As PTs continue to explore alternative, integrative, and holistic health in search of practice opportunities, they must consider risks such as those suggested by the questions above. This holds true, as well, for wellness and fitness activities. In the same way that PTs look to various sources to inform their clinical decisions, so, too, should they consult various sources to inform their risk management decisions. These sources include:

❖ APTA, including the resources noted in this column, for best practice standards and guidelines.

❖ State practice acts, to see if interventions

liabilityawareness

being contemplated are considered within the physical therapy scope of practice and, if so, the conditions under which such services may be provided.

❖ Professional liability insurers, to confirm what is covered by the patient's or client's professional liability policy.

❖ Payers and/or regulatory agencies, as necessary, to determine applicable guidelines or requirements.

❖ Risk management specialists who can discuss strategies related to PT practice, such as attorneys, independent insurance agents, and independent financial planners who are familiar with health care matters and state law.

Once the process of researching practice risks is complete, the PT's next step is to use the available evidence in conjunction with his or her best judgment and implement risk management practices that not only provide sensible and comfortable levels of protection but also are consistent with the profession's ethics and values. **(PT)**

Rita Arriaga, PT, MS, is an associate clinical professor in the Graduate Program in Physical Therapy and the director of rehabilitation services at the University of California, San Francisco, and is a former chair of APTA's Committee on Risk Management and Member Benefits. She can be reached at 415/476-3453 or arriaga@itsa.ucsf.edu.

Do you have risk-management questions or concerns? Insights into what PTs need or want to know will help APTA educate members about the types of incidents occurring in the workplace and about appropriate risk-management techniques. Contact Jennifer Baker, director of APTA Risk Management and Member Benefit Services, at 800/999-2782, ext 3145, or jenniferbaker@apta.org.

References

1. *Guide to Physical Therapist Practice.* Rev 2nd ed. Alexandria, Va: American Physical Therapy Association; 2003.
2. American Physical Therapy Association. Code of Ethics. [HOD 06-00-12-23] Available at www.apta.org/governance/HOD/policies/HoDPolicies/Section_I/ETHICS/HOD_06001223. Accessed April 13, 2004.
3. American Physical Therapy Association. Standards of Practice and the Criteria. [HOD 06-03-09-10] Available at www.apta.org/About/core_documents/standardsofpractice. Accessed April 13, 2004.
4. *Risk Management for Physical Therapists: A Quick Reference.* Alexandria, Va: American Physical Therapy Association; 2001.
5. American Physical Therapy Association. Guidelines for Physical Therapy Documentation. [BOD 03-00-22-54] Available at www.apta.org/guidedata/guidelines4ptpractice.cfm. Accessed April 13, 2004.

LIABILITY AWARENESS

by John J Bennett, Esq

APTA Examines Patient Abandonment

*PT presents an adapted version of
the House Report on RC 28-98.*

At the 1998 House of Delegates, the Connecticut Chapter of the American Physical Therapy Association (APTA) brought forward RC 28-98—Physical Therapists' Responsibility Regarding Abandonment—the replacement version of which would have charged the Board of Directors to "study the issue of abandonment and its ethical, legal, and other implications and ramifications as it applies to the delivery of physical therapy services."

Due to time constraints, the 1998 House was unable to consider RC 28-98. However, at its post-House meeting, the Board charged APTA staff to study the issue of abandonment and report to the November 1998 Board meeting.[1] The staff report discussed abandonment and the other concerns underlying RC 28-98, as reflected in the Support Statement submitted by the Connecticut Chapter in explanation of its motion. The staff report was the basis for the House Report on RC-28-98 that the Board of Directors submitted to the 1999 House of Delegates. This article is adapted from that House Report, which also appeared in the APTA 1999 House of Delegates Handbook.

Abandonment law is relevant in a variety of situations. Physical therapists stop treating patients without the patients' consent for various reasons, such as when a therapist decides to retire from practice or to move to a distant location, or when a PT falls in love with a patient so that continuing treatment would be unethical. In all such situations, PTs have an obligation to give the patient reasonable notice.

However, in view of the concerns expressed by the Connecticut Chapter in its Support Statement, this article focuses on the significance of abandonment law to PTs when treating patients who have exhausted the third-party coverage available to them. Because the law of abandonment provides little guidance with respect to such situations, this article also discusses a number of the Connecticut Chapter's other concerns, as reflected in its Support Statement for RC 28-98.

Patient Abandonment Law

Patient "abandonment" is a legal term developed primarily in medical malpractice litigation. According to the case of *Lee v Dewbre*,[2] abandonment is defined as "the unilateral severance of the professional relationship between [the physician] and the patient *without reasonable notice* at a time when there is still the necessity of continuing medical attention." (Emphasis added.)

Although most of the malpractice law concerning patient abandonment arises in cases involving physicians, the same legal principles undoubtedly apply to PTs.[3] Thus, it is fair to assume that the abandonment case law applicable to physicians is equally applicable to PTs.

Sufficient Notice. As indicated, the law does not obligate PTs to continue to treat a patient who needs further therapy but only to give *adequate advance notice.* As the court stated in *Sparks v Hicks*,[4] a physician is entitled to withdraw from a case at any time, but if a need for services still exists, the physician "is bound first to give

due notice to the patient and afford the latter ample opportunity to secure other medical attendance of his choice."

In general, if a patient is not in need of immediate attention (in some cases referred to as being at a "critical stage"), a physician may satisfy the notice requirement simply by giving the patient the names of other physicians. In *Miller v Greater Southeast Community Hospital*,[5] the court stated, "Where a patient is not in need of immediate medical attention, supplying the patient with a list of substitute physicians to replace the attending physician is a reasonable means of severing the professional relationship."

Relationship to Ordinary Negligence. A challenge to a physician's judgment as to the frequency of treatment is distinct from a claim of patient abandonment. Several courts have ruled that a lack of diligence in attending a patient does not constitute abandonment.[6,7,8] In one case, the court stated that malpractice, either stemming from a physician's failure to see a patient as often as necessary or from a physician's incorrect decision to discontinue treatment, is an act of negligence alone and not of patient abandonment.[9]

However, abandonment sometimes can be hard to differentiate from ordinary professional negligence. For example, in *Schliesman v Fisher*,[10] the court stated, "Whether a physician has abandoned his patient sometimes may be phrased in terms of whether he exercised ordinary skill and diligence in deciding to stop rendering service."

Proximate Cause. An essential element of an abandonment claim is "proximate cause." That is, a physician who is guilty of withdrawing without the required notice still will not be held liable unless the abandonment causes injury to the patient.[11,12]

Several courts have stated that in order for abandonment to be actionable, it must occur at a critical stage of the patient's disease.[13] In a nonemergency situation, the patient presumably has sufficient time to seek alternative care, even if the provider fails to give the requisite notice.

Since the care that PTs provide ordinarily is not of an emergency nature, their withdrawal without notice typically would not be at a critical stage and usually would not cause injury attributable to the patient's lacking the opportunity to seek care elsewhere. Such circumstances probably explain the absence of any reported cases in which a patient recovered damages attributable to abandonment by a PT.

Reason for Withdrawal. Abandonment law is typically indifferent to the physician's *reason* for terminating the physician/patient relationship, requiring only that sufficient notice be given. However, a physician's reason might prove to be relevant as a defense in a situation in which the physician withdraws without notice but argues that he or she is justified in doing so. For example, in *Allison v Patel,*[14] a town's only vascular surgeon, who was unavailable to respond to complications from an arteriogram, was permitted to show that his leaving town was justified when he went to a neighboring town to attend his gravely ill mother-in-law.

The fact that a patient may be unable to secure care from another source—for financial or any other reason—does not prevent physicians from terminating the physician/patient relationship, provided that adequate notice is given. Abandonment law, according to Hall, is thus "much more forgiving than is usually recognized."[15] This was affirmed in a California case involving a physician who refused to continue providing kidney dialysis to an indigent, extremely disruptive

patient with drug addiction but only after giving her a list of dialysis providers in the area and offering to assist her lawyers to find her alternative care.[16] The physician was found not responsible for the patient's being refused dialysis by any other provider.

One court has stated that the "patient's inability or failure to pay does not justify unilateral abandonment by the physician" (although, the issue in that case was that the defendant failed to give the requisite reasonable notice).[17]

Regulatory Law. State statutes and administrative regulations relating to patient abandonment do not differ in any significant way from the judge-made law (case law) developed in malpractice litigation. Although physical therapy practice acts identify various kinds of unprofessional conduct that may be grounds for licensing actions, only three state statutes refer explicitly to abandonment. The practice acts in Illinois[18] and New Mexico[19] simply mention abandonment without elaboration. The Colorado statute authorizes licensing action if the therapist has "abandoned a patient by any means, including, but not limited to, failure to provide a referral to another physical therapist or to other appropriate health care practitioners when the provision of such referral was necessary to meet generally accepted standards of physical therapy care."[20]

The New York Board of Regents' definition of unprofessional conduct includes "abandoning or neglecting a patient or

Liability Awareness

client under and in need of immediate professional care, without making reasonable arrangements for the continuation of such care."[21]

Ethical Principles. In addition to laws covering patient abandonment, physical therapists also are governed by an ethical system that gives directions on this issue. APTA's Code of Ethics[22] does not refer explicitly to patient abandonment, but its *Guide for Professional Conduct* (GPC) addresses the subject as follows:

> In the event of elective termination of a physical therapist/patient relationship by the physical therapist, *the therapist should take steps to transfer the care of the patient, as appropriate, to another provider.*[23] (Emphasis added.)

Other Concerns

Although the Connecticut Chapter's motion used the term "patient abandonment," the chapter actually had far broader concerns. The chapter's Support Statement raised a number of other issues, most relating to restrictions on patients' financial resources tied to limitations imposed by third-party payers. In particular, the Support Statement lamented what the chapter saw as the reality that PTs "have come to equate termination of [third-party] benefits with a reason for discharging the patient without providing the patient with options for continued care on a self-pay basis."

With respect to patients who exhaust their third-party benefits, the Support Statement emphasizes that PTs should:

❖ Exercise their clinical judgment in deciding when to discharge their patients, rather than relying on arbitrary insurance limits,

❖ Advise their patients of their clinical judgment that more therapy is needed,

❖ Assist their patients in insurance appeals processes, and

❖ Inform their patients of free or low-cost "community options" for obtaining further care.

Obligation to Exercise Clinical Judgment. PTs obviously have an ethical, if not legal, obligation to exercise their professional clinical judgment in treating patients. Under the heading "Acceptance of Responsibility," the GPC clearly outlines the obligation of PTs to exercise professional clinical judgment and not merely to defer to insurance contracts or insurance administrators.[24] PTs who simply treat up to the maximum allowed by the third-party payer (and not beyond) surely are not exercising professional clinical judgment.

Of course, the proper exercise of clinical judgment does not require PTs to disregard the cost of the therapeutic alternatives and the patient's financial resources, whether third-party or first-party. On the contrary, PTs should be mindful of the cost of therapy, since they have an ethical obligation, under the GPC, to be guided at all times by concern not only for the patient's physical well-being but also for the patient's socioeconomic welfare. Although this clause in the GPC applies more clearly to providing too much therapy than too little, proponents of RC 28-98 were correct to emphasize that insurance benefits should not be the *only* component of the decision-making process regarding frequency and duration of care.

Withholding Professional Opinion from Patients. The Support Statement implies that many PTs fail to communicate their clinical judgment that more therapy would be warranted to patients who have exhausted their third-party benefits. In general, PTs have an ethical, if not legal, obligation to communicate to the patient their judgment that the patient has a need for, or would benefit from, services beyond those covered by the patient's third-party benefits. As a practical matter,

therapists who withhold their professional opinion from a patient to protect their financial relationship with the third-party payer typically would be placing their own economic self-interest ahead of the patient's physical well-being.

A discussion of such conflict of interest is beyond the scope of RC 28-98. However, it should be noted that if a PT fails to give a patient his or her true clinical opinion, and such silence serves his or her economic self-interest, the PT would be at considerable risk of being liable for any resultant injury to the patient. Consequently, contractual provisions by which third-party payers purport to prevent health care practitioners from giving their professional opinion to patients have incurred almost universal condemnation, and a sizable number of states have enacted statutes that prohibit or render unenforceable such "gag rules."

Patient Advocacy. Quite apart from abandonment, the Support Statement states that PTs have a duty to "inform the patient of the insurance appeals processes and provide assistance as necessary." The Support Statement is correct in suggesting that PTs may have a legal obligation to testify on a patient's behalf in litigation. In *Spaulding v Hussain,*[25] a physician reneged on a commitment to testify in a patient's lawsuit against a third party, and the court upheld a verdict against the physician. However, although PTs may be obliged to testify for a patient[26,27,28] (but compare *Knight v Johnson*[29]) and not provide assistance to a patient's adversaries,[30,31] no authority holds that PTs have an obligation to counsel their patients about the appeals process of an insurer or otherwise to function as their patients' attorney in an insurance appeal.

The Support Statement's reference to PTs "provid[ing] assistance as necessary" perhaps was aimed less at testimony in formal proceedings, such as litigation, than at the more commonplace function of attempting to persuade insurance administrators and case managers to authorize additional treatment. In situations in which third-party payment for future physical therapy is dependent on the payer's deeming the treatment to be medically necessary, a patient often will need a PT's input to obtain any required advance authorization.

PTs' communications with the third-party payer, whether written or oral, on behalf of the patient are a kind of informal advocacy that can be crucial to the patient's receiving care—especially if the patient is unwilling or unable to proceed with therapy on a self-pay basis. The decision by a third-party payer to authorize further physical therapy may depend to some extent on the therapists' skill and persistence in arguing on the patient's behalf.

Can PTs be held legally liable to the patient for failing to provide such informal advocacy or for lack of skill or persistence in doing so? To date, no PTs have been held legally liable for failing to communicate to a third-party payer their clinical judgment that further treatment was medically necessary or for being culpably unpersuasive in communicating such judgment.

In *Wickline v California*,[32] a lawsuit against California's Medicaid program, the defendant sought to avoid liability by pointing to the role of the attending surgeon who failed to press for reconsideration of a denial of a requested extension of hospital stay, and the court's opinion contained "dicta"—language not necessary to the court's determination—suggesting that a practitioner could be held liable for being silent or unpersuasive. The opinion stated, "The physician who complies without protest with the limitations imposed by a third-party payer, when his medical judgment dictates otherwise, cannot avoid

his ultimate responsibility for his patient's care. He cannot point to the health care payer as the liability scapegoat when the consequences of his own determinative medical decisions go sour."

Since *Wickline* was not a claim against a practitioner, it is not an authority for the view that PTs can be liable to a patient for failing to use sufficient skill or diligence to persuade a payer to authorize additional treatment. Furthermore, in the subsequent case of *Wilson v Blue Cross of Southern California*,[33] the court emphasized that the *Wickline* language was merely dicta and rejected the argument of a utilization review organization that a treating physician has *sole* responsibility for the consequences when he or she decides to discharge a patient upon an insurer's refusal to pay benefits.

The evidentiary burdens of a patient seeking to hold a therapist liable for inadequate advocacy would be high, and the risk of liability correspondingly low. Nevertheless, the *Wickline* and *Wilson* opinions hold open the possibility—however remote—that a practitioner could incur liability to a patient for inadequate advocacy with a third-party payer, and, therefore, the dicta in *Wickline* should give pause to PTs.

Regardless of the risk of legal liability, PTs have an ethical obligation to make reasonable efforts to communicate with third-party payers in support of a request to authorize additional treatment—provided, of course, that they believe additional treatment is warranted. The GPC makes no explicit mention of such an obligation, but a duty to make reasonable efforts to communicate with payers on behalf of the patient seems clearly implicit in its principles.

First-Party Payment. The Support Statement for RC 28-98 states that PTs have a duty to inform a patient of the possibility of continuing treatment after

LIABILITY AWARENESS

exhaustion of third-party benefits on a self-pay basis. Research has not revealed any case law concerning a practitioner's duty to impart such self-evident advice. PTs who believe that a patient has a need for further treatment, despite the exhaustion of third-party benefits, obviously would do well to point out the possibility of continuing therapy on a self-pay basis.

Disclosure of Free/Low-Cost Alternatives. The Support Statement also states that PTs have a duty to inform a patient of "community options for continuation of services outside the resources of the patient." The passage evidently refers to options by which the patient might obtain physical therapy for free or at a lower cost.

Although the Support Statement focuses on patients who have exhausted their third-party benefits, its reference to community options raises the intriguing question: Do PTs have a legal or ethical obligation, from the outset of treatment, to tell a patient about alternative sources of therapy that would be cheaper than their own—a duty, in effect, to steer business to a competitor? That particular question was presented and discussed in a Judgment Call column in the July 1994 issue of *PT* Magazine.[34] The article was later reprinted in APTA's *Ethics in Physical Therapy, Part 2: Patient and Society.*[35]

Research has not revealed any case law concerning whether a practitioner has a legal duty to inform a patient of the availability of lower-cost treatment. Whether a PT has an *ethical* duty to inform a patient of the existence of lower-cost treatment is beyond the scope of this article. Of course, APTA's ethical principles would not prevent PTs from alerting a patient to the availability of lower-cost treatment, and doing so would be compliant with the basic principles of the GPC.

What Next?

As previously noted, the APTA Board of Directors has submitted a report on RC 28-98 to the members of the 1999 House of Delegates. Prior to the distribution of that House Report in the 1999 House of Delegates Handbook, the Connecticut and Missouri chapters sponsored RC 51-99, which would charge the Board to develop a position statement regarding PTs' responsibility for patient care when patients' financial resources from insurance are limited or depleted. The motion calls for the position statement to address the issue of abandonment and how third-party limitations may affect visit frequency, visit duration, plan of care, desired outcomes, and termination of care. The motion would charge the Board to report to the 2000 House of Delegates. The 1999 House of Delegates, which met in early June as this article went to press, had RC 51-99 on its agenda. *PT*

John J Bennett, Esq, is General Counsel for APTA. He can be reached via e-mail at jackbennett@apta.org.

References

1. B of D 6/98, V-18.
2. *Lee v Dewbre*, 362 SW 2d 900, 902, 1962 Tex App LEXIS 2004 (Tex Civ App 1962). See Annotation, "Liability of physician who abandons case," 57 ALR 2d 432 (1958).
3. *Crider v Bayard City Schools*, 250 Neb 775, 553 NW 2d 147, 1996 Neb LEXIS 173 (Neb 1996).
4. *Sparks v Hicks*, 912 P.2d 331, 333, 1996 Okla LEXIS 21 (Okla 1996).
5. *Miller v Greater Southeast Community Hospital*, 508 A2d 927,929, 1986 DC App LEXIS 352 (DC Ct App 1986).
6. *Glenn v Carlstrom*, 556 NW 2d 800, 803, 1996 Iowa Sup LEXIS 472 (Iowa 1996).
7. *Roberts v Wood*, 206 F Supp 579, 585, 1962 US Dist LEXIS 3774 (SD Ala 1962).
8. *Manno v McIntosh*, 519 NW 2d 815, 820 1994 Iowa App LEXIS 44 (Iowa App 1994).
9. *Smith v Lerner*, 387 NW 2d 576, 579, 1986 Iowa Sup LEXIS 1173 (Iowa 1986).
10. *Schliesman v Fisher*, 158 Cal Rptr 527, 532, 97 Cal App 3d 83, 1979 Cal App LEXIS 2152 (Cal App 1979).
11. *Skodje v Hardy*, 47 Wash 2d 557, 288 P.2d 471 (Wash 1942).
12. *Tompkins v Kusama*, 822 SW 2d 463 (Mo App ED 1991).
13. *Cox v Jones*, 470 NW 2d 23, 26, 1991 Iowa Sup LEXIS 175 (Iowa 1991).
14. *Allison v Patel*, 211 Ga App 376, 438 SE 2d 920, 1993 Ga App LEXIS 1521 (Ga App 1993) Cert denied 1994 Ga LEXIS 559 (Ga 1994).
15. Hall MA. A theory of economic informed consent. 31*Ga L Rev* 511 (1997).
16. *Payton v Weaver*, 182 Cal Rptr 225, 228, 131 Cal App 3d 38,43, 1982 Cal App LEXIS 1535 (Cal App 1982).
17. *Woodfolk v Group Health Association Inc*, 644 A2d 1367, 1368, 1994 DC App LEXIS 106 (DC App 1994).
18. 225 ILCS 90/17 (1)(N).
19. New Mex Stat Ann 61-12D-13(V).
20. Colo Rev Stat 12-41-115(1)(d).
21. 8 New York Code of Rules and Regs 29.2(a)(1).
22. HOD 06-91-05-05.
23. *Guide for Professional Conduct*, Section 3.3 (D).
24. GPC Section 3.1(A) (as amended January 1999). See also Section 7.1 (c).
25. *Spaulding v Hussain*, 299 NJ Super 430, 440, 551 A2d 1022, 1028, 1988 NJ Super LEXIS 464 (NJ Super 1988).
26. *Hammonds v Aetna Casualty & Surety Company*, 243 F Supp 793, 799 (ND Ohio 1965).
27. *Aufrichtig v Lowell*, 85 NY 2d 540, 546, 650 NE 2d 401, 404, 1995 NY LEXIS 1036 (NY 1995).
28. *Dickinson v Magaral*, 1993 US Dist LEXIS 13789 (DNJ 1993).
29. *Knight v Johnson*, 237 Mont 230, 233, 773, P 2d 293, 295 (Mont 1989).
30. *Alexander v Knight*, 177 A 2d 142, 146 (Pa Super 1962).
31. *Samms v District Court*, 408 P 2d 520, 1995 Colo LEXIS 768 (Colo 1995).
32. *Wickline v California*, 192 Cal App 3d 1630, 1645-1646, 239 Cal Rptr 810, 819 (Cal App. 1986).
33. *Wilson v Blue Cross of Southern California*, 222 Cal App 3d 660, 671, 271 Cal Rptr 876, 883 (Cal App 1990).
34. Judgment Call. *PT—Magazine of Physical Therapy*, 1994; 4(7):66-68, 70-71.
35. *Ethics in Physical Therapy, Part 2: Patient and Society.* Alexandria, Va: APTA; 1998. 26-30.

Sexual Misconduct

Sexual Harassment
HOD P06-99-17-06 (Initial HOD 06-94-33-04)

Environments in which physical therapy services are provided, or in which the work of the American Physical Therapy Association and its components is carried out, should be completely free of sexual harassment. Members of the Association have an obligation to comply with the applicable legal prohibitions against sexual harassment.

HABITS OF THOUGHT

By Ron Scott, JD, LLM, PT

Sexual Misconduct

One of the physical therapist's highest duties is to ensure that the professional-patient relationship does not become a sexual relationship.

Physical therapy often is referred to as a "hands-on profession." The adage goes, "If it's physical, it's therapy." The physical therapist-patient relationship may be one of the most intense among all the health care disciplines—in large part because of the length of time spent in close physical contact with patients during the rehabilitation process.

Physical therapists elicit and assess a large amount of personal information about the patient during the evaluation process, assimilating this information into the care plan. In what is an evolving relationship, physical therapists become privy to intimate details of their patients' lives. And—as in psychotherapy, other primary health care disciplines, and professions such as law and religion—patients who have shared their intimate thoughts may experience "transference" with their physical therapists within the therapeutic relationship.

A patient may be vulnerable to abuse because of the trust that he or she may place in the physical therapist. The patient may develop intense affection for the treating clinician and may feel an urgent need for approval, creating a kind of parent-child relationship or developing "romantic" feelings. These transference emotions are normal in a patient and should not be exploited by a physical therapist responsible for the patient's care.

The physical therapy clinician is a "fiduciary"—that is, *a professional having the legal and ethical duty to act primarily in the patient's best interests*. It therefore is one of the physical therapist's highest duties to ensure that the professional-patient relationship does not become an intimate, personal, sexual relationship. Any natural reciprocal or "countertransference" feelings that arise in the clin-

ician must be sublimated to prevent sexual abuse of a patient. Even when not *legally* proscribed, sexual relations with patients during the term of the therapist-patient relationship always are ethically wrong.

Legal Issues

From the legal perspective, there are two potential types of sexual abuse involving health professionals and patients. The first is *sexual assault or battery*, which involves any nonconsensual touching of a patient's or clinician's sexual or other body parts by the other party for the purpose of arousing or gratifying the sexual desire of either party or for the purpose of sexual abuse of the patient.[1] This intentional misconduct may give rise to civil liability for assault or battery, intentional infliction of emotional distress, or malpractice (substandard, negligent delivery of care).

A finding of civil liability against a physical therapist (or any health professional) for sexual assault or battery may result in a court award of punitive damages against the wrongdoer—in addition to the normal compensatory damages for pain and suffering, lost wages, and medical expenses incurred by the victim. This finding also may mean that the therapist's insurer is relieved from indemnifying the therapist against the loss, making the therapist personally liable for any money judgment rendered against him or her.

In addition to civil liability for sexual assault or battery, the therapist may face *criminal and adverse administrative actions* for misconduct, which can result in incarceration and suspension or loss of professional licensure. (Patients who have been sexually abused by a health professional may be reluctant to pursue criminal actions

in part because a finding of guilt for *criminal* activity arising out of the professional-patient relationship means that an insurer is less likely to indemnify the perpetrator—and therefore the patient will have more difficulty in collecting money damages awarded in the *civil* case.) Health professionals accused of sexual assault or battery also typically face adverse action regarding membership in professional associations.

The second type of sexual misconduct concerns relationships that could be construed as "consensual": The patient falls "in love" with his or her physical therapist, and the therapist reciprocates. Because of transference and the inherent vulnerability of patients dependent on therapists for care and support—and because of the fiduciary duty of trust and good faith imposed on health professionals—"consent" to sexual intimacy has no real meaning in a therapist-patient relationship. The therapist *always* is accountable for the creation of the relationship. Patients, however, are *not* bound by ethical codes or legal standards for behavior in the therapist-patient relationship.

The legal bar in California has attempted to fashion a regulation that expressly sanctions attorney-client sexual relations as long as the attorney does not "employ coercion, intimidation, or undue influence in entering into sexual relations with a client."[2] In the view of many legal commentators, this position fails to recognize that any sexual relationship between a professional and a client is inherently exploitive and therefore always to be avoided.

The more reasoned approach to both nonconsensual and putative "consensual" sexual relationships between professionals and patients may be the one recently adopted by the American Physical Therapy Association's (APTA) Judicial Committee. APTA's *Guide for Professional Conduct* was amended to include a new section under Principle 1 ("Physical therapists respect the rights and dignity of all individuals"). Section 1.3 (Patient Relations) reads:

> Physical therapists shall not engage in any sexual relationship or activity, whether consensual or nonconsensual, with any patient while a physical therapist-patient relationship exists.

Recognizing that a romantic attraction between therapist and patient occasionally may occur, Section 1.3 B. provides a means for preventing unethical conduct:

> In the event that a physical therapist and patient are about to begin a sexually intimate relationship, the therapist shall expeditiously disengage from care of the patient and coordinate the transfer of care of the patient, as appropriate, to another provider.

To help prevent allegations of patient abandonment in these circumstances, the new ethical standards address the legal and ethical duty to transfer care of a patient with whom the therapist is about to become sexually active. Several other key issues, however, are not addressed, including situations in which a patient is the spouse or fiancé (or fiancée) of the physical therapist. Also not addressed: Any suggested waiting period after severance of the therapist-patient relationship before commencing a sexual relationship with the former patient. (Some authorities suggest a waiting period of 6 months.[3])

Administrators and individual clinicians have an administrative, ethical, and legal duty to take appropriate steps to prevent both allegations of sexual abuse and actual sexual abuse of patients in the clinical setting. Some excellent guidelines for quality improvement and preventive risk management (eg, follow your instincts when you sense that a patient may present problems) have appeared in the physical therapy literature.[4] Other simple measures include: 1) a same-sex chaperone for observation of evaluation and treatment, available either on patient request or whenever a clinician believes the chaperone's presence is necessary; 2) a "knock-and-enter" policy under which any staff member who needs to open the closed door of a room in which patient evaluation or treatment is taking place may do so after giving due warning to the patient; 3) a policy ensuring that patients understand all therapeutic procedures and interventions—especially those that are intensively "hands-on"—and give informed consent to treatment; and 4) ongoing continuing education for professional and support staff on the appropriate handling of patients and prevention of sexual abuse and harassment.

Prevention of sexual abuse or of the allegation of sexual abuse serves the best interests of patient, provider, and profession. Sexual relations between physical therapists (or physical therapist assistants, physical therapy aides, or other support personnel) and patients is unethical. Its avoidance is the direct ethical and legal challenge to every person in the profession. *PT*

Ron Scott, JD, LLM, PT, is a Major in the Army Medical Specialist Corps, Brooke Army Medical Center, Fort Sam Houston, Tex. He is a member of APTA's Judicial Committee. The opinions expressed in this article are those of the author and should not be attributed to the US Army or APTA's Judicial Committee.

This column is coordinated by Ruth Purtilo, PhD, PT, FAPTA.

References

1 Adapted from Model Penal Code. Section 213.4, ALI (Proposed Official Draft 1962) and Colorado Rev Statutes, Section 18-3-401(4).
2 Defined, barred: sex with clients. Rule 3-120, State Bar of California. *National Law Journal*. May 6, 1991:6.
3 Stromberg CD, Haggarty DJ, Leibenluft RF, et al. Physical contact and sexual relations with patients. *The Psychologist's Legal Handbook*. Washington, DC: The Council for the National Register of Health Service Providers in Psychology; 1988:463.
4 Schunk C, Parver CP. Avoiding allegations of sexual misconduct. *Clinical Management*. 1989;9(5):22.

Suggested Readings

Campbell ML. The oath: an investigation of the injunction prohibiting physician-patient sexual relations. *Perspect Biol Med*. 1989;32(2):300-308.
Council on Ethical and Judicial Affairs, American Medical Association. Sexual misconduct in the practice of medicine. *JAMA*. 1991;266:2741-2745.
Gabbard GO. *Sexual Exploitation in Professional Relationships*. Washington, DC: American Psychiatric Press Inc; 1989.
Pitulla J. Unfair advantage. *Journal of the American Bar Association*. November 1992:78-80.
Samuelson RJ. Sex and psychotherapy. *Newsweek*. April 13, 1992:52-57.

This column is not intended as legal advice, which can be given only by your personal legal counsel, based on the law of your state or on federal law, as applicable.

Reported Incidents

The incidence of sexual abuse of patients is well-documented and publicized in many professions. Sexual abuse is estimated to occur in 7% to 12% of encounters between patients and psychotherapists, family practice physicians, gynecologists, internists, and surgeons. A similar prevalence is estimated for clergy, attorneys, social workers, and educators. Sexual abuse of these patients ranges from verbal abuse to sexual intimacies (such as kissing and fondling) to intercourse. Of the reported cases of sexual abuse among psychiatrists and their patients, 80% are estimated to involve male psychiatrists and female patients; 13%, female psychiatrists and female patients; 5%, male psychiatrists and male patients; and 2%, female psychiatrists and male patients.[1]

Although studies have not yet been conducted to provide detailed statistics on sexual relationships between physical therapists and patients, the number of reported incidents of sexual misconduct clearly is on the rise, as evidenced by cases brought before state licensure boards and the Judicial Committee of the American Physical Therapy Association (APTA). Many of the allegations have arisen because of intensive hands-on treatment in therapeutic procedures, especially those involving myofascial release or mobilization techniques performed near the patient's breast, genitals, or anus.

References

1 Sherman C. Behind closed doors: therapist-client sex. *Psychology Today*. 1993;26(3):67.

IN PRACTICE

by Claudette Finley, MS, PT

What is Sexual Harassment?

*Increasing awareness of sexual harassment
has caused changes in the law and in professional codes of conduct.*

In 1972, an amendment to the Civil Rights Act of 1964[1] formally added gender to the list of bases for illegal discrimination in the workplace. This law applies to all private and public employers whose businesses affect interstate commerce and who employ 15 or more persons. The Sex Discrimination Guidelines[2] published by the Equal Employment Opportunity Commission (EEOC), which are based on this Act, define sexual harassment as a form of sex discrimination and prohibit it in the workplace.

Sexual harassment is defined in the Guidelines as follows:

Unwelcome sexual advances, requests for sexual favors, and other verbal or physical conduct of a sexual nature constitute sexual harassment when (1) submission to such conduct is made either explicitly or implicitly a term or condition of an individual's employment, (2) submission to or rejection of such conduct by an individual is used as the basis for employment decisions affecting such individual, or (3) such conduct has the purpose or effect of unreasonably interfering with an individual's work performance or creating an intimidating, hostile or offensive working environment.

Following are the statements of several professional associations that have directly addressed this issue in their codes of ethics or their guidelines. Key words and phrases in these statements include *exploit, personal advantage, condone or engage in, deliberate or repeated,* and *demean the dignity.*

- "Clinical social workers do not exploit their professional relationships sexually, financially, or for any other personal advantage. They maintain this standard of conduct toward all who may be professionally associated with them, such as clients, colleagues, supervisees, employees, students, and research participants."—The National Federation of Societies for Clinical Social Work, *Code of Ethics,* Section 1.e.[3]

- "Members do not condone or engage in sexual harassment which is defined as deliberate or repeated comments, gestures, or physical contacts of a sexual nature."—The American Association for Counseling and Development, *Ethical Standards,* Section A, Number 9.[3]

- "A psychiatrist should not be a party to any type of policy that excludes, segregates, or demeans the dignity of any patient because of ethnic origin, race, sex, creed, age, socioeconomic status, or sexual orientation."—The American Psychiatric Association, *Principles of Medical Ethics with Annotations Especially Applicable to Psychiatry,* Section 1, Number 2.[3]

- "Psychologists do not exploit their professional relationships with clients, supervisees, students, employees, or research participants sexually or otherwise. Psychologists do not condone or engage in sexual harassment."—The American Psychological Association, *Ethical Principles of Psychologists,* Principle 7.d.[3]

- "Any kind of sexual, racial, or religious harassment should not be allowed. Appropriate channels should be provided for harassed persons to state their problems to objective officials..."—The American Society for Public Administration, *Code of Ethics and Implementation Guidelines.*[3]

In the above codes and guidelines, emphasis is placed on the problem of exploitation that is deliberate and repeated and demeaning and that is a purposeful act designed to elicit a reaction. Other professional associations address sexual harassment in the work environment in statements that are more general:

- "Members shall not discriminate in their professional activities on the basis of race, religion, gender, national origin, age or nondisqualifying handicap. Commentary: This rule applies to all professional activities of the member, including but not limited to dealings with clients, colleagues and employees."—The American Institute of Architects, *Code of Ethics and Professional Conduct,* R 2.501.[3]

- "[Conditions of employment must] enable the nurse to practice in accordance with the standards of nursing practice... Professional autonomy and self-regulation in the control of conditions of practice are necessary for implementing nursing standards."—The American Nurses Association, *Interpretive Statements,* 9.1.[3]

The *Code of Ethics*[4] of the American Physical Therapy Association (APTA) states in Principle 1 that "Physical therapists respect the rights and dignity of all individuals." Principle 1.1C of APTA's *Guide for Professional Conduct*[4] states, "Physical therapists shall not engage in conduct that constitutes harassment or abuse of colleagues or associates."

A booklet entitled *About Sexual Harassment in the Workplace*[5] describes a number of specific examples of sexual harassment. These examples include making offensive or suggestive comments, jokes, or gestures; teasing, staring or leering; leaving messages with sexual content; displaying posters, photographs or drawings of a sexual nature; pinching, grabbing or patting; touching in a manner that makes another feel threatened or uncomfortable; propositioning; and cornering or trapping a person. The *degree* and *frequency* of the behavior is the key factor. Activities that 1) occur accidentally, such as unintentionally brushing against someone, 2) are considered to be "normal" responses, such as looking up when someone walks by the desk, or 3) are terminated when a firm "no" response is given, do not constitute sexual harassment.

The trend for the legal standard for measuring whether sexual harassment actually has occurred in the work environment no longer is just whether a "reasonable person" would consider certain behavior to constitute harassment; it now is whether a reasonable person of the same gender as the person who allegedly has been harassed would perceive that sexual harassment had occurred. In one 1991 case, for example, the objective standard for determining whether harassment had occurred was whether a reasonable person of the plaintiff's gender (in that case, a woman) would have perceived that an abusive work environment had been created.[6] In a 1987 case involving a male supervisor's alleged harassment of a female subordinate, the court held that a "reasonable woman" standard should be applied because the plaintiff in the case was by definition female, whereas in a sexual harassment case involving a male subordinate, a "reasonable man" standard would be applied.[7]

Physical therapists and physical therapist assistants are not immune to sexual harassment. Situations both of *unequal* power, such as supervisor-employee or therapist-patient relationships, and of *equal* power, such as relationships between co-workers, hold the potential for sexual harassment. Women are not always the victims, and harassment by persons of the opposite gender is not always the pattern. Professional relationships between employers and employees, coworkers, faculty and students, and clinical supervisors and students may hold the potential for sexual harassment.

If your employment, raises, or promotions depend on a "yes" response to sexual advances, or if your work performance is affected by unwelcome sexual conduct, consider taking the following steps[5]:

- First, do not ignore the situation. If you experience sexual harassment in the workplace, give a firm "no," and communicate that the behavior makes you uncomfortable.

- Second, report the incident to someone in a supervisory position. Supervisors and administrators have a responsibility to know and understand the policies and procedures for dealing with sexual harassment in the workplace and to communicate them to employees. Any individual who has knowledge of sexual harassment taking place is obligated to report the incident. The responsibility to keep the workplace free from sexual harassment rests not only with the employer, but also with each employee.

- Third, it is essential that those parties involved in the investigation and disciplinary process protect the confidentiality both of the incident and of the names of the complainant and the accused until the complaint has been resolved. Protection of the rights of individuals involved is essential.

With the publication of the EEOC's *Sex Discrimination Guidelines*, physical therapy professionals' commitment to providing a workplace free of sexual harassment is no longer just a nice idea—it's the law. *PT*

Claudette Finley, MS, PT, is Associate Professor, Department of Physical Therapy, University of Florida, Health Science Center, Gainesville, Fla, and is a former member of the APTA Judicial Committee.

References

1 The Civil Rights Act of 1964, 42 USC §2000e, as amended 1972.

2 Sex Discrimination Guidelines, Equal Employment Opportunity Commission. (29 CFR 1604.11). *Federal Register.* November 10, 1980;45:74677.

3 Gorlin R. *Codes of Professional Responsibility*, ed 2. Washington, DC: Bureau of National Affairs Inc; 1990.

4 *Code of Ethics and Guide for Professional Conduct.* Alexandria, Va: American Physical Therapy Association; 1994.

5 *About Sexual Harassment in the Workplace: A Scriptographic Booklet.* South Deerfield, Mass: Channing L Bete Co, Inc; 1992:4-7.

6 *Robinson v. Jacksonville Shipping Yards, Inc,* 760 F Supp 1524 (MD Fla 1991).

7 *Yates v. AVCO Corp,* 819 F2d 630-631 (6th Cir 1987).

The information in this article should not be interpreted as specific advice for any particular practitioner. Personal advice can only be given by personal legal counsel, based on applicable state and federal law.

The views expressed in this article are those of the author and do not reflect official opinions of the APTA Judicial Committee.

by Ronald W Scott, JD, PT, OCS

Sexual Harassment: A Reminder for Managers

In the workplace, the primary responsibility for stopping sexual harassment rests with management.

*a*lthough sexual harassment has long been a widespread problem affecting productivity, morale, and every aspect of interpersonal relations in the workplace, only recently have allegations of sexual harassment against prominent public officials brought open discussion of this problem "out of the closet" and into every boardroom, work setting, and living room in America.

Sexual harassment and sexual misconduct issues have received increased attention from the American Physical Therapy Association (APTA). Articles on the subject have been published in the physical therapy literature,[1-3] and APTA's Judicial Committee recently amended its *Guide for Professional Conduct*[4] and *Guide for the Conduct of the Affiliate Member*[6] to reflect the wider spectrum of persons in the workplace who may be affected by harassment. The document now states that "Physical therapists [or physical therapist assistants] shall not engage in conduct that constitutes harassment or abuse of, or discrimination against, colleagues, associates, *or others* [emphasis added]."

APTA also recently produced an information paper, *Gender Issues in Employment Under Federal Law* ,[6] which addresses sexual harassment in the workplace in addition to other employment issues in which gender may be a factor.

Sexual Harassment Defined

The Equal Opportunity Commission (EEOC), the federal administrative agency responsible for promulgating and enforcing compliance with sexual harassment regulations, defines *sexual harassment* as:

> Unwelcome sexual advances, requests for sexual favors, and other verbal or physical conduct of a sexual nature... when (1) submission to such conduct is made either explicitly or implicitly a term or condition of an individual's employment, (2) submission to or rejection of such conduct by an individual is used as the basis for employment decisions affecting such individual, or (3) such conduct has the purpose or effect of unreasonably interfering with an individual's work performance or creating an intimidating, hostile, or offensive work environment.[7]

The EEOC definition of sexual harassment thus has a dual focus on 1) the types of inappropriate conduct that constitute sexual harassment and 2) the possible adverse employment consequences for victims of sexual harassment or others.

Conduct that constitutes sexual harassment in the work place could include:

- Unwelcome comments of a sexual nature about a victim's person or body parts.

- Solicitation of others for sexual relations.

- Inappropriate touching of another person on a private area of his or her body with intent to arouse or gratify sexual desires (ie, sexual battery[1,8]).

For more on specific conduct that may constitute sexual harassment, see Finley.[3]

Employment consequences fall into two categories: adverse employment decisions resulting from *quid pro quo* situations, and hostile work environments.

- *Quid pro quo* describes a situation in which a victim's response to sexual harassment is the basis for employment-related decisions involving the victim or other workers. A *quid pro quo* complaint typically is lodged either by an employee who has been denied opportunities because he or she refused a perpetrator's sexual advances or by an employee who has been denied opportunities because another employee obtained those opportunities by submitting to a perpetrator's sexual advances. Example: An employer's funding of a staff physical therapist's attendance at a professional conference depends on whether the physical therapist submits to the employer's sexual advances.

- In a hostile work environment, sexual harassment unreasonably interferes with either the "target" victim's or another person's work performance. Complaints related to hostile work environments can be lodged by any person in the workplace who is reasonably offended by a perpetrator's sexual harassment (of the complainant or of another person in the work setting) and whose work is impeded by that harassment. Example: A physical therapy aide is unable to concentrate on patient care activities because of the misconduct of a physical therapist who is making sexual advances toward a patient.

Assessing Whether Conduct Constitutes Sexual Harassment

Administrative agencies and the courts adjudicating sexual harassment cases traditionally have employed the "ordinary reasonable person" standard to evaluate whether an individual's conduct constitutes sexual harassment. This standard also is commonly used to determine whether a defendant in a tort case (eg, a malpractice suit) violated a duty owed to a plaintiff. Under this standard as applied in a sexual harassment case heard by a court or administrative official, a trier of fact (eg, a judge, jury member, or administrative official) puts himself or herself into the shoes of a "person of ordinary care and diligence,"[9] determines how such a person would be likely to perceive the conduct at issue, and decides the case accordingly.

The problem with the traditional "ordinary reasonable person" standard is that it frequently is translated into an "ordinary reasonable *man*" standard, with the result that the trier of fact assesses interpersonal conduct exclusively from the male point of view. To ensure that a gender-neutral standard is employed in administrative and legal sexual harassment cases, some federal courts have established a modified standard that eventually may supplant the traditional standard. Under this standard, the trier of fact still puts himself or herself into the shoes of an "ordinary reasonable person" when determining whether specific conduct constitutes sexual harassment, but that ordinary reasonable person must be of the same sex as the alleged victim of sexual harassment or misconduct.

Expert testimony has been presented in sexual harassment cases to support the opinion that men and women view sexually oriented conduct—in the workplace and elsewhere—very differently. In testifying in *Robinson v Jacksonville Shipyards* [760 F Supp 1486 (MD Fla 1991)], Alison Wetherfield of the National Organization for Women's Legal Defense and Education Fund cited a study in which 75% of men polled said they were flattered by sexual advances from women in the workplace; only 15% claimed they would be offended. Of women surveyed, however, 75% stated that they would be offended by such conduct.[10] In that case, a federal district court used the "ordinary reasonable woman" standard to hold an employer responsible for the sexually harassing conduct of male employees toward a female coworker.

In *Ellison v Brady* [924 F2d 871 (9th Cir 1991)], a federal appeals court evaluated what were labeled as "bizarre," repetitive, unwelcome love letters written by a male coworker to a woman in a federal government office. The lower court had found that the man's conduct did not constitute sexual harassment; in reversing that decision, the appellate court adopted the "ordinary reasonable woman" standard to assess whether the letters constituted sexual harassment. (Of course, this should not be interpreted to mean that such letters sent by a female coworker to a man would necessarily *not* constitute sexual harassment; in such a case, the "ordinary reasonable man" standard would have been applied by this court, and the case would have been assessed accordingly.)

Green Light, Yellow Light, Red Light

Another model for assessing interpersonal conduct was developed by the US Navy[11] after the Tailhook convention at which a number of male officers were accused of sexually harassing female officers. This model categorizes conduct as either "green light" (ie, conduct that is clearly acceptable behavior in the eyes of a reasonable person); "yellow light," (ie, conduct that may be unacceptable in the eyes of some reasonable persons); or "red light"(ie, conduct that is always unacceptable in the eyes of a reasonable person). Green light conduct might include such things as complimenting a colleague about his or her dress in an inoffensive and nondiscriminatory manner. Yellow light behavior might include soliciting a date from a coworker for the first time. And red light behavior might include such conduct as repeated solicitation of dates, indecent exposure, or sexual assault and battery.

Where the Buck Stops

In the workplace, facility managers and corporate managers bear the formidable responsibility of ferreting out, eliminating, and preventing sexual harassment. The buck *does* stop there. Managers may even be held liable for sexual harassment of which they were unaware, especially if their organization or work unit has no informal reporting or grievance mechanism in place to receive and investigate complaints of sexual harassment, or if management fails to take appropriate action after investigating such allegations.[12] Managers cannot assume an "ostrich defense"; they will be held responsible for what they should have observed and corrected.

The specific responsibilities of managers regarding sexual harassment include:

- *Sensitizing and educating employees about what constitutes sexual harassment, how men and women may differ in their attitudes toward sexual conduct, and the type of conduct that reasonable persons might find offensive.* This process not only should be part of new employee orientations, but also should be reinforced regularly as continuing education for all employees. Managers might choose to consult human resources management specialists to lead sessions at which employees are given information about current administrative and legal sexual harassment cases and asked to participate in group cooperative learning processes, such as brainstorming about what interpersonal activities constitute permissible and impermissible behavior in the workplace.

- *Expressing strong disapproval of sexual harassment and developing and enforcing appropriate sanctions to stop sexual harassment whenever it is found to exist.* Managers are responsible for taking immediate action to stop sexual harassment, regardless of who the perpetrator or the victim might be. Reporting, investigation, and grievance procedures for internal resolution of sexual harassment complaints should be in place. Managers must be fair and impartial in investigating such complaints, respecting the rights of all parties involved to the extent possible.[13] If employees and others view management's commitment as strong, the investigatory process as equitable, and the awarding of sanctions as appropriate, minor complaints stand a better chance of

What if it's the *patient* who is sexually harassing the PT?

Ronald W Scott, JD, PT, OCS, is Associate Professor and Interim Chair, Department of Physical Therapy, School of Allied Health Sciences, The University of Texas Health Science Center, San Antonio, Tex.

In a profession that involves a considerable amount of hands-on contact with patients, it is not surprising that the issue of sexual harassment of physical therapists by patients must be addressed. McComas et al[1] surveyed 118 physical therapists and 87 students, asking whether they had ever experienced inappropriate patient sexual behaviors (IPSB) ranging from telling suggestive stories or offensive jokes to rape. The results:

> Although 80.5% of all respondents indicated that they had encountered at least one of these behaviors, only 24.2% of those who reported experiencing any level of IPSB responded positively to the question, "Have you ever been sexually harassed by a patient?"

The researchers hypothesized that unwillingness to identify IPSB as sexual harassment is due to several factors, including a perception that inappropriate sexual behavior perpetrated by a person who is not in a position of authority over the target does not constitute sexual harassment.

Nevertheless, IPSB can create a hostile work environment for employees, and a manager's failure to stop sexual harassment of staff by a patient can lead to an actionable sexual harassment complaint. Although the EEOC has no authority to remedy inappropriate conduct of a patient toward a health care provider, it *does* have authority to remedy inadequate managerial response to that conduct.

Consider a case in which a patient makes inappropriate comments or gestures of a sexual nature to a staff member or touches or attempts to touch a staff member in an inappropriate way. What should the manager do? Some responsible actions include:

- Investigating the victim's complaint.
- Counseling the offender to cease and desist from further sexual harassment of the victim.
- Transferring the patient to another therapist's care.
- Consulting with other health professionals, the referring physician, human resources management, or an EEOC official, as appropriate, for advice.
- Removing the patient who continues to sexually harass staff from the clinic.

In any case, it is important for both managers and physical therapists to appropriately document any occurrence of IPSB in order to minimize the risk of liability if it becomes necessary to terminate a patient's care.

1 McComas J, Hébert C, Giacmin C, et al. Experiences of student and practicing physical therapists with inappropriate patient sexual behavior. *Phys Ther.* 1993;73:762-770.

References

1 Scott R. Sexual Misconduct. *PT—Magazine of Physical Therapy.* 1993;1(10):78-79.
2 Schunk C, Parver CP. Avoiding allegations of sexual misconduct. *Clinical Management.* 1989;9(5):19-22.
3 Finley C. What is sexual harassment? *PT—Magazine of Physical Therapy.* 1994;2(12):17-18.
4 *Guide for Professional Conduct.* Alexandria, Va: American Physical Therapy Association; 1995: Section 1-1.C.
5 *Guide for Conduct of the Affiliate Member.* Alexandria, Va: American Physical Therapy Association; 1995: Section 2-1.C.
6 *Gender Issues in Employment Under Federal Law: An American Physical Therapy Association White Paper.* Alexandria, Va: American Physical Therapy Association; 1995.
7 Sex Discrimination Guidelines, Equal Employment Opportunity Commission. (29 CFR 1604.11) *Federal Register.* November 10, 1980;45:74677.
8 Scott RW. *Health Care Malpractice: A Primer on Legal Issues.* Thorofare, NJ: Slack Inc; 1990:81-82.
9 *Black's Law Dictionary, 3rd ed.* St Paul, Minn: West Publishing Company; 1979:990.
10 Hayes AS. Courts concede the sexes think in unlike ways. *Wall Street Journal.* 1991;May 28:B1,B5.
11 Resolving conflict: following the light of personal behavior. *NavPers Bulletin* 15620. Washington, DC: US Government Printing Office; 1993.
12 Plevan BB, Borg JA. Employment Law: Rulings by several courts of appeals may lead to expanded employer liability. *National Law Journal.* 1994;Aug 8:B5, B8-10.
13 Lopez JA. Control the damage of a false accusation of sexual harassment. *Wall Street Journal.* 1994;Jan 12:B1.

Suggested Reading

Council on Ethical and Judicial Affairs, American Medical Association. Sexual misconduct in the practice of medicine. *JAMA.* 1991;266:2741-2745.
Komaromy M, Bindman AB, Haber RJ, Sande MA. Sexual harassment in medical training. *JAMA.* 1993;328:322-352.
Kruger P. See no evil. *Working Woman.* 1995;June:32-35, 64, 77.
Seventy-five percent of female physicians report sexual harassment. *PT Bulletin.* 1994;Jan 9:4.

being resolved at the organizational level instead of through the EEOC or the courts.

- *Alerting employees, as required by federal law, of their right to initiate formal charges with the EEOC.* Although victims of sexual harassment should be encouraged to resolve grievances at the lowest appropriate level, under the EEOC sex discrimination guidelines,[7] managers are responsible for making their employees aware of their right to pursue unresolved complaints at higher administrative or legal levels. Making employees aware of their rights could be a part of the sensitizing process described above; in addition, managers should ensure that both a statement of employees' rights and the organization's policy on sexual harassment with a description of the grievance process is posted in a prominent place.

Although managers have the primary responsibility to prevent and eliminate sexual harassment, responsibility ultimately is shared by everyone in the workplace.

This column is not intended as legal advice for any specific practitioner. Legal advice can only be given by your personal legal counsel, based on the laws of your state or on federal law, as applicable.

Sexual harassment occurs in all work settings,

and affects both men and women.

Physical therapists, physical therapist assistants,

and students need to be aware

of the nature of sexual harassment and

its legal ramifications.

∽

Confronting the Unwelcome: *Sexual* HARASSMENT

by Bradley Raymond, Esq,
and Marilyn Raymond, PT

Imagine yourself in the following situations:

- *A coworker who is having an affair with the department director is selected for a promotion instead of you.*

- *You are repeatedly patted on the shoulder, buttocks, and back by a coworker, even though you have asked that these actions be stopped.*

- *Sexually suggestive jokes, pictures, and stories that offend you and some of your friends are part of staff room discussions. Some of your other friends actively participate.*

- *You are constantly pressured to go out after work by a supervisor even though you have stated that you are not available.*

- *You witness a supervisor fondling a coworker in a treatment booth. She is resisting. You talk to the coworker later about the incident. She says that she will deny it if you report the incident. The supervisor gives you a poor performance review—the first difficulty you've ever experienced with the department.*

- *You are nearly raped by a hospital administrator after you stay late to catch up on some paperwork. There are no witnesses....*

© Chris McAllister

According to a 1996 survey of 400 APTA members, at least a quarter of those physical therapists, physical therapist assistants, and students surveyed indicated that they experienced situations similar to these (See "How Harassment Ranks as a Concern in the Profession," on page 49). And this may only be the tip of the iceberg. Sexual abusers tend to reinforce their misconduct with secrecy and silence.1 For those accused of or victimized by sexual harassment, the personal consequences can be long-lasting and potentially devastating. Chances are that you or someone you know has dealt with some form of sexual harassment.

Sexual harassment, and the ever-present threat of litigation, warrants the attention of the physical therapy profession. It is a human reality that can disrupt virtually any employment setting. It affects productivity, performance, interpersonal relationships, and the overall quality of work life.

Instances of sexual harassment also pose the possibility of significant bottom-line liability to hospitals, clinics, and other employ-ment entities in which physical therapists practice. Legal fees for defending an employment lawsuit can easily exceed $50,000—even in routine cases. Damage awards can exceed $1 million in some cases. This is serious business, regardless of how one views the broader moral and ethical issues associated with nondiscrimination in the workplace.

This article will provide an overview of sexual harassment in the workplace and suggest certain approaches to prevent, identify, assess, and resolve issues in a professional setting.

Defining the Conduct

The Equal Employment Opportunity Commission (EEOC)[2] has promulgated the following definition of sexual harassment:

> Harassment on the basis of sex is a violation of [Title VII]. Unwelcome sexual advances, requests for sexual favors, and other verbal or physical conduct constitute sexual harassment when: (1)

submission to such conduct is made either explicitly or implicitly a term or condition of an individual's employment, (2) submission to or rejection of such conduct by an individual is used as the basis for employment decisions affecting such individual, or (3) such conduct has the purpose or effect of unreasonably interfering with an individual's work performance or creating an intimidating, hostile or offensive working environment.[3]

The elements of the violation can be broken down as follows:

Unwelcome conduct: Logically, conduct that is welcome is not sexual harassment.

Of a sexual (or sexist) nature: Although hardly sexual in nature, workplace conduct that subordinates or humiliates women because of their sex may be a form of sexual harassment. The key is that the unwelcome conduct is engaged in because of the victim's sex.

"Quid pro quo" sexual harassment: This type of harassment is an explicit or implicit condition of employment or is used as a basis for employment decisions.

"Hostile environment" sexual harassment: Harassment of this nature affects or interferes with an individual's work performance or creates an intimidating, hostile, or offensive working environment.

"Quid Pro Quo" versus "Hostile Environment"

Legal principles are generally established incrementally, because judges render written decisions in concrete cases. Because sexual harassment is a real life event, specific categorizations developed in written decisions may nonetheless be somewhat artificial. The analysis can, however, be useful in determining whether a workplace issue that may, at "first blush," seem like a simple misunderstanding, has degenerated into a potential legal problem.

"Quid pro quo" harassment is probably the easiest form of sexual harassment to

identify. As the term implies, it involves circumstances in which a supervisor or other person in a dominant or management position has explicitly or implicitly conditioned work advancement, promotions, raises, or similar job benefits on the employee's submission to unwelcome sexual behavior. The courts generally require that there have been some tangible economic loss by the victim,[4] although this may not be required when the victim has actually submitted to the harasser's unwelcome advances.[5] Indeed, in a work setting in which "quid pro quo" harassment is occurring, workers who are not participating in the "transaction," and who have thus been denied the opportunity to achieve the same "bargain," may also have a claim.[6]

"Hostile environment" harassment is somewhat more elusive. It can range from a single incident of rape or attempted rape, to a work environment permeated with unwelcome sexual or sexist comments, pictures, jokes, or offensive touching. "Hostile environment" cases are evaluated from the perspective of a hypothetical "reasonable person." The US Supreme Court reasoned in a 1993 decision that:

Whether an environment is "hostile" or "abusive" can be determined only by

looking at all of the circumstances. These may include the frequency of the discriminatory conduct; its severity; whether it is physically threatening or humiliating, or merely an offensive utterance; and whether it unreasonably interferes with an employee's work performance.[7]

Not every inappropriate action by a supervisor toward a subordinate necessarily amounts to sexual harassment.[8] Isolated incidents of "sexual horseplay" occurring over a period of years may not, in some situations, be found to be so severe as to have permeated the work environment with discrimination.[9] Nor is mere crude or vulgar behavior necessarily actionable.

Nevertheless, situations involving unwelcome touching,[10] or pervasive and unwelcome exposure to pornographic or similar offensive materials,[11] or constant unwelcome exposure to sexual advances can result in liability.

It is unnecessary that the unwelcome conduct have been committed by a supervisor. It could be coworkers[12] or a third party such as a client.[13] In some situations, sexually offensive conduct by patients toward PTs or other employees, if not addressed by the hospital or clinic, could constitute actionable sexual harassment.

Who Can Be Liable?

The harasser, of course, can be held responsible for his or her conduct. Title VII expressly includes "agents" of an employer within the definition of employers who are covered by the statute.[14]

Employers are strictly liable, without regard to fault, for "quid pro quo" harassment. By definition, a person who commits "quid pro quo" harassment is a manager, supervisor, or other employer agent who "wields the employer's authority to alter terms and conditions of employment."[15] Thus, even when an employer is unaware that a supervisor is subjecting his subordinates to "quid pro quo" harassment, the employer is liable.

Determining employer liability is somewhat more complicated in "hostile environment" cases. Generally, the plaintiff must be able to show that the "employer, through its agents, knew or should have known of the charged harassment and failed to promptly implement an appropriate corrective action."[16] This might exist, for example, in a circumstance in which the unwelcome behavior is engaged in by a third party, such as a customer (or patient), and the employer refuses or fails to implement appropriate corrective action.[17] Employer liability may also occur where a supervisor has used "his actual or apparent authority to further the harassment, or if he was otherwise aided in accomplishing the harassment by the existence of the agency relationship."[18]

Defenses and Legal Remedies

In litigated cases, a number of defenses or bases for mitigating damages have been recognized—besides, of course, showing that the alleged conduct did not occur at all. They include:

- Facts showing that the employer implemented prompt remedial measures upon being informed of the unwelcome sexual conduct.[19] Failure to take remedial action, or inadequate remedial action may actually make a bad situation worse and exacerbate the liability.[20]
- Evidence that the conduct was welcomed. A complainant's provocative speech or dress may be relevant in determining whether the conduct was welcomed.[21] But caution should be used to avoid stereotypes. Thus, the use of "foul language or sexual innuendo [by women] in a consensual setting does not waive their legal protections against unwelcome harassment."[22]

Under Title VII, courts have addressed sexual harassment claims with various forms of relief. In cases involving employment practices that have pervasively "sexualized"

the workplace for a class of victims (eg, pervasive posting of pornography throughout the workplace, toleration of misogynist conduct and comments, insensitive responses to complaints, etc), structural injunctive relief may be used. This could include court-ordered implementation of sexual harassment policies, work rules containing schedule of penalties for sexual harassment, mandatory training of supervisors and employees, and mandated procedures for making and investigating complaints.[23]

In individual cases, in which a victim typically has experienced a forced or "voluntary" termination from employment, traditional forms of relief include reinstatement of the victim, back pay, front pay (for future wage loss), compensatory and punitive damages, interest, and attorney fees. Although psychological trauma or damage is not a necessary element of the violation,[24] the damage component in sexual harassment cases frequently involves conflicting claims of psychological trauma or

"posttraumatic stress" (and the predictable parade of expert witnesses for each side). In cases in which there is persuasive evidence of significant psychological injury to the plaintiff, large damage awards are possible.

Practical Considerations for the Workplace

Although sexual harassment complaints can spur emotional extremes, pragmatism should arguably remain paramount. Several practical considerations should be kept in mind by both victim and employer.

Human resources

Physical therapists and physical therapist assistants are usually not, and should not be expected to be, human resource experts or lawyers. A good human resources department should be able to objectively assist in resolving a potential problem before it erupts into a legal one. If you are associated with an institution that has a human resources department, contact those individuals for guidance.

Some employers also have an Employee Assistance Program (EAP) in which counseling can be obtained on a confidential basis. A good EAP program operates independently from the human resources function, and can be helpful in sensitive cases in resolving a sexual harassment situation before it becomes a lawsuit.

The sexual harassment policy

Most often, sexual harassment is committed by a supervisor against a subordinate without the knowledge of the employer's management. Courts have made it clear that when an employer takes prompt remedial action upon learning of a complaint, this may establish a defense at least to a charge of "hostile environment" harassment. And, while prompt remedial action might not be a defense to "quid pro quo" harassment, it could go a long way toward mitigating the harm caused. The first step to imposing prompt remedial action is to encourage employees to come forward and report sexual harassment. A written policy is a good way to encourage employees to report.

The elements of a good sexual harassment policy include the following:

PROTECT YOURSELF

Physical therapists need strategies to protect themselves against unwanted sexual behaviors from their colleagues, employers, and patients. Physical therapists also encounter false accusations of sexual harassment.

Protection begins with information. Raymond and Raymond in the accompanying article define the term "sexual harassment." Physical therapists should request a copy of their employer's sexual harassment policy and learn the procedure for handling grievances. Many employers run workshops or in-service programs to educate employees about the problem.

Physical therapists also face unwanted sexual behaviors from their patients. This is not technically sexual harassment, so McComas and her colleagues[1] coined a new term: inappropriate patient sexual behavior (IPSB). They surveyed 68 physical therapy students and 84 practicing physical therapists and found that 80% of their entire sample and 100% of all new graduates experienced IPSB.

To cope with IPSB, therapists should realize that they are not alone: They can turn to their colleagues for support. Usually patients who engage in IPSB have behaved similarly with more than one person. Ignoring the behavior usually does not make it go away. Some strategies for responding to IPSB include:

- Document the incident in the patient's chart, a personal journal, or an incident report.
- Discuss the incident with the patient, a colleague, a friend, a family member, a supervisor, a clergy member, or a security official, or, if you are a student, talk to your academic coordinator of clinical education or clinical instructor.
- Treat the patient in a more public area, at a more populated time, or by using a less "intimate" method (eg, home program vs in-office massage).
- Demand that the patient stop unwanted behaviors or you will discontinue physical therapy services.
- Discontinue treatment, and refer the patient to another therapist for treatment.
- Increase clinic security.
- File a formal complaint with the institution or police.

Physical therapists also face false accusations of sexual harassment. Legal experts[2] advise someone falsely accused to stay calm, inform his/her immediate supervisor, seek legal counsel, and use detailed records to support his/her statement.

Search the World Wide Web for more information on sexual harassment. Although Web pages change on a daily basis, try Capstone Communications (http://www.captson.com/), which offers a short quiz on sexual harassment. The Technology Law Bulletin (http://www.lgu.com/em49.htm) provides examples of sexual harassment and advises how to formulate a sexual harassment policy. The US Air Force site (http://www.aetc.af.mil/sh-policy.html) also describes how to identify the problem and what to do about it.

Sexual harassment, IPSB, and false accusations are part of today's clinical environment. Stopping these unwanted behaviors is difficult, but therapists can protect themselves with knowledge about the problem and coping strategies.

....

—by Jan Bruckner, PhD, PT, Associate Professor, Dept of Physical Therapy, Northeastern University. She conducts "Workshop on Sexual Harassment and Inappropriate Patient Sexual Behavior" in the physical therapy program. A commentary written by Bruckner on "Experiences of Student and Practicing Physical Therapists with Inappropriate Patient Sexual Behavior" (by McComas et al) was published in Physical Therapy *in November 1993.*

References

1   McComas J, Hebert C, Giacomin C, et al. Experiences of student and practicing therapists with inappropriate patient sexual behavior. *Phys Ther.* 1993;73:762-770.
2   Williams KG. Responding to false charges of sexual harassment. *Am J Hosp Pharm.* 1994;1:2004-2005.

- The conduct that is prohibited is expressly defined.
- There is a clear statement of what is prohibited.
- There is also a clear invitation to report unwelcome harassment.
- There are multiple avenues for reporting so that a victim is not required to start with the harasser himself—or with his best friend.
- There is consistent follow-through.[25]

Retaliation and Reaction

The danger that the person who is accused of harassment will retaliate against the person who complained can be vexing. Persons accused of sexual harassment can react with bitterness and seek retribution. Care must be taken to protect the victim's confidentiality and to ensure that she or he is not subjected to further abuse—just for complaining. Even if it turns out that there was no sexual harassment to begin with, a retaliation claim can still be brought under Title VII.

That sexual harassment can prove volatile and costly does not justify abandoning sound personnel administration practices. A careful and fair investigation before corrective steps are taken is almost always appropriate. Progressive discipline may be appropriate depending on the circumstances. Punishment for a first offense, particularly if it involves conduct that is more boorish than abusive, may itself result in litigation against an employer—by the accused perpetrator. As always, counseling and disciplinary actions should be adequately and clearly documented, usually in the perpetrator's employment file.

Follow-Through

The best sexual harassment policies are worthless if they are ignored—or treated as a joke. Managers and employees should, if necessary, be provided with appropriate training concerning workplace diversity and sexual harassment. Turning a complaint of unwelcome harassment into an attack on a trusted acquaintance—or a joke—can backfire into an expensive lawsuit.

Likewise, care should be exercised to ensure that steps taken have, in fact, abated the misconduct. It is not especially persuasive to a jury for an employer to say that "we talked to" the harasser, when there is evidence that the misconduct in fact didn't stop.

APTA's Policy

APTA's Judicial Committee has promulgated guidelines for member conduct in its *Guide for Professional Conduct*. The *Guide* states that "PTs shall not engage in conduct that constitutes harassment or abuse of, or discrimination against, colleagues, associates or others." Concerning patients, the *Guide* also provides that "PTs shall not engage in any sexual relationship or activity whether consensual or nonconsensual with any patient while a physical therapist-patient relationship exists." These provisions also apply to the physical therapist assistant as similarly stated in the *Standards of Ethical Conduct for the Physical Therapist Assistant*. Members who believe that another member has violated these provisions may submit an ethical complaint to his or her APTA chapter president. Also, members who have questions or concerns about sexual harassment should contact APTA's General Counsel and APTA's Department of Women's Initiatives.

Sexual harassment, and its legal ramifications, have significant relevance to the physical therapy profession. Although the profession is no doubt struggling with other issues, including a changing health care environment and constantly shrinking health care budgets, when sexual harassment occurs in the workplace and lands in the courtroom, everyone loses. *PT*

....

Bradley Raymond, Esq, is Attorney and Partner, Finkel, Whitefield, Selik, Raymond, Ferarra & Feldman, PC, Farmington Hills, Mich. His practice is devoted to labor and employment law. Marilyn Raymond, PT, is Adjunct Faculty, Oakland University Physical Therapy Program, Rochester Hills, Mich, and Doctoral Candidate, University of Mich, and School of Public Health, Ann Arbor, Mich. Her elective area is women's studies. She is a past member and chair of APTA's Advisory Panel on Women and currently is the APTA liaison to the Society for the Advancement of Women's Health Research.

References

1. MacKinnon C. *Feminism Unmodified*. Cambridge, Mass: Harvard University Press; 1987:104.
2. Sexual harassment may also be actionable under Title IX of the Education Amendments of 1972, 20 USC §§ 1618-1688, various state laws, and various other legal theories. We have confined the discussion here to Title VII because the principles established under this legislation are broadly applicable to virtually any employment setting.
3. 29 CFR§ 1604.11 (a).
4. *Kauffman v Allied Signal Inc*, 970 F2d 178 (6th Cir 1992).
5. *Karibian v Columbia University*, 14 F3d 773, 778-79 (2d Cir 1994).
6. *Priest v Rotary*, 634 F Supp 511 (ND Calif 1986).
7. *Harris v Forklift Systems Inc*, 126 LEd2d 295, 302-03 (1993).
8. *Saxton v AT&T*, 10 F3d 526 (7th Cir 1993).
9. *Candelore v Clark County Sanitation District*, 975 F2d 588 (9th Cir 1992).
10. *Campbell v Kansas State University*, 59 FEP Cases 1268, 1272 (D Kan 1992).
11. *Robinson v Jacksonville Shipyards*, 760 F Supp 1486 (MD Fla 1991).
12. *Robinson v Jacksonville Shipyards*, supra.
13. *Marantete v Michigan Host Inc*, 508 F Supp 909 (ED Mich 1980).
14. 42 USC § 2000e(b).
15. *Kotcher v Rosa & Sullivan Appliance Center*, 957 F2d 59, 62 (1992).
16. *Rabidue v Osceola Refining Co*, 805 F2d 611 (6th Cir 1986).
17. *Marantete v Michigan Host Inc*, 506 F Supp 909 (ED Mich 1980).
18. *Karibian v Columbia University*, 14 F3d 773 (2d Cir 1994).
19. *Saxton v AT&T*, 10 F3d 526 (7th Cir 1993).
20. *Robinson v Jacksonville Shipyards*, 760 F Supp 1486 (MD Fla 1991).
21. *Meritor Savings Bank v Vinson*, 477 US 57 (1986).
22. *Jenson v Eveleth Taconite Co*, 61 FEP Cases 1252, 1278-79 (D Minn 1993).
23. *Robinson v Jacksonville Shipyards*, 760 F Supp 1486 (MD Fla 1991).
24. *Harris v Forklift Systems Inc*, 126 LEd2d 295, 302-03 (1993).
25. Williams H. Model procedures for sexual harassment claims. *Arbitration Journal*. 1993;5:66-75.

Suggested Readings:

Gender Issues in Employment Under Federal Law. Alexandria, Va: American Physical Therapy Association; 1995.

Women's Issues Resource Guide. Alexandria, Va: American Physical Therapy Association; 1996.

Finley C. What is sexual harassment? *PT—Magazine of Physical Therapy*.1994;2(12):17-18.

Lake Research. *Presentation of Findings from a Survey of 400 Physical Therapy Professionals and Physical Therapy Students*. Alexandria, Va: American Physical Therapy Association; 1996.

MacKinnon CA. *Feminism Unmodified*. Cambridge, Mass: Harvard University Press; 1979.

MacKinnon CA. *Sexual Harassment of Working Women*. New Haven, Conn: Yale University Press; 1984.

McComas J, Hebert C, Giacomin C, et al. Experiences of student and practicing therapists with inappropriate patient sexual behavior. *Phys Ther*. 1993;73:762-770.

Ragins BR, Scandura TA. Antecedents and work-related correlates of reported sexual harassment: an empirical investigation of competing hypotheses. *Sex Roles*. 1995;32(7/8):429-453.

Schneider BE. Put up or shut up: workplace sexual assaults. *Gender and Society*. 1991;5:533-548.

Schunk C, Parver CP. Avoiding allegations of sexual misconduct: *Clinical Management*. 1989;9(5):19-22.

Scott RW. Sexual harassment: a reminder for managers. *PT—Magazine of Physical Therapy*. 1995;3(12):19-21.

Scott RW. Sexual misconduct. *PT—Magazine of Physical Therapy*. 1993;1(10):78-79.

Williams H. Model procedures for sexual harassment claims. *Arbitration Journal*. 1993;5:66-75.

Appendices

The Physical Therapist as Expert Witness

The Judicial Process of a Physical Therapy Malpractice Claim

> These articles were orignally written by Elaine W Selle, Esq, for use as part of the reference materials for the APTA Risk Management Seminars, which were conducted in the early 1990's. We are pleased that she has allowed us to include both of them in *Law and Liability, Part 1: Liability Issues*.

The Physical Therapist as Expert Witness

Elaine W Selle, Esq

The current focus on medical malpractice suits brings into sharp focus three inescapable facts for physical therapists. First, as health care providers charged with the legal and professional duty to render appropriate treatment within the standard of care, they are susceptible to becoming named defendants in medical malpractice suits. Second, physical therapists may also be called upon by either the patient-claimant or the sued defendant to serve as experts, that is, to testify as to the standard of care and whether the defendant-physical therapist breached this standard. Third, a physical therapist may become involved in a lawsuit as the treating therapist, giving testimony as to the current status and prognosis of the patient. In either of these three categories, the physical therapist, as a defendant or expert witness, must be both wary and prepared. These special roles will be delineated and discussed in full, with special emphasis placed on the deposition of a defendant-physical therapist.

I. The Physical Therapist as a Named Defendant

A.   Early Involvement With an Attorney

Unquestionably, one professional fear of all physical therapists, or any health care provider, occurs at that moment when the local civil sheriff serves a Petition for Damages on the individually named defendant-therapist. After the initial shock and great consternation, a therapist's second, natural inclination may be to discuss this matter with friends and/or colleagues. Given the vulnerability and emotional turmoil the therapist may feel at this particular time, it is easy to express certain regrets or self-doubts as to the treatment rendered to the plaintiff-patient. Although such mental ruminations and verbal expressions constitute normal human responses, this type of communication to anyone outside the attorney-client relationship is unwise and dangerous. Any and all such discussions do not qualify as legally "privileged" and, therefore, can be discovered by the opposing counsel during the course of litigation. Only communication between a client and an attorney remains confidential or "nondiscoverable." For this reason, a defendant-therapist must limit communications in both frequency and content until the suit is resolved through dismissal, settlement, or judgement at trial.

Upon receipt of a served suit, a therapist should contact his or her supervisor or employer immediately. In small hospitals or clinical settings, the therapist may directly contact the administrator. Where the therapist is an employee, professional liability insurance will be provided by the employer, who, upon notification of the suit, will directly contact the insurance company. The carrier will then assign local counsel to represent and defend the therapist against the malpractice suit. If the therapist is an independent contractor or the employer, then he or she will directly and immediately contact the insurance company so that an attorney can become involved as quickly as possible in this matter. Only an attorney can fully protect a therapist's interests once a claim is filed and served.

All states have strict time limitations, usually between 15 and 30 days, during which responsive pleadings, generally in the form of an answer to the petition, must be filed by an attorney. Service of the filed petition upon the defendant-physical therapist triggers the running of this deadline. Any delay on the part of the named defendant that causes further delay in the filing of responsive pleadings can result in plaintiff taking a Default Judgement. A Default Judgement, in essence, states that the named defendant failed to respond to the served suit within the prescribed time limits and, further, requests the court, upon this basis, to deem liability admitted on the therapist's part. The judge can then confirm this judgement, sometimes as few as 2 days later, precluding any later attempt by your attorney to argue any defense to liability. With a confirmed Default Judgement taken against you, the only legal issue is one of damages. Additionally, most insurance policies specifically except coverage for claims resulting from default judgements where the insured caused the delay in notification to the insurance carrier and ultimate tardiness in filing responsive pleadings. Therefore, under all circumstances, a physical therapist, as any named defendant, must respond immediately to a served petition by the civil sheriff. At this point, an attorney must become involved in order to represent the defendant's interests, as soon as possible.

B. Deposition of Physical Therapist as Defendant

Before the initial conference with your attorney, review all pertinent medical records and provide your attorney with a copy as well. During this meeting, you and your attorney will fully discuss all aspects of the case, including your treatment, the medical facts upon which the suit is based, and potential defenses. Following this meeting, your attorney will use other discovery devices, known as Interrogatories and Requests for Production of Documents, to gather other pertinent information, usually in the form of additional medical records. Discovery is that designated timeframe in which both parties, plaintiff and defendant, can learn the opponent's facts and information to establish their case (for plaintiff) or their defense (for defendant).

Perhaps the single most important event occurring during discovery is the deposition of the physical therapist, taken by opposing counsel. This event, the significance of which is often overlooked, should be correctly perceived as a minitrial. It is the first, and only, time that plaintiff's counsel can directly communicate with the defendant-physical therapist in the presence of the therapist's attorney and a court reporter. This question-answer format is ultimately reduced to a transcript by a court reporter, beginning after the witness is sworn. Although the deposition is certainly a fact-gathering discovery vehicle, it is also used by plaintiff's counsel to assess not only the substance of the therapist's testimony but also his or her strength as a trial witness. During the course of the deposition, plaintiff's counsel also tests the therapist's credibility, as well as his or her ability to withstand the rigors of tough questioning. The therapist's performance during a deposition may indirectly influence whether counsel for either party is willing to settle or try the case.

Despite an ostensibly friendly demeanor by plaintiff's counsel, you must always remember that this person is, indeed, the enemy. Although opposing counsel may appear solicitous and accommodating, it is critical to keep in mind that this is the individual who intentionally strives to elicit from you any and all information to build his or her theory of negligence by using your own sworn testimony. For this reason, the therapist must always remain focused and clear as to the purpose of the deposition and the opposing counsel's true intent. The deposition's significance is further underscored by the fact that this sworn testimony later becomes your script for trial. Whatever testimony you give during the deposition will be the same sworn testimony later given on the stand at trial. Any discrepancy between the deposition and trial testimony results in impeachment of your testimony and credibility in front of the jurors. Given the purpose, nature, strategy, and gravity of a deposition, it must be approached with serious consideration and careful planning.

For these important reasons, the attorney must meet with you 1 or 2 days before the scheduled deposition, not the day of the deposition. Proper preparation for this critical event involves your complete attention and thorough familiarity with your treatment and documentation appearing in the plaintiff's medical records. As the defendant, you should also know the plaintiff's other medical records relevant to your defense. These records should be brought with you to the deposition. Questioning by plaintiff's counsel will include all aspects of the nature, type, and basis of treatment rendered, your rationale in treatment decisions, and any improvement or change in the patient's physical status throughout treatment. Ideally, your medical records should complement and support your testimony.

During this predeposition conference, your counsel should also review with you anticipated questions by plaintiff's counsel, as well as your anticipated, always truthful, responses. This preparation should directly deal with any and all known weak or problem areas in your treatment. Obviously, opposing counsel will attack your weaknesses in order to strengthen his or her allegations of malpractice against you. During this portion of the deposition, never appear evasive or reluctant to answer these tough questions. Plaintiff's counsel will carefully assess the truthfulness of your testimony and your ability to handle thorny issues under pressure.

The rule of complete honesty in response to questions asked unequivocally extends to your own attorney. Never hide any unfavorable information from your counsel, who alone can assist you with ways to explain any problem areas. Most importantly, never allow your attorney to learn, for the first time during your deposition, damaging information that plaintiff's counsel has learned about you. Withholding any potentially harmful information only compromises your defense by handicapping your attorney's ability to protect you. Be completely open regarding any sensitive areas, such as prior malpractice claims, licensure restrictions, employment termination, psychiatric or chemical dependency problems, or complaints against you to a professional body.

During the deposition, you should remain direct, focused, poised, and confident. Your attitude should be open and forthright, indicating that you have nothing to hide and are willing to answer all questions truthfully. You should project professional concern for this patient's condition for which damages are being sought. However, you must remain steadfast in your knowledge that you treated this patient competently and within the standard of care at all times. Your demeanor should reflect this resolute belief, while avoiding any obnoxious, overbearing, or defensive posture. You must keep in mind that plaintiff's counsel continues to judge your strength as a trial witness and your ability to respond calmly under pressure. Your commitment to this advice characterizes you as a formidable opponent and greatly enhances your credibility as well.

In planning your deposition, select a date, time, and location convenient to you. Although most physical therapists feel comfortable being deposed in their office, they must also be careful to keep from the opposing attorney's view any textbooks or journals that may generate additional questions. For this reason, a conference room or neutral office is a preferable site; never agree to a deposition in opposing counsel's office. Physical therapists, as defendants, should reserve the right to read and sign their deposition. Although you cannot change the substance of your testimony, you are free to correct errors made by the court reporter appearing in a transcribed form. As mentioned earlier, bring with you any and all pertinent medical records for your ease of reference. You may always refer to these records before responding to any question. Of course, your file will be carefully reviewed and appropriately purged by your attorney for any confidential correspondence or other privileged information that is nondiscoverable.

Never bring with you to your deposition any textbooks, journal articles, medical literature, or citations therefrom, that you believe support your defense. Inevitably, plaintiff's counsel will attempt, and may succeed, in using against you these very articles, which you verified as authoritative. Once a textbook is deemed authoritative, then plaintiff can use any other section, chapter, or quote to refute your testimony. Bring with you an updated curriculum vitae, usually attached as an exhibit to the deposition. This CV will save time in questioning you on your medical and educational background.

You should arrive at your deposition in appropriate attire to create the specific impression that you are serious and professional in your approach. The following recommendations will also assist you in giving effective deposition testimony:

- Listen carefully to all questions asked and be sure that you understand each one before answering.

- Never hesitate to express your confusion over any question posed; never answer any question not fully understood.

- Never volunteer information; respond only to questions asked.

- Never be afraid to respond "I don't know," when appropriate.

- Never assume, speculate, or aggrandize your response; always testify from your own knowledge base, whether directly or indirectly acquired.

- Do not allow plaintiff's counsel to rush your answer; you are entitled to think carefully before responding.

- Allow all questions to be fully asked before responding; never assume you know what plaintiff's counsel will ask.

- Never argue with opposing counsel, maintain your focused attention, and allow your attorney to handle any problems or heated discussions.

- Allow your attorney to state objections on the record before responding; these objections will educate you as to the problem with the question as asked.

- In fielding hypothetical questions, be attuned to the generally overbroad and/or incomplete facts presented.

- Where applicable, state your inability to answer the hypothetical question as posed without further clarification or addition of specific facts.

- Be careful when answering questions couched in terms of "possibilities," "always," and "never."

C.   Trial of Physical Therapist as Defendant

If the case does not settle, a trial before a judge or jury will occur. Trial preparation requires that a therapist clear his or her calendar 2 days before, and the week of, the trial. Depending upon the number of defendants, a medical malpractice jury case can last anywhere from 3 to 5 days. Trial preparation includes your total familiarity with all aspects of treatment, medical records, and deposition testimony as well. Obviously, the deposition records your responses to specific questions asked by opposing counsel. Therefore, at trial, you may respond to new questions posed by your counsel and provide additional information to previous answers. However, at no time may you actually change your testimony on the stand. As earlier stated, trial testimony must be entirely consistent with earlier sworn deposition testimony. A copy of your deposition and pertinent medical records should be taken with you to the stand.

Your attorney will present your case and defense through you, bolstered by testimony from your expert witness and other necessary treating physicians. During this portion of the trial, known as direct examination, you must present yourself as a strong and confident witness. Through nonleading questions, your attorney will elicit from you all relevant aspects of your treatment, care, and treatment decisions. During this questioning, you should focus your attention on the jury, speaking directly to them. This approach establishes a rapport with the jurors and enhances your credibility in their eyes. Direct examination is the first and only opportunity you, as the defendant-physical therapist, have to indirectly address the jurors by responding to your counsel's questions.

Following completion of direct examination, your attorney will "tender" you as a witness to plaintiff's counsel who then will conduct cross examination (cross).

During cross, opposing counsel will concentrate primarily on those weak areas that surfaced during your deposition. Obviously, the plaintiff's mission is to cause uncertainty in the jurors' minds as to the type of treatment and care you rendered to plaintiff. Like the deposition, this cross examination represents yet another critical juncture in the litigation, when you must attempt to hold your own against this tough questioning. In order to successfully complete this portion of trial, you must remain focused, never losing your temper or becoming defensive. At times, plaintiff's counsel will deliberately attempt to provoke you in an effort to undermine your credibility and rapport with the jurors. Therefore, your assignment is quite clear: Remain responsive, firm, and polite to all questions asked. Your attorney can, and usually does, conduct "redirect" to rehabilitate any faltering that may have occurred and to reemphasize your strengths. Redirect is limited to the scope of questions asked during cross. At all times, before and after your testimony, remain attentive and interested in all aspects of the trial. Remember that the jurors continue to assess you and your reactions to determine whether you are a concerned and competent professional.

II. The Physical Therapist as an Expert Witness

In order for plaintiff to prevail in a medical malpractice case against a physical therapist, the law places the burden on plaintiff to prove certain essential elements of his/her claim, also known as a "cause of action." Specifically, plaintiff must prove that you had (1) a duty to the patient; (2) breached this duty (ie, were negligent in treatment); (3) caused harm as a result of the breached duty; and (4) caused specific damages, whether physical, mental, and/or economic, to plaintiff. Absolutely essential to plaintiff's satisfying all four elements in his/her burden of proof is the expert witness. Without this expert, plaintiff cannot prove that you breached your duty, which negligence caused the damages complained of in plaintiff's petition. As a matter of law, plaintiff must retain and produce at trial an expert witness (a physical therapist) who will testify that you breached your duty, or standard of care, and in doing so, caused injury to the plaintiff. This necessity of an expert is an established legal principle in medical malpractice litigation.

Unlike simple negligence cases, such as intersectional car collisions, medical malpractice claims often involve complex and difficult medical issues that only an expert in the field can adequately address. Thus, courts perceive a real need for, and require, such an expert, in the same medical specialty as the defendant, to explain these issues regarding the standard of care. Such issues lie outside the experience and expertise of the judge or jury. For this reason, plaintiff must retain an expert physical therapist to testify at trial against you. This expert witness must specifically state that you fell below the minimum standards established by the profession, thereby breaching the standard of care for physical therapists. This breach constitutes negligence that proximately caused, or contributed to, the damages that plaintiff claims.

Similarly, during the course of litigation, your counsel will also retain an expert to testify that you acted within the standard of care in treating the plaintiff-patient. Retaining this expert usually occurs after the therapist's counsel has deposed plaintiff's expert. Your expert witness will render an opinion that you acted within the standard of care and were, at no time, negligent in the treatment rendered to plaintiff. Without this expert, you legally cannot defend yourself against the adverse opinion of plaintiff's expert witness. Thus, you must, like plaintiff, retain an expert to testify on your behalf that the treatment and care rendered to plaintiff was well within the standard of care for physical therapists.

Thus, all medical malpractice claims necessarily involve expert witnesses, retained by both sides, who understandably will offer divergent opinions regarding the standard of care. The trier of fact, either a judge or jury, is then free to accept or reject the testimony of either parties' expert, ultimately deciding whether or not you breached the standard of care, that is, were negligent in treating the plaintiff. The jury will also decide the issue of causation, should they find that you breached the standard of care.

An expert is defined as a qualified individual who assists the untrained trier of fact in understanding the sophisticated, and often difficult, medical facts involved in the case. As stated earlier, these medical issues are often beyond the ordinary experience of lay jurors. Thus, the expert, required in all medical malpractice cases, testifies as to the standard of care, based upon his or her own expertise that lies within the same practice area as the defendant-physical therapist. The law acknowledges certain aspects of learning, skill, knowledge, training, and education that qualify a witness to serve as an expert. These qualifications are codified in Federal Rule of Evidence 702, used by most states to pattern their own rules regarding the admissibility of trial evidence and expert testimony. Upon the basis of Rule 702, both plaintiff and defendant can offer and qualify their respective witnesses as experts. Of course, the judge alone has the ultimate authority to qualify or strike a potential expert witness based upon these legally defined qualifications.

Generally, most expert physical therapists are found teaching in academia or practicing in private or public settings. Regardless of the particular setting, the law looks only to the expert's requisite knowledge, skill, experience, training, or education required by federal and state rules of evidence. Although courts broadly allow any of these sources of physical therapists to be qualified as experts, experienced medical malpractice attorneys always seek to match, as closely as possible, the practice areas of the expert with the same specialty practice as the defendant-physical therapist. Additionally, most experienced attorneys refrain from using the "hired gun" expert, whose primary income is derived from serving as an expert and testifying at trial. Jurors are generally not receptive to this type of expert who regularly solicits his or her experience in return for monetary gain.

As with the physical therapist as defendant, the physical therapist as an expert witness must also be familiar with the particular facts, issues, and medical treatment rendered to plaintiff by the defendant. Of course, this expert must be familiar with the standard of care for physical therapists and be able to apply this standard to the facts and specific issues of the case. Counsel for both parties will specifically look for an expert who also has the ability to synthesize complex information into simple, layperson's terms and communicate this digested information clearly to the jurors. Attorneys also look for experts who can establish rapport with, and relate to, the jurors at trial. A physical therapist, agreeing to testify as either plaintiff's or defendant's expert, must feel comfortable in the courtroom setting. Such characteristics in an expert are additional, invaluable assets for any trial attorney presenting or defending the malpractice claim. In considering physical therapists to testify on behalf of the defendant-physical therapist, defense attorneys avoid any individual who shares an employment, business, or extended social relationship with the defendant. Obviously, defense counsel must avoid the charge of bias, or even the hint of impropriety, in order to maintain the credibility of the expert. Only experts who present competently, honestly, and candidly should be considered by either party. Expert testimony should never be bought. Moreover, physical therapists considering acceptance of this position should personally and professionally believe in the worth and integrity of their offered testimony for which they get paid.

By law, experts are permitted to draw from a wide range of sources, including hearsay information, in reaching their opinions. Typically, experts rely upon their own knowledge and expertise in the profession, as well as the pertinent medical records of plaintiff, deposition testimony, journal articles, or other medical literature to support their conclusions. Experts may also consult with, and rely upon, other experts' written or verbal opinions regarding the standard of care. However, all experts, whether plaintiff's or defendant's witnesses, must be prepared to testify as to all sources upon which they base their opinion. Under federal and state discovery rules, opposing counsel has the right to explore, during this expert's deposition, every basis of every opinion offered by this expert.

Of course, it is the ultimate goal of all counsel to discredit, or at least to deflate, the testimony of their opponent's expert witness. This objective may be accomplished by obtaining and comparing copies of all previous deposition and/or trial testimony given by the opposing party's expert. A careful comparison of present and prior testimony may uncover inconsistent sworn statements that can reduce or destroy the credibility of an expert at trial. Additionally, detailed exploration of all bases of an expert's opinion during the deposition can reveal weaknesses or inaccuracies in this expert's understanding of the case. Perhaps, the expert was not given, or did not read, all pertinent records and documentation bearing on the issue of liability. Demonstrating an expert's lack of, or inaccurate/incomplete understanding of, the relevant medical facts and issues of the case greatly weakens the opponent's case.

At trial, plaintiff's counsel will conduct direct examination of plaintiff's expert witness, eliciting testimony that the defendant-physical therapist breached the standard of care and caused plaintiff's damages. Following this direct examination, plaintiff's attorney will tender this witness to defendant's attorney, who will then conduct cross examination. Similarly, counsel for the defendant-physical therapist will conduct direct examination of the defendant's expert and then tender this expert for cross examination by plaintiff's counsel. At trial, all experts must testify consistently with their prior deposition testimony, or suffer the consequences of impeachment. Both experts take with them to the stand their deposition testimony, as well as any pertinent medical records to which they may refer while testifying.

III. Physical Therapist as Treating Expert

Lastly, physical therapists may also serve as experts in the capacity of a treating health care provider. In this role, the physical therapist will be used primarily to obtain information regarding the nature and type of treatment rendered, as well as the progress and prognosis of the patient-plaintiff. Plaintiff's counsel will seek to establish their burden of proving damages through the physical therapist, hoping to elicit testimony that evidences the plaintiff's injured, impaired physical state. In contrast, defense counsel will seek to establish the patient's degree of improvement or success in treatment in order to mitigate damages. Generally, defense counsel will also seek information on the degree of plaintiff's compliance with treatment, regular office visits, medication, and any opinion that the patient may be a malingerer. Of course, physical therapists should be very careful to avoid use of such designations, testifying only to known facts, such as canceled appointments, inconsistencies between subjective complaints of pain and clinical findings, or a perplexing lack of improvement.

Cast in this role, the physical therapist has no partiality, bias, or vested interest in the outcome of the case. The therapist's only focus is the course of treatment rendered. In preparation for their deposition, for which they will be paid, the physical therapist must be familiar with the patient's medical records that reflect specific treatment rendered by the physical therapist. The therapist should also bring these records to the deposition for referral at any time. The party who issues a trial subpoena to the physical therapist will be responsible for payment of professional time and services rendered. Like the defendant-physical therapist and the expert-physical therapist, the treating physical therapist will also present to trial with his or her deposition testimony, as well as the pertinent documentation reflecting treatment rendered to the plaintiff-patient.

In order to prevail in a medical malpractice suit, the law places the burden of proof on plaintiff to establish certain essential elements of his or her claim, also known as a "cause of action." Failure to prove all four elements of (1) duty, (2) breach of duty, (3) causation, and (4) damages, prevents plaintiff from prevailing in his/her lawsuit. Like all health care providers, the physical therapist also has a legal, as well as professional, duty to render treatment and care to patients according to the standard set by their profession. This legal duty, expressed in terms of "standard of care," is that minimal level of professional performance at which all physical therapists must practice. A physical therapist may exceed the standard of care but must never fall below it. Failure to practice within this standard of care, or falling below this established standard, results in the therapist's breaching his legal duty to the plaintiff. This breach of the legal duty is also known as a breach of the standard of care, the second element in plaintiff's burden of proof. The law places the burden on plaintiff to prove that the defendant-physical therapist breached the standard of care in treating the patient-plaintiff. Further, a plaintiff must prove the third and fourth elements of his or her burden by demonstrating that the defendant-physical therapist's breach of the standard of care caused the plaintiff's damages, whether physical, mental, or economic. Testimony, or proof, at trial, as to these four elements permits a plaintiff to then have a jury decide the merits of the case. Failure to prove any of these requisite elements forecloses plaintiff from winning his/her malpractice claim against the physical therapist.

The Judicial Process of a Physical Therapy Medical Malpractice Claim

Elaine W Selle, Esq

I.   Definition of Medical Malpractice Claim

A medical malpractice, or negligence, claim is one brought against a defendant-health care provider, such as a physician, hospital, nurse, or physical therapist, for personal injury damages caused by the defendant's breach of the standard of care. As with all claims for negligence, including medical malpractice, the injured party-plaintiff must prove four elements in order to prevail. Specifically, plaintiff has the burden of proving:
  (1)   Defendant's legal duty to plaintiff,
  (2)   Defendant's breach of this duty,
  (3)   Defendant's breach causing plaintiff's injury, and
  (4)   Plaintiff's specific damages resulting from this breach.

Plaintiff must prove that the defendant-health care provider had a legal duty to treat a patient within the scope of the "standard of care." Further, plaintiff must prove the third and fourth elements of causation and damages by establishing that the defendant-health care provider's breach of the standard of care caused plaintiff's damages for which plaintiff now brings suit.

A.   Duty

Once a physical therapist undertakes, or engages in, rendering treatment to a patient, a legal duty is established immediately and continues throughout the course of treatment. If a plaintiff discontinues treatment, with or against the therapist's advice, then this professional relationship is severed, along with the legal duty. However, the physical therapist unquestionably has a duty to a patient for the duration of the treatment period. Thus, the first element in plaintiff's burden of proof is generally easy to establish.

In medical malpractice cases, the duty of all health care providers is couched in terms of the "standard of care." This legal term refers to a minimum standard, established by the profession, below which a therapist may not fall in treating a patient. This standard is a composite of the learning, knowledge, skill, and expertise that a therapist should possess and apply in treating patients. Some state statutes specifically set forth the legal definition of the standard of care to include the degree of knowledge or skills possessed or the degree of care ordinarily exercised by the health care provider acting within the scope of his or her medical specialty while treating a patient. Thus, a physical therapist must exhibit that same degree of skill, care, and judgement exhibited by other physical therapists treating a similar condition or medical problem. During litigation, both plaintiff and defendant will retain expert witnesses, in the same specialty as the defendant-health care provider, who will testify to and explain what standard was required of a defendant-physical therapist while treating the plaintiff-patient. In defining the standard of care, these expert witnesses may also refer to, or rely upon, medical and/or scientific data, studies, or articles in the field of professional literature addressing the same medical issue that forms the basis of plaintiff's lawsuit.

B.   Breach of the Standard of Care

In this second element of plaintiff's burden of proof, generally the most difficult, plaintiff must prove that the defendant-physical therapist failed to exercise that requisite degree of knowledge, skill, and expertise in treating the plaintiff-patient. This deviation, or breach of the standard of care, can take the form of an overt negligent act or a negligent omission, that is, failure to perform a necessary act. Plaintiff's allegations of negligence against a therapist can take many forms, including failure to properly treat, monitor, or supervise; improper use of equipment that causes injury; or failure to properly refer the patient to another specialty health care provider. In all of these possible scenarios of negligence, plaintiff must establish, through the use of expert testimony, that the professional conduct of the defendant-physical therapist fell below the minimum standard of care established by the profession, resulting in negligence, or medical malpractice. This second element of plaintiff's burden of proof becomes the true battleground of the lawsuit. In this arena, both parties' respective experts testify as to the standard of care and whether the defendant-physical therapist was negligent, that is, breached this standard.

C.   Causation

The third element in a medical malpractice cause of action is causation, or establishing the causal link between the defendant's breach of the standard of care, or negligence, and the plaintiff's resultant injuries. Plaintiff must prove that the defendant's conduct that deviated from the standard of care proximately caused, or substantially contributed to, the damages plaintiff claims in the Petition for Damages. A plaintiff may successfully prove a defendant-physical therapist's negligent act or omission; however, failure to establish a causal connection between the alleged malpractice and plaintiff's injuries dooms a plaintiff's lawsuit. Plaintiff must prove all four elements of a medical malpractice claim in order to prevail against the defendant. Thus, plaintiff's expert witness must also testify that the defendant-physical therapist's conduct resulted in, or caused, damage to plaintiff.

D.   Damages

At this point, plaintiff must prove damages, the fourth and last element in his or her cause of action, in order to successfully bring his or her case before a jury. Damages are divided into special and general, the former representing quantifiable economic losses, such as lost income, past, present, and future; medical expenses past, present, and future; and loss of earning capacity. The general damages include those subjective, personal injuries that are insusceptible to a specific quantum. These general damages include pain and suffering, mental anguish, loss of consortium (loss of sexual relationship, companionship), humiliation, and inconvenience. Like the first element in plaintiff's burden of proof, damages are also fairly easy to establish. However, a plaintiff's inability to demonstrate damages, whether special or general, directly resulting from the physical therapist's negligence will result in dismissal of the suit.

In summary, in order to successfully prosecute a medical malpractice claim, the injured party-plaintiff must prove:

1.   A duty existed between the plaintiff-patient and the defendant-health care provider;

2.   The degree of knowledge or skill possessed, or the degree of care ordinarily exercised, by the professional acting within their medical specialty (also known as the standard of care);

3.   The professional either lacked this degree of knowledge or skill, or failed to use reasonable care and diligence, along with his or her best judgement in applying that skill (ie, breached the standard of care); and

4.   The injured party actually sustained damages as a result of the professional's lack of knowledge or skill or failure to exercise this degree of care.

II. Documentation and Report of a Claim

As a general rule, therapists are unaware of potential medical malpractice claims until the sheriff serves a Petition for Damages upon them. This interval of time, from the date of the alleged act of negligence until service of the suit, generally results in poor or incomplete recollection of critical events not only by the physical therapist but by other critical witnesses as well. Recall of pertinent facts, including details of the patient's physical condition, aspects of treatment, or a patient's noncompliance, becomes more difficult with the passage of time. Therefore, the physical therapist must resort to, and rely upon, documentation that serves as the therapist's main line of defense against a claim for negligence.

Physical therapists should look for signs of any potential claims, such as injury during treatment, complaints about treatment or lack of progress, generally dissatisfied or disgruntled patients or family members, or newly created problems from treatment. Because physical therapy is a hands-on profession, the therapist is in a unique position to know when a patient has been injured as a result of any treatment rendered. Under these circumstances, physical therapists must thoroughly document all procedures taken, treatment rendered, and observations. However, the golden rule of documentation should prevail in all cases, not just for those situations portending potential claims. Excuses of insufficient time or inconvenience in charting can actually cost a therapist the proper defense to a lawsuit.

A therapist's failure to maintain proper documentation is a major obstacle to the physical therapist, the claims adjuster, and the attorney defending the therapist against claims of medical malpractice. When a physical therapist is aware of an incident that represents a potential suit, he or she should fully document the incident to include the following information:

1. Where, when, and how the incident occurred;
2. The specific circumstances surrounding the incident;
3. All witnesses to the incident;
4. Any equipment the patient may have been using or working with at the time of the accident, including the manufacturer's name;
5. All follow-up actions taken to mitigate the injury sustained;
6. All comments the patient may have made regarding the incident; and
7. Whether the patient may have contributed to his or her own injury, also known as comparative fault.

Depending upon the health care entity, incident reports will probably be required for any injury-producing occurrence. However, completion of incident reports does not preclude the need for thorough documentation in the patient's records. A physical therapist, like any health care provider, must think in terms of protection from the threat of future litigation and document thoroughly at all times. Of course, good rapport with the patient and the patient's family provides additional insurance against potential suits.

III. Litigation of a Medical Malpractice Suit

A. Filing of the Suit

The injured party-plaintiff must file a lawsuit in a court of "competent jurisdiction" that has the legal power to render a judgement against either party and the legal issues litigated. After the lawsuit is filed, it must also be served upon the individually named physical therapist, usually by a local sheriff, according to each state's Code of Civil Procedure. Service constitutes legal notice that then triggers a strict time frame, generally between 15 and 30 days from receipt of service, in which the defendant must file into the court's record responsive pleadings to this suit.

For this reason, a physical therapist who receives service of a filed Petition for Damages by a sheriff must immediately contact his or her insurance carrier so that legal representation may be obtained as soon as possible. At this point, the physical therapist will provide the insurer with a complete copy of the patient's file, which will also be forwarded to the attorney, selected by the insurance carrier, who will defend the interest of the sued therapist. The therapist will then meet with the attorney to discuss the facts of the case and plan a proper defense.

B.   Pre-suit Proceedings

Many state statutes require that claims against health care providers, such as physical therapists, be submitted first to a Medical Review Panel before legal action can proceed in a court of law. This panel consists of health care providers in the same specialty area as the defendant-therapist, governed by an Attorney Chairman who supervises the panel proceedings. The panelists receive and review written evidence submitted by both parties' attorneys and then render an opinion as to whether the defendant-health care provider, or physical therapist, breached the standard of care in treating the plaintiff-patient. The panelists also decide the issue of causation, should they find a breach. Only after the panel opinion has been rendered can the claimant then proceed directly into court with a filed and served Petition for Damages. Depending upon state law, this Medical Review Panel opinion may be admissible into evidence at a later trial.

C.   Discovery

Once responsive pleadings have been filed by the defendant-physical therapist's attorney, then the process known as "discovery" will proceed. Discovery describes the legal period and process whereby attorneys for both parties begin to learn relevant facts from the opposing side in order to build their case, if plaintiff, or defend the claim, if defendant. During this important legal phase, courts are guided by the well-established principle that information not privileged and relevant to the issues of the case is "discoverable," that is, it must be divulged to the requesting opponent. Federal Rules of Evidence, generally the model for a state's Code of Evidence, provide a broad scope of discovery to include information that may likely lead to admissible, unprivileged, relevant evidence. The discovery phase offers three major vehicles, known as Interrogatories, Requests for Production of Documents, and Depositions, that allow each respective counsel to gain access to pertinent information.

1.   Interrogatories

Interrogatories are written questions asked to an opposing counsel, usually limited to 25 in number, that are required to be answered in writing within a specific period of time, usually 15 to 30 days. Interrogatories seek to obtain general, background information that can lead to additional discoverable information. For example, in a medical malpractice case, attorney for the defendant-physical therapist will propound interrogatories to plaintiff inquiring into plaintiff's medical history, background, and physical/mental condition, including the identification of all of plaintiff's treating physicians and health care facilities that rendered treatment to plaintiff within the last 5 to 10 years from the date of the alleged negligence. Interrogatories regarding the identity of retained experts and other anticipated trial witnesses are also included in this list of questions. Interrogatories can also be used to provide information on employment, wage earnings (if claimed as an element of damages), marital status, and previous history of filing suit, if any. Plaintiff, too, may propound interrogatories to the defendant-physical therapist, who provides the answers to his or her defense counsel who then formally prepares answers within the designated period of time.

2. Request for Production of Documents

A party may also utilize the discovery vehicle of a Request for Production of Documents in order to obtain copies of any and all documents in the possession of plaintiff or plaintiff's attorney that are unprivileged and relevant to the therapist's defense of the malpractice claim. For example, defense counsel will generally request copies of all medical records, X-rays, pharmacy records (if relevant), coroner's report or autopsy report (where applicable), wage and earning statements (if lost wages are claimed), and any other documents that are relevant to any issue upon which the lawsuit is based. If such documents are not in the attorney's or plaintiff's possession, then counsel may subpoena such documents during the course of discovery.

3. Depositions

A deposition is sworn testimony given by the one "deposed," or questioned, by opposing counsel and later transcribed by a court reporter in a question-and-answer format. Depositions represent the first opportunity that opposing counsel has to question directly the opposing party. Depositions occur with both parties' attorneys and a court reporter in attendance. All parties to the suit are entitled to appear and participate in the deposition "noticed" by the party requesting this discovery vehicle. A Notice of Deposition is a formal pleading filed into the court's record, identifying the deponent and the date, place, and time of the deposition. Parties to the suit must appear voluntarily, without the issuance of a subpoena. All other important witnesses, such as treating health care providers and experts, usually agree to make themselves available at a certain time and place convenient to their schedule. Any such witness who renders a medical opinion is entitled to an expert fee paid by the party requesting the deposition. All nonparty fact witnesses over whom neither party has control should be subpoenaed to appear for their deposition on the designated date and time.

A deposition is the best discovery tool because it provides for a free exchange of information from an available source, sworn under oath to respond truthfully to all questions asked. Of course, certain questions seeking to discover legally privileged or irrelevant information will meet with objections from the deponent's attorney. Because most information is "discoverable," an attorney infrequently instructs a witness not to respond to questions posed. As sworn testimony, the deposition becomes the script for trial should the case fail to settle. All witnesses must adhere to the substance of their deposition testimony and avoid, at all costs, any deviation when giving trial testimony from the stand. Opposing counsel will seize upon any variance between deposition and trial testimony in an attempt to impeach, or discredit, the credibility of the witness before the judge or jury. Therefore, a witness's complete familiarity with deposition testimony is critical, especially for a party to the lawsuit, who can never afford to place doubts in the jurors' minds as to the accuracy or believability of their sworn trial testimony. For ease of reference, each witness should bring his or her deposition to the stand when giving trial testimony.

D.   Settlement

At any time during the discovery phase, up until the time a jury renders a verdict, the parties can agree to settlement of the claim. Frequently, judges exert pressure on each party to settle the case in order to avoid the time and expense of litigation. Long before a pre-trial conference with the judge occurs, both parties have carefully evaluated the strengths and weaknesses of their case and their probable chance of success at trial. Determinative factors in this decision include a party's presentation as a strong or weak trial witness, sympathy engendered for the plaintiff, degree of plaintiff's fault, strengths and weaknesses of each parties' respective expert witnesses, and the willingness of a defendant to subject himself or herself to the rigors of trial. Some physical therapists may decide to settle on the advice of counsel, or upon their desire to terminate a very upsetting ordeal. Other therapists may elect trial in order to defend their professional reputations. Of course, trial is inherently risky and always contains a factor of unpredictability, regardless of the degree of preparation and knowledge that precedes the actual trial process. Some insurance carriers may have a Consent to Settle clause that requires a physical therapist's written consent before the defense attorney can enter into settlement negotiations with plaintiff's counsel. Without this clause in the policy, the insurer can direct the therapist's attorney to settle the case, depending upon the degree of the therapist's exposure and the likelihood of success at trial. If a settlement is reached, the judicial process is then ended, pending execution of the settlement papers.

E.   Trial

If the case cannot settle out of court, then it will proceed to trial. In their first-filed pleading, either party can request a jury, absent which the judge will be the "trier of fact" who decides the case. All parties involved in the lawsuit attend each day of trial and participate by offering trial testimony. The most effective defense for multiple defendants, known as "co-defendants," is unity. Under this joint defense strategy, all health care providers adhere to their respective positions that they did not breach the standard of care in treating plaintiff. This approach then forces plaintiff to prove his or her case against each individually named defendant at trial. Comparative fault of the plaintiff, such as noncompliance with treatment, regular office visits, or medication, is also a highly effective defense. Of course, any inaccuracies in plaintiff's testimony, uncovered during the deposition, will greatly assist all co-defendants' attempt to impeach plaintiff's credibility as a trial witness and as a party litigant.

The first stage of trial is the selection of a jury, known as voir dire, that allows each attorney to question potential jurors in order to decide to keep or strike them. Specifically, each attorney tries to determine if these prospective jurors harbor any bias that would prevent them from impartially listening to and weighing all evidence presented during trial, before reaching their individual decisions. After the jury is selected, sworn in, and "empaneled," the attorneys will begin opening statements.

Plaintiff's attorney presents his or her opening statement first, followed by any and all defense counsel. This early part of the trial gives each attorney the opportunity to introduce themselves, their client, and all issues of the suit to the jury. At this stage, each attorney attempts to influence the jury with his or her particular presentation of the case, explaining anticipated testimony that will support his or her position. Following opening statements, plaintiff's attorney then will present his or her case first by calling the plaintiff and all other fact and/or expert witnesses to testify on plaintiff's behalf. Plaintiff's experts' testimony will be used to satisfy their burden of proving that the defendant-physical therapist deviated from the standard of care and, in doing so, caused plaintiff's injuries.

After plaintiff's counsel conducts direct examination of each witness, the opposing counsel, the physical therapist's attorney, then has the right to conduct cross-examination of each witness in order to uncover weaknesses in their testimony. Following plaintiff's presentation of the case, defense counsel then calls his or her witnesses, beginning with the defendant-physical therapist, followed by expert witnesses and other treating health care providers, who will render favorable testimony on the therapist's behalf. These defense witnesses are then individually tendered to the plaintiff for cross-examination. Cross-examination immediately follows direct examination and continues in that fashion until each parties' witnesses complete their trial testimony.

At the close of defendant's case, no further testimony or evidence will be presented for the jury's consideration. At that point, plaintiff then presents his or her closing argument, followed by all defense counsel. Plaintiff's attorney has a brief rebuttal closing argument, though defense counsel have no further opportunity for closing remarks. Following closing arguments by both sides, the judge will then instruct the jury on issues of law and allow them to deliberate in a closed and sequestered room. If the case is tried before a judge, the judge may render a verdict from the bench or take the matter under advisement. If the jury is the trier of fact, then the jury will reach a verdict on the issue of each defendant's liability. If the jurors find that any defendant breached the standard of care in treating the patient-plaintiff, then the jury must also consider the issue of causation as to each individually named trial defendant.

If causation is found, then the jury will also decide quantum, or damages, and assign that amount. Upon the judge's reading of the verdict, the litigation is then ended at the trial-court level.

F. Appeal

Once a verdict is rendered, the trial portion of a case is concluded. However, the losing party, designated the "appellant," has a legal right to appeal his or her loss to the next highest court, usually the appellate court for each state. Some state appellate courts also have the authority both to review issues of fact and of law and to render legal findings in both areas. Appeals, framed in terms of legal issues, can also be taken to the State Supreme Court by the losing party at the appellate court level. Appellate courts can affirm or reverse the lower trial court, and the State Supreme Court can affirm or reverse the decision of the appellate court. Once the Supreme Court has ruled, the decision is final and binding. Should the defendant-health care provider become the losing party at this highest level, then the insurer for the defendant will be liable for all damages awarded by the jury or court, including interest that begins to accrue from the date that the verdict is entered.

IV. Conclusion

The judicial process can be slow and confusing and often takes years to complete. The keys to successfully defending a case are proper documentation, communication, and preparation. A therapist should always thoroughly document in every situation, not just with suspicious cases that may result in litigation. In the event that a lawsuit is filed, the therapist should immediately report and transmit the lawsuit and all pertinent records to the insurer and the assigned attorney. Once the litigation process begins, the therapist should work closely with the attorney to enhance understanding of the medical issues and to prepare a strong defense for trial. This defense team, joined in strategy and purpose, perseveres throughout trial until the verdict is rendered. If unfavorable, the defendant can appeal the decision to the state's highest court, where it becomes final.